Ring the Bell

Ring the Bell

HOW THE PHILADELPHIA PHILLIES BUILT BASEBALL'S BEST FAN BASE

KEVIN REAVY AND JACK FRITZ
FOREWORD BY SCOTT FRANZKE

Copyright © 2025 by Kevin Reavy and Jack Fritz
Foreword copyright © 2025 by Scott Franzke

All rights reserved. No part of this book may be reproduced in any manner without the express written consent of the publisher, except in the case of brief excerpts in critical reviews or articles. All inquiries should be addressed to Sports Publishing, 307 West 36th Street, 11th Floor, New York, NY 10018.

Sports Publishing books may be purchased in bulk at special discounts for sales promotion, corporate gifts, fund-raising, or educational purposes. Special editions can also be created to specifications. For details, contact the Special Sales Department, Sports Publishing, 307 West 36th Street, 11th Floor, New York, NY 10018 or sportspubbooks@skyhorsepublishing.com.

Sports Publishing® is a registered trademark of Skyhorse Publishing, Inc.®, a Delaware corporation.

Visit our website at www.sportspubbooks.com.

10 9 8 7 6 5 4 3 2 1

Library of Congress Cataloging-in-Publication Data is available on file.

Cover design by David Ter-Avanesyan
Front jacket photographs: Getty Images
Back jacket collage, "Phanatical Devotion," courtesy of Dan Zdilla

Print ISBN: 978-1-68358-497-1
Ebook ISBN: 978-1-68358-498-8

Printed in the United States of America

To Phillies Fans, for Whom the Bell Tolls

CONTENTS

	Foreword by Scott Franzke	ix
	Introduction	xi
#1	1964 (by Kevin Reavy)	1
#2	1980 Franchise Pillars (by Kevin Reavy)	5
#3	1980—The First One (by Kevin Reavy)	21
#4	The Phillie Phanatic (by Kevin Reavy)	36
#5	1983 (by Kevin Reavy)	42
#6	1993—Worst to First (by Kevin Reavy)	45
#7	Harry Kalas—Voice of the Phillies (by Jack Fritz)	69
#8	The Fans	85
#9	The 2008 Pillars (by Jack Fritz)	93
#10	2008—"World Champions, World F%$&in' Champions" (by Jack Fritz)	116
#11	Post-2008 Years—No Cigars (by Jack Fritz)	178
#12	The Harper Pursuit (by Jack Fritz)	254
#13	2022 (by Kevin Reavy)	262
#14	2023 (by Jack Fritz)	278
	The Lists: The Best and Worst of Times	305
	Acknowledgments	314
	Endnotes	315

FOREWORD

I was still relatively new to the Phillies, and to Philadelphia, when the 2007 Phillies ended a 13-year playoff draught by coming back from 7 1/2 games down in September, stunning the Mets, and winning the first of five straight division titles.

The stadium was alive every night with the hopeful energy that something special was in the making. But it was a quiet park bench, miles away from the roar of the stadium crowds, nestled in Fairmount Park, that caught my attention. My wife had sent me a photo of the bench on which someone had painted an old-school Phillies *P* logo. And while I certainly don't condone defacing park property, it said something to me about the city: people here cared about the Phillies. It mattered.

And I think that is what impressed me the most over the nearly 20 years that I've had the privilege to broadcast Phillies baseball, and it is really all that someone in my position can ask for: listeners who care. They want their teams to win, and they *always* want their teams to win. Even when the sport takes 162 different outcomes to decide the fate of a season, Phillies fans passionately feel the wins and losses of every game.

And I hope you'll enjoy finding that passion all wrapped up in the following pages of *Ring the Bell: How the Philadelphia Phillies Built Baseball's Best Fan Base*. I think you will find that Jack and Kevin have dug deeply into the stories that have resonated with multiple generations of fans over the past 60-plus years, from the heartbreak of 1964 to the heart-stopping Harper home run in 2022, and so much in between.

Personally, to have been given a front-row seat for so many of the moments you will read about in this book has been an honor and certainly the greatest thrill of my professional life. As broadcasters, we're there for every game, but like you, we can't change the outcome. We are merely along for the ride. But what a ride it has been, watching up close the great 2007–11 era, including the magical run to the 2008 World Series championship, or the more recent run of three consecutive playoff appearances, and with all those moments burned in our memories for years to come.

When I meet listeners, they're usually quick to point out a radio call of mine and tell me why it's their favorite. I think people just assume it's what us broadcasters want to hear. And no doubt it is flattering. But what always stands out to me is how people usually add *their moment* into the story:

"I was watching with my dad . . ."
"My kids and I were at the game . . ."
"I was with my buddy when . . ."
"My mom was sick, and we listened . . ."

It stood out to them because they shared it with someone meaningful. It mattered. And for me to be connected to *your moment* in some small way—well, talk about humbling.

We have all come to love our team from different directions and unique perspectives. And while fandom usually starts with success—from the enjoyment of something—for us here in Philadelphia, much of the passion is also forged when things go wrong. We share that too. We lean on each other in those moments. We help each other stay hopeful that another memorable moment is waiting around the corner. And because we're Phillies fans, we can't wait to once again hear that bell ring.

—Scott Franzke

"It's bedlam at The Bank!" was Franzke's iconic call following Bryce Harper's game-winning home run in Game Five of the 2022 NLCS. *Incredible Baseball Stats* author Ryan Spaeder used it for his signature wedding cocktail (signed and dated). The call, and the cocktail, were incredibly strong. (*Ryan Spaeder*)

INTRODUCTION

Ralph Waldo Emerson, a great American intellectual, famously said, "It's not the destination, it's the journey." He must've been a Phillies fan. The Philadelphia Phillies, a franchise nearly 150 years old, has only reached its grand destination twice (World Series wins in 1980 and 2008). Two times. That's it. Yet, this city's fans—gruff, loyal, and louder than any other—keep showing up, generation after generation, like it's a religious mandate. How?

Well, Olive Garden, a great American impressionist Italian restaurant chain, famously said, "When you're here, you're family." The Phillies, warts and all, have been an inextricable part of the city and of the lives of the fans who cheered them on. The team's story isn't just stats and box scores; it's our story, forged in heartbreak, triumph, and a stubborn refusal to walk away.

This book is an encyclopedia of sorts, but it's more of a family history. We won't get into the really old stuff. Let's face it—while I'm sure the 1915 World Series loss was painful, no one's calling local sports talk radio to curse out Eppa Rixey. We'll mostly delve into the memories that formed this generation's deep bond with its ballclub, the kinds of happenings, good and bad, that somehow manifested an unrivaled home-field advantage.

What's your Phillies origin story? Did you fall in love with the 1964 club, only to have your heart broken in the end? Did you idolize the 1993 Phillies, only to have your heart broken in the end? Yeah, unfortunately, that plot repeats a lot in this city; still, the fans never give up hope and never turn down the volume.

The Phillies are 29–14 at Citizens Bank Park in the postseason. That .674 winning percentage is a record for any stadium in Major League Baseball history (minimum 20 postseason games).

Lately, its home-field advantage has been highlighted by Philadelphia's unlikely lengthy postseason runs in both 2022 and 2023. It wouldn't be possible without clutch road wins, but Philadelphia cut opponents' margin for error razor thin with its home dominance.

Postseason games at Citizens Bank Park in 2022 touched on levels the game has rarely experienced—literally. Philly fans' steady commotion during the World Series could be heard from over a mile away, relentlessly sustaining ear-splitting decibels that would make European football rioters wince. Phils announcer Scott Franzke coined it "Bedlam at the Bank," in stark contrast to Atlanta's ballpark, where one could easily take a phone call without leaving his or her seat. *Hey, some people prefer a quiet night out.*

At any game, in any city, a stadium media crew can ask its fans to scream as loudly as possible, but they can't make them care. The Phillies have the best home edge in baseball because, through it all, the fans never stopped bleeding for 'em.

That moment and emotion in 2022 were real and powerful. But alas, like for the vast majority of MLB seasons, the Phils were not ultimately victorious. And if pain builds character, it certainly explains why Philadelphia has so damn much of it.

The team's history includes a ton of rough patches, including a 31-year stint with just one single season above .500 (1918–48). Per US statistics, the average male born when that slump started in 1918 would be more likely to die before seeing two winning Phillies seasons. In 2007, the Phillies became the first professional team with ten thousand losses. *Yikes.*

Phillies fans wear their disappointment like a tattoo, and it makes sense. Players spend countless hours on the field, in the gym, and in the film room, putting in the work for future glory. The fans put in a different kind of work, carrying the emotional baggage of a team that's way more "wait till next *generation*" than "wait till next *year*." There's pride for having gone through it. Like a family—dysfunctional and sometimes emotionally abusive—the Phillies and their fans have stuck together.

This book will cover the moments and emotions that define the modern Phillies fan. Through the collapses, the close calls, the high hopes, and the champagne-soaked moments of glory, Phillies fandom is a family.

And this is our collective story.

#1

1964

> This was the pivotal event in my life. Nothing good that has ever happened to me since then can make up for the disappointment of that ruined season, and nothing bad that has happened since then can even vaguely compare with the emotional devastation wrought by that monstrous collapse.
>
> —Joe Queenan[1]

Whether in jest or not, fans today are quick to argue professional sports are scripted. And while the vast majority of us know it's a silly supposition, we still carve out a little room for fate, cosmic favoritism, or whatever it is that convinces us the scales are tilted and the thumb is certainly not attached to a Phillies fan.

We romanticize hope into fate—it's the kind of spiritual magic that permeates (to varying degrees) every one of Kevin Costner's sports movies. But, alas, the 1964 Phillies story is a tale more cautionary than fairy. It was as cold and harsh as reality often is. We hope for the best, but in the real world, the voices in Ray Kinsella's head are far more likely the result of a serious neurological condition, and, if he builds it, the foreclosure letters will most definitely come.

The Phils were in their 82nd season, having only logged two World Series appearances and one measly Series game win in that entire span dating back to 1883. To make matters worse—something Philadelphia sports has a penchant for—The Phillies were often not even the best ballclub in Philly.

From 1901 to 1954, the city was home to both the National League Phillies and American League Athletics. We'll dive more into that later in the book, but it's an important setup to the '64 squad. Just a decade removed from evicting it's AL roommate, it looked like the Phils were building something real and resilient.

The A's, despite five championships in Philadelphia, were chronically feast or famine. The 1950 season proved extremely pivotal for both clubs, as the A's (52–102 record) slumped back in the tank, and the Phils soared to the World Series, capturing the hearts and minds of Philly fans for good. It seemed as though the fans had made their choice, and just four seasons later, the A's were off to Kansas City, and the Phils looked to turn the page and set out on their own.

The Phillies finished at .500 or better six times from 1951 to 1963. It's not much to brag about, but consider the pedigree—just about a decade before the 1950 Whiz Kids' surprise World Series run, the Phillies became the only team in modern baseball history with a five-year stretch, from 1938 to 1942, that had a winning percentage under .300 (.295, for a season average of 45–107). Mediocrity was a win by comparison, but there was reason to hope for more.

In 1962 Johnny Callison joined the team and became an All-Star. That same season, Chris Short started making a name for himself in the rotation, winning 11 games with a 3.42 ERA. In 1964 they added future Hall of Famer Jim Bunning to the rotation and handed a full-time gig to Dick Allen, who was elected to the National Baseball Hall of Fame in late 2024. The pieces were certainly coming together, but fans still didn't anticipate the Fightins would compete for the World Series in '64.

Legendary Philly sportswriter Ray Didinger, a young Phillies fan at the time, idolized the upstart National League contenders:

> The Philly fans fell head over heels in love with the '64 Phillies because their success seemed to come out of nowhere. The Phillies were the worst team in baseball in the late 1950s and early 1960s. It was to a point where the fans had pretty much given up. The attendance figures at Connie Mack Stadium will attest to that.
>
> But 1964 changed all that. The Phillies did more than play winning baseball—they restored hope to a forlorn city; they made the spring and summer fun again. Total strangers struck up conversations on the street, on the buses and subways: "Hey, did you see the game last night?" Everyone was a Phillies fan.[2]

They caught fire early, going 9–2 in April, their best start to a season since they went 11–1 through the first 12 contests in 1915.

By the All-Star break, the National League title seemed like a two-horse race, with the Phillies (47–28) nursing a 1 1/2-game lead over the San Francisco Giants (47–31). Both teams had battled for the top spot all season; it seemed inevitable that the pennant would go to one or the other. Callison won the franchise's first and only All-Star MVP award, so karmically, advantage Philadelphia. Even though fans had been burned before, the universe kept dropping fate signs. This was a Costner movie in the making.

"Jim Bunning pitches the perfect game on Father's Day. Callison wins the All-Star game with a walk-off home run. Allen runs away with Rookie of Year. The team turns three—that's right, three—triple plays," said Didinger, playing the hits from the near-picture-perfect season. "Even the most skeptical fans began to think there was a special kind of magic at work—that the Phillies were having one of those years where the baseball genie comes out of the bottle and grants your every wish; '64 was that year for the Phillies."

And then, it wasn't. Just as the universe had sent signs all season that things were going great, there was one very literal sign that a fall was coming. The Phillies, up 6 1/2 games in the NL, lost on September 21, and about 12 hours later, the autumnal equinox marked the official start of fall.

Fall, they would. The Phils dropped 10 straight games in all, ending the slide 2 1/2 games behind.

During the Phillies' 10-game losing streak, the Reds won eight in a row and the Cardinals won 9 of 10. In the blink of an eye, a 6 1/2-game Philadelphia lead ended up with St. Louis in the World Series and Cincinnati tied with the Phillies at just a single game behind. Some blame a man called Chico "Effing" Ruiz.

Knotted up at 0–0 in the sixth inning of a September 21 game against Cincinnati, Reds third baseman Chico Ruiz successfully stole home—with *two outs* and Frank Robinson, one of the greatest hitters in baseball history, in the prime of his career, at the plate. That wasn't a traditionally heady play, but the Reds were desperate, Ruiz was a rookie, and Twitter wasn't invented yet. It was perhaps the perfect time for a low-percentage bonehead play.

The Reds took that game 1–0, and several Phillies in the years that followed would admit that it shook their confidence a bit. But after that, everyone blamed Gene Mauch.

The Phillies' thirty-eight-year-old manager was a hothead, known for doling out harsh criticisms and trashing clubhouses—think Tom Hanks's Jimmy Dugan in *A League of Their Own*. In a *Philadelphia Inquirer* interview after the

All-Star break that season, he singled out his Rookie of the Year–to–be, Dick Allen, saying, "Nobody has any idea what he has meant to this team. He's really something, and he's just going to keep getting better." Just after that, he told *Inquirer* reporter Allen Lewis that Allen was playing hurt, because, if he came out of the lineup, he might not get back in. A trope, maybe—a holdover sentiment from the days of Wally Pipp—but, Mauch demanded toughness, and he held grudges.

Reliever (and 1980 World Series champion manager) Dallas Green told Fox Sports in 2014 that Mauch got so upset with his top relief man Jack Baldschun after a September 19 loss that he erroneously opted for less-experienced, less-capable arms the rest of the season. Baldschun led the team in relief innings and saves that season (118 1/3 innings pitched, 21 saves), but only saw 7 2/3 innings of action during the 10-game slide.

Mostly, Mauch got the blame for repeatedly pitching his two aces (Bunning and Short) on short rest down the stretch. This time, the grudge turned on Mauch, and a lot of Phillies fans took their ire to the grave.

Of course, as is usually the case with drawn out team sport collapses, there was plenty of blame to go around. According to Bobby Shantz, former league MVP pitching his final season that year for the Phillies, it wasn't on the skipper:

> The fans were looking for someone to blame, and they seemed to blame Mauch, with how the pitching was used and all that. But I don't think it was his fault. He was doing his best to get us out of it, and nothing worked. No one complained when the moves were working all season.[3]

On the flip side, the Phillies' loss was the Cardinals' gain, and maybe the Mound City Rebound *is* the storybook, too-good-to-be-true World Series run that's made for the silver screen.

Nah.

When Mudville's Mighty Casey struck out, Ernest Thayer never even bothered to mention who they were playing—because it wasn't about them. The 1964 season wasn't about St. Louis. The story—the *tragedy*—was about the Philadelphia Phillies and how, sometimes, things go mightily wrong in spectacular ways.

#2
1980 FRANCHISE PILLARS

MIKE SCHMIDT

Philly is a sports debate town. With a ballclub that goes back to 1883, and a football team that predates the first canned beer (1933 Eagles vs. 1935 Krueger's Ale), the players, moments, teams, and accomplishments are simply too numerous to have a consensus on any*thing* or any*one*—except in the case of Michael Jack Schmidt.

The knee-jerk, glass-half-empty instinct might be to say that Schmidt is the franchise's clear top dog because of the overall dearth of game-changing players to wear Phillies pinstripes. Sure, Philadelphia has no Babe versus Mick, Musial versus Pujols, or Mays versus Bonds, but that doesn't mean Schmidt is out of the conversation with every one of those sluggers. He's widely considered the greatest third baseman in baseball history, and as far as franchise pillars go, he's load-bearing.

Here are the numbers:

- In career franchise WAR (wins above replacement), Schmidt (106.8) is ahead of Phillies Wall of Famers Richie Ashburn and Bobby Abreu *combined* (57.7 and 47.2, respectively).
- He is the franchise leader in games played (2,404), runs (1,506), total bases (4,404), home runs (548), RBIs (1,595), walks (1,507), and even a bunch of those dorky stats that probably aren't real, like base-out runs added (55.4).

- Schmidt led the 1980s in home runs (313), and hit more as a third baseman than anyone else (509). Only Babe Ruth led the league more times (12 to 8).
- He's a 10-time Gold Glove winner and leads the franchise in dWAR (defensive WAR, 18.4).

Baseball is a team game, but a lot of Philadelphia's best moments were made possible because of their second-round draft pick in 1971—a freakishly athletic *shortstop* out of Ohio University.

The MLB draft is always a bit of a crapshoot. Sometimes the stars align, and the top pick is obvious (e.g., Bryce Harper, Nationals, 2010), and other times its slim pickings, and the top selection is disastrous (e.g., Mickey Moniak, Phillies, 2016). The 1971 draft had a fairly miserable first round entirely.

Frank Tanana was the first player off the board to put together a stellar MLB career (13th pick, 21 years, 241 wins), followed by the great Jim Rice (15th, Hall of Fame, .298/.352/.502) and Rick Rhoden (20th, 16 years, 3.59 ERA). That leaves 26 other guys that never made a big name for themselves in the big leagues—including the Phillies' first pick, Roy Thomas.

Thomas, selected sixth overall, has a name that sounds more like a ChatGPT-created fast-food burger-chain operator, and career stats don't do much to dispel the notion. We implore you to check out his Baseball-Reference.com page, where his player photo features a face that looks like Roy Thomas is looking at Roy Thomas's career stats. Nearly every Googleable picture of the man resembles Phil Hartman's unfrozen caveman lawyer, confused and frightened by the witchcraft of modern flash photography.

Eventually, Philadelphia selected Schmidt in the second round, 30th overall. Schmidt had just led his Ohio Bobcats to the College World Series and was a shortstop on the 1970 College Baseball All-America Team. He stayed at shortstop almost exclusively during his 1971 Double-A season and then mostly played second base during his breakout 1972 Triple-A season, where he slashed .291/.409/.551 with 26 home runs in 131 games. The Phillies, at the time, had Larry Bowa at short and Don Money at third, two players in their prime who would have nine All-Star selections between them before 1980 (five to four, respectively). Unfortunately for the Phils, all of Money's All-Star seasons were with the Milwaukee Brewers.

> Don Money was the centerpiece of the 1967 trade between the Phillies and Pirates, with Philadelphia sending reigning MLB strikeout king and NL Cy Young runner-up Jim Bunning to Pittsburgh. Money was the Carolina League MVP and seemed like a shoo-in for instant stardom in the big leagues. What happened instead is every baseball fan's worst nightmare—Money, in four full seasons with the Phillies, hit just .242/.302/.371, and then immediately became one of the best third basemen in baseball after being traded to Milwaukee. From 1973 to 1978, he hit .281/.346/.428, which is just rude if you think about it. This wasn't a Ryne Sandberg or Fergie Jenkins situation, where the Phils lost dice rolls on high-value untested prospects. Philadelphia, patiently and politely, gave Money *four seasons* to figure out how to play baseball. In return, spoiled Milwaukee fans got a great player with easily the coolest name in sports. If his name was Dick Ferkis, the Phils would have traded him in '68, easy.

It would have been an interesting infield if the Phillies had stuck with some combination of Schmidt/Money/Bowa long term, but it's hard to lament potentialities when a nearly centenarian franchise was welcoming its best player. Plus, the Phils acquired second baseman Dave Cash from the Pirates in 1974, and all he did was make the All-Star team each season he spent with Philadelphia (1974–76). In both 1974 and 1976, the Phils sent their second baseman (Cash), shortstop (Larry Bowa), and third baseman (Schmidt) to the midsummer classic. The '76 team featured nearly the entire Phillies infield, with catcher Bob Boone getting a reserve selection.

Famously, Schmidt, twenty-three, struggled in his first full year with the ballclub, hitting .196/.324/.373, but time has shed a kinder light on Schmitty's first go-round. Hell, Kyle Schwarber batted .197 in 2023 and received MVP votes. Jimmy Rollins, who broke Schmidt's franchise hits record in 2014, had a lower OPS at the same age and still made the All-Star team that season (.686 to .697). To be fair—probably too fair, but who cares?—Schmidt's OPS was a respectable .737 on September 22 before he ended the season in an 0-for-26 rut. Regardless, Schmidt became a superstar the following year.

"The Phillies were coming off that brutal 1972 season, and the club was looking for someone to tout other than Lefty [Steve Carlton]," said longtime

Phillies broadcaster Chris "Wheels" Wheeler. "So, when Mike hit .196 in 132 games, there was concern. But he showed so much potential with his bat and glove the organization really felt they had a player."[1]

They were right. Schmidt led the bigs in homers each of the next three seasons following his rookie campaign. He had a three-year late start and still managed to hit the fourth-most homers in the National League in the 1970s. But, of course, he was no one-trick pony. He was very flashy with the leather, and we're not just talking about his glove. Channeling Mars Blackmon in that famous 1991 Air Jordan commercial, "It's gotta be the shoes!"

Schmidt is not remembered for his speed and quickness in the way that greats like Barry Bonds and Mickey Mantle are, but he probably should be. He had as many seasons with 35-plus home runs and at least a dozen stolen bases as Bonds (six).

The following players had the most career seasons with 30-plus home runs, 100-plus walks, and 10-plus stolen bases:

Bonds, eight
Schmidt, five
Mantle, five
Babe Ruth, five
Jeff Bagwell, five
Lou Gehrig, three

Schmidt's speed and quickness helped him become elite in every facet of the game, which is why, before Bonds kicked things off in 1990, Schmidt's three MVP awards were a major-league record (Bonds, seven; Mantle, Mike Trout, Albert Pujols, Álex Rodríguez, Yogi Berra, Roy Campanella, Stan Musial, Joe DiMaggio, Jimmie Foxx, three). In total, he finished in the top ten in MVP voting nine times.

Statistically, Schmidt is the franchise's best player, and it's not close. Any Mount Rushmore debate of Philly athletes is really just deciding which three come after MLB's greatest third baseman. Curious, then, that it seems—no matter who you'd pick to fill those three vacancies—Schmidt would likely be the least beloved player of the quartet.

"Mike Schmidt was the greatest third baseman in the history of the game . . . and it wasn't until maybe toward the end of his career that people started to realize it," said longtime *Inquirer* reporter and WIP sports talk host Glen

Macnow. "He was never good at expressing himself and said some regrettable things over the years.

"He played the game with such ease and grace. . . . He didn't appear to be hustling out there, because he didn't have to. He knew where to be; his instincts were so good that he could read the ball off the bat and put himself in a position where he could make a great play without diving. As his career [wound] down, people started to realize what a good thing they had. I think both sides—Schmidt and the fans—would like a do-over on that."[2]

As the legendary Huey Lewis reminds us, the power of love is a curious thing. Schmidt is now, generally, given his flowers and adoration from fans, and however unlikely it may have seemed during his mostly stoic playing career, he's now a dynamite Phillies broadcaster. We can't go back in time, but the reciprocal relationship between Michael Jack and the fans feels right, presently.

"[Schmidt] was very introverted and didn't spend a lot of time trying to let people get to know him," admitted Wheels. "All I can say as someone who spent a lot of time around him, I knew we had an amazing all-around player who was going to be a first ballot Hall of Famer.

"No doubt he is more loved now than when he played. And Mike now is very comfortable in his own skin and loves life."[3]

In 2006, Schmidt said, "Sure, I was disappointed in not being considered for the Phillies [managerial] job in 2004, even though I understood at the time why I wasn't. Their number one priority was prior experience managing in the big leagues, and I had none. End of story."[4]

Still, Schmidt has never doubted his ability. "Times change. Situations change. But one thing hasn't changed: I haven't forgotten how to win. It's in the blood."

STEVE CARLTON

When the Phillies dealt their ace, Rick Wise, to the St. Louis Cardinals in 1972, Cards GM Bing Devine was asked about the difference between the pitcher they were trading away and the pitcher they were receiving: "One's right-handed, and the other's left-handed."

Sure, it was *a* difference, but the lefty that arrived in Philadelphia turned out to be *the* Lefty, with a capital *L*, maybe the best the game has ever seen.

Hindsight is 20/20, so it's hard to disagree with Devine's assessment at the time. Wise, just twenty-five years old, had a 2.88 ERA on the season, his first as an All-Star. He also cemented himself in Phillies history on June 23 of that year by pitching a no-hitter while also slugging two home runs.

> **FUN FACTS:** Wise is often, erroneously, credited with being the first pitcher to homer in his no-hit game, but he was the *fourth* to do so (Wes Ferrell, 1932; Jim Tobin, 1944; Earl Wilson, the first black player in the AL with a no-no, 1962). Wise was, however, the first and only one to go yard twice, and considering the MLB-wide DH designation currently in place, it may forever be considered the greatest all-around pitcher's performance ever recorded. Fittingly, Wise's big game was 54 years to the day of the only no-no credited to Babe Ruth, the game's original two-way star. Oddly, Ruth recorded *zero* innings pitched that day, having gotten tossed after an opening walk. He was relieved by Ernie Shore, who went perfect the rest of the way to cement the game's first official combined no-hitter. Odder still, of the 322 total no-hitters pitched in major-league history, these are the only two to fall on June 23. Apologies for the tangent; back to Lefty!

At the time of the trade, the twenty-seven-year-old Carlton had already pitched three All-Star seasons and was coming off his first 20-win campaign. It was an even trade on paper, but few could have foreseen that Carlton would immediately record one of the most dominant seasons in MLB history. Rumor has it, the Cardinals had been encouraging Carlton to ease up on his slider (recognized today as one of the game's best in history). The Phillies thought that was a dumb idea.

> So, I'm sitting in the coffee shop of the Jack Tarr Hotel in Clearwater on a February morning in 1972. It was my first spring training. My boss at the time, Larry Shenk, walks up and sits down. He has a strange look on his face. He says, J.Q. (GM John Quinn) just traded Rick Wise for Steve Carlton. What do you think? My initial reaction was the fans aren't going to like trading Rick, who was coming off a no-hitter and a 6 HR season. But as a fan, I thought about this tall, skinny left-hander with the big Adam's apple who could really fire. And I told the Baron I liked the deal. And, no offense, we were very

lucky back then not to have talk shows and social media. We just had our beat writers. It was a little easier to control the narrative.

—Chris Wheeler[5]

Carlton—unleashing his unhittable slider—was 27–10, with a 1.97 ERA and 310 strikeouts in 1972, winning the National League Cy Young Award and Triple Crown (NL lead in wins, ERA, strikeouts). It's easily one of the greatest seasons ever pitched, but what makes it uniquely Philly is that he accomplished this feat on one of the worst ballclubs imaginable.

Aside from Carlton, the Phillies were terrible that year. Their No. 2 starter won just two games (Ken Reynolds, 2–15), and their No. 3 and No. 4 starters each only won four (Bill Champion, 4–14; Woodie Fryman, 4–10). Larry Bowa led the team in plate appearances (633) and hit just .250/.291./.320. It's a situation that is oddly unique to baseball because, in every other major sport, it's nearly impossible to be the worst team with the best player. Technically, the Texas Rangers finished with a worse win percentage (.351 to .378), but that was the Rangers' first-ever season, and cost-cutting led to them fielding one of the worst offensive squads to ever grace the diamond (.217 team batting average and 38 games with zero extra-base hits, a Live Ball Era record). The Phillies lost just three fewer games than Texas—gross!

It's just not supposed to happen that way. Kelly Leak signs up, and the Bears reach the championship. Roy Hobbs catches lightning in a 40-ounce hickory bottle, and the Knights win the pennant. The 1972 Bad News Phils acquire the best player in baseball and finish dead last in the NL—*naturally.*

The Phillies' Hollywood ending would have to wait a few years, but Lefty's season is a triumph unto itself:

- Carlton's 27 wins accounted for 45.8 percent of the team's victories.
- He set a Phillies record for pitching WAR (12.1), besting Grover Cleveland Alexander's mark from 1917 (10.9). Eight years later, he notched the franchise's third-best WAR (10.2), and Aaron Nola is the only Phillie since to have sniffed double digits (9.2, 2018).
- Since 1972, no one in baseball has matched or bettered Carlton's ERA and strikeout total in the same season (1.97 ERA, 310 Ks).
- Thirty complete games are the highest MLB single-season total in 70 years (tied with Juan Marichal, 1968; Fergie Jenkins, 1971; and Catfish Hunter, 1975).

The team was bad, but according to Wheeler, the vibe shifted when Carlton took the mound.

"When Lefty pitched on what we would call 'win day,' the team was different. They knew all they had to do was score a few runs and catch the ball. Carlton would do the rest. The Vet really rocked on the nights he pitched."[6]

Lefty had a shockingly pedestrian follow-up in 1973 and actually led the league in losses (13–20, 3.90 ERA). It ended up being a common theme of Carlton's career—inconsistent greatness. The ups and downs were evident not just on the field but also in the clubhouse. Beginning that season, Carlton would become a problem for the press.

"Lefty was burned by a sportswriter in 1973," said Wheeler, perhaps tactfully avoiding any reference to infamous *Inquirer* columnist Bill Conlin (more on this later). "So, he just decided to shut down completely with the media."[7]

An outspoken former teammate of Carlton's, Larry Bowa, was less diplomatic in his assessment of the situation: "He gave the media every opportunity. I think it was Bill Conlin that wrote an article about where he went after a game he pitched. And if he went out and had a few drinks after a night he pitched, it was nobody's business. So, from that day on, he said, 'I don't need to talk to you guys if you're going to write something like that.'"[8]

Carlton admitted as much in a rare candid interview with *Philadelphia Inquirer* writer Stan Hochman in 2013: "Winter of '72, I was everywhere. Doing everything I shouldn't be doing. Got to Spring Training with walking pneumonia. It set me up to have the problems I did. . . . I don't believe in good and bad; I believe life is about lessons, and these guys (cynical writers) wanted to tee off on me.

This is my problem with the media. They chop off heads of others to make themselves taller. This is where we're not uplifting society."[9]

That's awfully deep for an athlete, but it's kiddie pool stuff for Lefty. He refused to talk ball with the media but would often muse about science, nature, and a whole wide array of existential gobbledygook that was surely strange for the time but might fit perfectly today in a three-hour slot on *The Joe Rogan Experience*.

It's fascinating looking back on Carlton's impact with a modern eye. Hall of Fame manager Tommy Lasorda credited him with completely changing the way pitchers train and prepare for the rigors of a 162-game season. Inspired by martial arts training, Lefty was in tune with his body and environment in ways that were way ahead of his time. The 1970s judged him harshly, but by today's standards, he'd surely be just another of many athletes with his or her own fitness company, wellness drink, and Spotify podcast.

> In Bill Conlin, Carlton couldn't have picked a better villain. For most of his career, Conlin was credited as one of the best in sports writing—maybe ever. As a kid, he was my favorite writer, and I enjoyed his curmudgeonly miserable attitude on episodes of *Daily News Live*. He was good at his job, but he really seemed awful to be around—and that played well on TV. Of course, his grouchy demeanor isn't what ultimately cemented the heinous chapters of his Wikipedia bio. His fall from grace is very Googleable, but it's far too heavy for a book that strives to keep the morally distressing topics in their appropriate spaces.

Upon tabulation, Lefty's career had way more ups than downs, and he retired as one of the best pitchers in baseball history. The MLB career strikeout record traded hands between Carlton and Nolan Ryan several times in 1983 and 1984, but age seemed to favor The Express. Carlton, perhaps stubbornly, logged 430 innings in his 40s, with a dreadful 5.21 ERA, while Ryan pitched 1,271 2/3 innings in his 40s with a 3.33 ERA. Old baseball cards featuring Lefty in White Sox, Giants, Indians, and Twins jerseys during those later years have become a fun fixation for fans, like one of those creepy AI photos that doesn't look quite right. Collectively, everyone seems to prefer, and willfully accept, the alternative reality where the National League's greatest left-hander finished things off in a Phillies uniform. Regardless, his legacy is untarnished.

Carlton was one of the last of his kind. He is the last pitcher to log 300 innings pitched in a single season (1980). Much of baseball history was played with blissful ignorance of both preventative and reparative therapies to combat physical wear and tear. Many players, Carlton included, played until their proverbial arms fell off.

Philadelphia A's and Phillies star Bobby Shantz had this to say:

"When you started a game, you expected to finish it. In 1952 [with the A's], I pitched 14 innings of one-run ball and got the win. The Yankees starter [Tom Morgan] pitched into the 14th. We won it 2–1. I had to have thrown over 350 pitches that game."[10]

Regarding the whole arm-falling-off thing, that's the scenario that ended Shantz's career. "My last year, ending up with the Phillies, I was still pitching pretty well," and the former AL MVP was right, as he posted a 3.12 ERA in 60 2/3 innings of relief, to go with one of the lowest WHIPs of his career (1.170). "I just couldn't do it anymore. The thought of coming back [in 1965] never crossed my mind because my arm just hurt too much."

It really seemed like that's what Carlton was going for, pitching until his age forty-three season in 1988. His career would have looked much better (statwise, and baseball-card-wise) if he just would've woken up one morning in 1985 with Shantz Shoulder and called it a career.

PETE ROSE

In late 1978, just the fourth year of free agency, the Phillies landed arguably the franchise's most influential free agent in Pete Rose. He was thirty-seven years old when the Phils signed him on December 5, 1978, and his thirty-eighth birthday would be just a week following opening day of the 1979 season—he was no spring chicken. To that point, he had amassed 3,164 hits in his career and a .310/.379/.432 slash line, all with the Reds. In many ways, however, his MLB story was just getting started.

Rose, also known as Charlie Hustle, was a dangerously fierce competitor with a knack for winning; he was among baseball's best leaders. Ironically, Charlie Hustle also seems like the perfect name for a degenerate gambler who bet on the teams he played for, and quite possibly bet *against* the teams he played for, lying about it for a super long time. Yes, in more ways than one, Rose was certainly a hustler.

The details surrounding the nickname's origin have been debated, but Rose, in fact, got it from Yankee legend Whitey Ford during spring training in 1963. Ford was certainly mocking the rookie's over-the-top effort and competitiveness, but Rose owned it and made it his alter ego. It's just a sad coincidence that the name also looks like an alias on some local bookie's ledger sheet.

Before we get to the scandalous, here's a look at the stats, which are undeniable:

- Rose batted .331 his first season in Philadelphia, leading the NL in OBP (.418).
- Also in his first year, he became just the third player in MLB history with multiple 163-game seasons (1974, 1979; Brooks Robinson, 1961, 1964; Billy Williams, 1968, 1969).

1980 FRANCHISE PILLARS

- He led the league in doubles in 1980 (42), playing every possible game for the sixth time in seven seasons.
- Pete batted .326 in the postseason in 1980 and is largely credited with being a key catalyst to getting the Phillies over the hump for their first championship.
- He racked up 826 of his MLB-leading 4,256 career hits with Philadelphia, batting .291/.365/.361 in his five years. Over three postseason trips with the Phils (1980, 1981, 1983), he batted .326.

Rose was released by the Phillies following the 1983 season, and he exited Philadelphia a hero. He helped the franchise get its first title and nearly tacked on another one after a failed World Series effort in 1983.

That's where our story takes a turn. Following a short stint with the Expos in 1984, Rose was traded in-season and finished his playing career with the Reds as a player-manager (1984–86; very cool by the way). He stayed on as manager until 1989, when rumors of his gambling spurred an intense investigation by Major League Baseball.

On August 24, 1989, he was handed a lifetime ban by Commissioner Bart Giamatti for illegally betting on baseball and spent most of the next two decades denying it while continuing to be denied entry back into the MLB fold. His ban includes his removal from Hall of Fame consideration. Since then, he admitted to betting on baseball while he played and managed but to his dying day, insisted he never bet against his team.

> Gambling addicts are not known for having much restraint. Also, documented habitual liars are not very trustworthy. Keeping these two facts in mind, I can't imagine a scenario in which Rose *didn't* ever take the under in a game where he could pencil himself in at leadoff—just my opinion. It's also important to note that Rose could have been theoretically telling the truth while still indirectly cheating; all he would have to do is let his bookie know when it might be an advantageous time to place a bet against his team . . . for a small fee. In such a case, Rose would be able to honestly claim he never personally bet against himself. Whatever the case may be, his legacy is forever muddled. His gambling woes were not even the most egregious of his alleged transgressions, but history has taught us repeatedly that heroes disappoint, and that can be true of

> anyone. We've tried here to focus mostly on what happened between the white lines regarding Phillies legends, but Rose's misdeeds bleed into both territories. Love him or hate him, we can't blame you.

Major League Baseball has a long history of stars who lived hard, played hard, and were eventually taken out by their lifestyle. In some cases, it only seemed to add to their legend:

- Babe Ruth and Mickey Mantle are two of the most beloved, storied characters in MLB history, but their vices (e.g., alcohol consumption) likely hindered their careers and shortened their lives.
- Lou Gehrig tragically died of Lou Gehrig's disease (ALS)—right? Well, a Harvard study in 2022 suggested the possibility that the Iron Horse's toughness is what actually took him out. Gehrig played hard and famously played every day. Multiple concussions over a long playing career (as well as his collegiate football career at Columbia University) may have led to ALS-mirroring symptoms that eventually caused his untimely demise.
- Roberto Clemente, through no fault of his own (aside from being a great dude) perished in a plane crash in 1972 while on his way to deliver aid to hurricane victims in Nicaragua. Sometimes, the good guy gets taken out. But he'll forever be remembered as one of baseball's greatest *actual* heroes.

Now, Pete Rose lived until 2024, but the abrupt end to his career, and absurd twists and turns that followed, make it feel as though Charlie Hustle died by Giamatti's pen that day in 1989, and the fans were left with just Pete from then on. As it turns out, "just Pete" was a pretty lousy trade-off.

Still, perhaps he does belong in the Hall—not for Pete's sake, but for the fans and for the crystalline memories that, through the natural laws of time and space, cannot be altered by the revelations that followed. When he played, he was great and beloved. It changes how we look back on it, but even then, there are many unknowns. As far as former players are concerned, no one ever seems to have a negative thing to say about the man—at least, not regarding the times when he was legally permitted to step foot on a Major League Baseball field.

Bob Boone (Phillies catcher, 1972–81) said of Rose's absence from the team's 20th anniversary of 1980 celebration, "I'm sad about what happened to him. But I'm also resentful that we have to talk about it on the reunion of us winning the World Series."[11] And that's just it: once you know of the existence of Mr. Hyde, no one's as interested in Dr. Jekyll's glory days back in medical school.

It's hard to quantify if or how Rose's misdeeds would have altered the course of history. Through all the years and lies, the questions will never have satisfying answers. Hall enshrinement was Rose's concern, but it shouldn't be the fans'. The commish can't ban the memories. To that point, the league explained in a statement made on May 13, 2025, "Commissioner Rob Manfred has concluded that MLB's policy shall be that permanent ineligibility ends upon the passing of the disciplined individual." So, for the first time ever, there is no official obstruction to Rose's Hall of Fame entry. Of course, Barry Bonds, Mark McGwire, and Gary Sheffield know that it's still no guarantee.

LARRY BOWA

When the Phillies finally hoisted the Commissioner's Trophy in 1980, some of the biggest names in franchise (and baseball) history adorned the red pinstripes. Most fans probably think first of Mike Schmidt, Steve Carlton, or Pete Rose, but baseball is fundamentally a team game. There's a slew of unheralded players from that team and era, and Larry Bowa tops the list. He was the ultimate teammate. And he was better than you probably think.

Schmidt, the game's greatest third baseman, overshadowed the outstanding shortstop who played alongside him for nine seasons in Philadelphia. The truth is, besides Schmidt, Bowa was probably the most consistent two-way player throughout the team's dominant stretch in the late 1970s and early 1980s.

During that era, the Phillies had a little bit of an identity crisis:

- In 1976 Philly had one of the best starting rotations in baseball and won a franchise-record 101 games, leading the NL in starting pitcher wins with 75.
- Although the 1977 rotation was a massive disappointment, the team tied the 101-win mark behind the best offense and bullpen in the

league (.279 BA, first in NL; four relievers with a qualified ERA under 3.00, leading MLB).
- In 1978 the rotation drastically improved (96 quality starts, compared to 88 in 1977 and 91 in 1976), but the team batting average plummeted 20 points (.258).
- The bullpen collapsed in 1979 (last in NL in holds; Ron Reed led bullpen with 4.15 ERA).

One of the team's strengths that never really seemed to falter was its defense. Bowa played a very big part in that.

Bowa, a five-time All-Star, won two Gold Gloves, but was not a one-trick pony. During the 12 years he spent with Philadelphia, Dave Concepción and Garry Templeton were the only shortstops with more .280 seasons (Bowa, four; Concepción and Templeton, six). He actually led the Phillies in batting average in 1975 and 1979. He was no Cal Ripken Jr., but these were different times.

Shortstops simply were not expected to hit back then. Consider that from 1964 to 1983, the Baltimore Orioles posted a remarkable .588 collective win percentage, which averages out to 95 wins per full season. Mark Belanger logged the most innings for them at shortstop during that storied 20-year run, and he batted just .227 (1965–81). To Baltimore, Belanger's eight Gold Gloves weighed way more than his bat ever could.

Bowa's bat was the occasional cherry on top of his defensive prowess, as he led all NL shortstops in the 1970s in defensive WAR (15.6). These days, Cardinals wiz Ozzie Smith gets all the love, but Bo retired with the NL record for career games at shortstop (2,222) and the MLB career fielding percentage mark (.9797).

But that's enough stats. Stats don't tell the whole story, and Bowa's is a lot of story to tell.

Rocky analogies get old quickly, but truly, Larry (Bal)Bowa is a real Philly guy—an underdog, overachiever, and leader who used every bit of his ability to excel repeatedly in the City of Brotherly Love. He's the kinda guy who gets hit and keeps moving forward.

As long as we're doing movie analogies, Rudy might be a more apt comparison (think "Five feet nothin', a hundred and nothin'"). Bowa was cut from his high school team three years in row after being considered too small (his official MLB weight is listed at just 155 pounds). He eventually played, and played well, earning a spot on the hometown Sacramento City College team, where he was twice named All-Conference. He always had his sights set on the big leagues, but smaller guys who get cut in high school and go to community college don't generally get to play for the Phillies—unless, very loosely umbrellaed under *play*, we include slinging bags of peanuts and Miller Lites up in the 700 level.

It's not a glitch on his Baseball-Reference page (or much of a surprise); Bowa went undrafted. Rumor has it, the Phillies were the only team to show interest in him in free agency, after sending their California scout, Eddie Bockman, to see him play a doubleheader while at SCC. Naturally, Bowa got tossed from both games for arguing with the umpire. For better or worse, Bowa always seemed to lead with his fiery impulses.

At the 20th anniversary celebration of the 1980 championship team, Tug McGraw commented on Bowa's (and Pete Rose's) absence: "We called them the soup spoons. Because they were always stirring things up. Twenty years later, nothing's changed."[12]

Of course, Rose was banned from baseball, so he had an excuse. Bowa, however, was merely pissed off at the organization—just because. Phillies chairman Bill Giles said at the time, "Bowa claims he's mad at me for whatever reason—I'm not sure why."[13] That's just Bo.

Whatever it was, it blew over, and Bowa got the Phillies managerial job a year later. And years earlier, when he got thrown out of that doubleheader in front of Bockman, he still ended up getting signed. That was just Bo being Bo, and it was part of his competitive edge.

He consistently climbed the ranks through the minor leagues from 1966 to 1969, earning the starting shortstop job in 1970 and never looking back. Over the next 15 seasons (12, Philadelphia; 4, Chicago Cubs), he played in 91.2 percent of his team's games (2,131 of 2,370 possible). Longevity and durability would be one of his hallmarks, both during and after his playing career.

Bowa, senior advisor to the Phillies' GM as of publication, racked up an impressive postplaying career, coaching for the Phils (1989–96, 2014–17), Anaheim Angels (1997–99), Seattle Mariners (2000), New York Yankees (2006–07), and LA Dodgers (2008–10). His managerial stops included the San Diego Padres (1987–88) and Phils (2001–04), where he earned NL Manager of the Year for the 2001 season. He bounced around a bit, but through it all, he always seemed to be with Philadelphia for the biggest moments.

"It means a lot to me," said Bowa when asked about the personal importance of being in uniform for the opening and closing of the Vet and opening of Citizens Bank Park. "It means I was here a long time, and I had to do something good to stay here that long. I was also [with Philadelphia] for the last game at Connie Mack . . . and then I went down to Clearwater and was there for the opening of the spring training site. We played the last spring training game at Jack Russell. So, I had a lot of openings and closings in my career, which, I thank the Phillies, and I thank the good man above for keeping me in good health."[14]

Hopes and expectations vary from player to player. Mike Schmidt's impact on the organization was almost ordained. But few would have guessed an undrafted free agent from Sacramento City College would Forrest Gump his way into some of the most pivotal moments in franchise history. (And that's not a dig—Gump had game.) "The fact that I've been with the organization for a very long time, some of those things just fall into place, and they did."[15]

#3

1980—THE FIRST ONE

"The love affair between the Philadelphia fans and that ballclub was something I'll never forget."

—Harry Kalas[1]

THE PRELUDE: 1977

Spiritually, the tale of the 1980 Phillies began in 1977. As with most stories—this book, especially—failure and pain typically preempt glory. On its face, the 1980 season feels like the end of a bad joke. The franchise was closing in on its 100-year anniversary, with zero championships to show for it. But it's hard for any fan to shoulder a load of that magnitude. The wounds of the 1977 season were still fresh at the time, and whether it's real or make-believe (again, think *Rocky I*), it certainly seems as though *what* is meant to be in Philadelphia doesn't always happen *when* it's meant to be. In 1977 the Phillies were *supposed to be* MLB champions. In the end, just like Balboa, the Phillies would have to wait three years to get their happy ending.

The Phils won a franchise-best 101 games in '77. The pieces had been falling into place for most of the decade, and the team's trajectory seemed destined to conclude with a World Series trophy by season's end. The club had seven consecutive losing seasons from 1968–74, but then everything seemed to click at once. Mike Schmidt emerged, collecting three consecutive home run titles from 1974 to 1976; Steve Carlton, after leading the league in losses in 1973 (20), put together a nine-year run from 1974 to 1982 with a cumulative 2.99 ERA and three Cy Young Awards; outfielder Greg Luzinski put together four straight All-Star seasons from 1975 to 1978. For a very long time, the Phillies seemed to come out on the losing end of roster building, but two trades in 1975 brought, arguably, the league's best center fielder (Garry

Maddox) and best relief pitcher (Tug McGraw) to the City of Brotherly Love. The rotation *may* have been their only weakness, as GM Paul Owens built a venerable superteam.

"The bullpen was stacked, the bench was stacked, the lineup was stacked," said Mitchell Nathanson, author of *The Fall of the 1977 Phillies*. "Baseball will never see a complete club like that again." (Nathanson said this in 2019, prior to Shohei Ohtani signing a team-friendly deal in 2024 to make the Dodgers, on paper, a nearly perfect ballclub. Never underestimate a professional sports team's ability to throw money at a problem.)

The Phils led the league in RBIs, runs scored, batting average, on-base percentage, and slugging that year, but the bullpen was the not-so-secret weapon. They had the best 'pen in baseball, and they used it well. Those were the days when the bullpen was primarily a place for players who were not quite cutting it in the starting rotation—think backup singers who didn't have the chops for center stage. Of course, that's not how the bullpen is used today, and that's not how Phillies manager Danny Ozark used his throughout the 1970s.

Aside from Cy Young winner Carlton, the rotation was a bit of a mess. Larry Christenson won 19 games despite a 4.06 ERA, but Jim Kaat and Randy Lerch were just 16–17 combined, with a cumulative 5.22 ERA.

The team's top four relievers got plenty of work and dominated, with Ron Reed (124 1/3 innings pitched), Gene Garber (103 1/3), McGraw (79), and Warren Brusstar (71 1/3) sporting a collective 2.59 ERA. Those four horsemen were among just 12 relievers in the National League with an ERA below 3.00 (minimum 70 IP), and no other team in all of baseball had more than two! They had a generational ace in the rotation, but it was the four relief aces stashed up their sleeve that made for a very unfair game. It all added up to a team-record 101 regular-season wins. Of course, none of that stuff carries over to the postseason.

The Phillies entered the five game National League Championship Series as prohibitive favorites, but the Dodgers were no pushovers. They won 98 games and were the only NL team to top the Phils in homers. Let's be honest—it was obvious both then and now that sure things don't exist when it comes to Phillies baseball. Aside from maybe death itself, 95 years of failure is a universally depressing feat. Still, with all their strengths, the Fightins had the feel of a team that was too big to fail. Because the bullpen played a major part

1980—THE FIRST ONE

of Philadelphia's success that regular season, it was no surprise that Garber and company would factor in heavily in the NLCS, for better or worse.

"The series was tied at 1–1, and whoever won that third game went up 2–1 in the best-of-five series," recalled Garber. "We had Lefty going the next night. . . . [T]hat made Game 3 so important. In a short series, whoever wins two games has a decided advantage."[2]

For most of the game, the pen was as advertised. Brusstar and Reed relieved Christenson early, surrendering zero runs in 2 2/3 innings of work, handing the ball off to Garber in the seventh with the score tied 3–3. In the eighth, the Phils scored two to make the score 5–3, which was seemingly more than enough cushion.

Garber, affectionately known as "Geno" by the screaming Vet Stadium fans, dominated. He induced eight groundball outs in a row and was one more away from closing out the game and delivering a crucial 2–1 series lead. Ninth inning, two outs, 0–1 count, best changeup, groundball pitcher in baseball on the mound—what could go wrong? *Every $%&ing thing.*

"[Dodgers pinch-hitter Vic Davalillo] lays down a perfect drag bunt," Garber said. "He could not have rolled it out there any better. He got it past me, and the first baseman, Richie Hebner, couldn't get it. Ted Sizemore tried to scoop it over, and Davalillo was safe. That's when the nightmare started."[3]

Credit Manny Mota, the next LA batter, for somehow getting under Garber's deadly changeup, and lifting it to deep left field. Luzinski leapt slightly to snag it, but the ball popped out of his glove and off the wall. Davalillo scored, and an error on Sizemore from Luzinski's throw moved Mota to third base.

KEVIN'S NOTE

Manager Danny Ozark routinely replaced lumbering "Bull" Luzinski in left with the more sure-handed Jerry Martin as a late-inning defensive upgrade. Not doing that here was an obvious mistake that Ozark never really owned, telling reporters after the game, "If they tie it [or go ahead], Bull's up third [in the bottom of the ninth]."[4] That's a silly supposition, but I'll grant that it's hard to predict that exact scenario, with a groundball pitcher throwing to a guy that was not at all a dead-pull hitter. Forget all that. Maybe I'm a victim of the conspiratorial question-everything, don't-believe-your-lying-eyes affliction that has infected all aspects of

> modern discourse, but *are we sure Bull didn't catch that ball?* The replays are from the 1970s—it's grainy, and I feel like the ball might never actually have touched the wall. It landed in the very top of Luzinski's glove, the glove hit the wall, the ball popped out, and finally, it landed in Bull's hands. It seems possible that the ball never connected with a foreign surface, but the wall simply jarred the ball out of the glove. I'm not a flat-earther, but I'm all-in that #BullCaughtIt, even though he, himself, seems to be pretty sure it hit the wall. At the very least, I just wonder if maybe he could have *pretended* it never hit the wall and gotten the out call. The game came down to a blown call anyway.

Davey Lopes then came up and ripped a grounder to golden-gloved Schmidt, who was playing in. It ricocheted off his leather, and Larry Bowa barehanded it and fired to first, in time to get the batter and end the game—if the call had been properly made. It was not.

Said Larry Bowa, "Everything happened so fast. The ball came to me on one hop, I barehanded it, threw . . . and he was out. I just watched it again [in 2024]. But at the time, there is no replay rule, and the fact that [umpire] Bruce Froemming anticipated Lopes being one of the fastest guys in the National League, he just thought there was no way that could happen. But, it was a perfect storm, and it did happen. The call just didn't go our way."[5]

The result was heartbreaking because Hebner knew the throw beat Lopes—and Harry Kalas called it that way, at first, on the broadcast—but only one person's opinion matters in times like these, and this time, it was the out-of-position umpire.

After recording the shoulda-been out, Hebner's right hand shot up. Alas, the instinctual celebratory gesture quickly turned to fist-of-fury. Hebner was all over Froemming. Garber and Sizemore (each in a better position to see the play) were also furious. And after a fruitless Ozark protest, the insanity proceeded onward.

A botched pickoff attempt moved Lopes to second. A base hit up the middle just barely past the glove of Garber scored Lopes, and the Dodgers secured the lead and eventually the game, 6–5.

No, Luzinski batting third in the bottom of the ninth did not affect the outcome of the ballgame. In tragedies such as these, even the best-laid plans are destined to go up in smoke. It's hard to blame him, just as it would be hard to blame Wile E. Coyote—the plot, it seemed, depended on him failing. Baseball is a funny game that way.

Truly, it was cartoonish the way things conspired against Ozark and the '77 Phils: the best groundball pitcher in baseball gave up four groundballs, one catchable pop fly, and zero walks, somehow surrendering three runs and tanking a season 95 years in the making.

"I still wake up with nightmares from that game,"[6] admitted Garber 30 years later. Garber pitched well, but no pitcher can hold their own against the LA Dodgers *and* fate.

Alas, what probably lessened the sting was the familiarity of outcome: 95 years, same result. That's a lot of years to wait. So, what's three more?

THE PRESTIGE: 1980

On paper, it would seem, that the Phillies were always building toward championship success in 1980. In reality, hopes were pretty low. The Black Friday collapse felt more like the beginning of the end, as the 1978 squad lost the NLCS again to the Dodgers, and 1979 culminated with just 84 wins, sending Ozark to the unemployment office before September call-ups.

Carlton was still an ace, but the thirty-five-year-old entered 1980 coming off the third-worst ERA performance of his career (3.62).

Pete Rose, who dominated in his first season in Philly (.331/.418/.430 in 1979), would turn thirty-nine before the team's fourth game of the season.

They fielded the oldest batters in baseball that season (30.6 years, weighted by at-bats and games played). Bowa was thirty-four, Tugger thirty-five, and Reed thirty-seven—you get the idea. Time, a familiar foe for the winless franchise, was threatening to forcefully close Philly's window.

Phillies fans were reading the room and were hesitant at first to buy in. Who could blame them? Outsiders are sometimes too quick to label Philly fans as fair-weather, but the context clearly pointed elsewhere—rationality be damned, the fans demanded excellence. The Cubs may have carried baseball's most storied championship drought (1909–2015), but its ineptitude bred a palpable degree of benevolent apathy. Before winning it all in 2016, Chicago seemed awkwardly proud of its failure. Sure, fans wanted to win, but they also seemed comfortably wrapped up in the victimhood of their idiotic Curse of the Billy Goat. Fans in the City of Brotherly (Tough) Love just desperately wanted a winner, and nothing else would satiate.

On the eve of the opening game of the season against Montreal, the Phillies held an open practice for about four thousand fans, and Phils VP Bill Giles had a literal message for the Philly faithful: PLENTY OF GOOD TICKETS LEFT. That's what was printed on the sign hanging from Giles's neck as he watched batting practice. Opening Day, typically an easy sellout for even the lowliest teams in baseball, was projected to be light on ticket sales. Giles, clearly sensing his aging squad needed a refresh, was marching into the 1980s with "New Hair, New Me" vibes.

Giles held a sort of spring cleaning sale before the start of the season, selling off all relics of the past, including their mascots. Phil and Phillis, most notably part of a home-run spectacular beyond the outfield wall since the Vet's inception, were sold to a New Jersey amusement park (see photo in insert). To those not alive at the time to personally witness it (the writers of this book included), the description of the display's capabilities sounds like a ChatGPT conjuring from the prompt "Make up a home run celebration display as aggressively 1970s and Philadelphia as physically possible." Bill Giles's description of the spectacle to the press in 1971 was *a lot*:

> They are part of my home-run spectacular. When a Phillie hits a homer, Philadelphia Phil will appear between the boards in center field and hit a baseball. It will travel toward the message board in right center and strike a Liberty Bell. The bell will glow and its crack will light up. The ball will continue and hit little Philadelphia Phillis in the fanny and she will fall down. As she falls, she will pull a lanyard on a cannon and the cannon will explode. After smoke and sound effects, a Colonial American flag will drop down. Then my dancing waters will come into play to the tune of Stars and Stripes Forever.

Sports Illustrated staff remarked in the April 19, 1971, issue, "[W]hen Third Baseman Don Money produced a Phillie homer against Mauch's Expos, 'the ball' (a light running unobtrusively along a track between Phil and Phillis) was barely visible, the bell failed to glow, Phillis struck a thoroughly warranted blow for Women's Liberation by declining to fall down and the cannon smoke and the cannon noise went off independently of one another." Bill Conlin noted of the display's demise that it "functioned properly maybe three times in nine seasons."[7]

Yikes.

While the front office seemed preoccupied with the past, the question of whether it had exorcized old demons was not top of mind for the players. "It was a good clubhouse," according to shortstop Larry Bowa. "We had a lot of different personalities. We could be difficult [for the media] to deal with, but everybody stood up, especially when they wanted to compare us to the '64 Phillies.... But none of us were around for all that. By the end of the summer, they made sure we knew *everything* about the '64 Phillies."[8]

The 1980 team certainly was not the most talented in team history, but experience was their 10th man, their secret weapon. Some reliable vets like Garber and Hebner were gone, but the front office filled the gaps with attitude.

Rose was added via free agency the previous season, and Dallas Green began his first full season as manager after a successful stint closing out the final 30 games of 1979. These additions—Green especially—represented tidal shifts in how the team operated, according to Bowa: "Danny [Ozark] was a real good manager; he let us play, left us alone. Dallas brought a little energy in there. He'd tell us, 'You guys think you're great. You've been reading your press clippings, but you haven't won anything.'"[9]

The Phillies were used to having one of the most talented lineups in baseball, but time and economics put a natural shelf life on that kind of thing. It's extremely difficult to keep great teams together nowadays, when even the eight-hole hitters are getting eight-figure contracts. But, a budget—albeit much, *much* smaller—was a factor to be dealt with in 1980 as well.

The Cincinnati Reds surely felt the financial strain when they broke up the Big Red Machine in 1979, and that led to Rose signing the biggest contract in sports (four years, $3.2 million—that's not a typo). If Phillies president and owner Ruly Carpenter insisted on fielding the best players in the game, the same financial fate was eventually going to befall Philadelphia. There was a palpable feeling among fans, players, coaches, the front office, spouses, hot dog vendors ... that it was now or never.

"Ruly would come down to the clubhouse all the time and talk to us," said Bowa. "And that spring training, he goes, 'You know, we need to get this thing straightened out here, because I'm going to have to break this team up if we don't go deeper into the playoffs.'

"It was understood. When he told us that in '80, we realized he was giving us every opportunity to get to the World Series, and we just hadn't done it. It wasn't an ultimatum, but he planted a seed."[10]

From the outset of the '80 season, Green was planting seeds of his own—only, it was more of the Jack's beanstalk variety. Green made his giant presence known. "In prior years, it seemed like tee times were more important than batting-practice times," Green said. "In 1980, that was going to change."[11]

The Phillies had proven time and again that talent acquisition alone was not enough to deliver the world championship. Green helped tighten the screws to squeeze a little bit more out of the outstanding players already in place.

> In September, he took Maddox out a couple times; he took Luzinski out a couple times. He just got everyone's attention real quick. He was a different personality, and it was clear there would be a different set of rules. It caught a lot of guys off guard, but not me—my personality was a lot like his. But [for] guys like Maddox and Schmidt, I don't think it rubbed them the right way right away. But I think at the end, they understand what he was trying to do, to light a fire under us.
>
> —Larry Bowa[12]

Though it had a storybook ending, the 1980 season was a boring read for much of the regular season. Many area sportswriters picked Philadelphia for fourth place in the Eastern Division, and for good reason. That was the position they finished in 1979, and the team seemingly wasn't getting any younger or better. At the onset, that prediction seemed spot-on, as the Phils struggled out of the gate, going 6–9 in April. They followed that up with a 17–9 May, which was the pattern of inconsistency that defined the season. They were good enough to stay in contention but were not nearly as dominant top to bottom as they were in 1976–77.

A 10–3 stretch from June 4 to June 18 was immediately followed by a 2–8 stretch through June 28. They started August 3–6, and then won eight of the next nine.

The team's future Hall of Famers made sure the pennant race always stayed tight. Schmidt (.286/.380/.624, 48 HR, 121 RBIs) was having his first MVP season, and Carlton (24–9, 2.34 ERA, 286 Ks) was on his way to collecting his third Cy Young Award. The Phillies turned the last couple weeks of the schedule into a postseason push.

On September 28, the Phils lost to the Montreal Expos, surrendering first place in the division to Canada by half a game. It would be the last meaningful game the Phillies dropped that season.

After sweeping the Cubs at home, the Phillies traveled to America's Hat for a three-game series that would decide the division. The Phils and Expos both were 89–70. For all intents and purposes, this was the NL's divisional round that wouldn't officially exist until 1995, and the Phils were ready for it.

That year, Pete Rose (.282/.352/.354) was having a paltry season by his lofty standards, but he had been routinely telling teammates to just get him to the postseason, and that's where he'd shine.

He wasn't lying (*wink*). Rose went off, batting .636/.667/.636 in his final 12 plate appearances of the regular season, leading Philadelphia to wins in the first two games, and the Eastern Division crown. He followed that up by batting .400/.520/.400 in what Mike Schmidt considered "without question, the most action-packed League Championship Series in history."[13]

> We got the feeling that those games could go on, and on, and on . . . like a heavyweight championship bout where both fighters could withstand a bunch of punches.
>
> —Tim McCarver[14]

Houston matched up well with Philadelphia. The Phillies led the NL in total bases, 2,248, and the Astros led all baseball in ERA, 3.10, and WHIP (walks and hits per inning pitched) of 1.236. While the 'Stros had less power than an Amish schoolhouse—Schmidt hit more dingers than Houston's top four "sluggers" *combined* (Schmidt, 48; Puhl, Cruz, Morgan, Howe, 45)—they also had one of the greatest pitching rotations of all time—in the first half of the season, anyway.

That team is perhaps remembered most for Nolan Ryan's brilliance on the mound, but his rotation mate, J. R. Richard, bested The Express in ERA three of the previous four seasons before Ryan joined the club in 1980. Richard, after appearing in his first All-Star Game, suffered a stroke on the sidelines on July 30, 1980, and never pitched in the big leagues again. The thirty-year-old ended his last season with a 10–4 record and 1.90 ERA. His 0.924 WHIP that year was better than any season from Hall of Famers Roy Halladay, Tom Seaver, and Ferguson Jenkins.

RING THE BELL

The NLCS, and season, may have turned out differently if Richard was in the postseason rotation, but the Astros had plenty of aces left in the deck. Their other four primary starters combined for a 3.19 ERA (Ryan, 3.35; Vern Ruhle, 2.37; Ken Forsch, 3.20; Joe Niekro, 3.55). By comparison, the Phillies' top four starters not named Steve Carlton (2.34) had a combined ERA of just 4.27 (Dick Ruthven, 3.55; Larry Christenson, 4.03; Bob Walk, 4.57; Randy Lerch, 5.16).

The Phillies hadn't appeared in a World Series since 1950. The Astros hadn't ever previously played in the postseason. On paper, these two very different ballclubs seemed destined for an extremely competitive and entertaining series. It didn't disappoint.

GAME ONE (OCTOBER 7):

PHILLIES 3, ASTROS 1 (VETERANS STADIUM)

Carlton outdueled Forsch, pitching seven innings, surrendering the lone Astros run in the third. Greg Luzinski's two-run home run in the sixth—the only homer of the entire series—gave the Phillies a lead they would not relinquish. Tug McGraw closed it out for the two-inning save.

GAME TWO (OCTOBER 8):

ASTROS 7, PHILLIES 4 (10 INNINGS, VETERANS STADIUM)

For the second straight day, the Astros took a 1–0 lead in the third inning, and once again, Luzinski was responsible for the two runs that gave the Phillies the lead, this time knocking in the tying run and scoring the go-ahead run on a Garry Maddox single. In what would become a trend in this series—the game ultimately headed to extra innings with the Astros pounding Phils relief pitching for four runs in the top of the 10th.

GAME THREE (OCTOBER 10):

ASTROS 1, PHILLIES 0 (11 INNINGS, ASTRODOME)

More extra innings! Niekro was masterful for Houston, pitching 10 innings of scoreless ball—a completely foreign concept to modern MLB pitchers. (The 2023 NL Cy Young winner, Blake Snell, didn't complete 10 innings total until his third start of that season.) Christenson wasn't too shabby himself, exiting the game after six innings of scoreless ball. The game remained knotted up at nil until the bottom of the 11th, when Tugger surrendered a leadoff triple to Joe Morgan and the eventual game-winning sacrifice fly to Denny Walling. Dave Smith got the win after pitching just one single inning following Niekro's gem, because baseball is weird and the rules don't care about feelings.

GAME FOUR (OCTOBER 11):

PHILLIES 5, ASTROS 3 (10 INNINGS, ASTRODOME)

Extra, extras! Read all about it: Houston took a two-run lead into the eighth inning, chasing Carlton from the game before the end of the sixth. Consecutive singles by Greg Gross, Lonnie Smith, Rose, and Schmidt tied it up, and a sacrifice fly by Manny Trillo gave the Fightins the lead, 3–2. After Brusstar shut down the Astros 1-2-3 in the bottom of the inning, Dallas Green stuck with the hot hand and left Brusstar out there to finish it off in the ninth. It didn't go according to plan.

Houston eked out the tying run on just a walk and single in the ninth, and, again, the game was headed to extra innings.

Clutch two-out doubles by Luzinski and Trillo gave the Phils the lead in the top of the 10th, and Tug closed it out it out in the bottom of the inning. Brusstar was credited with both the blown save and the win because, again, baseball is weird and the rules don't care about feelings.

GAME FIVE (OCTOBER 12):

PHILLIES 8, ASTROS 7 (10 INNINGS, ASTRODOME)

If you're not a big fan of extra innings, you would have hated this series. For everyone else, Game Five was an epically entertaining conclusion to one of the greatest battles in baseball history.

The Astros started quickly, getting a run off of Marty Bystrom in the first inning, but the Phils responded with a two-run single from Bob Boone off Nolan Ryan in the top of the second. The Astros tied it in the sixth, and tacked on three more in seventh, handing the would-be MLB strikeout king a 5–2 lead into the eighth.

Imagine—Nolan Ryan, literally, was the toughest pitcher to hit. He leads all pitchers in baseball history in batting average against (.204), just a tick below Sandy Koufax (.205). Ryan led the league in fewest hits per nine innings

12 times, and Koufax only played 12 total *seasons*. In 1980, The Express was at the height of his powers, and a 5–2 lead late in the game *should have been* insurmountable. Of course, both the Phillies and the series itself were too good to go down that predictably.

The Phils scored five in the eighth (all earned runs, charged to Ryan), but surrendered two tying runs to Houston in the bottom half of the inning, and, again, the game was headed to extras.

Maddox knocked home the go-ahead run in the top of the 10th, just under center fielder Terry Puhl's glove, and Ruthven retired Houston in order to send Philadelphia to the World Series for just the third time in franchise history.

Harry Kalas had the call: "3-2 pitch, swing and a drive, right-center field, Maddox is there . . . The Phillies are in the World Series!"

> When we beat Nolan Ryan, that made us feel like we were going to win the whole thing. To come from behind and beat him, I had a feeling this was going to be our year.
>
> —Larry Bowa[15]

It was the greatest NLCS in baseball history, but they don't hand out trophies for that distinction. A lot of work was left to be done, and the American League champion Royals (97–64) had just swept the Yankees, which had finished a monster 103-win regular season. George Brett, the 1980 MVP, was enjoying his best major-league season that year, leading baseball in batting average (.390), on-base average (.454), slugging (.664), and POS+ (on-base plus slugging plus) of 203), but just as Brett was the second-best third baseman on the field (to Schmidt, of course), the Royals would finish in similar standing by Series end. It was a great matchup, but there was no stopping the Phillies that season.

GAME ONE (OCTOBER 14):

PHILLIES 7, ROYALS 6 (VETERANS STADIUM)

Rookie Bob Walk (11–7, 4.57 ERA) was not the ideal choice to start the Phillies' first World Series game in 30 years, but the rest of the rotation was gassed. He performed admirably, though, surrendering four runs through seven innings, and two more to start the eighth before handing the ball over to Tug for the two-inning save.

1980—THE FIRST ONE

Bake McBride's three-run home run in the third gave the Phillies a 5–4 lead, and they held on to win it in the end, 7–6.

GAME TWO (OCTOBER 15):

PHILLIES 6, ROYALS 4 (VETERANS STADIUM)
The Phillies were a pain in the ass to opposing teams all year, but it was a literal pain in the ass that became a key factor in Game Two. Brett was forced out of the game after the sixth inning with what would later be confirmed as hemorrhoids. The Phillies had another come-from-behind victory in this one, taking the lead with four runs in the posterior half of the eighth before shutting Kansas City out in the ninth. Smooth number two for Philadelphia.

GAME THREE (OCTOBER 17):

ROYALS 4, PHILLIES 3 (ROYALS STADIUM)
New locale, new outcome—hemorrhoid-free Brett (Ace Ventura voice: "That kinda surgery can be done over the weekend!") set the tone with a home run in the first inning, and Willie Aikens hit a walk-off single with two outs in the ninth for the KC victory.

GAME FOUR (OCTOBER 18):

ROYALS 5, PHILLIES 3 (ROYALS STADIUM)
This one was ugly, and it very easily could have turned the series in the Royals' favor, if not for one sneaky pitch.

Christenson didn't make it out of the first inning, surrendering four earned runs to the Royals and recording just one out. By the fourth, it was 5–1, and Dickie Noles, allegedly, decided it was time to send a message. On an 0–2 pitch, Noles fired a fastball at Brett's head, sending the MVP flying wildly backward to the dirt to avoid getting hit. Royals manager Jim Frey stormed out of the dugout, screaming at umpires, Noles, and even Pete Rose.

After the game, Noles denied intentionally throwing at Brett, with all the fervor of a chocolate-stained toddler pleading innocence in *The Case of the Missing Good Humor Bar*. Whatever the intent, this is largely considered the moment the series dynamics turned decisively toward Philadelphia.

RING THE BELL

The Royals won the game, but the war was up for grabs.

GAME FIVE (OCTOBER 19):

PHILLIES 4, ROYALS 3 (ROYALS STADIUM)

Two big *what-ifs* are in this one:

- Schmidt led off the ninth with the Phillies down one run. Amazingly—and certainly not something you'd see against a star slugger in today's game—Brett played up on Schmidt to take away a potential bunt. Bunting was the furthest thought from Schmidt's mind, as he ripped a leadoff single just past Brett, which would have otherwise been an easy catch for the third baseman had he been playing in his regular spot. Schmidt scored on a double by Del Unser, and Unser scored the eventual game-winner.
- The box score shows McGraw surrendering just one hit in three innings to close this one out, but his turn was *wild*. Tugger, who eventually walked the bases loaded, surrendered a near game-ending home run to Hal McRae with two men on and one out in the ninth. Maybe 20 feet the other way, the Royals would have been headed to Philadelphia needing just one win to take the Series.

"It looked like it was going to go out of here," said McGraw, reflecting on McRae's deep shot. "It started to curl like a five-iron shot and went foul, but boy it had my heart jumping there for a while.

"[Catcher] Boonie comes out to the mound and says, 'Isn't this exciting?'—that's an understatement."[16] The heart attack lefty struck out José Cardenal, the city of Philadelphia collectively exhaled, and the Phillies were just one win away.

GAME SIX (OCTOBER 21):

PHILLIES 4, ROYALS 1 (VETERANS STADIUM)

Everything was set up perfectly for the Phillies, with the series back in Philadelphia and ace Carlton on the mound. Lefty rose to the occasion, pitching seven scoreless innings, surrendering just one earned run in the eighth—an inherited runner once McGraw took over.

Leading 4–1 in the ninth, Tugger made it interesting once again, loading the bases with one out. Then, two of the most memorable moments in Phillies history happened in succession.

Frank White popped it up to the first-base side, and Boone called off first baseman Rose to make the catch. The ball popped out of Boone's glove, but Rose alertly reached out and snagged it before it hit the ground, for the second out of the inning.

Things like that don't happen to losing teams. Rose dashed toward the mound, gave the ball a quick little dribble, and the Phillies were one out away. Willie Wilson, Babe Ruth, Mighty Casey, even God Himself—it didn't matter who was up next; the Phillies were winning this game.

In what would be the defining snapshot of the Phillies' 1980 season and franchise, Tug thrust his arms into the air in victory after striking out Wilson and giving the city of Philadelphia its first World Series—well, unless you count the Athletics. We don't.

When the A's left town in 1954, they took their championships with them. It's a little odd that a Connie Mack statue sits just outside the gates of Citizens Bank Park, as the Athletics icon was once sued in Pennsylvania Supreme Court for repeatedly raiding Phillies rosters of star players, most famously Napoleon Lajoie. Whatever.

Ultimately, the fans chose the Phillies, warts and all. It only took 97 years to be rewarded with a championship, but good things come to those who wait—and are still alive to witness it.

Two days later, the Phils marched down Broad Street.

Though the Flyers had experienced some championship success at the time, the celebration that followed the Phillies victory was unlike anything the city had ever seen.

Police inspector William Lindsay, who estimated the parade crowd to be over one million fans, said at the time, "It's a sea of humanity; it's unbelievable . . . It's bigger than the Mummers; it's three or four times bigger than the crowd for the Flyers."[17]

Tugger, who had spent the first eleven years of his career with the Mets organization (1964–74), told the feverish Philly crowd, "All through baseball history Philadelphia has had to take a back seat to New York City. Well, New York can take this world championship and stick it 'cause we're number one!"[18]

#4

THE PHILLIE PHANATIC

The first mention of the term *phanatic* in Philly newspapers was in the *Philadelphia Inquirer* on September 12, 1941. It appeared in a satirical Complaint Department insert in the sports pages, just below a comment lamenting Adolf Hitler's costly scourge of Europe. It was a different time.

> Somehow Shibe Park doesn't seem the same without Danny Murtaugh.
> —Phil Phanatic

Here's a little context: These days, Murtaugh is a much more familiar name on the left side of the state, having managed the Pittsburgh Pirates to two World Series victories, in 1960 and 1971. But in 1941 he was a pesky rookie second baseman on arguably the worst Phillies team ever fielded. The Fightins lost a franchise-record 111 games that season, so it's fitting that one of the team's fan favorites was also possibly its worst player—"The Whistling Irishman," Danny Murtaugh.

Murtaugh ended up leading the league in steals (18), after not making his MLB debut until June—impressive, but he also led the league in caught stealing (13), so it was much more likely due to reckless disregard than sheer talent. The Chester, Pennsylvania, native was beloved by fans, who were understandably starved for entertainment from a team that was on the tail end of a ten-year stretch during which the Phils *averaged* exactly 100 losses per season (1933–42, 1,000 losses). For context, the Cincinnati Reds, founded in 1882 (one year prior to the Phillies), have just *two* 100-loss seasons in their entire existence. *Yikes.*

Baseball-Reference.com didn't get many page views back in 1941, so fans weren't as savvy to stats as they are now—not that it mattered, considering the team was awful and it wasn't as important for Murtaugh to put up a shiny OBP as it was to simply run like hell at every available opportunity. Like bluffing on the river with 7–2 offsuit, sometimes getting thrown out foolishly trying to steal home can be a real cool hand.

Simply put, Murtaugh's popularity should have been inexplicable, considering he finished the season with the twelfth-lowest OPS in all of franchise history (.523, with a minimum of 375 plate appearances), a mark that's only been "bested" twice in the 84 years since (Bobby Wine, 1967; Larry Bowa, 1973). What doesn't show up in the box scores, though, is showmanship.

This chapter is all about showmanship. More specifically, this chapter is about baseball's Pattison Street Prankster, Galapagos Goof, Jawnsonville Brat—the Phillie Phanatic, the greatest mascot in professional sports.

Generally speaking, mascots exist in the periphery. They're an added layer of entertainment, but a *way-off-to-the-side* show, oftentimes cheaply and transparently there to encourage parents of little ones to bring the whole family out—and charge the ensuing tickets, food, drinks, foam fingers, ice cream, and officially licensed MLB merchandise to the Amex. This is the territory of Stomper, Billy the Marlin, Bernie Brewer, and the lot of barely-out-of-beta ballclub clowns. The Phanatic is just built differently.

THE ORIGIN STORY

After 1941 the word *phanatic* wouldn't show up in Philly papers again until spring of 1978. The Phillies promotions department was eager to expound on, or move on from, the dull duo of Philadelphia Phil and Phillis,* and it tasked Muppet designers Harrison/Erickson with designing and building the franchise a mascot to rival the Padres' famous San Diego Chicken. Intern Dave Raymond adorned the would-be iconic suit for the first time on April 25 that year, but it's unclear if the front office knew just how electric the Phils' mysterious furry friend would be.

The very first time *Phillie Phanatic* appeared in type on a newspaper canvas was not even to promote the big green guy himself. It was a season primer article on April 5, 1978, detailing the year's scheduled promotions: "Poncho Day—July 23 . . . A red and white vinyl poncho with 'I'm a Phillie Phanatic!' stenciled on front goes to all youngsters."[1]

The next day, the Phillies took out a full-page ad in the *Philadelphia Daily News* to promote ticket purchasing, with the sales pitch, in giant bold letters,

---

*The two are pictured in the insert.

Be a Phillies Phanatic!" along with Phil and Phillis, Major League Baseball's slightly-less-raggedy Ann and Andy.

Two straight days of the Phanatic sales pitch saw no mention of the would-be pitchmonster. Of course, the actual Phillie Phanatic was a massive hit once he took the field, but it certainly seems as though the guys and gals in marketing were more focused on the slogan than the ballfield jester who would steal its thunder. The reason was simple: the suit wasn't ready, and no one was certain it would work.

"They didn't settle on Dave Raymond until just before that game," said the Phanatic's current best friend* Tom Burgoyne, "and the costume didn't really come until the day of or the day before. There wasn't a big marketing push.... He just put on the costume, and they said, 'Okay, go out there and have fun—G-rated fun.'

"He was kind of making it up as he went along. Bill Giles calls down during the game and says, 'Why don't you go out there when the ground crew goes out in the fifth inning to sweep the bases? Go and mess around a little bit.' So, that became a fifth-inning routine every game. And it all picked up steam and kind of happened by accident."[2]

With the fans, the Phanatic was an instant hit. Raymond, twenty-two at the time and still in college, had the right combination of youthful energy and strategic naïveté to make the flightless bird take off. As goofy and frivolous a venture it may have seemed at the time, Raymond took the unserious challenge seriously, perhaps in a way that only a college kid could.

"I sort of had to grow into the part," Raymond said in the first-ever interview of his rookie season. "When I first started, I would just sort of stand around or wave and stuff. Then, gradually, I developed this dance and this routine with the ground crew.... The ball players are really nice, too.... They let me know it's alright to fool around and stuff. [W]hat gets a good reaction from fans, I keep doing."[3]

To be honest, the article that resulted from that interview was condescending and perhaps a little demeaning to the big guy. Purists—sportswriters certainly included—have historically resisted change in baseball, and a college kid in a bird suit was certain to ruffle a few fundamentalist feathers. Regardless, Raymond eventually won over just about everyone.

---

*Playful title used by the portrayer of the Phillie Phanatic. Of course, the Phanatic is more than just a suit...

Raymond brought the character to life in a way that went far beyond its initial design. He transformed the Phanatic from a simple idea into a full-fledged personality, capable of engaging fans, entertaining audiences, and becoming a central figure in the Phillies' brand. His creativity and dedication set a new standard for what mascots could achieve. And when it was time to pass the torch, miraculously, the Phanatic soared to new heights.

Burgoyne, after a stint as the backup, took over "best friend" duties full-time in 1993, and he's been doing it ever since. "For 47 years, it has been primarily Dave Raymond and [me] working the games," said Burgoyne in 2024. "So it's been very consistent."

THE MAKING OF A MASCOTEER

I went to Saint Joseph's Prep High School, and I was the mascot. My senior year, we got a new Hawk—which was a hand-me-down Hawk costume from the college. . . . It was very comical and cartoonish, and I thought, *Oh, I can be the Phanatic in this thing.* I really did pattern the Hawk after the Phanatic that year. In fact, I was interviewed for the school paper and I said, "I'm going to be the Phanatic one day." I brought that article when I interviewed for the Phillies job.

I went to Drexel after high school (I was not the Dragon), and I took a job in sales for six months and wasn't doing a very good job at it. Then, going through the want ads in the *Inquirer*, I see a Mascot Wanted ad. I sent a résumé and a letter to the listed P.O. box that I didn't know was for the Phillies—there was no mention of any of that. The Phillies eventually contacted me, and it was just the right place at the right time.

I also brought to the interview this big, eight-by-ten color photo that was in the *Inquirer* two days after the Phillies championship parade in 1980; my friends [and I] were on top of a statue in Center City—I tell people I was the original pole climber—and it landed on the back page in this big color photo. So, I was trying to convey to the team that I was a huge Philadelphia sports fan, which I was. I was a nut.

I think the Phanatic represents the fans. He lives and dies with the team just like the fans do. —Tom Burgoyne, the Phanatic's Best Friend

There's the ATV, the hot dog cannon, the dugout roof opposing pitcher psych-outs—so many signature moves are in the Phanatic's repertoire, which have been honed to perfection over the years. Gimmicks and schtick are part of the job, but at the heart of it all is the literal heart beating beneath Harrison/Erickson's fine stitchwork.

The Phanatic is the best in sports because he's always been the team's best fan and the fans' best friend. Harry Kalas could be described the same way: they are both just *part of it*—part of the history, the lore, and the identity of Phillies baseball, past, present, and future.

And that might be too dramatic if this were a book about our Queens borough brethren, discussing the revelatory historical significance of Mr. Met; in fact, it would be really sad. No offense to Mr. Met and his creepo mug, but not all sideshows were meant for the main stage.

Here are some big honors for the big bird:

- ***Forbes* magazine**: In 2008, the magazine named the Phanatic the best mascot in sports.
- ***Sports Illustrated for Kids***: The Phanatic was voted Best Mascot Ever by readers.[4]
- ***Good Morning, America***: In 2015, ABC's *Good Morning, America* honored the Phanatic as the best mascot in baseball.
- **National Baseball Hall of Fame and Museum**: The Phanatic is one of only three mascots on display (with the San Diego Chicken and the Expos' Youppi!).
- **Mascot Hall of Fame**: In 2005, the Phanatic was inducted as a charter member, highlighting the mascot's significant impact on sports entertainment.
- ***Business Insider***: In 2020, Meredith Cash of *Business Insider* ranked 110 sports mascots, with the Phanatic finishing second—to the Philadelphia Flyers' Gritty, an acceptable miscalculation.
- **Fox 29 Philadelphia**: A 2024 study reported by the TV station, named the Phillie Phanatic the best mascot in Major League Baseball, based on a survey of two thousand baseball fans.

"There has been that consistency," Burgoyne asserts, after almost 50 years of primarily just Raymond and Burgoyne on mascot BFF duty. "I hear it all the time. There will be crowds of kids running after the Phanatic on the concourse, high fiving him, and dads will say, 'Hey, I did this when I was a kid.' Consistency has been a real key over all this time, and the Phanatic has been there with and for the fans."[5]

#5
1983

"It's so funny because the team took forever to get to the World Series, and that was the goal. Then, they do it again three years later and it's like, 'Oh, all right, no big deal."

—Glen Macnow[1]

If you're a 1983 Phillies superfan—which, unless you're related to John Denny or you *are* John Denny, you shouldn't be—this chapter's for you. People don't talk about the 1983 Phillies. Fans don't seem to care all that much. Still, it would feel like a glaring omission to skip over an NL pennant-winning club, so, we decided to cover the bullet points and write 721 words (or so) on the subject—a word for every run scored by the Fightins that season.

The team found success thanks to the usual suspects:

- Mike Schmidt led all baseball in home runs (40) and walks (128) and topped all National League hitters in OPS+ (156).
- Steve Carlton, thirty-eight but still an absolute horse, won 15 games with a 3.11 ERA, leading the NL in innings pitched (283 2/3) and all baseball in strikeouts (275).[*]
- The Phillies had one of the best bullpens in baseball, as had been a trademark of the team for nearly a decade to this point. The Philly pen led the majors in wins in relief (33) and topped the National League with the fewest losses in relief (16). Al Holland, new to Philadelphia

---

[*]Only three pitchers have pitched over 280 innings since Lefty in '83 (Bert Blyleven, 1985; Roger Clemens and Charlie Hough, 1987). In retrospect, Lefty may have been pushing too hard in his advanced age. His productivity dropped the following year (3.58 ERA, 163 Ks), and then he tallied a 5.21 ERA for the final 84 games of his career.

after tallying a career 2.60 ERA in 164 games prior, was a first-time full-time closer and shined, saving 25 games with a 2.26 ERA.

If that was it, the 1983 Phillies would be rather unremarkable. This is where John Denny comes in.

Denny, thirty, was in his first full season with Philadelphia, after nine seasons of injuries and wild inconsistency. His talent was clear—he led the NL in ERA in 1976 (2.52)—but he was just 75–71 with a 3.81 ERA before his thirtieth birthday. No one expected he'd have one of the most dominant pitching seasons in Phillies history.

After surrendering four runs in six innings of work in his first start of the season, Denny went 7–2 over his next 10 outings, sporting a miniscule 1.42 ERA. He rode that wave to a 19–7 record on the season, with a 2.37 ERA, leading the NL in wins and taking home the first Cy Young Award in franchise history to a Phillie not named Steve Carlton (Carlton four, Denny one, Steve Bedrosian one, Roy Halladay one).

WAR can be a fickle stat, but Denny led all MLB pitchers (7.5). Regardless of its efficacy, conventional wisdom would suggest that if Denny had pitched that season like his rotation mate Marty Bystrom (-0.5 WAR, 4.60 ERA), the 90–72 NL East winners would likely have finished around .500.

> Denny, a groundball pitcher, didn't give up a lot of homers. He had the lowest HR per nine innings in the bigs in '83 (0.3) and finished his career *just* ahead of Greg Maddux in the category (0.57 to 0.63). In total, he surrendered just two grand slams in his 13-year MLB career. The first one Denny served up was in August of 1977, exactly two months after the debut of Denny's Grand Slam Breakfast—proof that we live in a simulation.

Alas, baseball is a team game, so there was a lot more to it than Lefty, Schmitty, and Denny.

In a nod to the 1950 NL pennant-winning Whiz Kids, the '83 squad was coined the "Wheeze Kids" by *Daily News* writer Stan Hochman. It poked fun at the advanced age of the club, which featured three rusted-out cogs from the 1970s Big Red Machine (Pete Rose at forty-two, Joe Morgan at thirty-nine, and Tony Pérez at forty-one) and outfielder Von Hayes, twenty-four, the only player among the starting eight under thirty. They fielded the most quadragenarians in Phillies history (Rose, Pérez, Bill Robinson at forty, Ron Reed at forty).

The geezer squad scratched and clawed their way to 90 wins, which was just one game behind their 1980 total. They might have seemed like an even match on paper with the 91-win Los Angeles Dodgers, but the Phillies managed just one single win against LA in 12 contests during the regular season. But that didn't matter.

The series was surprising, but mostly forgettable, save for a 1–0 opening win for Philadelphia behind ace Carlton (7 2/3 IP, seven hits). Phillies took the pennant, 3–1, outscoring LA in the series, 19–5.

They ran into a buzzsaw in the World Series, losing it 4–1 to AL MVP Cal Ripken Jr. and the Baltimore Orioles. The O's scored 832 runs that season; the Phillies, 721.

#6

1993—WORST TO FIRST

The 1992 Phillies finished dead last in the NL East, but it was not a squad devoid of potential. Darren Daulton, John Kruk, Lenny Dykstra, and Mitch Williams were legitimate stars in their prime, and young talents like Dave Hollins and Curt Schilling brought a lot to the table. On paper, the worst-to-first transition from 1992 to 1993 seems improbable, but a foundation was already in place to win.

DARREN DAULTON

Daulton was a Phillie for a long time, but his stint as an impactful Phillie was a very slow burn. He had a cup of coffee with the pennant-winning '83 club (two games) and then served primarily as a backup catcher from 1985 to 1988, hitting just .208/.321/.342 over that time. No one expected greatness from Dutch, and if things had gone according to plan, he never would have gotten a chance to start for the Phillies at all.

The thirty-one-year-old backstop Lance Parrish was Philadelphia's big free-agent signing in 1987, a six-time All-Star with the Detroit Tigers and winner of five of the previous seven AL Silver Sluggers. For the Phillies, he's remembered as one of the greatest talent acquisition failures in Philadelphia sports history.

Philadelphia Daily News sportswriter Bernard Fernandez wrote of Parrish in July 1987, "Phillies fans waited and waited for him. . . . They waited for the genuine All-Star article to show up and replace the muscled impostor who struggled to hit .200, rarely went deep, and only occasionally threw out brazen baserunners who appeared oblivious to his reputation. And when the impatient patrons of Veterans Stadium could wait no longer for the newcomer's production to match their expectations, they proclaimed him a false prophet and booed his every action until his wife felt compelled to stop attending home games.

"If Philadelphia's courtship of Lance Parrish started out as a love affair, the union seemed headed for divorce court."[1]

Yikes. Parrish and the Phillies got their divorce on October 3, 1988, by way of trade with the California Angels (for "promising" pitching prospect David Holdridge, who proceeded to compile a 5.53 ERA in 362 2/3 minor-league innings with the Philadelphia organization, from 1989 to 1991). After the deal was done, Parrish said, "I've thought a lot about what went wrong with Philadelphia and why it went wrong. . . . People weren't very patient. They expected results right away."[2]

Losing ballgames is one thing; losing the fans is a mortal sin in Philadelphia. His final stat line with the club, over 253 games, was .240/.304/.385. *Ew.*

After the ink dried on Parrish's walking papers, Lee Thomas said, "We're definitely in the market for catcher."[3] He didn't know what he had.

The Phillies were never able to trade for a starting backstop and seemed resigned to the rebuilding process, standing pat with Daulton in 1989, who started . . . middled . . . and ended slowly, finishing the season hitting .201/.303/.310. In 1990 some potential blossomed, as the twenty-eight-year-old led all National League catchers with a .783 OPS, oddly finishing with the exact same batting average that year as Parrish, who had a similar OPS (.268, .789). His production plummeted again in 1991 (.196/.297/.365), but then, the following season, a star was born.

In 1992 Daulton became just the second player in baseball history to lead the league in RBIs playing just the catcher position (109; Roy Campanella had 142 RBIs in 1953). With the DH in both leagues now, this will likely remain a two-man club. He inked a deal worth $18.5 million in the offseason to make him the highest-paid catcher in baseball at the time.

JOHN KRUK

If not for a string of robberies on the West Coast, John Kruk probably never would have ended up in a Phillies jersey.

When Kruk got the call-up to the big leagues in 1986, there was a lot of buzz. In 1,288 minor-league at-bats from 1983 to 1986, he had recorded a monster .343 batting average (498 AB at Double A; 790 AB at Triple A).

He fit in seamlessly at the next level, batting .309 in 278 at-bats in 1986, receiving just one Rookie of the Year vote despite having the highest OPS of any eligible rookie hitter, on a list that included Barry Bonds, Will Clark, and Kevin Mitchell.

In 1987 Kruk led all National League first basemen with a .313 batting average. Then, in the spring of 1988, Kruk learned that the FBI was looking for a recent roommate of his who had committed several armed robberies.

"I just didn't care about playing anymore," said Kruk. "I'm not going to make excuses for anything, but yes, all of this was on my mind. I was scared. Yeah, this guy was my friend. But if he did some of the things they said he did, you never knew what he might do to me. . . . I have never been so scared in all my life."[4]

Kruk was spooked, and it affected his play on the field, turning his .313/.406/.488 in '87 into a .241/.369/.362 in '88. After a slow start the following season (.184 average in 76 AB), the Padres shipped Kruk to Philly, along with Randy Ready, for outfielder Chris James—a deal that seemed kinda even at the time. Twenty-four-year-old James hit .293/.344/.525 in 358 at-bats in 1987, but he only lasted a half-season in San Diego in 1989 and was a utility outfielder by 1992.

Kruk made three straight All-Star teams from 1991 to 1993 and, of course, is currently a fixture in the Phillies broadcast booth. San Diego got swindled.

If Kruk hadn't had the slump, the Phillies never would have gotten Kruk. If the armed robberies never happened, Kruk wouldn't have had the slump.

Those robberies were very lucky for the Phillies—especially that last one with the Pads.

DAVE HOLLINS

In another boneheaded move by San Diego in 1989, the Padres let third baseman Dave Hollins go to Philadelphia in the Rule 5 Draft.
Whoops. Hollins hit 27 homers in 1992 and was an All-Star in 1993. Hollins ended up with a solid 12-year career, hitting .260/.358/.420, and he joins a long list of players Tony Gwynn would have loved to play with.

RING THE BELL

LENNY DYKSTRA

Mike Schmidt retired on May 29, 1989. The front office marked the occasion by having one of the best transactional Junes in franchise history.

Kruk was acquired on June 2, and two weeks later the Phils traded for future All-Stars in Terry Mulholland and Lenny Dykstra. Without these moves, 1993 surely would have been just another nondescript state of Phillies history.

> I have some thoughts on Mulholland: The lefty doesn't get as much respect or credit as some of the other main players from the Macho Row '93 Phils, but he was crucial to their success. In the four full seasons of his first stint with the club (1990–93), he averaged 30 starts a year with a 3.52 ERA and 1.182 WHIP, which was the lowest WHIP of all qualified NL lefty starters over that period. The dude was a workhorse—over the same four-year stretch, Mulholland led the league in complete games with 33—one more than Braves legend Greg Maddux.
>
> He doesn't get remembered as much because he was kinda normal; he was delightfully miscast amongst a band of miscreants, like a Red Ryder Carbine Action 200-shot Range Model air rifle mistakenly banished to the Island of Misfit Toys.

Lenny Dykstra was surely undervalued with the Mets, platooning when his skill set was clearly best utilized as an everyday leadoff man. Of course, that's easy to say today, 20-plus years after Michael Lewis's *Moneyball: The Art of Winning an Unfair Game* helped change the way we value players. Dykstra's .377 on-base average in 1986, in 498 plate appearances at the age of twenty-three, on a championship team, should have made him a Met for life. As it was at the time, he was a *not-quite* star—*not quite* a .300 hitter, *not quite* a speedster, *not quite* a slugger, *not quite* a slick fielder. He was just a solid ballplayer.

In 1989 the Mets couldn't see past his limitations. Now, it's clear to see they were underutilizing one of the best leadoff men in baseball. *Moneyball* did for OBP what Jordan did for Nike.

Whether it was luck or skillful management, GM Lee Thomas fleeced New York for Dykstra and uber-reliable reliever Roger McDowell for good measure. All it cost Philadelphia was Juan Samuel, who was an All-Star in 1987, leading the league in extra-base hits but also strikeouts (80, 162). It might have seemed like an even swap at the time, but Samuel would average just 279 plate appearances per season for the remaining nine years of his career. Dykstra gave Philly what it hadn't had since Pete Rose—a leadoff hitter and a leader.

"Our first need has been pitching, and it remains so," said Thomas after striking the deal. "But we've also desperately needed a real leadoff hitter, someone who can get us going—and Dykstra fills that bill. . . . I think he will become very important for us."[5]

On the intangibles side, Nails was cocky and self-assured. He led the charge toward getting the Phillies' groove back.

After arriving in Philly, the 5-foot-10, 160 pound center fielder said, "Every team I've ever played for has won. I don't know what it's like to lose, and it's not something I want to learn."[6]

Dykstra certainly can't be accused of not trying to win at all costs. "I started [taking steroids] because I had to," Dykstra admitted in an interview in 2016. "I was too small. I didn't forget how to hit. I was too weak.

"[Phillies general manager] Lee Thomas said, look, we're going to give you 1990. You'll be our everyday guy. So I knew '90 was it for me. . . . I literally called up some doctor in Mississippi and told him the story. . . . I have a family. I have a chance to make a lot of money."[7]

Nails led the league in hits and on-base average in 1990 (192, .418), making his first All-Star team and *Sports Illustrated* cover.

Ethics and morality can be subjective, but the hard facts remain: Major League Baseball did not begin testing for steroids until 2003.

MITCH WILLIAMS

Let's get this out of the way—Mitch Williams is the guy who gave up the 1993 World Series–winning home run to Toronto Blue Jays slugger Joe Carter. He'll never live that down. It's the fourth sentence of his Wikipedia page. It happened, and he was never the same pitcher afterward, but it shouldn't take away from the fact that he was one heck of a major-league reliever.

Williams's effectively wild delivery, and effectively wild results, made him a poster boy for the quirky, hard-throwing, menacing closers that began to emerge in the late 1980s and early 1990s. He missed the strike zone an awful lot, but he also missed a ton of bats.

In his very first season, he led the league in games pitched (80, 1986; Texas Rangers), with a 3.58 ERA. By 1989, with the Chicago Cubs, Williams was an All-Star, leading all baseball in games pitched (76), saving 36 of them with a 2.34 ERA. When he joined the Phillies, the success continued, and he actually had one of the strangest, most dominant months in Phillies pitching history.

Through a wild set of circumstances, Wild Thing Williams started the month of August 1991 with wins in his first five appearances. He ended August 8–1 with a 1.21 ERA in 22 innings pitched. That's the last time any pitcher has recorded eight wins in a single month, and it's only been topped once in the Live Ball era, by Grover Cleveland Alexander in 1920 (nine wins).

Effectively wild gets thrown around a lot, but it should really be a badge on Williams's Baseball Reference page. He's the only pitcher in baseball history with less than 700 innings pitched and more than 500 walks surrendered (691 1/3, 544). Mitchy Poo did it his way and was successful, completing his 11-year MLB career with a 3.65 ERA and paltry .218 batting average against.

"Take a bunch of has-beens, oddballs, and no-hopers, put them in a baseball team, and you'll be on a home run to coming last in the league!" No, that is not a poorly written 1993 Phillies season preview by a person who's never watched professional sports. It is the first line of the description for the film *Major League*, from the back of its 1990 VHS jacket—and is also poorly written, probably by a person who has never watched professional sports.

Still, in terms of expectations, the line fits the patchwork 1993 Macho Row Phillies. The comparisons to the film are uncanny:

- Tom Berenger's character, Jake Taylor, couldn't be more of a match for Daulton—a team captain catcher with aching knees, a South Beach tan, a swooning female following, and maybe a few good seasons left in the tank.
- Jim Fregosi wasn't exactly managing a Tire World, like James Gammon's character, Lou Brown, before taking helm of the Phillies in 1991, but his fiery personality was a dead match.

GLEN MACNOW VERSUS JIM FREGOSI, AS TOLD BY THE PROF

Fregosi hated us [reporters]. Before a game, in the bull session that reporters used to hold with the manager—typically off the record—a topic that we discussed on WIP radio comes up. Fregosi says, "The people who listen to WIP are people who live in South Philly who sleep with their sisters, and the people who are on WIP are people who f*ck their mothers."

Someone in that session told it to someone at WIP. We were of the mind that if someone says something about us, we are going to play that up. And we pumped it up for days. Early in '94, at a press conference, Fregosi says, "I'm going to read a prepared statement." And he sits there and reads the thing, obviously written by Larry Shenk [Phillies PR director] because they weren't words Fregosi would ever use. And it said something along the lines of, "I slipped in my characterization of Philadelphia fans. At the same time, I feel betrayed that someone would leak out a private conversation, and that's all I'm going to say about that." And that was it.

So I said to him, "In any of that, I didn't hear an apology to the fans from South Philadelphia. Do you feel you should apologize to them?" He looked at me and gave me the evil eye and said, "Everything I had to say was in that statement."

Silence. Fifteen seconds pass.

Nothing.

So, I figure I've got to ride this thing and said, "When you said people on WIP are f*cking their mothers"—I may have censored myself, with there being cameras in the room—"did you think that you were besmirching them?"

He's boring down on me with his evil death eye and says, "Everything I planned to say is in the statement. If anyone has questions about the team, I'll answer them."

The whole room is intimidated by this jackass, so I wait about ten seconds and say, "All right, so how's the team?" He was not a friendly, fun kind of fellow.[8]

- Mitch Williams used the same nickname as Charlie Sheen's character, Rick "Wild Thing" Vaughn. But it was actually Vaughn who was the copycat, as Williams earned the moniker in 1986, due to his quirky delivery and control issues, three years before *Major League* hit theaters in 1989. It's been suggested that Williams was actually the inspiration for Vaughn, though Williams wouldn't wear the same No. 99 jersey until 1993 (a nod to his favorite football player, Mark Gastineau).
- Outfielder Pete Incaviglia might not be a dead ringer for Dennis Haysbert's character, Pedro Cerrano, but they both shared monster trouble-with-the-curve power and intimidating personas at the plate.
- Lenny Dykstra might be a stretch comparison to Corbin Bernsen's character, Roger Dorn, but if Dorn were a real person, I would imagine his tweet history would be every bit as wild and divisive as Nails's. The salacious, divisive stuff aside, ya gotta appreciate the candor:

I tried to boycott a Sunday afternoon game vs the pre-indoor-option @Marlins when it was brutally hot & I had partied the night b4. Viciously argued w [umpire] Eric Gregg RIP that the first pitch was a ball. But Fregosi had tipped him off what I was up to, and he wouldn't eject my ass.[9]

That's classic Dorn and Lou Brown behavior.

Personality was the intangible so overflowing on the roster that it seemed to make a stout, tangible effect on their standing in the National League East. The players knew it, and they knew how to use it to their advantage.

[This team] is kinda like family, ya know, they're all a bunch of sick bastards.

—John Kruk[10]

I think the warden—I mean, the general manager—of this club has done a fine job of assembling a prison squad.

—Mitch Williams[11]

I've never seen so many guys so excited every day to get up and come to the clubhouse. You never know what's going to happen; it's like a zoo.

—Pete Incaviglia[12]

I think we proved you can be loose and still play hard, and that getting along as a team really brings out the best in players.

—Lenny Dykstra[13]

The 1993 rags-to-riches swing, really, was kind of a classic band-of-misfits Hollywood tale. The Phillies were like P. T. Barnum scouring the world for oddities and stitching together the Greatest Show on Earth. Somehow or another, the Phillies had rounded up some of the weirdest, wildest personalities in baseball who just so happened to be great at playing the sport—for one season, anyway.

THE HOT START

The Phillies closed out spring training with a 16–10 record, which was part of manager Fregosi's strategy to help jumpstart a winning atmosphere. And, for what seemed like a rarity for the centennial-plus franchise, the plan worked, and the Phillies brought their newfound winning ways with them up I-95 to Philadelphia.

The Phils won eight of their first nine contests and finished out the opening month 17–5 overall. It's still their best April all-time (.773 win percentage, with a minimum of 15 games) and was most recently challenged by the 2024 club, which holds the April club record for wins (19–9, .679). It was a hot start, but it was no fluke.

Through June, the Phils were 52–25, which is their second-best record heading into July in team history (.675; 1976, 50–20, .714). The club record for wins through June? You guessed it—those 2024 Phillies (55–29, .655). Oh, what could have been.

Everything clicked for the Phillies at once, and the city was quick to take notice—not just that the Phillies had started 8–1 and had the best record in baseball but also of how odd that was for the oft-downtrodden organization.

Jayson Stark wrote the following for the *Philadelphia Inquirer* on April 16:

RING THE BELL

This is all really happening. You do not need smelling salts. This is not a dream.

The Phillies are 8–1. They have been keeping records back to 1911, and only once in those 82 other seasons have they ever started a season 8–1. That was in 1915, when they played at Baker Bowl, when Grover Cleveland Alexander was still known as "Pete" and they had an outfielder named Possum Whitted.

> Fun Possum Facts: George "Possum" Whitted is one of only five major leaguers in history to play at least 40 games at every position except pitcher and catcher. It is rumored that, at six months of age, he fell out of a second-story window and was unharmed; he was kicked by a mule, and the mule sustained a leg injury; he did not like to go to school, and the school subsequently burned down.[14] He might be Chuck Norris's illegitimate grandfather. That was a fun aside. Back to '93!

"The Vet—people have strong feelings positive and negative about it—was insane during that time. People really came out; forty thousand people every day," said outfielder Jim Eisenreich. "We didn't really have many slumps, but they turned up, win or lose."[15]

The Phillies might have been a hard sell in spring training, but fans didn't take long to catch on. Dollar dogs and DJ Jazzy Jeff bobbleheads are all well and good, but nothing packs a stadium better than a hot start.

The first sign of turnstile uptick? Maybe April 27, when 34,005 fans packed into the Vet on a *Tuesday*. They began a seven-game road trip the next day, sitting at 14–5. In the 12 games they played at home to that point (discounting the 60,985 on Opening Day), they averaged just 25,420—not terrible, but tickets were about to get much hotter.

After the 5–2 road trip, the 19–7 Phils were the hottest team in baseball, and they would only slip below 30K in attendance eight more times that season—all Mondays, Tuesdays, Wednesdays, and Thursdays, by the way—hey, Must See TV had just premiered on NBC, and *Seinfeld* was at the height of its powers. Whatever the reason, people occasionally had better things to do, not that there's anything wrong with that.

Fans were embracing the team after years of mediocrity, and it was accentuated by one of the greatest media turning points in the city's history: the rise of WIP sports radio.

WIP VERSUS MACHO ROW

In 1990, when 610 WIP was getting its sea legs as an all-sports station, it made a concerted effort to focus more an entertainment than a straight journalistic, informative approach.

> We were struggling, so we brought in a guy named Tom Bigby as originally a consultant and eventually full-time. He said, "Listen, it's not about sports, it's about entertainment. It's a sports theme, a sports backdrop, but it has to be entertaining."
> —Jay Snider, then part of the WIP ownership group.[16]

"The people I had hired are criticizing the Phillies like hell," said majority owner of WIP and the Philadelphia Flyers Ed Snider, "criticizing the Eagles, criticizing the Sixers before we owned them, and here I am [the station owner]. I couldn't change that. I didn't want to tell people what they had to say, but my [fellow] owners know I own it and they're getting the hell kicked out of them. The truth of the matter is I could have taken anything [the hosts and callers] threw at me, if I was the only [team] owner in town. I was a little bit embarrassed that I was the owner of something that was kicking the hell out of [the other teams]. At the time, the Sixers weren't doing well, the Phillies weren't doing well and even though I knew I wasn't responsible [for the criticism], I was also getting a lot of crap. I just didn't feel comfortable in that regard."[17]

It was common at the time for the relationship between the city's athletes and WIP to be tumultuous, and for good reason. WIP was the voice of the fan when sports-talk radio was essentially an unrivaled social-media platform. At a purely binary level, blaming the station for adversarial takes and energy seems appropriate, but over time, the nuance is clearer.

Today, we are in the age of Twitter/X, Facebook/Meta, Instagram, and such. Individual feelings about them aside, it's probably fair to assume the majority of social media users consider the entire platform genre to be a steaming garbage dump of unfettered—and oft-unwanted—opinion. If WIP was the Old West of sports talk, social media is just the New Old West, with way more Starbucks, craft breweries, and cell phone–addicted cowboys. It's a sleeker, shinier environment but can be just as dingy. The biggest difference between now and then is that the players maybe weren't as savvy to the hustle back in the early 1990s.

"We were coming in to establish ourselves as a big adversarial voice that wasn't going to be a bunch of lapdogs," said Glen Macnow, who started with the station in 1993. He continued:

> We were going to be the independent voice of the fan, sucking up to no player, no manager, no team. And it worked because we built a really powerful institution of a station that all these years later continues to thrive. But caught in the wash on that one was [the 1993 Phillies], which was a really fun team that we could've left our foot off the negative gas pedal a little bit.
>
> I don't get the sense that WIP was anti–that team. Everybody was loving what was going on. We were just critical, and I don't think the players were used to getting critical coverage.[18]

WIP certainly didn't invent the concept of oppositional sports coverage in Philly; it just changed the format. Before radio and television, it was the newspaper sports section, as evidenced by the previously covered press boycott by Steve Carlton. What made it a fascinating team to cover and talk about was that the '93 team was every bit as tough as any adversarial media that came its way.

Macnow, pulling double duty covering the team on the air and in the paper, recognized the team was a force, on and off the field: "You would go in that clubhouse, and it was, 'Who's tougher than who? Who's got bigger balls?' They were hostile with the press, but they were scrappy and beloved—and deserved to be beloved. [Longtime sports radio host] Mike Missanelli gave them the nickname 'Macho Row.'"

THE MISFITS OF MACHO ROW

Ballplayers were always—and will always be—deified to a certain extent, but the relationship between the fans and players has metamorphosized over time. In *Field of Dreams*, which hit theaters in 1989, the character Ray Kinsella treats baseball as a kind of religious entity. Legendary film critic Roger Ebert, at first screening, assumed the "If you build it, he will come" line was a literal reference to both church and God Himself. Absent in the movie is any mention of multimillion-dollar endorsement deals or generational wealth handed out like Tic Tacs to fourth outfielders and situational lefties.

James Earl Jones laid down a quote for the ages at the end of the film, with so much romance and intensity; one could simply change a few words, and the sentiment would fit seamlessly within the dialogue of *Fifty Shades of Grey*:

"People will *come*, Ray. People will most definitely *come*." Sorry for that!

Mike Schmidt was the first MLB player to be paid over $500,000 when the Phillies inked him to a multiyear deal worth $561,500 per season in 1977. His career earnings were $17,035,010, which, even with skyrocketing inflation and Netflix fees going up again, is a ton of money. Still, 1977 wasn't exactly the Stone Age, and it's mind-blowing to consider that *eight* members of the 2024 Phillies earned annual salaries greater than Schmidt's career total (Bryce Harper leading the way with $27.54 million). The reality is, that kind of money changes things, and makes it that much more difficult for the average blue-collar fan to relate. In 1993 some of that movie-like magic was still kicking around in the bottle.

Sure, the team featured 11 millionaires (from Ricky Jordan earning $1 million annually to Mitch Williams making $3.5 million), but the players otherwise seemed about as proletariat as a championship level team could be. Players today have personal trainers, stylists, and private chefs. In 1993 *macho* was the operative word. Kruk, once spoofed by heavyweight comedian Chris Farley on *Saturday Night Live*, looked as though he'd never done a sit-up and followed a strict diet of Bud Lights and Big Macs. Daulton looked like he could have been a regular on *Miami Vice*. Danny Jackson would, on occasion, rip his shirt off and do WWE pump-ups. Speaking of blue collar—even for the mid-1990s, the team featured a shocking number of mullets.

There was a lot of late-night drinking and good old-fashioned toxic masculinity. But let's face it—toxicity is the spice of life. Make no mistake about it, the clubhouse would get wild, and things could get out of hand—like that time in 1991 when Dykstra was drunk behind the wheel, wrecked his car, and nearly killed himself and passenger Daulton—but, when it didn't stray into illegality, there was a refreshing honesty and relatability to the brash machismo. Call it "intoxicating masculinity." Men wanted to be them; women wanted to be *with* them. As former *Deadspin* editor A. J. Daulerio has described it,

57

"Philly's ladies fawned over the players like New York's women did over firefighters after 9/11."[19]

The 1994 strike, and the rift it would cause with the fans, was still a dormant volcano. And here were the 1993 Phillies, existing simultaneously within the best of all possible worlds. They were winning, beloved, admired, and still somehow perceived as just regular dudes. Perception is one thing; reality is another.

That season, Glen Macnow interviewed utility man Wes Chamberlain for an *Inquirer* article on how fans relate to players as their salaries continued to skyrocket: "Chamberlain says to me, 'It must be tough for the average guy to get by on the average salary.' And I asked him, what do you think the average salary is? He said, 'I don't know . . . $125K a year?"

And that was over 30 years ago.

Now, of course, the team was not a monolith. Several players strayed from the Row, perhaps none more notable than the ever-friendly, gracious, unassuming fan favorite Jim Eisenreich—the man the team nicknamed "Dahmer" after a serial murdering cannibal. Of course.

EISEY'S PATH

That season's Phillies featured a lot of castoffs who turned out to be diamonds in the rough. Eisenreich was one of them, and that was not an unfamiliar position for the old vet.

"I was fortunate to go to the Phillies," recalled Eisenreich, the unlikely hero who led the '93 team in batting average (.318). "I was already thirty-four years old and was glad to have the opportunity."[20]

The Saint Cloud, Minnesota, native was always a wiz on the ball field. His talent was never a question. In 1984 the then owner of the Twins, Calvin Griffith, said of Eisey, "A natural ballplayer like this might only come once in a lifetime."[21] However, *ability* is a complex word, and as natural and capable as he was physically, a lifelong disease was naturally, physically working against him every step of the way.

What we know now is that Eisenreich had, and has, Tourette syndrome, defined by the Mayo Clinic as "a disorder that involves repetitive movements or unwanted sounds (tics) that can't be easily controlled." Eisenreich had been misdiagnosed and struggled for years to get a handle on the effects of the disease while trying to maintain a career in baseball.

"Growing up, it didn't really bother me playing sports as much as it did in the classroom," said Eisenreich. "I think with sports, because you're always moving, I was able to kind of hide the tics and stuff that I did. In the classroom, when the teacher is speaking, you can't [hide]. Or in church. I was interrupting but trying not to."

What was happening between his ears seemed to have very little effect on his play between the foul poles, so Eisey pushed forward. "I did all these things [tics] in the minor leagues, and high school and college too. People would ask me why I do that, and I didn't know. I had no clue. I didn't want to do those things, but I did."[22]

After being drafted by the Twins in the 16th round of the 1980 MLB draft, he batted .309 in 763 minor-league at-bats over two seasons. In Single-A ball in 1981, he hit .311/.407/.507 with 23 home runs, and that was all Minnesota had to see. He would start the 1982 campaign with the big club.

"So, when I got to the big leagues with the Twins that first year, there was something that made me think, *Are the people watching me play baseball, or are they watching me with my tics and making all the noise?* Mentally, I started to worry about my health. I always did, but when it started to affect me in the sporting world—that's why I left."

Yep, Eisenreich did the unthinkable—he had reached his dream of making it to the major leagues, and he walked away. "I needed to be healthy," he said. "I felt I physically couldn't go out and play."[23]

On May 4, 1982, playing on the road in Boston, Eisenreich was pulled early for the fifth-consecutive game. Dan Shaughnessy of the *Boston Globe* covered his exit the following morning:

> Last night was the saddest and ugliest of scenes thus far. One pitch into the second inning, Eisenreich, his shoulders twitching uncontrollably, came in from center field. He was again victim of a mysterious disorder, perhaps exacerbated by the taunts of some unspeakably insensitive "fans" who in the first inning had yelled, "Hey, Eisenreich, how many innings tonight?" and "It's a little cold, I'm shivering, too," and "Are you epileptic?"[24]

It was still a mystery to everyone at the time what was wrong with the twenty-three-year-old rookie, and his season was shut down after an 0-for-3 showing on June 10. After just two games into the 1983 season, Eisenreich was convinced he was done for good.

"Part of it was, I was mentally tired of it. I wanted my health more than I wanted to play baseball."[25]

He returned in 1984 and played just 12 games before getting serious about retirement and looking after his mental well-being, sitting out all of 1985 and 1986. Obviously, he didn't stay retired, luckily for the Phillies—but first, the Royals.

In 1987, this time with Kansas City, Eisenreich had a proper diagnosis and a plan to move forward with his MLB career. Despite having to compete for playing time among some of the best outfielders of the 1980s (Bo Jackson, Willie Wilson, Danny Tartabull), Eisey had a three-year stretch from 1989 to 1991 batting .291 while averaging 490 plate appearances per season. He led all Royals batters in WAR in 1989 despite being the club's fourth outfielder (3.1)!

A down season in 1992 paved the way for the Phillies to take a flyer, and as it turned out, that early time away from the game left plenty of tread on the tires. In 1993 with the Phillies, he led the club in batting at .318 and ultimately finished his Phillies career in 1996 with the highest franchise batting average of any Phillie since Hall of Famer Chuck Klein hung 'em up way back in 1944 (with a minimum of 1,500 PA; Eisenreich, .324; Klein, .326).

THE POSTSEASON

SEPTEMBER 28, 1993:
Philadelphia Phillies 10, Pittsburgh Pirates 7

> The Phillies are the '93 Eastern Division Champions! This wonderful band of throwback players has won the NL East, mobbing one another on the field! . . . What a fun team to be around and what a fun year, and it's not over yet.
> —Harry Kalas, calling the final out, Phillies TV broadcast.

A season after finishing dead last in the NL East and a decade removed from their last postseason appearance, the Fightin' Phils were finally back to playing meaningful ball in October. The Phillies (97–65) were facing off against the NL

West champion Atlanta Braves (104–58), sliding right into their familiar position as underdogs. Sure, the Braves owned the best record in baseball, two full games better than the Phillies have ever been—to this day, in their entire history dating back to 1883 (102 wins, 2011). But this was an even match on paper. The Phillies scored the most runs in the NL (877), and the Braves surrendered the least runs in the NL (559)—unstoppable force versus immovable object.

GAME ONE (OCTOBER 6):
Phillies 4, Braves 3 (10 innings, Veterans Stadium)
Curt Schilling probably didn't know it when he toed the rubber to kick off the 1993 NLCS, but he was taking the first step toward becoming arguably the greatest postseason pitcher of all time. After a lackluster 4.02 ERA during the regular season, Schilling struck out the first five Bravos he faced, and a star was officially born.

Schilling pitched eight innings, surrendering two earned runs and striking out 10, handing the ball off to Mitch Williams to close it out. Wild Thing walked the first batter he faced (as was his way) and ultimately allowed the Braves to tie it up in the ninth. Alas, the Phillies deep bench of unlikely heroes this time produced Kim Batiste, who smacked a walk-off double (in his only plate appearance of the series) in the 10th to cap the opening upset blow.

GAME TWO (OCTOBER 7):
Braves 14, Phillies 3 (Veterans Stadium)
Nothing against Game One starter Steve Avery, but Atlanta's Greg Maddux was way, way better. The MLB ERA leader (2.36) had a 7–0 lead after three innings, and it was essentially over from there. Maddux was not historically known as a great postseason pitcher, but he wasn't exactly Clayton Kershaw (sick burn).

> **KEVIN'S NOTE:** Sure, Maddux would go on to win his second of four consecutive Cy Youngs that season, but it was his first year with Atlanta. He previously pitched in relative obscurity for the Cubs for seven seasons, the first six of which were fairly pedestrian until he broke out in 1992. He was no superstar yet—just a quiet, calculating master of his craft,

happy to let the baseball world take its time to notice. I remember early in 1995 watching an ESPN feature on Maddux; the players' strike was over, the league needed upstanding superstars, and he was dealing, on a consistently winning team, en route to his fourth consecutive Cy Young. The league decided it was time to anoint Greg Maddux. I was 11 at the time and knew he was good, but until that five-minute feature it hadn't quite clicked that I was watching the greatest pitcher of a generation. News travels fast these days, but back before broadband, greatness took a little longer to download.

GAME THREE (OCTOBER 9):
Braves 9, Phillies 4 (Atlanta–Fulton County Stadium)
Terry Mulholland pitched five shutout innings and had a 2–0 lead to start the sixth. Then, Atlanta's offense exploded for five runs, and then four more in the seventh (four earned runs charged to Mulholland, five charged to Larry Andersen). Braves starter Tom Glavine earned the win, surrendering two runs over seven innings of work.

GAME FOUR (OCTOBER 10):
Phillies 2, Braves 1 (Atlanta–Fulton County Stadium)
Phillies starter Danny Jackson outdueled the third ace in Atlanta's deck, John Smoltz. Jackson pitched 7 2/3 innings of one-run ball, and Mitch Williams closed out another hairy nail-biter after allowing the first two batters to reach base in the ninth. The Phillies were 1-for-11 with runners in scoring position, while the Braves were just 1-for-15.

GAME FIVE (OCTOBER 11):
Phillies 4, Braves 3 (Atlanta–Fulton County Stadium)
"Another boring one-run win," as Larry Andersen would frequently announce after close victories in spring training.[26] Schilling pitched another beaut, going eight shutout innings before allowing the first two batters to reach base with a 3–0 lead in the ninth. Wild Thing couldn't hold it this time, and the Braves scored three to take the game into extras.

Dykstra gave the Phillies the lead again in the 10th with a solo home run, and the wily sage Andersen pitched a delightfully boring bottom half of the inning, shutting down the Bravos in order and putting the Fightins on the brink of a World Series berth.

GAME SIX (OCTOBER 13):
Phillies 6, Braves 3 (Veterans Stadium)
Atlanta sent Maddux to the mound in Game Six, but Mickey Morandini shot his fifth offering of the night off the ace's leg. He stayed in the game but was clearly affected by the comebacker, surrendering six runs in 5 2/3 innings. All-Star Tommy Greene pitched strong, earning the win after going seven innings, surrendering just three runs.

Williams struck out Bill Pecota in the ninth to end the game and the series, sending the Phillies to back to the World Series after a mostly tumultuous decade. In an iconic moment of jubilation, Wild Thing did a kind of leaping split that, after all these years perfectly reflects the enigmatic closer's fiery personality and steadfast commitment to never skipping leg day.

Schilling (16 IP, 1.69 ERA, 19 Ks) earned NLCS MVP honors, the first pitcher to do so without earning a single win or save. (Schill ended his career 11–2 with a 2.23 ERA and 0.968 WHIP through 133 1/3 postseason innings. For that alone, he's long overdue for Hall of Fame induction.)

THE WORLD SERIES

The 1993 World Series, the second consecutive appearance for the AL champion juggernaut Blue Jays, is a fascinating Series to look back on. It's remembered mostly for one single swing, but there was so much more to the story.

GAME ONE
Toronto Skydome
Blue Jays 8, Phillies 5
Naturally, Schilling got the start, and in typical hard-luck Phillies fashion, he surrendered the most runs of his 19-start postseason career (seven, six earned). The Phils held leads at two separate points in the contest but couldn't hold off the high-powered Blue Jays lineup that had led the major leagues in batting average and slugging percentage during the regular season (.279, .436).

GAME TWO
Toronto Skydome
Phillies 6, Blue Jays 4

Jim Eisenreich famously crushed a three-run homer in the top of the third inning to give the Phillies a strong 5–0 lead and silence the Toronto crowd. As he crossed home plate, the stoic outfielder simply strolled back to the dugout as if he had just scored on a sacrifice fly in an otherwise meaningless mid-May ballgame—a sign of the times.

Mulholland pitched a bend-don't-break 5 2/3 innings, letting up three runs on seven hits. Williams pitched his patented 1 2/3-inning save, letting up zero hits and zero runs while walking two.

GAME THREE
Veterans Stadium
Blue Jays 10, Phillies 3

Rickey Henderson, Paul Molitor, Roberto Alomar—three Hall of Fame hitters—combined for nine hits in this one (two, three, four, respectively). Conversely, the Phillies were held scoreless through five, and the three runs they did score were relatively meaningless in terms of mounting a potential comeback. Pat Hentgen, a 19-game winner, surrendered just one earned run in six innings pitched.

GAME FOUR
Veterans Stadium
Blue Jays 15, Phillies 14

At the time, it seemed like it couldn't get more gut-punchy than this.
To date, it is the highest-scoring World Series game in baseball history. Neither starter made it out of the third inning, but the Phillies bats were awakened and resilient. Already at a 3–0 deficit when the Phils came to the plate in the first, they answered with four runs of their own, after four walks and a bases-clearing triple by Milt Thompson.

After trailing 7–6 in the fourth, the Phillies tied it up and then scored five more in the fifth. They added a run in the sixth and another run in the seventh. By then, the Fightins had a 14–9 lead going into the eighth—which, tragically, is the only time in all of World Series history to date that a team has failed to get a victory after leading by five or more runs after seven innings (or four runs, for that matter). Toronto's six-run explosion off Andersen and

Williams in the eighth erased the heroism of Milt Thompson's five-RBI effort and Dykstra's two homers and 10 total bases.

GAME FIVE
Veterans Stadium
Phillies 2, Blue Jays 0
This was a statement game that could have, *should have*, defined the Phillies' clutch, gritty season. Schilling pitched a complete-game shutout of one of the hottest offensive teams in World Series history. It was the first World Series complete-game shutout pitched in four seasons and just the tenth since 1967.

The 3–2 hole was still steep, but there was an odd sense of optimism, both within the team and the fan base, that the Phillies would find a way and overcome, as they'd done all season.

Ominously, Mitch Williams told reporters after the game, "We've found the key to winning: Keeping me out of the game."[27]

GAME SIX
Veterans Stadium
Blue Jays 8, Phillies 6
Terry Mulholland ended up with a very fine career, pitching 20 years in the big leagues. This was not his finest moment.

The Jays jumped out to a 3–0 lead in the first off the All-Star lefty and added two more in the fifth, before handing it off to the beleaguered bullpen. Down 5–1 in the seventh, the Phils called on a familiar hero.

Dykstra, who ended his career batting .321/.433/.661 in 136 postseason plate appearances, gave the Phils a much-needed jolt in the seventh, launching a three-run homer off Dave Stewart to cut the lead to 5–4. The regular season, the postseason, the World Series—the message was clear and consistent: when the moment calls, The Dude abides.

The flood gates opened that inning and the Fightins scored five overall, ultimately carrying a 6–5 lead into the ninth, where things usually got pretty wild.

With one out and two men on, Toronto slugger Joe Carter cemented his legacy, launching a 2-2 pitch into the stands for the 8–6 victory. To this day, it is the only World Series to end on a come-from-behind home run.

> Before I was a host on the radio, or a member of the Philadelphia media, I lived and died with our teams, season after season, a devoted fan. And many of those years had always seemed to end the very same way: in heartache. But this was a different kind of hurt.
>
> The year 1993 was one of the most memorable of my life. In June of that year, while the Phils were putting together their magical season, I met the woman who I would I eventually marry. And I found out she was an absolute keeper, just seconds after Joe Carter's series-clinching home run sailed over the left field wall in Toronto. She was not then, nor is she now, a sports fan. However, she did seem to enjoy how crazy I was about the '93 Phils. I'm an open book, and I wear my emotions on my sleeve. For five months, we watched baseball together—as if she had a choice. That team was something else, and I brought her along for the ride. We were out at the bar that night, cheering along with the rest of the crazies, thinking the Phils would force a seventh game. They were just three outs away but that ninth inning was nerve-racking as hell. And then it happened. Carter, with his shit-eating grin, began dancing his way around the bases, crushing my dreams of a Phillies parade. With my heart sinking to my stomach and the feeling of utter despair so overwhelming, the emotion was just too much. I cried like a big frigging baby. It was over. The finality of it all hit me with the force of a Louisville Slugger. I was dead inside. Twenty-two-year old men shouldn't cry over a game. After all, there's no crying in baseball. But this one hurt so much. I loved that team. As I looked across the table at my girlfriend, Andrea, she glanced back at me with an expression of understanding; she grabbed my hand, tilted her head, and said, "I'm so sorry, babe." She was as sincere as one could be. I thought I may have embarrassed her.
>
> I asked her if she thought I was crazy getting that worked up. And she replied, 'Yes, you are; that's why I love you so much.'
>
> —Brian Startare[28]

The finality of it, for Phillies fans, was like a head-on collision; in the end, the gang had found themselves in a pickle from which they could not escape. Williams took the brunt of the blame, but for better or worse, he was exactly as advertised.

Although Mitch "Wild Thing" Williams was effectively erratic, he *was* effective. He closed out 43 victories in 1993, giving him a total of 186 career saves to that point, with a paltry .213 batting average against. His control issues are what frequently contributed to his downfall, but the Phillies were both chock-full of flawed vets and well aware of the buyer-beware tags on every one of them.

> I was nine years old when the season began in 1993. I was a little too young to have gotten swept up in the Randall Cunningham "Ultimate Weapon" era, the Flyers were just on the verge, and there was absolutely nothing interesting about the Sixers.*
>
> I can't recall the exact moment, but as the Phillies caught fire to start the '93 season, my Philly sports fandom was like a gasoline-soaked wick standing in its wake—school was almost done for the summer, and my metaphorical appointment book had giant swaths of fertile free time not already designated for the neighborhood pool and Nintendo.
>
> I would watch all the games, read all the articles, and cut out all the photos I deemed cool enough to adorn my bedroom wall. I became completely obsessed with the Phillies and baseball.
>
> That season set the bar so unrealistically high for me because I very truly believed every season that followed could be a winner. I thought Ron Gant and Danny Tartabull were the answer. Remember Garrett Stephenson? It's better if you don't. Before the internet picked up speed, I would check the league leaders printed weekly at the back of the sports page of the *Philadelphia Inquirer*—it was like a reaffirmation of everything I'd learned from my morning classes of SportsCenter summer school. Phillies players were in bold, always exciting to check for the homies. Just one gripe I've held onto after all these years: Why, in the *Philadelphia Inquirer*, the news organization tasked with covering the *National* League Phillies, were the American League leaders listed first?
>
> ---
>
> *This would change on June 30 when the 76ers drafted Shawn Bradley, a 7-foot-6 center who would wear No. 76. The synergy of this 76-fecta would dominate playground scuttlebutt later that fall. In retrospect, it was almost as if a *Beavis and Butt-Head*–addled preteen made the pick, selecting The BFG over OMFG-level talents like Penny Hardaway and Jamal Mashburn.

Given it was the last part of the section, NL stats would routinely be cut short (and stolen bases were very important to me). Maybe no people over there ever noticed, or maybe they were just very staunch loyalists to alphabetical order. But I never got over it, and now it's in a book.

Anyway, like Startare, I cried when Joe Carter hit that home run, under far different circumstances and for far different reasons. He was being vulnerable (humiliating himself?) in front of his wife-to-be, because this thing he wanted for so long ended painfully. I bawled my eyes out in my mother's arms, perhaps for the very last time, because my shiny new toy had just been broken. It's sadness all the same. Brian had surely known my version, and I would grow to know his.

#7
HARRY KALAS—VOICE OF THE PHILLIES

OUR VOICE

It's impossible to tell the story of Phillies baseball without the voice that many of us grew up listening to: Harry Kalas, known more concisely as H.K.

From 1971 to 2009, H.K. was the voice of our summers. Whether you were down the shore, hanging outside having a few, or just getting home from baseball practice (like I usually was), you always knew that at 7:05, or 1:05, that beautiful and sultry voice would crack the mic and say something along the lines of, "Good evening everyone, from Citizens Bank Park, welcome to Phillies baseball." It was perfect.

In a way, Harry made it feel like home for a lot of us. With Harry on the mic and the Phillies on our screen, you knew you could take your mind off of everything else and just enjoy a baseball game.

It's easy to understand why he was so beloved. He was funny, he was always there, he had great chemistry with whomever he worked with, he always met the moment, he had the catchphrases, and, most important, he loved us back as much as we loved him.

Who could forget that day up in Cooperstown when our voice was inducted into the National Baseball Hall of Fame and he unleashed this wonderful poem (good luck not reading this in H.K.'s voice):

> This is to the Philadelphia fan
> To laud your passion as best I can
> Your loyalty is unsurpassed, be the Fightins in first or last
> We come to the park each day, looking forward to another fray

> Because we know you'll be there, and we know you really care
> You give the opposing pitcher fits, because as one loyalist shouts,
> "Everybody hits!"
> To be sure in Philly, there might be some boos, because you passionate fans, like the manager—hate to lose
> Your reaction to the action on the field that you impart spurs us as broadcasters to call the game with enthusiasm and heart
> *We feel your passion through and through, Philadelphia fans—I love you*

With a lump in his throat and some water in his eyes, H.K. was giving the emotion back that everyone here felt while watching him up there being immortalized amongst the greats.

THE EARLY YEARS

The story of H.K. in Philadelphia is a long one, but we can thank two specific people for us enjoying 38 years with our voice: Mickey Vernon and Bill Giles.

You might ask, "Who the hell is Mickey Vernon?" Mickey Vernon was the first baseball player who ever interacted with a young Harry Kalas. All the way back in 1946, Harry's dad took him to see the White Sox play the Washington Senators at Comiskey Park in Chicago. Mickey saw a young Harry, picked him up, brought him into the dugout, introduced him to all of his teammates, and gave him a signed baseball. From that moment on, Harry knew he wanted to get into baseball.

Bill Giles, the second person, famously brought Harry from Houston to help open Veterans Stadium and be a part of the Phillies broadcast team. It's funny, the guy that Harry was replacing was none other than Bill Campbell, whom the Phillies were forced to move on from by their new lead beer sponsor—Christian Schmidt Brewing, makers of Schmidt's beer.

The story goes that Campbell identified as a Ballantine Beer guy and that offseason the Phillies inked a $13.5 million dollar deal with Schmidt's to become the new official beer sponsor of the Phillies (big money at the time!) and the brewing company wanted their own guy in there.

In comes a young Harry Kalas to replace a legend. I'm sure the reaction wasn't over the top—not in this city! No, I'm sure Harry was welcomed in with open arms. (Can you sense my sarcasm?)

Oh how little did people know at the time the type of legend that was about to begin. At this time, Harry first partnered with Whitey—Richie Ashburn.

Harry and Whitey entertained us for 26 years. There were some highs, like from 1976 to 1983 and, of course, 1993, but what really created the bond of Harry and Whitey to the audience was the lows. Maybe the most iconic and memorable call from that early run of Kalas and Ashburn was Whitey cackling in the background as the Phillies came back against Nolan Ryan and won Game Five of the 1980 NLCS in what many have called one of the greatest baseball games ever played.

"Three-two pitch . . . swing and a drive, right-center field . . . Maddox is there [Whitey cackles.] The Phillies are on their way to the World Series!" Perfection.

Of course, Kalas's 1980 run would end there, as Major League Baseball did not allow the local radio stations to produce live coverage of the World Series games. So all we have is an audio recording of what Harry *would* have said had he been allowed to call the game. Unfortunately, we would have to wait 28 more years for Kalas to deliver a World Series final call, and I think we can all say our guy came through.

Now, back to the lows. We had some bad baseball teams during his early years here. Heck, in Kalas's second year on the job, the Phillies won only 59 games. After 1983 the Phillies went 10 years without making the postseason and had back-to-back mid-60-win seasons in 1988 and 1989. The '93 season was magic. From 1994 until Whitey's passing in 1997, the Phillies were mired in three straight mid-60-win seasons. But through it all, you could count on Harry and Whitey to keep us entertained and make bad baseball enjoyable. That was their brilliance.

You didn't think I'd just skip over '93 did you? Maybe the most iconic Harry and Whitey year was the 1993 Phillies. Kalas and Ashburn were built to call that baseball season. A team full of castoffs, who were equipped with beer guts and mullets, went from worst to first and, thus, completely took over this town for an entire summer. (And rain delay theater followed until Bryce Harper was signed.)

To this day, people who were alive for the '93 Phillies will tell you it was one of the most enjoyable teams this city has ever seen. For a lot of kids it was the first time they could consciously remember a competitive baseball team in this city.

How come it's always a decade or more in between playoff appearances for this baseball team? I mean it's gotta be some kind of sick joke that between 1983 and 1993 no playoff baseball was here. We went from 1993 to 2007 without playoff baseball, and a few years before I wrote this, we had just ended another 11-year playoff drought from 2011 to 2022. I hope that whenever you're reading this book we are not in the midst of another 10-plus-year playoff drought, and at the risk of having my old takes exposed, I will *not* jinx it now.

Anyway, from Mariano Duncan on Mother's Day, to Larry Andersen's single against the Cubs, the Mitch Williams Walk-Off at 3:30 in the morning, and eventually winning the National League pennant, the season built for those Harry and Whitey.

"What are the odds the Wild Thing can work a one-two-three ninth here, Harry?"

"No chance."

"The oh-two pitch—"

"This wacky, wonderful, bunch of throwbacks has just won the National League pennant!. It's bedlam here at Veterans Stadium!"

I would talk about what happened after that, but we don't need to talk about 15–14 or Joe Carter here. This is about Harry.

Unfortunately, '93 would be the duo's last playoff season. Richie Ashburn tragically passed away on September 9, 1997, at a hotel in midtown New York. Harry described it as losing his "best friend in the world," as he talked to reporters in his hotel room while taking a long drag of a cigarette and with tears filling his eyes. Gone were the days of hearing about the '62 Mets, the worst team in the history of baseball that Ashburn starred on, or the story of him hitting the same woman twice with foul balls in the same at-bat, which caused her to leave the game on a stretcher. Yes, a part of the Phillies died that day with Richie Ashburn; however, to this day people still bring up the magic those two created—a rare feat that truly shows how special those two were. It was a bond between broadcasters and city that has been so rare throughout the years. Luckily for us, Harry kept rolling on, just then without his counterpart for the last 26 years.

HARRY 2.0

With Ashburn's passing, the broadcast booth took new shape, but unfortunately for Harry, and us of course, the Phillies were still mired in their losing ways.

Often with athletes, we talk about moments that show just how special they are. I think we can do that with broadcasters too. Sure, we all remember their memorable calls and their catchphrases. But what makes and connects a broadcaster to an audience is moments of vulnerability and realness. No moment summed that up more than Harry addressing the city after the tragedy that was 9/11.

With a country in mourning and in attempt to get back to normalcy, Harry took to the microphone and spoke directly into households all across the Delaware Valley with sincerity and thoughtfulness. With a crackle in his voice, Kalas said, "From the cradle of Liberty, Philadelphia, Pennsylvania. Do we have closure? No. No, the heinous acts of terrorism of last Tuesday will be with us for as long as we all shall live. We have earned a greater respect and love for the men and women of our fire departments, our police departments, and our emergency-rescue squads. We are all Americans, and we are proud to be Americans, and we must never resort to the thinking that created Tuesday's acts of terrorism. They were born of hatred; we as individuals, we as a nation, must never hate. More than ever before, we must stand together and live by His words, 'Love one another.'" Simple and yet powerful, that was the Harry Kalas way. It's hard not to watch that video every year on that anniversary.

One moment that I thought summed up how the players felt about Harry was actually when Philadelphia showed how we *really* are. Scott Rolen had been our only hope from 1997 to 2001, but with a baseball team that wasn't fully committed to winning, Rolen didn't want to sign away the rest of his career to an organization that, at the time, had more of a small-market mindset.

> Imagine if the Phillies had been able to convince Rolen to stay. What would that team have looked like? It would have been arguably the greatest infield ever assembled: a Hall of Fame third baseman, a Hall of Fame–caliber shortstop, an eventual (as of this writing) Hall of Fame second baseman, and a slugging first baseman who was the game's most feared slugger from 2005 to 2011. Damn it.

The Mike Schmidt prodigy was traded in 2002 to the St. Louis Cardinals even though Citizens Bank Park was only a year away and the Phillies were showing signs of a team ready to spend—they eventually spent the Rolen money on Jim Thome. After Harry's Hall of Fame induction, he was honored at Veterans Stadium with a slow ride around the stadium so the sold out crowd could give him a warm ovation. Their opponent that day? None other than the St. Louis Cardinals and our brand-new enemy.

With the boos raining down, Rolen ran onto the field and opened the door for Harry to get in the car, making sure he honored a broadcaster who introduced the city to a Hall of Fame talent.

The early 2000s had some bad baseball, but some great Harry moments. Who could forget Robert Person's two-home run game, Kevin Millwood's no-hitter, and the Bobby Abreu inside-the-park home run? All those moments seemed built for the legendary broadcaster.

Still, even with the team not breaking through to the postseason yet, some serious roots were growing underneath the surface that would help carry the franchise through the best run in team history. The calvary of Rollins, Utley, Hamels, and Howard were coming, and only one man was needed to usher in this new and exciting era of Phillies baseball. Harry 2.0 was off and rolling.

THE GOLDEN YEARS

For my generation, the Millennials (insert angry old man yelling at a cloud here), Harry truly became our voice with pillars of Rollins, Utley, Howard, and Hamels joining the fold. However, it really started with Jim Thome.

For us kids around that time, Jim Thome was a God. Not only chicks dig the long ball, but so do kids, and Thome hit them better than most. Jim Thome is also an underrated great H.K. name.

"Swing and a long-drive, deep right-center field. . . . That ball is outta here. . . . Three run home run, Jim *Thome*." Extra emphasis was on the Thome.

With the slugging first baseman in the fold, it was the kids turn to show the city what they got. Jimmy Rollins was the first of the future trio to reach the majors. In 2001 he had already made his first All-Star team and quickly had formed a connection with the city. We had hope again.

With Rollins established, next to come up was Chase Utley. We all still remember Harry's call of Utley's first career home run in his first career start at second base—a grand slam over the head of future Phillies manager Gabe Kapler. "Welcome to the show, Mr. UT-ley."

While Jimmy and Chase were putting their mark on the new era of Phillies baseball, a guy was putting up historic numbers in Reading, but we'll get to him in a little bit.

Harry got to open the Vet in 1971 and close it in 2003. While it was only home to three World Series appearances and one championship, the Vet was a home away from home for a lot of Philadelphians, and Harry got to call all of it.

The 2003 season was another that ended without a playoff appearance, but it was also one that you left filled with hope for the future: a new ballpark and a new group of stars, but with the same man there to call it all. Welcome to the Golden Years.

THE GOLDEN YEARS

Not very often does a broadcaster get to usher in two new ballparks in their career, but Harry was able to do it.

Citizens Bank Park *officially* opened on April 12, 2004. It's fitting that the first home run at the new ballpark was off the bat of a first ballot, all–Harry Kalas name in Phils right fielder Bobby Abreu. Can't you just hear him saying that name right now?

The town was fired up about baseball again, but the story of the Phillies from 2004 to 2006 could be summed up in one phrase: *close, but no cigar.* The Phillies were good, just not good enough. They won 86, 88, and 85 games from 2004 to 2006. Even without reaching the postseason, there were some fantastic moments during those years, like Thome's 400th home run, an underrated Kalas call, and "number fifty-*eight* for the big man" during Ryan Howard's 2006 MVP campaign. But the Phillies just couldn't capitalize on that offensive firepower—that is, until their shortstop, their leader and spark plug, uttered the phrase *the team to beat.*

God, I loved the '07 Phillies. The team gave me my first taste of postseason baseball and the first time I truly got to experience Kalas calling a division race. Couple that with one of the biggest chases in a division in baseball history against your most hated rival, and you had yourself quite the summer in 2007.

From August 27 to the end of the regular season we got some *prime* Kalas moments. *Why August 27?* you might ask. That was when, while entering the weekend trailing the Mets by five games in the division, the Phils completed the four-game sweep and thrust themselves right into the heart of the division race.

In the final game of that series, with just over forty-two thousand in the ballpark and stressed-out Mets fans all over the stadium, Chase Utley, fresh off returning from his broken hand, ripped a single just past the outstretched arm of Carlos Delgado into right field. A sun-drenched Citizens Bank Park was in a frenzy, and Harry the K belted out, "Line-drive hit to right field, here comes Iguchi, the throw to the plate . . . *late!* The Phils win, eleven to ten, on an RBI single by Chase Utley! What a huge win, what a huge series by the Fightin' Phils, who sweep the New York Mets. *Wow!*" Division race was on.

What happened in the final month of the season was nothing short of excruciating, invigorating, and stressful. The Phillies, while trailing the division by seven games with 17 games left, took advantage of the one of the biggest collapses in baseball history. Did it make up for '64? No. But was it sweet? It sure was.

All of this culminated on September 30 of that year. With the division race tied, at the start of the day, the Phillies needed to win and have the Mets lose for them to claim the division crown.

Before the Phillies even took the field, the Mets were down 7–0, and Citizens Bank Park was in a full-on frenzy. What transpired was 2 hours and 58 minutes of pure jubilation down at the ballpark. For a thirteen-year-old me, I was finally able to see my team make the playoffs. It was a special day that was capped off in a special, special way.

On the mound, drenched in a sea of white rally towels, Brett Myers—the team's former-starter-turned-closer because of a rough stretch in the middle of the season—had Willy Mo Pena in a 1-2 hole. It was a culminating moment, the young kids who provided so much hope were starting to grow up, they had fully chased down the Mets, Rollins's prophecy had come to life, and finally, there was Harry—welcoming us all back to playoff baseball for the first time since 1993.

With Pena down 1-2 in the count, Myers unleashed his patented knuckle curveball, and H.K. belted out in his ever most excited and velvety voice, "Curveball, struck him out! The Phillies are National League East *champions!* Look at the scene on the field; look at the scene in the stands. This is incredible! The Phillies have won the National League East and will go to the postseason for the first time since 1993." Aah, the '07 Phillies.

Do we have to talk about the Rockies series? You know the story, they got *smoked* by the red-hot Rockies, which ended up in the World Series only to fall to the Boston Red Sox, winning their second title in four years. What were they whining about up in Boston again? Some curse? Seems like it was lifted.

Regardless, the '07 Phillies brought baseball back to Philadelphia and had the city believing that with a few tweaks maybe, just maybe, 2008 would be their year. And however right they were.

THEY DID IT

"Fans on their feet, rally towels are being waved. . . . Brad Lidge . . . stretches. The oh-two pitch . . . swing and miss! Struck him out! The Philadelphia Phillies are 2008 world champions of baseball!" The call we had been waiting a lifetime (and a rain delay) for was finally delivered. And boy, did Harry deliver. Why wouldn't he? Let's just step back and realize how special that moment truly was for a broadcaster and the city.

Harry Kalas had been this team's broadcaster since 1971. When the Phillies won the title in 1980, he couldn't even call the game live due to Major League Baseball restrictions. He had '93, but they ultimately fell short, and then endured a playoffless streak until 2007 that was fresh off a playoffless streak from 1984 to 1992. The team sure didn't make it easy on old Har.

For us, 1983 (!) was the last time we had a parade down Broad Street. Sure, we had '93, we had Buddy's Eagles, the Lindros Flyers, the '01 Sixers, and the Donovan and Andy Birds, but it all led down the same path: heartbreak.

When I was growing up, Negadelphia still existed. Generations hadn't seen a Philly team bring home a title, and you mean to tell me the Phillies, *the Phillies*, were going to be the team to break the curse of Billy Penn?

Well, I'll be damned.

All the years Harry put in, all the years of heartbreak or just incompetence these teams here put us through, all seemed to be washed away with that call that we all have ingrained into our brain.

We were champions. We had finally done it, and Harry finally got the call.

Also, who could forget Chris Wheeler freaking out right beside Harry in the booth? "On the final call in 2008, I caught my mind wandering when the Rays had a runner at second and one out in the ninth," Wheeler said to us when asked about his thinking during the final out. "I thought about how local broadcasters weren't even able to do radio during the World Series in

1980. Harry later did a re-creation of the Series, which was great, but it was a re-creation and not live. So I said to myself, *If we somehow get two more outs and win the World Series, just be quiet and make sure Harry has his moment.* Of course he was great, and the call lives on. It sure was the right decision on my part."

Wheels's reaction was like a snapshot into every single bar, living room, or wherever else you were when the Phillies had finally delivered the first title to the city of Philadelphia since 1983.

THE END

I don't think we saw it coming. I know I didn't.

Before a game against the Nationals in DC on April 13, 2009, fresh off a dramatic late-inning home run by Matt Stairs in Colorado (Harry's last "Outta Here!"), the great broadcaster collapsed in the broadcast booth and, unfortunately, passed away.

Larry Andersen was one of the first to see Kalas. He remembered running into the booth, with Kalas on the floor staring blankly into the sky. Andersen immediately started attempting to administer CPR, but he just remembers Kalas being gone. In L.A.'s words, Harry was looking towards the heavens as if to say, "I'll see you soon, partner."

Much like you reading this, I remember exactly where I was when I heard that our voice was gone. I was sitting in some pointless assembly before heading out to baseball practice as the school day was wrapping up when the alert popped up on my phone. I remember going through the motions at practice that day not realizing that the loss of someone I hadn't really known could affect me so much. But that was the power of H.K.

THE CALLS

All right, let's pick the spirits back up here; I know that was a somber last paragraph. What is a chapter on the voice of the Phillies without a detailed breakdown of his most famous calls?

"OUTTA HERE"

You can hear it right now can't you? That deep, hearty call used to fill up our summer nights. Even in sitting down to write this chapter I forget how good and strong Harry's "Outta here!" call was until I heard some of them again.

"Outta here!" is iconic. Heck, they *still* play it in the ballpark after a Phillie hits a home run.

But how did it start? It was with none other than the legend himself, Larry Bowa. "We were behind the batting cage taking batting practice, and I was with Harry [Kalas], and Bull [Luzinski] hit a ball, and I went, 'That ball's outta here.' Harry gives me a staredown and goes, 'I like that,'" Bowa said when asked about the iconic call. "I didn't think anything of it. . . . And then when he started using it, it became unbelievable."

You could make a case that Larry Bowa is the most important Phillie of all time. World Series–winning shortstop, coach on the '93 team, manager in the early 2000s. And he helped give Harry his hallmark call? Sounds like a case to me!

He was often imitated, never duplicated. "Outta here!" was ingrained into our souls growing up. Hit a home run in the neighborhood wiffle ball game? "Outta here!" Need Harry to be the voice on your cellphones voice mailbox? "Sorry, Jim can't get to the phone right now. He is "outta here!" Looking for the best imitation to try and win a contest on WIP? The phones would light up with people waiting to give their impressions of the call.

Harry had a ton of memorable calls, and narrowing them down to five feels wrong in a way, but they didn't pay us the big bucks on this book to not come up with the *correct* top-five list of Harry Kalas's best calls as voted by . . . me.

5. THE BIGGIO HOMER

A call about a home run that essentially sunk the Phillies chances to make the postseason? *That's* on my list of the five best Harry Kalas calls? Yes, because it was so, so Harry, and I think summed up why we loved him so much.

With the Phillies leading the Astros by a half-game for the wild card in 2005, Houston came to town for a big late-season tilt. After dropping the first two games of the series, the Phillies were trying to salvage game three and had Billy Wagner on the mound trying to preserve the lead. Up walked Craig Biggio to hit a go-ahead home run off Wagner, which sparked this pure disgust from Harry: "You're kidding me; you are *kidding* me. Home run, Craig

Biggio, to give the Astros an eight to six lead. All the runs are unearned, but who cares?" He felt our pain and summed it up perfectly.

4. KIM BATISTE PLAYS HERO

The 1993 Phillies were littered with moments, many of which them documented throughout this book, but when we're talking about Harry calls, I think one jumps out above all else.

Leading in the ninth inning of Game One in the 1993 National League Championship Series against the Braves, Jim Fregosi did what he usually did when looking to preserve a lead: he put in some defensive replacements. One of those was Kim Batiste to play third base. Before the acronym GOAT was overused to describe innocuous things, the word *goat* in sports described someone who cost the team the game.

After Mitch Williams walked the leadoff hitter, Batiste got a tailor-made double-play ball hit to him, only he threw the ball into right field, allowing the runner to get to third base with no outs—brutal.

But Kim Batiste would have a chance to go from goat to GOAT. In the bottom of the 10th, John Kruk hit a one-out double. The scene was set. Now usually this would be Dave Hollins's spot in the lineup. Hollins was an All-Star that year and drove in 93 runs. I think the Braves would take that tradeoff.

In a classic "how can you not be romantic about baseball?" moment, Kim Batiste just squeezed a ball past the diving Terry Pendleton at third base (why wasn't he guarding the line?), and Veterans Stadium was euphoric.

Of course, as always, H.K. nailed it. "Here's the stretch. The one-two pitch, swing—a hard groundball . . . *Base hit! Base hit down the left-field line! Kruk scores. Phils win four to three on the RBI hit by Kim Bah-tiste!*" I had to add the extra emphasis on "Batiste" to really capture how Harry called that one—a GOAT-worthy call.

3. THE TRILLO TRIPLE

Of all the games in Phillies history, I think Game Five of the 1980 National League Championship Series is the one I wish I could have lived and experienced. Again, the Phillies, a team that had been around for almost a hundred years at that point were *still* searching for their first title. Talk about pressure to get the job done.

Now ultimately, they did get the job done but not without some stress-filled high-wire acts, like in Game Five of the NLCS. By the way, the NLCS was only five games back then, so Game Five was an elimination game.

The 1980 Phillies sure didn't make it easy on themselves in this one. They were down 5–2 in the eighth against none other than *Nolan freakin' Ryan*. This game was *over*. No shot in hell the Phillies were coming back against "The Ryan Express" down three in the Astrodome.

Well, they did it. They led off the eighth with three straight singles off of Ryan, and Pete Rose walked with the bases loaded to make it 5–3. Just like that, the big right-hander was out of the game. With two outs and the Phillies still trailing 5–4, Manny Trillo laced a ball down the third-base line into the corner, and he was off.

With a shriek of enthusiasm, H.K. belted out, "Trillo! Line drive down the left-field line! Avila scores. Here's Del Unser being waved around. He's going to score. Manny Trillo at third with a triple! Phils lead it, seven to five. What a comeback by this Fightin' bunch of Phils!" Even though it was 14 years my prior, Harry's call still gives me chills.

The crazy part about that game was that it wasn't a deciding play or anything. The Phillies blew that lead, which was 7–5 at the time. Tug McGraw allowed two in the eighth to make it 7–7. Eventually in the top of the 10th, Garry Maddox hit a sacrifice fly that scored Del Unser, and with Dick Ruthven on the mound the Phillies closed out the Astros in the bottom of the 10th and advanced to their first World Series since 1950. The Trillo triple.

2. SCHMITTY'S 500TH

I always wonder at what point the Phillies fans who hated Mike Schmidt realized they were probably a little tough on the guy. I'd like to think that when he hit his 500th home run a lot of them looked in the mirror and said, "Hand up; the guy was pretty good."

If not for number one, the most iconic Harry call would be the call of Mike Schmidt's 500th home run. After all, for a franchise that has been around for almost 150 years, Schmitty is the only Phillie to hit 500 homers. (Is Bryce next?) It's a *big* deal, and one can only imagine the buildup and the angst for the greatest player in Phillies history to accomplish his biggest personal feat.

Do you want to know my favorite part about Schmitty's 500th? It was a clutch homer. Mike Schmidt hit his 500th home run in the ninth inning with the Phillies down one run. It wasn't just some random game where he hit the home run in the fifth inning. This gave the Phillies a win. That is awesome. Now, the 1987 Phillies ultimately ended up finishing under .500, but on April 18, it was a big win.

The good part about it being so clutch and in a big moment is that I believe it got *even more* passion and emotion from Harry. Again, Harry would have nailed the call anyway, but giving him a top-of-the-ninth, go-ahead home run was serving it up on a tee.

As usual, H.K. knocked it out of the park: "Here's the stretch by Robinson, the three-oh pitch . . . swing and a long drive! There it is, number five hundred! The career five hundreth home run for Michael Jack Schmidt! And the Phillies have regained the lead here in Pittsburgh, eight to six, and the Phillies dugout comes swarming out to home plate."

I have three thoughts. One, calling the guy Michael Jack Schmidt is so unique by a broadcaster, but it just flowed so perfectly and really stuck. I still take calls to this day from people who experienced the Schmidt era, and they all call him either Schmitty or Michael Jack Schmidt. A lot of that is credit to Harry.

Two, the "eight to six" that Harry let out in that call was just all-time. So raspy, so deep, so passionate.

Three, regarding Don Robinson, although I'm sure it hurt in the moment, would you want to be the guy who gave up an iconic moment to an iconic player? Think about it.—for the rest of eternity, or until baseball dies, your name would be synonymous with the best third baseman to ever play the game. I'll have to ask Don, but I don't think it would be the worst thing in the world.

1. WORLD CHAMPIONS OF BASEBALL

Just writing out that put a smile on my face. Because Harry could not be on the call for the 1980 World Series due to MLB rules and regulations, he had to go from 1971 to 2008 without being able to say the Phillies were world champions of baseball. Heck, we couldn't even get Harry a World Series call without it being delayed an extra night.

Why do the sports gods hate us? Why can't it just be easy? Did we really need the first rain delay in World Series history to make us wait even longer for the first title in Philadelphia since 1983? The answer is no, no we didn't.

One of the coolest things for broadcasters that have been around the team for a long time and have entered into our homes on a nightly basis has to be that fans want to win the title not only for themselves but for the legends who call these games as well. I remember during the 2017 run for the Eagles fielding hundreds of calls from people talking about how obviously they wanted a Super Bowl for themselves and, almost more important, for the iconic Merrill Reese.

The same thing happened in 2008. We all wanted to win the World Series, but we all wanted Harry to have that moment too, and given that it's number one on this list and I still get chills listening to it, I'd say he lived up to the moment.

With Citizens Bank Park in a frenzy and waiting to explode, Harry Kalas, the team's broadcaster since 1971, barred from calling the 1980 World Series, falling just short of having this moment in 1993, really being the face of the franchise during some lean years, *finally* got his moment.

"Fans on their feet, rally towels are being waved. Brad Lidge . . . stretches. The oh-two pitch, swing and a miss! Struck him out! The Philadelphia Phillies are 2008 world champions of Baseball! Brad Lidge does it again and stays perfect for the 2008 season—forty-eight for forty-eight. And let this city celebrate."

I have two thoughts on the call. One, the way he says, "Brad Lidge . . . stretches" creates even more suspense. It is just brilliant.

Two, the count being 0-2 made it even cooler. We've all been in the backyard playing baseball with our friends and pretending we're about to close out a World Series game. The count that's always in our head? It's 0-2. Having the World Series end on a strikeout is a chef's kiss as well—just perfect.

Larry Andersen remembered that day well. L.A. was just like us—thrilled the Phils won the World Series, of course, but even more thrilled that Kalas got to have that call. He remembered just looking at Harry and smiling.

FAVORITE HARRY STORIES FROM INTERVIEWEES

We compiled some great Harry stories while interviewing people for this book. Here are a couple. The first is from Larry Bowa, who remembered a legendary time in Chicago:

> We were in Chicago, and at that time they played all day games, and Tug [McGraw] and Harry liked to have a few drinks out there, and the bars were open all night. [Because of that] Tug just couldn't pitch

in Chicago—in fact, Dallas Green would just tell him to forget about it, he wasn't going to use him.

So, Bull [Luzinski] and I are going to the park for the game that day; it's about 8:30, and as we're going through the lobby, we see Harry and Tug, and they're going to the front desk, and they say, 'We'd like to leave a wake-up call for nine o'clock.'

The lady says, 'Tonight?'

And they say, 'No, the morning.'

So, she says, 'Well, it's 8:30 right now, so—'

And Bull and I just cracked up laughing. They had no idea what time it was, where they were. They loved to go out and have a few pops. That's the reason Tug never pitched there after a while, because Dallas said, 'No, no, no. If you like to have fun in Chicago, we'll go in another direction.'

If you look at his numbers pitching at Wrigley, they weren't very pretty.

The other was from Andersen, who grew close with Kalas during his time with the team in '93 and while broadcasting games alongside the legend. (Broadcasting with Kalas was tough for L.A. because, in his words, "I just wanted to listen to him too!") Part of what made Kalas so beloved by the players in the eyes of L.A. was that he would never criticize them on the air and would always look for the bright side, even if a player wasn't all that great. Also, he truly was one of the guys, as evidenced by Bowa's story.

My favorite L.A. and Harry story was when they were sitting on the tarmac in Philly waiting to take off for a road trip. Harry passed out in his seat before the plane even took off, woke up an hour or so later, and said to L.A. "Well, 'Breakdown,' (L.A.'s nickname because he would often have computer troubles and yell at the thing) a pretty smooth flight so far." The plane hadn't moved.

It's wild that a whole generation of Phillies fans are going to grow up now knowing about Harry. While it's tough to do it justice in writing, especially with some of the calls, I hope this book helps people understand how much he meant to this town, and his legend will live on. Thankfully, Harry has been replaced by the wonderful Tom McCarthy, who is well on his way to becoming a legend in his own right in this city. There's a bond between a broadcaster and a city; the broadcaster is a friend on a journey through a game and a season. In a sports-crazed place like this, the person gets immortalized. Rest easy, H.K., and thank you.

#8
THE FANS

"I felt as if I'd died and gone to baseball heaven."

—Scott Rolen

Hall of Fame third baseman Scott Rolen didn't say this upon being drafted by the Phillies in June 1993. Nor did he say this upon being called up to the Phillies in August 1996. No, he said this to the press immediately after being traded *by* Philadelphia *to* the St. Louis Cardinals in 2002. He didn't mince words.

"I can't wait to get on the plane and get to Florida to join the Cardinals," said Rolen. "[St. Louis] may be the best place to play in the game, and it's the place I always dreamed of playing."[1]

This was after having spent a decade with the Phillies organization, winning Rookie of the Year and three Gold Gloves at third base. Rolen, once a finalist for Indiana's Mr. Basketball award in high school, just dunked on Philly on his way out the door. *Dang.*

Before Rolen, third baseman Mike Schmidt said, "Philadelphia is the only city where you can experience the thrill of victory and the agony of reading about it the next day."[2]

After Rolen, third baseman Alec Bohm said, "I f*cking hate this place" on a hot mic during a three-error game in April 2022.

The truth of the matter is, it's not for the players to decide. Fans don't get to see things from an athlete's perspective; as such, athletes don't get to be the arbiters of a metaphorical baseball heaven simply by participating in a game that's existence predates the first zipper (invented by W. L. Judson in 1893, FYI).

Fans appreciate being liked by athletes as much as athletes appreciate being adored by fans. But every successful relationship has its ups and downs.

It's hard to blame Rolen, Schmidt, Bohm, or nearly any athlete (except J. D. Drew; he sucks) that gets bristly with the team, the city, or both, because pushback is required. It's tough love, tried and true.

If unconditional support and adoration is what you seek, then St. Louis's Busch Stadium should rightly be lined with gates of pearl. But those fans will never cheer as hard or care as much as the ones who, just like Bohm, sometimes f*cking hate this place too.

The day after Bohm had his slipup, the fans gave him a standing ovation. After a prolonged slump by shortstop Trea Turner in 2023, fans turned boos to cheers to help turn his season around. It's all about the team, and Phillies fans will do whatever it takes to support the cause.

This is perhaps most evident in what's become one of the city's greatest rooting traditions—fan groups. The oft-costumed collections of fans that would flock to the Vet or CBP with a giant sign and punny title, signaling their devotion to specific players, both stars and benchwarmers alike.

> Always loved the upper deck fan clubs. Wolf Pack. Duck Pond. Byrd Nest. Padilla Flotilla.
> —Former Phillies center fielder Doug Glanville.[3]

Remember the classics? The devoted fan groups like the Wolf Pack for Randy Wolf, the Schill-o-Meter for Curt Schilling, and the Padilla Flotilla for Vicente Padilla became staples of the game and broadcasts.[4] These groups highlight the duality of Philly fandom—brutally honest with the team as a whole but deeply affectionate toward players who earn their respect, whether through talent, grit, or sheer personality.

Matt Albertson, Society for American Baseball Research (SABR) member and Philly SABR cochair, started researching and cataloging all the fan groups in 2022. When the national media pelts the nation with negative reminders of Eagles fans pelting Santa with snowballs a bajillion years ago, it's fun—and more accurate—to look back at this enduring tradition that highlights the best of the best fans in baseball.

"I'm a fan, and I like fans doing fan things," said Albertson. "I was intrigued and sought out the biggest list I could find but was disappointed in what was out there. . . . I wanted to know more.

"Having discovered three unique Phillies fan groups while researching the 1895 Favorite Phillie contest, I knew I could take on the side project and put together something useful, fun, and concrete. I didn't just want names of what groups may have existed, I wanted photographic evidence or firsthand accounts from people in those groups. I wanted to build the most authoritative chronicle available."

Albertson's *27th and Jefferson* blog on MattAlbertson.net is the authority on the Phillies' most phanatical, and it's growing and evolving.

"I'm still finding more groups, but the pace is slowing down . . . I've scoured the internet and found old websites that included pictures of a few groups. When I posted a bunch en masse on Twitter, the thread went viral, and people came out of the woodwork to tell me about the group they were in and even sent me pictures to include."5

THE STATS

Number of groups: 92
Most popular year: 2002 (27 groups)

THE LIST (SO FAR):

2024:
    Nola's Gondolas—Aaron Nola
    Stubbs' Club—Garrett Stubbs
    Ranger's Rangers—Ranger Suárez

2023:
    Stott's Tots—Bryson Stott
    Harper's Hounds—Bryce Harper
    Marsh's Maniacs—Brandon Marsh
    Marsh's Marshmallows—Brandon Marsh (Twitter: @Marshs_Mallows)
    Marsh's Marshans—Brandon Marsh

2022:
    Jean's Jeans—Jean Segura (Twitter: @JeansJeans302)
    Harper's Heroes—Bryce Harper
    The Knapp Sacks—Andrew Knapp

2020:
    The Phandemic Krew—Phillies (Twitter: @PhandemicKrew)

"If there was an award for Most Valuable Fans, the Phandemic Krew would win hands-down!"

—Ken Rosenthal, *The Athletic*[6]

It's no surprise that 2020 was a weird time for baseball and every single thing else about normal everyday life. Stadiums were empty, and teams sold spaces for cutouts of fans' faces for the stands because, otherwise, it would look weird.

During that season, fans Oscar Alvarado and Brett MacMinn started gatherings outside of Ashburn Alley at Citizens Bank Park, deciding to cheer from *outside* the stadium while the COVID-19 lockdowns kept fans from being allowed in.

"Hey, they're not letting us in the park, but what if we stood outside?" Alvarado pondered with his friend, MacMinn. "Are they going to say anything? Are they going to let us watch? Are they going to kick us out? We decided to do it until they pushed us out."[7]

They were allowed to stay and were actually encouraged by the front office, players, and coaches, who could hear their cheers in an otherwise eerily quiet playing environment. From there, the group grew bigger and beyond its original scope.

Through the 2024 season, they attended 414 games (inside and out of CBP), were the subjects of two MLB-licensed bobbleheads, and used their influence to support Bette's Triples, a fundraiser that supports the Pennsylvania Society for the Prevention of Cruelty to Animals.

2016:
Ruppies Puppies—Cameron Rupp (Twitter: @RuppiesPuppies)

2011:
Cliff Hangers—Cliff Lee
Vance Worley's Greek Warriors—Vance Worley
Francisco's Benny Franks—Ben Francisco
Chooch's Conductor's—Carlos Ruiz
Orr's Oars—Pete Orr
Stute's Fruits—Michael Stutes

2010:
Doc's Patients—Roy Halladay
Polanco Heads—Placido Polanco

THE FANS

2009:
- Bako's Tacos—Paul Bako
- Rodrigo's Amigos—Rodrigo López
- Werth's Smurfs—Jayson Werth
- Kendrick's Hendrix—Kyle Kendrick

2007:
- Phlyin Hawaiians—Shane Victorino
- Red Army—Phillies
- Chase's Chicks—Chase Utley
- The Coste Guard—Chris Coste
- Flash's Followers—Tom Gordon

2006:
- Sal's Pals—Sal Fasano
- Howard's Homers—Ryan Howard
- J-Roll's Bakery—Jimmy Rollins

2005:
- Abreu's Amigos—Bobby Abreu

2003:
- The Pratt Pack—Todd Pratt
- Millwood's Militia—Kevin Millwood
- Turk's Turkeys—Turk Wendell
- Byrd's Nest—Marlon Byrd
- The Generic Fan Group—Phillies
- Thome's Homies—Jim Thome
- Thome-Nators—Jim Thome
- Bowa's Boys—Phillies
- Cormier's Crazy Crew—Rheal Cormier

2002:
- Kalas's Krew (We're Way Out of Here)—Harry Kalas
- Pat's Bat-Men—Pat Burrell
- Burrell's Bomb Squad—Pat Burrell
- Burrell of Monkees—Pat Burrell

The Duck Pond—Brandon Duckworth
Duckworth's Quack Pack—Brandon Duckworth
Padilla's Flotilla—Vicente Padilla
Giambi's Zombies—Jeremy Giambi
Burrell's Squirrels—Pat Burrell
Burrell's Girls—Pat Burrell
J-ro's Bros—Jimmy Rollins
Bobby's Bobbies—Bobby Abreu
Mesa's Faces—José Mesa
Marlon's Magician—Marlon Anderson
Perez's Fezes—Tomás Pérez
The Adams Family—Terry Adams
Lieberthal's Little Phan Group—Mike Lieberthal
Dolla Dog Pound—Dollar Dogs
Amigos de Areu y Pérez—Bobby Abreu and Tomás Pérez
Coggin's Corner—Dave Coggin
Lieberthal's Neanderthals—Mike Lieberthal
Polanco's Posse—Placido Polanco
The Casey's Kalas Krazies—Harry Kalas
Myer's Suppliers—Brett Myers
Roa Boat—Joe Roa
Harry's Hoodlums—Harry Kalas
Burrell's Bunch—Pat Burrell

2001:

The Dave Kave—Dave Coggin
Daal House—Omar Daal

2000:

Chen Pen—Bruce Chen

1999:

The Wolf Pack—Randy Wolf
This is the group that started the sensation and is the most well-known. Matt Breen, of the *Philadelphia Inquirer*, wrote the following:
The Wolf Pack never missed an inning Wolf pitched in Philadelphia after showing up 25 years ago to the 700 level with a spray-painted bedsheet. Wolf

spent eight years with the Phillies after reaching the majors in 1999. The Wolf Pack—a group of eight Wood brothers and their Thompson cousins—howled every night."[8]

> Person's People—Robert Person
> Ogea's Orangemen—Chad Ogea
> Byrd's Nest—Paul Byrd
> Gomzee's Homeez—Wayne Gomes
> Abreu's Army—Bobby Abreu
> Glanville—Doug Glanville
> The Scott Squad—Scott Rolen
> Gant's Gang—Ron Gant
> The Byrd Cage—Paul Byrd

1998:
Dutch Wonder-Land—Darren Daulton

1997:
The Schill-o-Meter—Curt Schilling

The Schill-o-Meter was the OG in the category. Unfortunately for Schill and the team, most of the right-hander's best seasons were spoiled by some pretty awful Phils teams, but it provided ample (and cheap) seating opportunity for a couple of fans to start hanging K signs on the wall to mark Schilling's strikeouts.

It got a lot of airplay on Phillies broadcasts and caught the attention of the Phillies' single-season strikeout leader. Schill got the duo a pair of Diamond Club seats for Fan Appreciation Night in 1998 and flew them out to Miami at season's end, where they hung their Schill-o-Meter sign with a new 300 banner to mark the pitcher's 300th and final strikeout of the season.

Jeltz Fan Club (JFC)—Steve Jeltz (Twitter: @JFC_2023)

1966:
Allen's Alley—Dick Allen

1895:
Morris Guards and Kelly's Rooters—Phillies

Donaghy's Rooters—Phillies

A *Philadelphia Inquirer* article appeared in 1895, detailing the growing popularity of the Phillies' burgeoning fan clubs:

> There is every indication that a very large number of Philadelphians will go to Baltimore on Thursday to witness the opening championship game between the champion "Orioles" and the Phillies. The Morris Guards have twenty-two men enrolled, and Colonel Billy Morris hopes to increase his company to fifty. Kelly's Rooters are about twenty strong, but Colonel Ed J. Kelly has established a recruiting station uptown and he is hustling to take down a bigger delegation than Morris. There is great rivalry between the two companies, but they are enlisted in a common cause and there is no danger of bloodshed.[9]

#9
THE 2008 PILLARS

Jimmy, Ryan, Chase, and Cole—you say those four first names in the city of Philadelphia, and people know exactly who you are talking about. That's what a Phillies 2008 pillar is: players who held up the building and were stalwarts for the *other* greatest run in Phillies history.

And for people who are thirty-five and under, those were *the guys*—the guys who made baseball exciting, the guys who made local kids everywhere fall in love with the game, the guys who we'd get to tell our kids and grandkids about.

> One of the coolest parts of being a Phillies fan is hearing older fans talking about their favorite players when they were kids. More often than not, I see the older generation light up when they get to tell you what it was like watching a young Dick Allen or Schmitty and Carlton. Maybe it's because I love the game—I feel like baseball players are gods to kids, and I certainly felt that growing up with Jimmy, Ryan, Chase, and Cole.

They were drafted here, developed here, became leaders here and were the backbone of this city's first title since 1983. (I know it was the Sixers and not the Phillies in '83, but listen, it had been a long freakin' time.)

Having been developed here, with stories of them coming through the minor leagues, they connected much deeper to the fanbase. Bryce Harper has done such an unbelievable job connecting with the fan base that I sometimes even forget he played for the Nationals. But I think a majority of people love the homegrown guys. Fans will revere the stars choosing us. But going through the ups and downs with players who have been here through the mud and watching them turn into champions? That's special.

RING THE BELL

This chapter covers the origin stories behind these pillars and some of their journey before 2008. Obviously, 2008 deserves a whole chapter by itself, but so do the guys who helped carry that team to a championship.

Who better to start off a chapter on the pillars of a championship team than its leadoff hitter and the guy who got the ball rolling?

Scott Rolen. I'm kidding! Here's Jimmy Rollins.

JIMMY ROLLINS, A.K.A. J-ROLL

Aah, J-Roll, the straw that stirred the drink for the '07–'11 Phillies. When it was all said and done, here is the Jimmy Rollins résumé:

- Franchise leader in hits (2,306)
- Franchise leader in doubles (479)
- Franchise leader in leadoff home runs (46)
- Franchise leader in total at-bats
- Franchise record holder for longest hitting streak (38 games between two seasons, 2005 and 2006)
- Second in franchise history in games played, total bases, extra base hits, and stolen bases
- Third in franchise history in runs, singles, and triples
- A 20 doubles, 20 triples, 20 home runs, and 20 stolen bases season (2007)
- An NL MVP (2007)
- Four-time Gold Glover
- A walk-off in the NLCS
- Undefeated prediction king (the team to beat)
- The one who made every throw right to the *P-H-I-L-L-I-E-S* across Ryan Howard's chest for 10 years (a fake stat, but prove it wrong, I dare you)
- One of the best Harry Kalas nicknames (J-Roll)
- And, finally, the most iconic smile in Philadelphia sports history

Pretty impressive, no?

THE 2008 PILLARS

> I really took Rollins's defense for granted after he left. Having a guy who could get to every ball, seemingly never make an error, throw the ball right on the money, and make turning double plays look easy was really valuable. Freddy Galvis was very, very good at it, but he just couldn't hit. The post-Galvis and post-Rollins shortstop days were a tough watch.

For parts of 15 seasons with the Phillies, Jimmy Rollins electrified the Philly faithful. With game-changing speed, a fantastic glove, a surprising amount of pop for a smaller guy, and a flair for the dramatic, Rollins was the perfect catalyst to usher in a new era of Phillies baseball. He was also the right leadership complement to Utley, the ultimate lead-by-example guy, and Howard, the quiet-like slugger. That was *not* Rollins, whose confidence and swagger you could feel from miles away.

But how did this all start? How did the Phillies end up with the franchise's best shortstop in the second round of the 1996 MLB draft?

> Interestingly enough, the Phillies took Adam Eaton in the first round that year. Yes, that Adam Eaton, the guy who stole money from the Phillies in 2007 and 2008 and the guy who got booed while accepting his '08 World Series ring. Yes, I was there that day and yes, I did let out a hearty boo for Adam Eaton. To this day, that was my proudest boo.

One guy who knew how they ended up with Rollins in the second round of that draft was former Phillies director of amateur scouting Mike Arbuckle, who scouted and ultimately ended up drafting the high school shortstop. Arbuckle oversaw the Phillies drafts from 1993 to 2008 and was responsible for all of the homegrown talent that helped build the 2007–11 Phillies.

He still remembers what it was like watching a young Jimmy Rollins and what the sentiment was around the game when they took him. "I had people tell me after the draft, other scouting directors say, 'I can't believe you took him in the second round—he's a little guy,' Arbuckle recounts. "Well, Jimmy wasn't a little guy; he was a short guy, but he had body strength and athleticism. Those things I loved. I loved the presence; he always had a little swagger about him that he knew he could play the game, and so it was kind of that combination of the physical tools, athleticism, and the makeup that jumped out at me."[1] And man, did Arbuckle nail it.

The Bay Area kid would have to leave home and travel to the complete opposite side of the country to play for an organization that was in the midst of a 95-loss season and had a ballpark that was begging to get torn down. I'm sure he was excited, right?

"When I got drafted to Philly I was not happy—at all," Rollins told the *Player's Breakdown* podcast, "Philada-who? I watched the All-Star Game that year in '96 and you had the turf field, the yellow seats, green seats, brown seats, all types of colors and I'm like . . . Nah."[2]

While Rollins wasn't excited, the Phillies were.

"It was an easy pick for me because not only did I like him but my key guys (Marti Wolever, Dean Youngward, Jim Fregosi Jr., Bob Poole) loved him as well, said Arbuckle. "So it was kind of unanimous; everybody that had seen him really wanted him and really thought he was going to be a good big leaguer. And when I got to know Jimmy and to know his parents, his parents were extremely positive people, really good people. So once you got to know the whole family and the whole picture you felt even better about it."[3]

Speaking of his parents, according to Rollins, again speaking to the *Player's Breakdown* podcast, his mom told him upon being drafted to Philadelphia, "Well, babe. There's really no one in front of you, so if you look at it that way you can get to the big leagues a lot faster than being stuck behind people."

That line right there, his mom said, "changed his whole attitude." Shoutout to Gigi Rollins.

Rollins was off to the East Coast, rural Virginia to be exact, to start his pro journey. The Martinsville Phillies of the Appalachian League were awaiting Rollins, and the road to the major leagues was set.

After spending the 1997 season for the Piedmont Boll Weevils (what a name), where he was the youngest player on the team at eighteen years old, Rollins put up a stash line of .270/.330/.370. But that offseason, when Rollins went down to the Instructional League, Mike Arbuckle first thought, *Oh, this guy might be different.*

"We were down in Florida; we'd have our organizational meeting in the morning so our scouts could watch our guys play in the afternoon," Arbuckle said. "I don't remember who we were playing, but we were down in the ninth inning, and we got a runner on, and Jimmy comes to the plate with two outs. He takes a pitch that's not a strike, and the next pitch he lets it fly, and the ball is out of the ballpark, and we win it. You know, it just kind of showed everybody in the organization, even as a young kid, that he was a guy that liked to rise to the moment, and he carried that all the way through."

With that, Rollins was off. He would spend the 1998 season in Clearwater (along with Pat Burrell, Brandon Duckworth, and . . . Adam Eaton); in 1999 at the age of twenty, Rollins would play the entire season at Reading (with a brief stint up in Wilkes-Barre). Then after spending a majority of the 2000 season in Scranton/Wilkes-Barre, the 62–86 Phillies decided it was time to call the kid up and have him make his major-league debut. Gigi Rollins was right.

Was there ever anything more fitting than Rollins's first hit being a triple?

> Sarah Langs, a sportswriter, says there's just no other sport like baseball where things just weave together so perfectly and romantically. "How could you not be romantic about baseball?" She couldn't have said it better. Not only was Rollins's first hit in the big leagues a triple, but so was his last hit as a Phillie—perfection.

His manager at the time, Larry Bowa, was impressed. "He had an arrogance about him that was good if you played on his team, similar to Pete [Rose]. If you played against him, you hated him. But he played the game hard, and right away I knew he was going to be something special."

Simply put, Rollins had swagger, and he believed in himself. As we would learn, he would talk the talk and walk the walk.

Talking was definitely never an issue for a young Rollins except for one time. "Jimmy is very outspoken. You never get the last word in on Jimmy." Bowa recounted when I asked about his favorite memory of early Rollins. He continued:

> I remember sitting in the clubhouse—I used to go out in the clubhouse and BS with the players. Jimmy had a knack where, if they had to be dressed and out on the field at 4:00 p.m., he would come in at ten minutes to four—every day. And he comes walking in—he has this swag about him.
>
> And I said, "There he is! J-Roll! Hey, I got your walk down good, man." And everybody's watching. So, I'm imitating him walking,

and he says, "No, no, no, Bo. You've gotta drag that right foot a bit longer."

So I said, "Why don't you try dragging your foot across home plate every now and then?" And the clubhouse erupted because he wasn't hitting very well at the time. And to this day, he'll tell you—that was the only time he was ever held speechless.

Welcome to the big leagues, kid. And with that, much like how, on the field, Rollins was the table setter for an offense that put fear into opposing pitchers' eyes, he was also the table setter for kicking off the other best run in franchise history.

"He brought a lot of energy to the park. I think he made things go over there," said Bowa. "Chase was great, [Ryan] Howard was great; they had some great players on that team, but Jimmy was the guy that—Reggie Jackson might say—Jimmy was the straw that stirred the drink."[4]

Jimmy Rollins was here, their franchise shortstop was ready, he just needed his calvary behind him.

CHASE UTLEY, A.K.A. THE MAN

Led Zeppelin's "Kashmir" immediately starts blaring in the background. Chase Utley is the man.

Before we get into the origin of Utley and the city of Philadelphia, let's check the résumé:

- The man
- Second most All-Star appearances as a Phillie (six-time All-Star Game starter: 2006–10, 2014)
- Four-time Silver Slugger Award winner (2006–09)
- Tied for most home runs in a World Series with five, alongside Reggie Jackson in 1977 and George Springer in 2017
- Second in WAR in franchise history
- A grand slam in his first game over the head of Gabe Kapler, who has no significance at all to the history of the Phillies
- One broken opponent's leg (*He was a Met, and Utley never meant to hurt him; it was a baseball play!*)

- Phillies leader in WAR, batting average, on-base percentage, and wRC+ during 2007–11
- One famous deke to help the Phillies win a World Series
- A shoulda-been MVP if not for John Lannan (He ended the year hitting .332 with a .976 OPS and 22 homers while missing a month of the season, essentially.)
- And finally, one unbelievable World Series speech (This is a family book, but world bleeping champions.)

His career started with a grand slam, and for parts of 13 seasons Chase Utley provided the most exemplary way to play baseball in the city of Philadelphia that we may have ever seen.

> Utley was my favorite Phillie growing up, and I don't think local Little League and youth coaches had ever unanimously loved a player more than him. Aah yes, the white New Balance kicks, tucked-in-T-shirt-wearing, pepper-playing dads all over the Delaware Valley loved telling you how Utley played the game the right way. "Like Pete Rose used to play" was a common phrase among the locals. But they were right; he was the best, and hopefully one day we will see his name immortalized with the game's greats in Cooperstown.

How did Utley end up in Philadelphia? It actually ended up being a stroke of luck in two separate cases. The first was a bit of a shock.

Utley was born in Southern California and grew up a diehard Dodgers fan. Surely he would sign with his childhood team if it selected him in the MLB draft, right? Not so fast, my friend; even though the Dodgers selected the hometown kid in the second round of the 1997 MLB draft, Utley turned them down to attend UCLA—a massive break for the Phillies.

One guy who was excited that Utley turned down the Dodgers was Mike Arbuckle. "The first time I saw Chase, it was at Blair Field in Long Beach, California, and what really stuck out was his bat," Arbuckle said. "He just centered everything, and he was a skinny kid, didn't look like he had any body strength, but the ball really jumped off his bat. He hit a ball out of Blair Field, which has heavy marine air because it's right by the ocean. It's known as a graveyard for hitters because you just never see guys hit the ball out in that park, but he hit one out and immediately got my attention."

However, Arbuckle thought he had lost the talented prep infielder when the Dodgers took him. "After getting to know him, I was shocked that he didn't sign, because if there was ever a baseball rat it was Chase Utley," said Arbuckle.

Utley was off to UCLA, and the Phillies and Mike Arbuckle breathed a sigh of relief.

Utley wasted no time at UCLA. He set the freshman record for home runs with 15 and earned a spot on the freshman All-American team. His sophomore year, he was a first-team All-American and played in every single inning of that season for the Bruins. And finally, his junior year, Utley led the Bruins to their first Super Regional in school history, all while being a first-team All-American yet again.

Once again, Arbuckle and the Phillies were watching. "I had seen Chase as a freshman at second base, and he was better defensively than he was the year before [while still in high school]," Arbuckle remembered when speaking with us. "Then I saw him as a sophomore, and he was better again defensively. Finally, I see him as a junior, and he's way better defensively again. Well, that showed me a couple of things. One, he had work ethic, and number two he had aptitude. So he had improved so much defensively, and I still loved the bat."

Now, it was part two of the luck that was required to make Chase Utley a Phillie. The Phillies were torn between two players at the time of the 2000 MLB draft: Rocco Baldelli and Chase Utley. Thankfully, the Rays took Baldelli sixth overall and left the Phillies with a clear-cut choice at 15.

> Had a rare illness called channelopathy never happened to Baldelli, he very well could have ended up a great, great player, one of the better what-ifs in recent baseball history. Plus, who could forget his game-tying home run in Game Five of the 2008 World Series before the Phillies ultimately scratched across the go-ahead and winning run?

Here's how Arbuckle remembers the night they drafted Utley:

We thought we were either going to get Chase or Rocco Baldelli in that draft, just because of the way we thought the clubs were going to pick ahead of us. But as it shook out, Tampa had come in and seen Rocco in a playoff game right at the end; they even left their draft meetings to go see him. So they took him ahead of us. Ultimately, I think history would indicate that we made the right choice, or lucked into the right choice, because honestly, had they both been on the board I'm not sure which way I would have gone because I really liked both of them.

The biggest question Chase had around his game was his defense. What position was he going to play in the big leagues? Could he stick at second base? Would he be better suited at another position? Would the Phillies have to trade him to an American League team with the DH option?

Early in his minor-league tenure, the doubters might have been proven right. Utley hit; that was never a doubt. In his first full minor-league season in Clearwater in 2001, Utley hit .257 with a .746 OPS and 16 home runs. However, he did make 17 errors at second base. This, and the trade for Placido Polanco (a great second baseman in his own right for the early 2000s, whom the Phillies got in the Scott Rolen trade with the Cardinals), prompted the Phillies to try to make Utley a third baseman at Scranton/Wilkes-Barre in 2002. That . . . did not go well. Utley hit again, a .263 average with an .813 OPS but 28 errors at third base.

Thankfully, that experiment ended, and Utley would be back to second base for the spring of 2003. He actually made the team out of spring training as a bench player but only got one at-bat in the first five games of the season before being sent down to Triple A when the team needed an extra bullpen arm.

As chronicled by Matt Gelb of The Athletic during the week of Utley's retirement, Charlie Manuel, who was hired as a special assistant to the general manager that year, was in the room when Utley got sent back to the minor leagues. Utley looked every single one of the people in the room that day and said, "You f*ckers must not want to win."

Different.

Even though he was sent down at the beginning of the 2003 season, Utley did come up for a brief stint in late April while some of the regulars were banged up and gave us a glimpse into who he ultimately would be. In his first career start in the big leagues, the legend of Chase Utley would begin.

With two outs and the bases loaded in the bottom of the third and the Everybody Hits, Woohoo guy just finishing up his routine, Utley unloaded on a pitch from Aaron Cook and drove it over the head of Gabe Kapler and the Colorado Rockies for his first big-league home run. In the most Chase Utley thing of all time, he sprinted around the bases.

We asked Bowa if he'd ever seen a quicker trip around the bases for a home run, and he said, "I think Pete [Rose]. Even on a walk, Pete would spring down to first. Other than him, no. But, Chase was that kinda guy. He didn't want to show anybody up. He played the game the right way. He respected the game. That's what you gotta admire about him. Not only was he a great player, but he respected the game of baseball."

Utley ultimately got the call up on August 14 of the 2003 season to help put the team over the top. The Phils were 66–54 when Utley got called up and were fighting for a wild-card spot. The newly acquired David Bell had been dealing with injuries for a majority of the 2003 season, so while he was out, Utley handled second and Polanco took down third.

> Aah, yes another, "How could you not be romantic about baseball" moment—in five seasons after Polanco was ultimately traded, he would be back with the Phillies again and, yes, still playing third base.

The Phillies gave Utley a shot to play pretty much every day from that point on until the end of the season. Unfortunately, the Phillies and Utley fell short. They lost seven of their last eight games, and Utley only hit .244 with one home run in his first big audition with the big-league club.

With Bell at third and Polanco at second for the 2004 season, Utley was forced back to Triple A. Fortunately for us, and ultimately for the Phillies (although I'm sure they were a little stressed at this time), Utley was ready for the big leagues. At twenty-five (!) and still in Triple A, he hit .285 with an .880 OPS; the problem was, he was blocked at the big-league level by Polanco and David Bell, who actually enjoyed a nice 2004 season despite what people said about him.

> Please note that the comment about David Bell was made in jest; if you know me at all, you know he was my least favorite Phillie of all time. Maybe because, at ten years old, I (Jack) was furious that Utley wasn't a big leaguer (I'm *sure* this is what it was) or because Bell just looked miserable being here, I was not a David Bell guy. However, the real reason

> for this Jack note is the Utley and, eventually, the Ryan Howard situations set back baseball talk in this city for at least two decades, so I am mad at the Phillies for that. Why? Because whenever there's a new young prospect coming through the system that people are excited about, the detractors still throw out the age-old tripe of "cAn'T wAiT tO sEe hiM whEn hE's twenty-five," in a tone that I *know* is snarky. So thank you, Phillies, for that and no, this isn't true anymore. Please retire it. Also, Utley and Howard were blocked.

Utley would ultimately hit .266 with a .776 OPS in 2004 and showed enough to become the everyday second baseman in 2005. That's what everyone was saying after another playoffless season in 2004, right? As the story goes, Placido Polanco was slated to become a free agent, so the Phillies offered him arbitration so they could get some compensation picks back when he signed elsewhere. Much to the Phillies' surprise, Polanco didn't have much of a market, so he accepted their qualifying offer to return for the 2005 season. Gulp.

What would the Phillies do? Utley was clearly ready, so surely general manager Ed Wade would trade the oft-injured Bell and eat the rest of his contract to extend the guy that was younger and hit close to .300 during his time with the Phillies right?

[Game-show buzzer] *Wrong.*

Nope. After some attempts to play Polanco in left field, the Phillies traded Polanco to the Detroit Tigers on June 7 for Ugueth Urbina and Ramón Martínez. (Do not Google Ugueth Urbina.) Polanco would sign an extension with the Tigers and hit over .300 during his four-and-a-half seasons there before the Phillies brought him back in 2010 to play third base.

Regardless, the charade was over. Utley was *finally* the everyday second baseman. He hit .291 with a .915 OPS in 2005, and the love affair between a city and its second baseman was off and running.

RYAN HOWARD, A.K.A. THE BIG PIECE

There wasn't a more feared home run hitter in baseball than Ryan Howard from 2006 to 2010. His 2006 season? We may never see another season like that by someone in a Phillies uniform for a long, long time.

RING THE BELL

> While the ending wasn't the best (the Achilles tendon injury and the big new contract on top of it), there was nothing like Ryan Howard at his peak. Were Jimmy and Chase considered *better* players? Sure, but Ryan Howard was box office, with the wiggle of the bat, the emphatic bat drop when he knew he crushed one. Ryan Howard was the guy kids in the backyard were trying to be. It got ugly toward the end here, but I think people have gone back and properly appreciated Howard, and they should.

Let's start off with the résumé:

- Three-time National League All Star
- NL Rookie of the Year in 2005
- NL MVP, 2006
- NLCS MVP
- Second in franchise history in home runs (382)
- Most home runs in a single season in franchise history (58)
- Fifth in franchise history in total bases
- Third in franchise history in RBIs
- Fastest player in MLB history to 100 home runs, 200 home runs, and 1,000 RBIs
- Most grand slams in franchise history (15)
- Most home runs at Citizens Bank Park (198)
- One famous quote, "Get me to the plate, boys"
- Owner of Chris Volstad (Sorry, Chris, but eight home runs and a stash-line of .519/.594/1.481 with 2.075 OPS—holy cow!)

With the last offensive pillar, Ryan Howard, three core offensive pieces really came together and gave the Phillies one of the best offenses in the sport for a five-year span. You have Rollins with the speed and pop at the top, the pure hitter in Utley, and then the thump from Howard. It really was perfect.

But unlike Rollins and Utley, Howard was not a top pick—not even in the top three rounds. Yes, the Phillies were lucky enough to land their final piece in the fifth round of the 2001 MLB draft. How did someone with that much pop not go earlier than he did?

"He had a horrible spring his junior year," Phillies director of amateur scouting Mike Arbuckle remembered when talking to us "He had been a name heading into that year. But clubs were starting to backpedal because he was just swinging through balls over and over."

The Phillies liked Howard. Their area scout, Jerry Lafferty, had been on Howard since high school, but whether it was—perhaps the pressure of the draft year weighing on him—he was scuffling.

"When I went in to see him (in a fall-league game at Missouri State, where Howard attended), he [was] punched out twice, and he hit a soft, little groundball to the infield and just looked lost at the plate," Arbuckle recounted. "So, I'm scratching my head. I did see BP, and I could see he could launch 'em. I mean, he had big, big raw power. But . . . is it usable?"

It must have been usable enough. Even though teams were scared off by Howard's struggles in his junior year, the Phillies still made him their pick in in that fifth round.

"We're sitting there in that fourth- or fifth-round range, and Marti Woelver says to me, 'Well here's a guy with double-plus power,' Arbuckle said to us about draft night. "So, I said, 'Okay, we'll roll the dice here.' . . . We know he can hit the ball out of the ballpark; it's just a matter of if he'll make enough contact to do it. So we got him signed and sent him to Batavia, New York, and he never missed a beat. He hit from day one and all the way through the system."[5]

Ryan Howard's minor-league career was the stuff of legends. After a short-season stint in Batavia, where Howard hit .272 with an .840 OPS and six home runs, he was off to Lakewood for his first full season of minor-league baseball in 2002. There, Howard hit .280 with an .828 OPS and 16 home runs, and the Phillies officially had a decision to make.

Would they take a chance on Howard and bet on his future, maybe sign a stopgap first baseman and bide their time, or should they sign the biggest free agent on the market that offseason in future Hall of Famer Jim Thome? Considering that they needed a box-office player to draw fans to the new ballpark that was opening in 2004, it's really hard to blame the Phillies for signing Thome, who by the way was awesome as a Phillie. As always, hindsight is 20/20.

So for the 2003 season, Howard was off to Clearwater, where he really started to explode as an all-around great hitter, slashing .304, with an .889 OPS, and 23 HR. For the 2004 season, Howard was sent to Reading; there, he turned into the Babe Ruth of Baseballtown.

> I was 10 in 2004, but I still remember waking up one morning and, on *Sports Rise* on Comcast Sportsnet, watching a full-length feature on Howard and the gargantuan-like things he was doing up in Reading. This was around the time the Eagles got Terrell Owens, the Flyers were making playoff runs, and the Allen Iverson Sixers were doing well, so to fit that in to the programming meant he had to be pretty special.

While in Reading, Howard hit 37 home runs in 102 games and had a stash line of .297/.647/1.033—ridiculous. Obviously, he had outgrown Baseballtown, so the organization decided to send him to Triple A, where Howard continued doing Howard things, hitting nine home runs in 29 games, with an OPS of .966.

This forced the Phillies to call Howard up when rosters expanded in September 2004. With Thome still in the fold, Howard was mostly used as a pinch-hitter until they were eliminated from playoff contention, and he finally got some starts the last week of the '04 season.

Across three levels in 2004, Ryan Howard slugged 48 home runs and 33 doubles and drove in 136 runs. It was the greatest minor-league season a Phillie has ever had.

Once again, the Phillies had a decision to make. Howard was clearly ready. They knew, Thome knew, the fans knew, and Howard knew. Would they trade Ryan Howard and commit to Thome as their first baseman or let him just continue to put up historic numbers in the minor leagues?

It was a choice talked about within the walls of Citizens Bank Park. "I remember we were in the offices in the offseason, and we were debating on whether or not we should trade Ryan [Howard] and keep Jimmy [Thome]," Arbuckle recounted in his conversation with us. "We said to ourselves 'Okay, if we got enough for Ryan, maybe it *would* make sense to move him because he had just hit all the way through the minor leagues. I remember a few good baseball guys that I trusted who told me, 'Eh, he's hit well in Triple A, but we're not sure it's going to carry over, so we won't give you a whole lot for him.' That really shows you the inexact science that we deal with."

Talk about another bullet being dodged when building this core.

> It truly is one of the greatest what-ifs about this Phillies core. What if the Phillies *had* traded Ryan Howard? I'm sure there was public pressure to do it. This team hadn't made the playoffs in a decade, Thome was a Hall of Famer, they paid him a ton of money to take this franchise from a small-market mindset to the big leagues. Howard was raking in the minor leagues but had questions about his defense and was an older prospect. During a time when fans want prospects traded as fast as possible, the Phillies deserve credit for sticking to their guns, knowing what they had and not trading Howard, or Utley, for that matter. The other biggest what-if is whether they would have won the World Series with Thome. I guess we'll never know.

Things were tense around the Howard-Thome situation. First, though, the Phillies decided to move on from team great Larry Bowa as manager after falling a couple of games short of the postseason in the 2004 season. In came Charlie Manuel to take over the ballclub. What makes this interesting is that Manuel was Thome's hitting coach with the Cleveland Indians from 1994 to 1999 and his manager from 2000 to halfway through the 2002 season. Obviously, they were keeping Thome and moving Howard, right?

To add another level of intrigue to all of this, Howard changed agents in that offseason, a move usually made when the player is unhappy in his current situation and would like a change of scenery. Howard was even quoted about this in the *Inquirer* in 2004 by Todd Zolecki: "[T]he ultimate goal is to get to the big leagues, whether it's via a trade or being able to play in Philadelphia. That's the ultimate goal. But that's out of my hands as far as to what's involved there." Howard never requested a trade, but he sure wanted it to be clear that he thought he was ready for the big leagues.

Ultimately, the Phillies decided to hold on to Howard and run the risk of having an unhappy player at Triple A. Howard was full-on blocked. Thome was paid through 2008, he was a favorite of the now manager, and he was key in helping garner excitement at the new Citizens Bank Park. But the Phillies couldn't just wait around forever; another decision would eventually have to be made.

Thankfully for the Phillies, and unfortunately for Thome, the 2005 season would shed a clearer light on what the team should decide about the situation.

> I *remember* the Howard-Thome situation, but while researching it I could only imagine how excruciating this had to be for fans. My favorite part was when I read what the Phillies were saying. It was always some version of "Yeah, we think he needs more time in the minor leagues." Meanwhile, the guy was putting up historic minor-league seasons. If this were today, Howard would have been up in less than a year. Man, could you imagine if the National League just had a frickin' DH? Thome and Howard could have stayed, and we could have ridden off into the sunset, murdering baseballs and winning titles. *But I digress.*

Howard was optioned back to Triple A at the end of spring training in 2005. Coincidentally—and file this one away for future Phillies trivia contests—Howard was optioned the same day Shane Victorino was told he wouldn't make the big-league roster. The Phillies had acquired Victorino in the Rule 5 draft from the Los Angeles Dodgers. If a player is selected in the Rule 5 draft and he does *not* make the big-league roster, by rule he has to be offered back to the original team for $25,000 after they also pass through waivers. Luckily, the Dodgers turned down the opportunity to bring back Victorino, and the Flyin' Hawaiian was sent to Triple A along with Howard.

Down there, Howard continued to show the Phillies that the minor leagues were simply no match for him anymore. The twenty-five-year-old Howard hit to a tune of .371 with 16 home runs and an OPS north of 1.100 at Wilkes-Barre in '05.

At the big-league club, their slugger was starting to show signs of a body that *might* be on the verge of breaking down. Thome's back was becoming an issue. He hit the IL early in '05 season with a sprained back, which he would deal with for most of the year. In his place, Howard was the obvious choice, although in his brief shot he only hit .214 with one home run in 12 games, which was not exactly what the Phillies were hoping for. Thome reentered the fold on May 21 but never really got going. After hitting .211 with only six home runs from May 21 to June 30, Thome's season ended. He was placed on the disabled list with an elbow injury that was on top of his back issue. Thome's season was over; it was time for the kid to shine.

And shine he did. Finally, in an extended run at the big-league level, Howard took off. From July 2 on, Howard hit .296 with an OPS around .950

and 21 home runs. For his efforts, Howard was awarded the National League Rookie of the Year, the fourth in franchise history.

Ultimately, the '05 Phillies would fall two games short of the NL East and a game short of a wild-card spot. Brutal. The Phillies moved on from longtime general manager Ed Wade and brought in Hall of Fame executive Pat Gillick.

Gillick's first decision was where to trade Jim Thome. It took about a month after his hiring—Gillick finally pulled the trigger. On November 25, 2005, the Phillies traded Thome to the Chicago White Sox for Aaron Rowand a couple of minor-league pitchers. Instead of being bitter about the Phillies trading him away and going with someone else, the always-classy Thome said this to local reporters on the phone:

> When I leave the game of baseball someday, I want people to recognize that I always put my teams first. That's what I love about the game—being a part of the team. I see in Ryan Howard what someone saw in me when I broke into the big leagues, and now it's time for both of us to seize the opportunity ahead of us. It's a win-win situation. I really enjoyed my time in Philadelphia, and I want to thank my teammates and the fans for a heck of a ride.

Well, we all know what ensued next, don't we? Howard was the full-time starter in 2006, and he would have arguably the single most dominant season a Phillies hitter has ever had: 58 home runs, 149 RBIs, a .313 AVG, an OPS of 1.084, and, ultimately, the 2006 National League MVP—a truly remarkable season.

It *might* be hyperbolic—and if it happens we might need to add another chapter to this book—but I'm not sure we'll ever see another Phillie have the type of season that Howard did in '06. It was ridiculous. Howard was box office, and his 2006 season was especially so.

Shoutout to the big piece.

COLE HAMELS, A.K.A. HOLLYWOOD

The Phillies had all the offensive firepower needed to win, but what's a good offense without an ace?

RING THE BELL

> At the time of writing this chapter, the Phillies are two days removed from losing to the Mets in the 2024 NLDS. I hope that when you read this book 5, 10, 15, 20 years from now we have a World Series title to show for it because this stretch has been brutal. But the point of the Jack note here is to simply thank Cole Hamels for being the missing piece on a team that actually has won a championship here. Maybe it's the emotions of the loss, and the losses of the last couple of years, haunting me, but I am extra thankful for Hamels and what he was able to do in the fall of 2008. Thank you, Cole.

Let's start with the résumé:

- 2008 World Series MVP
- 2008 NLCS MVP
- Three-time All-Star (2007, 2011, 2012)
- Six 200-inning seasons (2008, 2010 through 2014)
- Three 200-strikeout seasons (2010, 2012, 2013)
- Third in franchise history in 10 or more strikeout games (29)
- Fourth in franchise history in games started (294)
- Sixth in franchise history in wins (114), innings pitched (1,930), and ERA (3.30)
- Third in franchise history in strikeouts (1,844)
- Tied for first in franchise history in postseason games started (13). First in postseason wins (seven) and strikeouts (77). Third in postseason ERA (3.09)
- One no-hitter (July 25, 2015, in what would be his last start as a Phillie against the Cubs)
- One unforgettable Bugs Bunny changeup

The *majority* of the fans of Philadelphia will forever be indebted to two men for what they did in their efforts to bring this city a title: Nick Foles and Cole Hamels.

Sure, this is a team game, and both rosters were pretty loaded. But when you talk about going on a run and delivering in the clutchest ways possible on the biggest stages, it's those two.

But much like the stories of Rollins, Utley, and Howard the origin story of Hamels and the Phillies is one filled with happenstance and a lucky . . . break?

No, literally, a break. During his junior year at Rancho Bernardo High School in Southern California, the already prized left-hander was going out for a pass while having a football catch with his buddy and collided with the mirror on a parked car. What resulted was a broken arm and MLB teams being scared off because of it. Hamels, who without the broken arm would have been gone long before the Phillies were slated to pick, was officially a risk for teams in the draft.

Unlike Howard, Utley, and Rollins, Hamels was viewed, as a top-of-the-rotation pitcher, as a lock to be a top-five pick. That's because, as Phillies fans would come to know very well, he had a unicorn, Bugs Bunny changeup that you just didn't see from high school kids.

"He looked like a thirty-year-old big leaguer throwing his changeup in high school," Mike Arbuckle said to us. "So you're saying to yourself, *I don't have to project that it's going to get better because it's already major-league quality—plus* major-league quality, if you wanted to say that. So it was an easy scout because you didn't have to dream on what it's going to look like in four to five years because it's already there. . . . Very few high schoolers I've ever seen had a changeup like Hamels did."

But it wasn't just the changeup that scouts loved. Hamels was tall and lean, his mechanics were repeatable, he was up to 94 with his fastball, he had feel for his curveball, and everything with him was just smooth and effortless.

Most teams were scared off with the injury. Most teams didn't include the Phillies.

"I will give full credit to our club physician at the time, Mike Ciccotti," Arbuckle said of the process of getting medical clearance to draft Hamels. "Mike knew the guy that did the surgery out in San Diego, and Mike said to me, 'I have no problem whatsoever in taking him.' He said, 'That arm is going to be stronger than it was before the break.' So we had full clearance from our medical staff to take him, which a lot of other teams didn't have."

The Phillies had their medical clearance; now they just hoped he would get to the 17th pick in the draft. "We started to get a pretty good feeling that there would be a good chance he'd be there because of the conversations we were having with crosscheckers and scouting directors from other teams," Arbuckle reminisced. "We were getting feedback from a lot of those teams that were saying, 'Man, we like this guy but our medical guys won't approve him.' So we were kind of homing in on him because we were getting enough feedback to feel like there was going to be a pretty good chance he was going to get to us."

The Phillies were all in. While rare, it was truly a unanimous decision in the draft room that day. With the 17th pick in the 2002 MLB Draft, Hamels was officially a Philadelphia Phillie. How about a special shoutout to Hamels's buddy who couldn't throw a football well that one day, which led to him becoming a Phillie—send him a World Series ring or something!

> I was eight years old when the Phillies drafted Hamels, but I could only imagine what early 2000s prospect huggers, like myself now, were saying about the Phillies minor-league system. "We're going to have Howard, Utley, and Rollins to go with Scott Rolen, Marlon Byrd, and Pat Burrell, plus a rotation with Gavin Floyd, Brett Myers, *and* Cole Hamels?" What a time that must have been. By the way, for those of you who don't remember, Gavin Floyd was drafted a year before Hamels at fourth overall. He never lived up to the hype for the Phillies and was traded along with Gio González (what a mistake) to the White Sox for Freddy García. You could make the case that Gavin Floyd was most notable as a Phillie for serving up the pitch to Xavier Nady that he smoked to the wall and Aaron Rowand eventually chased down before slamming his head into the Citizens Bank Park fence, causing a broken nose and an all-time Phillies moment.

Because Hamels took so long to sign with the Phillies, he wasn't able to start his minor-league career until the 2003 season, and it sure didn't take long for the team to realize they might have found something special in the young lefty.

Hamels dazzled in his first minor-league season. In his first 13 starts with Lakewood, Hamels pitched to a 0.84 ERA and struck out 115 batters in 74 innings (!) before being rewarded with a promotion to Clearwater to round out his nineteen-year-old season in the minor leagues. Hamels was on the fast-track to the big leagues.

The hype continued to build in the spring of 2004 as Hamels, now twenty, was pitching in a spring-training game against the behemoth New

York Yankees—yes, the '04 Yankees, who were showing off their shiny new toy, Álex Rodríguez. Hamels, who entered in the game in the fifth inning, got to face Jeter and A-Rod in that inning and struck out both on that world-class changeup.

After the game, Jeter was asked if Hamels's changeup looked like a big-league pitch to him. The captain flashed his iconic smile and said, "It looked like one today."

While he was very impressive, and the Hamels hype train had most definitely left the station, the Phillies did not keep him on their Opening Day roster, and it was back to Clearwater to start the 2004 season. Surely, this will be a short stint in Clearwater before he was in Reading and maybe, just maybe, he could finish the year in Wilkes-Barre?

Well, as the iconic Lee Corso would say, "Not so fast, my friends." Hamels was dealing with elbow soreness. He was actually dealing with elbow soreness during spring training with the big-league club, but since it was his first camp with the team, he didn't want to tell the Phillies. I'm sure they were thrilled about that.

Tommy John surgery wasn't required, but Hamels was shut down to kick off the '04 season. He made a couple of starts finally in Clearwater, for new manager Mike Schmidt, before having to be shut down again with an inflamed joint in that same elbow. In the four starts prior to the setback, Hamels was Hamels, pitching to a 1.13 ERA.

But that was it—16 innings and four starts were all Hamels would throw in the 2004 minor-league season. He had tried to rehab and get back for a couple starts in August, but again, while just having a catch, he still felt soreness in his elbow. His goal of reaching Triple A was dashed, as was his goal of pitching in the Futures Game. The fast-track to the big leagues was delayed.

> I'm sure Negadelphia was handling this one well. I can just *hear* the calls into WIP around this time. "See, this is why you never get excited about prospects," or the old classic "Once again, Angelo, this is why you trade prospects. *They're prospects for a reason!*" It never fails that an uberhyped kid with arm injuries is not the best match for a baseball town that hadn't seen playoff baseball in over a decade.

RING THE BELL

After a forgettable '04, Hamels moved on to 2005. He was already invited to big-league camp and was slated to start the season in Reading. He's going to end the year in the major leagues, right? We're back? Once again, ole Lee Corso lines rent-free in our heads: "Not so fast, my friend."

This time however, the injury was not to the elbow, and it didn't even occur on the baseball field. Hamels was involved in a bar fight down in Clearwater at around 2:00 a.m. when he and four other players were attacked from behind by a group of drunk guys. Hamels, who was the designated driver that night, ended up with the worst result: a broken hand and another setback for the prized, and now snake-bitten, lefty.

Did the Phillies have to add maturity questions to the list of injuries Hamels was dealing with? They certainly weren't happy with their young phenom. In a quote to Todd Zolecki of the *Inquirer* in the early summer of 2005, Mike Arbuckle said, "No question, he's used up some margin for error."

After stern talking-tos from Arbuckle and Ed Wade, they felt like the message had gotten through to Hamels, and he was ready to resume his track to the big leagues.

Now twenty-one, Hamels only needed three dazzling starts at Clearwater to get promoted to Reading. And guess what? Hamels only needed a couple of starts there before having back spasms.

> Again, I can just *hear* the WIP calls. Hamels was dealing with back issues around the deadline too at a time in which the team had opened a new ballpark and was dying to make the playoffs?! Aah, it's sports radio heaven! "Angelo, they *have* to get this guy Hamel, or whatever his name is, *out* of here ASAP. He's hurt all the time!"

Unfortunately for Hamels, who had goals of being a September call-up for the '05 Phillies, he didn't make another start after dealing with the back issues. After shining in his first minor-league season, shining in his first big-league camp, and looking like a guy who could make his big-league debut before he was legally allowed to drink, Hamels had made 10 starts in two minor-league seasons. It was concerning.

Finally, in 2006, the tide started to turn. Hamels was healthy. After spending the offseason rehabbing his back, Hamels had no setbacks during spring training and started the season in Clearwater, where of course, it was warm.

The Phillies didn't need Hamels in the cold northeast with a shaky back to start his season.

It was all shaping up to be the season Hamels reached the major leagues. *It was time.*

He only needed four starts in Clearwater before taking the jump to Wilkes-Barre. He was *that* close to the big leagues and the Phillies needed him, but they just couldn't rush him, given his injury history. So Hamels waited, and dominated, the competition in Triple A.

After a complete-game shutout against the Braves' Triple-A affiliate, some minor-league manager who definitely wouldn't come up in future Phillies-Braves postseason lore, Brian Snitker, said, "I thought that was Steve Carlton pitching against us. This kid's good. He's everything he's cracked up to be."

Finally, on May 11 the Phillies had seen enough. Could he have seasoned a bit more in the minor leagues? Sure, but *it was time.* Hamels, after a pretty remarkable minor-league career that saw him go 14–4 with a 1.43 ERA and striking out 273 in 195 innings, was finally a big leaguer.

It was an interesting journey for Hamels. From fast-tracked to sidetracked, and everything in between, the Phillies never gave up on Hamels and believed he would get healthy and mature.

He wasted little time introducing himself to the fan base who had been drooling over the potential for years, tossing five innings of shutout baseball and only allowing one hit. Little did we know at the time that a mere two years later, he would be immortalized in this city forever.

#10

2008—"WORLD CHAMPIONS, WORLD F%$&IN' CHAMPIONS"

Twenty-five years. Twenty-five long, godforsaken years since the city of Philadelphia had last won a title.

Sure, there were good runs: the '93 Phils, the '01 Sixers, the early 2000s Eagles, and the early 2000s Flyers. But none of them had achieved the ultimate goal: bringing the city of Philadelphia its first title since 1983.

The city was ready, damn near starving to finally get a taste of what it was like to be a champion again. Twenty-five years is a long time in a city as passionate as this one. The teams here are like extended families. We can rip them, but an outsider can't. During the drought, the kids became the adults, the adults became the parents, and before we knew it a whole new generation was here. Heck, many of this area's loved ones had passed during the time it took for one of the teams to bring home a title, and you can bet they were bitching about it on their way out.

But how did we get here? How did the losingest franchise in the history of sports finally get it right? Let's get into the story of the 2008 Phillies.

THE BUILD

The 2008 Phillies were not put together overnight. They didn't all of a sudden get hot and ride that wave into a world title. No, this team was built over time, and its core that we saw parading down Broad Street had plenty of ups and downs along the way.

The story of the slow-built 2008 Phillies really begins with one man: Mike Arbuckle. Arbuckle is responsible for drafting the homegrown core that carried

2008—"WORLD CHAMPIONS, WORLD F%$&IN' CHAMPIONS"

this team from 2006 to 2011. But it wasn't just Rollins, Utley, Howard, and Hamels that Arbuckle was responsible for. No, Arbuckle was responsible for nine homegrown Phillies on the 2008 roster, and it could have been ten if Rolen had seen the vision, but we don't need to go down that road again.

Pat Burrell, Cole Hamels, Ryan Howard, Ryan Madson, Brett Myers, Jimmy Rollins, Carlos Ruiz (not drafted but signed), Chase Utley, and J. A. Happ were all drafted or signed under Arbuckle's watch.

It's rare to see the ace, the number-two starter, three-fourths of the starting infield, the catcher, the starting left fielder, and a key bullpen piece all be homegrown in today's game, but the Phillies were able to do it and, arguably more important, not trade them away when they were in desperate spots before the '08 season.

So the Phillies had talent, sure, but did they have the right man in charge to put it all together? In comes a guy who already had his bust being made in Cooperstown: Pat Gillick.

The Phillies were stuck. They had a good and young roster, were *finally* started spending money (Jim Thome, David Bell, Billy Wagner), and had a new ballpark with fans coming in to check it out, but they hadn't made the playoffs since 1993. Even though they were knocking on the doorstep of the playoffs, they decided it was time to move on from Ed Wade.

> It is amazing to see the parallels between the early 2000s Phillies and the late 2010s Phillies. Both were pretty much stuck. They had talent, but other teams around them just *seemed* better. Both teams moved on from a GM who was integral in signing or drafting most of the talent on the roster for proven Hall of Fame worthy executives like Pat Gillick and Dave Dombrowski to put them over the top. Dombrowski hasn't yet, but much like the town now celebrates Ed Wade for his accomplishments as Phillies GM, I believe there will be a similar sentiment toward Matt Klentak if the Phillies end up winning the World Series. (Please win a World Series.)

On November 2, 2005, rumors began swirling that David Montgomery had hired Pat Gillick. He wanted a winner and no one on the market was quite like Gillick, who won back-to-back titles with the Blue Jays in 1992 and 1993, won divisions with the Orioles, and was the man behind the 116-win 2001 Seattle Mariners.

Even though in the industry he had garnered the nickname "Stand Pat," meaning he rarely made the big move to put his team over the top, Gillick could hardly do that now. He was walking into the situation of needing to trade Jim Thome and to decide whether to re-sign high-priced closer Billy Wagner.

Ultimately, the Phillies did trade Thome, of course, to the White Sox, which paved the way for slugging phenom Ryan Howard to take center stage. Point number one for Gillick. And he decided to not re-sign Wagner and instead sign former Yankee Tom Gordon—not a point for Gillick.

Gillick was rolling; now he had to put the finishing touches on a team and a city desperate for playoff baseball. Although they weren't all winners (signing Adam Eaton, trading for Freddy García, not getting a whole lot in return for Bobby Abreu), here are the moves, and non-moves, that solidified Pat Gillick as a Hall of Famer and forever endeared him to the city of Philadelphia.

KEEPING CHARLIE MANUEL AS MANAGER

Manuel was already in place when Gillick took over as general manager, albeit for only one season, and given Gillick's long career in baseball, I'm sure he could have turned to other managers after falling short yet again in the 2006 season.

> I was alive during this time, but I didn't *experience* what it was like watching and reacting to Phillies moves then. So in writing about this portion, I'm trying to put my current self (thirty years old, father of two) back in time to see how I would have reacted. You mean to tell me this team was supposed to compete in 2006 with a rotation of Jon Lieber, Brett Myers, Randy Wolf, Cory Lidle, Gavin Floyd, and, for 17 starts, Ryan Madson? It would have been a meltdown *especially* with what that team was capable of offensively. You give '06 Howard, Utley, and Rollins *that* pitching staff? Criminal.

Gillick seemed unsure with Manuel. He let him enter the 2007 season without a contract extension, which made him a lame-duck manager—not good. Manuel had to prove himself to Gillick, who didn't hire him. According to Jim Salisbury of the *Inquirer* at the time, it was looking like Manuel wasn't going to come back heading into the final month of the 2007 season. "Organization insiders say Gillick was uncertain about retaining Manuel during the final month of the season," Salisbury wrote in October 2007. "Among Gillick's concerns were Manuel's handling of the bullpen and the team's readiness for the season coming out of Spring Training."[1]

Well, the last month of the season did happen. The Phillies chased down the New York Mets to win their first division since 1993, and the Phillies rewarded Manuel with a two-year contract extension.

The old adage is that managers can't win you games; they can only lose you games. But who knows how this era of Phillies baseball would have gone without Manuel in charge. Keeping Manuel around was a win for Gillick.

SIGNING JAYSON WERTH

Much like the pillars of the '08 championship team discussed in the previous chapter, a lot of luck was involved in the Phillies' signing of Jayson Werth.

Werth was a super-talented kid out of high school, which is why Pat Gillick made him the Orioles' first-round pick in 1997. He had speed and power and could flat-out hit. Oddly enough, Werth was actually a catcher coming up through the minor leagues before eventually making the transition to outfield. Anyway, Gillick clearly always had an affinity toward Werth.

It was why after Werth missed most of the 2005 season (after A. J. Burnett hit him in the wrist during a spring training game in the spring of '05) *and* the entirety of the 2006 season with more wrist issues Gillick swooped in and signed his former prospect. "Jayson is a young outfielder with a combination of power and speed," Gillick said at the time. "He's had some injuries over the past couple years but we think he has tremendous athleticism and we're very happy to have him in a Phillies uniform. He's a great addition to the club," Gillick said to reporters upon signing Werth.

Safe to say Gillick nailed that one.

Werth would go on to spend four years with the Phillies and hit .282 with 95 home runs and an .885 OPS, all while playing a stellar right field. Heck, before Bryce Harper and Kyle Schwarber showed up, Werth was the Phillies' all-time leader in postseason home runs.

> For my money, Werth was the most underrated Phillie of that run, and had he been on the '11 team, who knows what would have happened? He was just so good during that stretch from '08 to '10. It's a shame how it turned out when he went to Washington, although he didn't help matters with some of his comments. But overall, Werth was a great Phillie; the club wouldn't have won the World Series without him. Nor would it have had the run it did the next two seasons had he not been on the team. When he got a huge ovation at the 10-year reunion of the 2009 Phillies in August 2019, that was really good to see.

Did Gillick hedge on Werth when he signed Geoff Jenkins in the offseason heading into the 2008 season? *Sure he did*, but I don't want the facts get in the way of a good story. And, (*whispering*) Werth battled wrist injuries again in '07. But who cares? Werth eventually took the job and ran with it, and Jenkins still had the big double in Game 5. It all worked out.

That's still a point for Gillick.

LETTING AARON ROWAND WALK AND GIVING VICTORINO THE KEYS TO CENTER FIELD

Around the same time Jayson Werth was going from relatively unknown to a key part of the Phillies core, so was Shane Victorino.

The luck I've been mentioning lately was on display again in the case of Victorino. At the cost of the $50,000 selection fee, the Phillies picked Victorino in the Rule 5 draft back in the winter of 2004. Was he really going to make the team with a center field mix that already had Kenny Lofton (what a throwback!), Jason Michaels, and Marlon Byrd? Ultimately, the answer was no, and the Phillies had to offer Victorino back to the Dodgers for $25,000. They declined, he cleared waivers, and the Phillies were able to keep Victorino and send him up to Scranton/Wilkes-Barre to begin the 2005 season.

In the case of both Victorino and Werth—Thanks Dodgers! However, we haven't gotten to the decision that Gillick deserves credit for. That came two seasons later.

Aaron Rowand had been a crowd favorite ever since he rammed his nose into the center-field wall at Citizens Bank Park and saved what would have

2008—"WORLD CHAMPIONS, WORLD F%$&IN' CHAMPIONS"

been a bases-clearing double for the Mets' Xavier Nady. Of course, who could forget after the game when asked why he did it? He uttered the now-famous, "For who? My teammates. For what? To win." Talk about a quote that can win over an entire city.

But now the decision was whether to pay Rowand. He had been a good player for the Phillies. He played a solid center field and was an All-Star in 2007, hitting .309 with an .889 OPS and 27 home runs.

Meanwhile, Victorino had been a surprise. He played a lot of right field in '06 and '07, with Rowand in center, and did a good job. Obviously he played his usual phenomenal defense, but he hit too, batting .287 and .281 in those two years.

At last, Rowand decided to leave Philadelphia. He got a five-year deal with the San Francisco Giants worth $60 million. The Phillies only offered three years and $33 million. Had they not been more comfortable with Victorino in center field, *maybe* they would have tried to match it. But they did not, and the keys were handed over to Victorino.

> Obviously, hindsight is 20/20, but I think if you put truth serum in the Phillies brass at that point, they would have been nervous about their outfield situation. Rowand, who just helped them win their first division in 14 years, was gone; Burrell only had a year left on his contract. Werth had shown good signs, but was he going to hit right-handed pitching enough and stay healthy? Sure, they signed Geoff Jenkins, but that was just as a platoon option. It all worked out, but man, I'm sure there were some tense times around the ole ballpark in the winter of 2007–08.

Victorino would reward the Phillies by playing a Gold Glove center field in '08 and stealing 36 bags while hitting .293. Victorino would go on to make two All-Star teams with the Phillies and bring home two Gold Gloves. He went from Dodgers castoff to integral part of a title team and the lockdown center fielder of one of the best teams in franchise history.

That's baseball.

RING THE BELL

TRADING FOR JAMIE MOYER

Gillick's first season was a doozy. He had a world champion–caliber offense and a rotation that was among the worst in baseball. The starters' ERA in 2006 was 5.08. That's right, 5.08!

The rotation was a collection of older innings-eaters with no real upside, some projects—like Madson as a starter and Scott Mathieson (remember him?)—and two young guys figuring out their way, in Cole Hamels and Brett Myers.

They finished the first half 40–47 and eventually fell to nine games under .500. Things were looking bleak. That was, of course, before they ripped off a 5–1 stretch heading into the July 31 trade deadline.

All of a sudden they were 49–54 and playing good baseball. Was it enough to not sell at the deadline?

Nope! Gillick pulled the plug. He traded Bobby Abreu and Cory Lidle to the New York Yankees for a collection of nobodies in the hope of replenishing the farm. Hopes were so low around the Phillies at this time that Gillick threw this out there: "Realistically, it's a stretch to say we'll be there in 2007," the Phillies GM said after the trade. "I think it's probably going to go a little slower. Realistically, the holes we have to fill, it's going to take a while."

While that quote, as the kids say, didn't age well (and thankfully so), his other quote that stuck out on that day would age well, and it would help jump-start a middling franchise. "I don't think it's out of the picture," Gillick said of the National League wild-card race. "We haven't won with this group. Consequently, you've got to change the mix."

Why is that important? In subsequent years many came to believe this was the time that Howard, Utley, and Rollins truly felt like it was their team. Abreu was a great player, but he was the leader because he was the elder statesman. Now it was the kids' turn to guide the franchise and boy, did they do a good job.

One guy who definitely was not a kid was Jamie Moyer. The Phillies were still playing good baseball and all of a sudden found themselves only 2 1/2 games behind the Reds for the National League wild card. Instead of just closing the book on the pesky 2006 Phillies, Gillick acquired a man who made his big-league debut the same year that Bill Buckner became a household name in the New England region.

> You might be asking yourself, *How did they acquire someone after the trade deadline? That makes no sense!* Well, there used to be something called the waiver deadline that would usually be on August 31, when a team could place a player on waivers, a team could claim him, and the two organizations would have an allotted time to make a trade. If they could not come to a deal, the player would simply return to his team. I miss the waiver deadline.

Moyer, the Souderton High School kid and former Saint Joseph's Hawk, *finally* returned home and brought some stability to a rotation that badly needed it. The minor leagues didn't offer much for the rotation, so in October 2006 the Phillies inked Moyer to a two-year extension that would have him stay with the Phillies through the 2008 season.

Unfortunately, the '06 Phillies fell three games short for the NL wild card, but even so, they finally injected some life into the fan base. They had their young ace, they had a younger guy with some upside in Brett Myers, and they finally were able to get some quality innings from the veteran in Moyer. There was a semblance of a quality major-league rotation; now, Gillick just had to add to it.

And add to it he would! That offseason Gillick traded for another former Mariner, and White Sox at the time, Freddy García, who pitched to a crisp 5.90 ERA in 11 starts. Gillick also gave Adam Eaton a three-year $24.5 million deal; Eaton pitched to an ERA over 6.00 in 2007 and an ERA over 5.80 in 2008. *Barf!*

These last two weren't home runs by Gillick, but trading for Moyer was a big win.

ACQUIRING BRAD LIDGE (AND ERIC BRUNTLETT)

Aah, the final (offseason) move for the 2008 Phillies happened, and boy, was it a big one. Because Billy Wagner walked, Gillick looked elsewhere for someone to lock down the ninth inning. He thought he found it with the veteran Tom Gordon, who had been Mariano Rivera's set-up man with the Yankees for the previous two seasons. Initially, "Flash" Gordon was a good signing. He made the All-Star team in 2006 and saved 34 games.

Unfortunately, that would be Gordon's last real hurrah in the major leagues. He entered the 2007 entrenched as the Phillies' closer only to battle a shoulder injury that would linger throughout the season, and eventually the keys to the closer role were handed to former starter Brett Myers, who was dealing with his own struggles.

Even though Myers did well in the closer's role, saving 21 games and pitching to an ERA around 3.00, they needed the young right-hander back in the rotation. So it was back to the drawing board for Gillick, and his move was definitely a shot in the dark.

Brad Lidge had battled injuries throughout the minor leagues after being selected in the first round of the 1998 draft by the Houston Astros out of Notre Dame. Lidge was known for his high-90s fastball and wicked slider (hmm, sounds familiar). Given his injury history, the Astros transitioned Lidge to the bullpen, where he took off. In 2003 he joined a bullpen of Billy Wagner and Octavio Dotel as the third back-end option and finished the year fifth in Rookie of the Year voting.

In 2004, with Wagner obviously in Philadelphia, Lidge was moved to the setup role behind Dotel. However, in June of that season the Astros traded Dotel to Oakland A's, which opened up the closer's role for Lidge. The former first-rounder ran with it, pitching to a 1.49 ERA and saving 28 games. In 2005 Lidge really took off for the 'Stros, as he made his first All-Star Game, saved 42 games, and pitched to a 2.29 ERA on a Houston team that would end up winning the National League pennant.

Lidge looked like he was well on his way to becoming the next most dominant closer in baseball. However, that was halted in Game Five of the 2005 National League Championship Series against the St. Louis Cardinals.

Leading 4–2 in the top of the ninth with a chance to send the Astros to the World Series, Houston sent out its All-Star to face the bottom of the Cardinals order. Lidge struck out the first two batters, easy-peezy. This one's over, right? Well, David Eckstein singled to left, Jim Edmonds drew a walk, and all of a sudden the National League's Most Valuable Player, Albert Pujols, stepped up to the plate.

Pujols hit .330 in '05, with 41 homers and an OPS north of 1.000. It was certainly not the easiest spot for Lidge. As fate would have it, on an 0-1 pitch, Lidge hung a slider, and Pujols hit what was maybe the most squared up baseball in the sport's history, traveling an estimated 455 feet and well over the train tracks at Minute Maid Park.

2008—"WORLD CHAMPIONS, WORLD F%$&IN' CHAMPIONS"

> If you haven't seen the Pujols home run off Lidge, please put this book down. (Make sure you open it back up, please! Have Kevin and I mentioned that we're both young fathers just trying to make it?) Fire up the ole YouTube, and watch that home run. *Sure,* Jorge Soler hit a similar one in the World Series in '21, but that Pujols home run was different. Off the top of my head, the most squared-up baseballs ever hit were that one, Stairs off Broxton in '08, and Schwarber off Darvish in '22. I'm not biased or anything, I promise.

Unfortunately for Lidge, that wasn't the end. The Astros would bounce back in Game Six, beating the Cardinals 5–1, behind the arm of Roy Oswalt, to win the pennant. Their opponent in the World Series was the Chicago White Sox.

With Game Two tied 6–6 heading into the bottom of the ninth, Astros manager Phil Garner summoned Lidge again. Only this time he wasn't facing Albert Pujols. No this time, Lidge was facing a man who hit exactly zero home runs during the regular season in 2005. That would be light-hitting, but All-Star that season, Scott Podsednik. In an improbable turn of events, Podsednik turned around a 95 mph offering from Lidge and hit what was at the time the thirteenth walk-off home run in World Series history. It also sent the White Sox to Houston up 2–0 in the Series. Poor Lidge.

Surely, that was it, right? Garner couldn't bring him out again, could he?

Nope, Lidge wasn't out of the woods yet. With the Astros now down 3–0 in the Series, he was brought on yet again by Garner to try to extend Game Four. In a 0–0 game entering the top of the eighth, Lidge was brought in. The leadoff hitter, Willie Harris, singled to left; Podsednik bunted him over; and Carl Everett grounded out to the second baseman, moving Harris to third base. The stage was set. All Lidge had to do was get out White Sox outfielder Jermaine Dye and he would keep the game alive for the Astros. Welp, Lidge allowed a single up the middle, Harris scored, and after the Astros couldn't muster up a run in the bottom of the eighth or ninth, the World Series was over, a 4–0 sweep by the Chicago White Sox.

To say it was a postseason to forget for Lidge would be an understatement. He allowed an iconic home run and, essentially, lost two World Series games. Tough.

Lidge was broken. He came back in 2006 ready to round back into form as the Astros closer, but he lost that job *three* times during the season and pitched to a 5.28 ERA. In '07, Lidge fluctuated between the closer spot and late-inning reliever on an Astros team that only won 73 games and was trending toward hitting the reset button, as their great duo of Craig Biggio and Jeff Bagwell were winding down.

After the 2007 season, Lidge got another surgery, this time on his right knee to repair some torn cartilage.

Lidge hadn't looked right since Pujols launched a baseball to the moon, and now, the oft-injured closer needed another knee surgery. Yes, trading for Lidge certainly was a shot in the dark, and one Gillick deserves a lot of credit for.

On November 7, the deal was done. Lidge and Eric Brunlett (also important) were shipped to Philadelphia for Michael Bourn, Geoff Geary, and Mike "Don't Call Me George" Costanzo.

> The man making the trade for Houston at the time was none other than Ed Wade, who had now taken over as the general manager for the Astros. This wouldn't be the first time Wade would throw the Phillies a bone. The Phillies seemed to never lose a trade with the Astros during this time; he also would send them Roy Oswalt and Hunter Pence in subsequent years. Maybe Wade did earn a World Series ring after all?

The organization felt like it had gotten a closer who had some red flags but also some upside. According to Phillies scouts, that traditional Lidge-like bite to his slider was back late in the season, and even with the knee injury the arm was healthy, which was ultimately all that mattered. The roster was set, the team was ready, the city was hungry. It was time to play.

THE 2008 REGULAR SEASON

If the baseball season is a journey, then so is this chapter. We can't just fast-forward to the playoffs! Baseball, and the telling of it, is a marathon, not a sprint.

Obviously, a lot of hope preceded the 2008 regular season. Sure, there were question marks. Could the rotation hold up? How would Myers transition back into the starting rotation? How would Lidge look? Was he over what happened in '05 and ready to get back on track?

Let's not forget, however, that the Phils had back-to-back MVPs in Jimmy Rollins and Ryan Howard. Was '08 Utley's turn? (It sure looked like it for a little bit.) Hamels was ready to take off in his third year in the big leagues. Werth and Victorino showed a ton of promise in '07 and would get an expanded role in '08. And, finally, the squad was now veteran-like with a core that had been together for a better part of four seasons.

The time was now, and Manuel set the tone early in his message to the team to kick off spring training. "How bad do we want it?" Manuel said. "We have a couple more steps to go. I know the type of guys we got, and believe me, if we want it, we can go get it. That's all I gotta say." Please read that in Charlie's West Virginia accent, would ya?

The Phillies were ready to head north for the season, but their closer was not. Yes, Lidge was hurt again, this time with a torn meniscus in the same knee he had just had surgery on. He would miss six to eight weeks and ended up being back in early April. Still, for a team with World Series aspirations and a closer looking to get right with his new team, it certainly was an ominous start.

Here are the most notable things that happened in the first half of the 2008 regular season:

MYERS STARTS ON OPENING DAY AGAIN; BULLPEN SHELLACKED

It sure seemed like the Phillies wanted to show confidence in Myers after his down 2007 that ended with him in the closer's role. They backed that up by giving him his second straight Opening Day start even with the emergence of Hamels.

The reality was, they *needed* Myers to get back on track as a starter. Hamels and Moyer were established, but after them Myers was a question mark, Eaton couldn't be trusted, and Kyle Kendrick, despite a nice 2007, was more of a fifth starter than anything else.

For this team to reach their ultimate goal, it needed Myers to get back to the pre-2007 form. Unfortunately, in his first opportunity back in the starting rotation, he allowed four runs in five innings to the light-hitting Nationals.

Worse off for the Phillies on Opening Day was their bullpen, which ended up being really good, obviously. However, during the first game of the season it was not.

Tom Gordon allowed five runs in the top of the ninth, and the Phillies dropped the opener, 11–6. Another slow start for this group?

THE LAST HOME OPENER AT SHEA

> Rarely do I open up a section with a Jack note; however, this was important. The Mets from '07 to '11 were the absolute worst, but it made everything during that time that much more fun. In my lifetime, the Phils and Mets during that time was the best rivalry this city has had. I know, *What about Eagles-Cowboys?!* you are currently screaming in your mind. The Cowboys have sucked my entire life, they've never been a real threat, and it truly has not had the mid-'90s juice it had for a lot of people. Phillies-Mets had real juice and real animosity. To make it even more fun, before 2008 the Phillies had played the Mets home opener in 2007 right after Rollins said the Phillies were the team to beat (he got booed), and the Phils famously chased down the Metropolitans to end that season in one of the biggest collapses in baseball history. To be the opponent during the last home opener at Shea was perfect. Aah, the Mets—forever corny.

The Mets were good. David Wright and José Reyes were developing into stars; maybe the most underrated slugger of the 2000s, Carlos Delgado, was still doing his thing;, and Carlos Beltrán could do it all in center field. However, with Pedro Martínez winding down in his career, the Mets needed a new ace. So they acquired Johan Santana for four prospects and subsequently signed him to a six-year deal.

The stage was set: stars on both sides, teams that weren't fond of one another, and fan bases that couldn't stand the sight of the other's logo.

Oh yeah, back to the corny part. While the Phillies did the talking in 2007, it was the Mets this time around that tried to create some magic of their own. "This year, to Jimmy Rollins, we are the team to beat," Carlos Beltrán said in February of '08.

2008—"WORLD CHAMPIONS, WORLD F%$&IN' CHAMPIONS"

Very cute.

Brett Myers seemed to speak for the entire team when he quipped back, "He's just trying to pull a Jimmy when you can't have a sequel. Sequels are always terrible."

It was on.

Everything was going well for the Phillies to kick off the last home opener at Shea. Jamie Moyer got the start and was pitching well, as he gave them six innings of two-run ball. They had just taken the lead with a three-run top of the seventh. However, that good feeling turned to concern in the top of the eighth. Their fearless leader, and enemy number one in New York, Jimmy Rollins, was on second base when Aaron Heilman made a pickoff attempt. Rollins scampered back in an awkward fashion. He would end up scoring that inning but was replaced in the bottom half of the inning.

After the game, it was determined that Rollins had a sprained ankle and would, eventually, go on the disabled list for the first time in his career.

Two Jack notes in one subchapter? Oh, well! I do find it funny that during those times that Rollins and Burrell were really enemy numbers one and two for Mets fans, while Utley just lurked. Burrell owned the Mets and is still seventh all-time in home runs against them. And, of course, we've detailed Rollins. But it would be Utley, both with the Phillies and the Dodgers, that most Mets fans would say they hate the most.

After injuring his ankle on April 8, the Phillies didn't put him on the IL until April 21. That's nuts. It was early, but playing without their shortstop for an extended period was the first real hurdle the 2008 Phillies had to overcome.

THE EARLY HEROES

With Rollins out and Ryan Howard battling his semi-usual slow start to the season (he was hitting .167 with a .608 OPS on May 9), it was on some other guys to step up and carry the team for a bit, and carry them they did.

Pat Burrell was in an interesting spot in 2008. He was once dubbed the future of the franchise, and the hopes and dreams of the Phillies returning to glory rested on his shoulders. He was the number one overall pick, and he had all the power in the world. But as Rollins, Utley, and Howard became more established, Burrell fell out of the spotlight. For a guy like Burrell, maybe that was a good thing. Not everyone is built for having the weight of the franchise on his shoulders. We saw it in 2003 after he had seemingly *arrived* in '02. Burrell had gotten his big contract (a six year, $50 million deal in the offseason), and he would go on to hit .209 with a .713 OPS.

Now, the thirty-one-year-old left fielder was entering the last year of his contract with the Phillies. With big future contracts eventually coming to Howard, Utley, Rollins, and Hamels, the team couldn't pay everybody, and after '08 it looked like Burrell was going to be the first member of the core to leave the nest.

> Pat Burrell in a roundabout way was actually my first memory of "real" Philadelphia. After he hit the big double in Game Five and led the parade down Broad Street, Burrell was a legend in Philadelphia. *However,* I remember how Burrell had been ridiculed before all of that: "Why does he jump out of the way on fastballs inside?" One day during the summer, I was at a random night game with my parents, who didn't get down to many games; we were in the 400 section of Citizens Bank Park. The 400 section was not like the 700 level at the Vet. It was much tamer. But after Burrell struck out in a big spot, someone yelled, in the most beautiful Delco accent imaginable, "How about instead of paying $50 million for Burrell we get some f***ing pitching!" It was about as intense as my ten-year-old self could experience. That was my first introduction into "real" Philadelphia.

Contract-year Burrell was a problem, in a good way, for the Phillies in '08. With Rollins down and Howard struggling, No. 5 picked up the slack. From the start of the season until May 9 (the date Rollins returned to the lineup), Burrell hit .303 with a .440 OBP and an OPS over 1.000.

He was certainly doing his part—but he wasn't the only one.

It really looked like it was going to happen. It really did. After Howard won the MVP in 2006 and Rollins followed that up with an MVP season of his own in '07, it really looked like 2008 was going to be Utley's turn.

Utley was on fire. From the start of the season until May 9, Utley was hitting .336 with a .706 SLG and 13 (!) home runs. Utley was so hot it even caught the attention of arguably the greatest offensive second baseman of all time: the great Joe Morgan.

During this time, *Sunday Night Baseball* was Jon Miller and Joe Morgan, and boy, were they a treat. Sunday Night Baseball *felt* big. During a game against the Mets in late April, after Utley hit his second home run of the night, Morgan said this on the ESPN broadcast that night:

"Jon, he might end up as the greatest-hitting second baseman ever."

He was hot.

He would eventually cool off, however, and the dream of three straight MVPs didn't happen, but still in the early season when they needed him, the man was the man.

CHARLIE WINS NUMBER 500, AND THE PHILS ENTER HITTIN' SEASON

Now, managerial win-loss records are not counted in the annals of baseball history quite like the 500 home run club or 300 wins, but for a team that loves their manager, 500 wins meant something.

On May 4, after a Geoff Jenkins walk-off base hit, Manuel got his 500th win as a manager. Of course, this led to a nice celebration in the clubhouse, and the skipper told his players, "Screw five-hundred; I want a thousand,"[2] in the most Charlie way possible.

The win even led to this quip from the usually soft-spoken Utley, who handed Manuel a Phillies white home jersey with 500 on the back to commemorate the moment: "You know what that means? It means you had some damn good players,"[3] which got a great laugh out of everybody.

Chuck stamping home win number 500 during hittin' season is poetic. What is hittin' season, you might ask? According to Manuel, "Hittin' season is anywhere from the end of May, June, July, August when the hot days of summer roll in. The ball carries better, and everything about it has more energy. It's summertime and they get into it. That's what I call hittin' season."[4]

Well, it certainly was that time of the year. From May 1 until mid-June, the Phillies hit .270, launched 58 home runs, and scored 240 runs. Things were going well.

RING THE BELL

VICTORINO HELPS LIDGE STAY PERFECT

> Now, I'll be honest. This is a very minor story in the grand scheme of things for the 2008 Phillies, but I think it's a cool one, *especially* with regard to how the season ended for Lidge.
>
> By now, everyone knows how the season ended for Brad Lidge in 2008. It was perfect (besides the All-Star game, but who cares?).

Do you know how uncool it would be had Lidge gone 40 for 41 in save opportunities during regular season instead of 41-for-41 and then eventually 8-for-8 in the postseason? Sure, it still would have been a great year, but the *lore* of the perfect season would have been gone. Instead, thanks to Shane Victorino, we weren't robbed of that, and we get to pass down to future generations the story of Lidge's perfect season.

Victorino was manning center field in a game against the Braves in which he had already tripled twice, including during the top of the 10th to put the Phillies ahead. Lidge was on to try to protect a 4–2 lead at Turner Field in Atlanta.

Lidge struck out Brian McCann to start the inning, but then Josh Anderson singled to left and Grégor Blanco got a bunt base hit, which allowed Anderson to go to third base. Blanco then stole second to put two runners in scoring position. Lidge struck out Greg Norton. There was light at the end of the tunnel. All Lidge had to do was get out Yunel Escobar.

He didn't. Escobar ripped a base hit up the middle, Anderson scored, and Blanco was sprinting around third base. Unfortunately for the Bravos, the man of the hour was in center field, and after an extra little bounce in his crow hop for his throw home, Victorino delivered an absolute BB shot to Chris Coste at home plate.

The ballgame was over, perfect season still intact. Whereas Lidge ended up 41-for-41 in the regular season, maybe Victorino deserves credit for one of those saves?

After the game Lidge said, "The Force was with us tonight," and he wasn't wrong.

2008—"WORLD CHAMPIONS, WORLD F%$&IN' CHAMPIONS"

WE SAW SOME HIGHS, NOW HOW ABOUT THE LOWS

Every season, even the most *perfect* ones, are filled with bumps and bruises along the way. This group wasn't exempt.

The first bump in the road involved their shortstop, except this time it wasn't an injury.

When you think of Charlie Manuel as a manager, you assume he's laid-back and even-keeled and trusts his players to police themselves. While that was mostly true, he would get on these guys as well. It's part of what made him so beloved by his players. He was jovial and fun but had a standard that if players didn't meet they would be held accountable. Players knew exactly where they stood.

Manuel, famously, had two rules: be on time and hustle.

As great managers and coaches know, stars need to be held accountable; otherwise, other players would not follow their lead.

Manuel did just that on June 6, 2008. While in Cincinnati, Jimmy Rollins hit a pop fly to short left field with Carlos Ruiz on second base and two outs. Paul Janish, the Reds' shortstop, dropped it, which allowed Ruiz to score from second base. But Rollins was only at first base when he easily could have been on second.

Manuel yanked him. It's easy to bench role players; it takes guts to bench stars.

The aftereffect could have gone one of two ways. Rollins could have been pouty. He could have gone to the front office and demanded that Charlie be fired, and the whole situation could have turned ugly.

Instead, Rollins showed great leadership.

"It's my fault," Rollins said after the game. "I can't get mad at him. That's like breaking the law and getting mad when the police show up. You can't do that."

The next part of the quote really showed how much respect the guys in that clubhouse had for Manuel.

"With this team you don't get away with anything anyway, but he's the manager and that's what he's supposed to do when a player isn't hustling. He has to take the initiative to make sure you play the game the right way."[5] Stars know they have to be made an example of sometimes, and how they handle it resonates throughout an entire clubhouse.

The next bump in the road for the first half of the '08 regular season was simply how they were playing. The Phillies hit their offensive funk in late June and early July.

After scoring 20 runs against the Cardinals on June 13, the Phillies went 3–11 in their next 14. The stretch included a road trip against the American League that saw the Phillies go 3–9 and get outscored 57–37. One had to wonder how they would fare in the World Series given how much they struggled against the American League in the regular season, going 4–11.

The team average during that time was the worst in baseball, at .218, and the Phils scored the third fewest runs during that stretch. That's shocking considering how potent that lineup was on a night-in-night-out basis.

Given how the pitching staff was faring—more on that soon—the Phillies simply could not survive if the offense wasn't going to produce.

The big piece needed to get going. Up until July 1, Howard was hitting .215 and was on pace to strike out over 200 times, which at the time was a huge deal.

> I know, it's almost impossible to see the big picture when you're going through it. Nevertheless, this portion of the book should remind fans not to freak out when a good team is playing badly. Every team goes through it. That goes for players as well. *I can only imagine* what people were saying about Howard during this time: "Drop him in the lineup," "He's a flash in the pan, a strikeout king," "Where's Thome?" I wrote this right after the Phillies in 2024 could not pull themselves out of whatever funk they were in, so maybe freakouts are sometimes fine.

The offense ended up being more than okay, but for a team built to slug, I'm sure this was a worrisome time around the ballpark.

The final issue the Phillies had to deal with in the first half of the 2008 season was one of their starters—Brett Myers, who was moved back into the rotation after serving as the team's closer during the stretch run of the 2007 season. Myers loved that role and was disappointed when the Phillies traded for Lidge and moved him back into the rotation. Gillick, at the time, said that there wasn't a starter on the market who was as good as Myers when he was right. So they gambled on Myers getting back into form. Unfortunately, it wasn't going well. In his first 17 starts of the season, Myers had an ERA approaching 6.00.

Was he broken? Did they have to invest in a starter at the trade deadline? CC Sabathia was available. Was it time to gut the farm system to get him? I'm sure these were questions asked behind the walls at Citizens Bank Park. The Phillies couldn't make a trade just yet, but they couldn't keep rolling him out there, so the brass pulled their last string. On July 2, a mere nine months after he had lit up Citizens Bank Park by striking out Wily Mo Peña to end the Phillies' 13-year playoff drought, Myers was demoted to Lehigh Valley in a move rarely seen for an established player. In fact, once a player reaches a certain amount of service time, he would have to agree to be sent down to the minor leagues.

Myers was lost mentally. The always confident Myers had missing his spark, and pitching coach Rich Dubee said, "I think confidence-wise this is probably the lowest I've seen him."

Why? Myers gave these pretty revealing comments to Jim Salisbury: "I want to be great, and honestly, I realized last year that I'd only be a good starter. I felt like I had rock-star status as a closer. I wasn't prepared to become a starter because my heart and my mind-set were still in the bullpen. That's my fault."[6]

So it was off to Lehigh Valley for Myers to get right. He okayed the demotion.

Heading into July, the Phillies offense was causing panic in the city by not scoring as much as they should, the rotation seemed to be hanging on by a thread, and the division lead was down to one game. This once-promising season that had the town dreaming of an October parade all of a sudden was looking shaky.

THE ALL-STAR GAME

Oddly, you can't tell the story of the 2008 Phillies without a quick mention of the All-Star Game that took place that year. If you don't remember it, is fire up YouTube and look at the show that Josh Hamilton put on in the Home Run Derby. Insane.

The All-Star Game itself was the final one at old Yankee Stadium, so, of course, the pomp and circumstance was a lot. Forty Hall of Famers were in attendance that night, including, from the Phillies, Schmidt, Carlton, and Robin Roberts. It's safe to say that none of them were around when it finished.

RING THE BELL

The All-Star Game took *4 hours and 50 minutes* to play. It ended at 1:38 in the morning. What a nightmare. Of course, the game couldn't be called, which would have saved teams from burning pitchers who might be in post-season runs. And, who could forget, the winner of the All-Star Game determined home-field advantage in the World Series.

And that, right there, is why mentioning the '08 All-Star Game in this chapter is noteworthy.

Clint Hurdle went to Brad Lidge earlier in the afternoon on the day of the All-Star Game and told the Phillies reliever to be ready for the ninth. He wanted him on the mound if the National League had the lead. Lucky for us, the game just kept going and going, and Hurdle had Lidge warming up multiple times throughout.

> I wish I was back then how I am now, because had this warm-up thing happened now, I would see red. Did we need to have our All-Star closer, who had a magical season up until that point, warm up multiple times to try to win what should be a meaningless game? Oh, I would have been seething. Nevertheless, the game did count, the NL squad had to have to Lidge warm up multiple times, and Hurdle had to eventually pitch him.

Finally, Hurdle called Lidge's number for the bottom of the 15th. Justin Morneau singled, Dioner Navarro followed up with a single of his own, Lidge walked J. D. Drew, and then, mercifully, Michael Young hit a sac fly that ended the game.

Lidge lost the All-Star Game. Technically, it wasn't a save, so the perfect season lived on, but all things considered it is pretty funny that the only game Lidge "blew" the entire season happened in the 15th inning of the All-Star Game, and it cost the Phillies the opportunity to have home-field advantage should they make the World Series.

THE TRADE DEADLINE

Aah, the deadline. What was "Stand Pat" Gillick going to do?

The big names around the trade deadline were CC Sabathia and Manny Ramírez. In Philadelphia, the player everyone wanted the team to mortgage the farm for was Sabathia. He was an ace, a true horse, and, if paired with

Hamels, a difference-maker come October. But he was a free agent at the end of the year. The prospect cost for his services, likely only for the remainder of that year, probably would have been too high.

Three weeks before the deadline, the Brewers pulled off the blockbuster trade for Sabathia. The old adage is that the blockbuster trade rarely ends in a world championship for the team that acquires the player, but man, Sabathia pitched to a 1.65 ERA as a Brewer and was pitching on three-days rest to get that team into the postseason. He was a behemoth. Thankfully, we know what happened in October; however, Sabathia in '08 lived up to the hype.

So, the Phillies missed out on Sabathia and also missed out on the other big-fish pitcher at the deadline—Rich Harden. Where were Gillick's lonely eyes going to turn to now?

How about back to the Bay Area for a guy that just threw seven innings of one-run ball against the Phils in late June? That would be the one and only Joe Blanton.

The sound heard was parade balloons deflating all over the Delaware Valley. From hopes and dreams of CC Sabathia to "Average" Joe Blanton—surely there's no way this will end in a World Series, right? Right?

Yes, before the second half of the season even started, the Phillies acquired the twenty-seven-year-old right-hander.

They were aggressive in acquiring Blanton, who up until that point of the season was 5–12 with a 4.96 ERA. They believed that those numbers were a bit deceiving and that he would pitch better in the second half, plus they had him under control for a couple of years after that. He wasn't one of those high-price rental types.

The one thing Blanton could do really well was eat innings. Since 2005, he ranked third in the American League in innings pitched, behind Mark Buehrle and Jon Garland. The Phillies were getting a steady hand in Blanton, but was he truly enough to put this team over the top?

Time would tell.

MYERS'S RETURN

Maybe the Phillies' biggest deadline acquisition was getting the old Brett Myers back. Simply put, Myers was the linchpin of World Series aspirations in 2008. If he was the same as he was just before he got sent to the minor leagues, you could kiss this season goodbye. The lineup was rounding back into form, the bullpen was having a historic season, but without Myers being competent the rotation was an arm short.

Thankfully for the Phillies and Myers himself, he did come back from the minor leagues looking like the old Myers. Whether it was the humiliation of going to the minor leagues as a tenured big leaguer or his acceptance of not being this team's closer, Myers looked the part, and that was huge for this team.

Even though he only had two starts before the trade deadline, it sure seemed like the Phillies had seen enough. The trade deadline came and went with no further trade for a starter. These were the guys they would ride with, hopefully, into October:

Hamels, Myers, Moyer, Blanton, and Kyle Kendrick or J. A. Happ.

Buckle up!

A TIGHT AUGUST

August began with the '08 Phillies a game up on the New York Mets for the division lead. Was it the Mets' turn to get some payback after what the Phils had done to them last year? They sure thought so.

The Phillies still weren't playing their best baseball to start the month of August, but things didn't get really bad until they went out to Los Angeles for a four-game set with the Dodgers. The Dodgers were certainly feeling good about themselves. They had just acquired Manny Ramírez, which seemed to revitalize both him and the Dodgers.

> Dodgers Manny was a problem. For my money, Dodgers Manny was one of the five best right-handed hitters of my lifetime. He was just incredible in his career, but his time with the Dodgers might have been the best we've ever seen him. As a Dodger, he hit .396, slugged .743, had an OPS of 1.232, and hit 17 home runs in only 53 games. It was absurd. We'll obviously detail this later when talking about the '08 play-offs, but I don't think I've ever feared an opposing player quite like him. Maybe Rob Gronkowski in the second half of the Eagles Super Bowl in 2018, but those are the two. Manny hit .520 in the postseason that year—.520! In the NLCS alone, he hit .533 with a 1.749 OPS—video game numbers.

2008—"WORLD CHAMPIONS, WORLD F%$&IN' CHAMPIONS"

Although the Phillies didn't have to deal with playoff Manny for a little bit, they did out in LA in August, and that didn't go so well. The Dodgers swept them out of LA and the division lead in one four-game set.

Sure, losing four straight to the Dodgers was bad and so was losing the division lead, but the worst thing to happen out in Los Angeles might have been Jimmy Rollins's appearance on a sports program.

It had been a roller coaster of a season for Rollins. After being the hero in 2007 with bold proclamations and an MVP award, Rollins was having a down '08 season by his standards. On top of that, he got benched for not hustling in Cincinnati and benched again for being late to a game against the Mets in early June, and it seemed as if every day there were questions as to whether he and the manager were getting along.

Things came to a head for Rollins when, again, he and Ryan Howard went on the *Best Damn Sports Show Period* while the team was out in LA. "I might catch some flak for this," Rollins said when asked about what it's like to play in Philadelphia. "But, you know, they're front-runners. When you're doing good, they're on your side. When you're doing bad, they're completely against you. You know, Ryan [Howard] is from St. Louis. St. Louis it seems like they support their team. They're out there, and they're encouraging." The match was lit.

Shockingly, that comment didn't sit well back in Philadelphia, and Rollins had to spend the next couple of days cleaning up that mess.

Even though he clarified what he meant about front-runners, Rollins' message was clear:

Support us. If we deserve to be booed, it's all good, but don't just kick the game off by booing someone. Things were rocky in Phillies land.

Out of first place and their franchise shortstop in a war of words with the fans, the Phillies had hit their second big piece of adversity during the '08 regular season. This quote by Charlie Manuel to reporters after losing to the Dodgers to complete the four-game set really summed up the subtle ways that the skipper would motivate his ballclub:

"If you want to know the truth, I think it's a good test for our team. If you stay in the hunt and you battle it out and we win, I think that tells us what kind of team we are. . . . There's two ways to look at it. If we get down and we don't come back, we're not champions and we're not men."

He was relaying the same message to his team. How would they respond?

After completing their road trip by taking two of three from the Padres in San Diego and then returning home to take two of the three from the lowly Nationals, it was the Phillies' turn to have a home four-game set against the Dodgers.

> The funniest part for me in writing this chapter has been remembering that even the best Phillies offense I've seen in my lifetime wasn't perfect. Guys who I have immortalized had slumps. The biggest benefit of being a sports fan when you're a kid is seeing your guys as infallible. You brush off the losses and just look forward to seeing the boys play again the next day. You may wonder why Dad is so upset, but you chalk that up to a bad day at work. He's not really upset over the baseball game, is he? It's crazy that the talking point around the Phillies in mid-to-late August was whether the big four—Utley, Rollins, Howard, and Burrell—were going to heat up. But people were right to wonder that. The quartet was hitting .197 in August until the Dodgers series that started on the 22nd, and Rollins specifically was hitting .081 since he called the fans front-runners. Aah, the benefit of hindsight. I *never* doubted these guys. You believe me, right? Right?

The lineup needed a spark. They say managers can't have that much of an effect on the outcome of the game, but you know what they can do? Shake up a lineup that had been scuffling. For years, Utley and Howard hit three and four for this team; after the struggles they'd had, Manuel decided it was time to split them up heading into the four-game stretch with the Dodgers by batting Pat Burrell third. Whether it was the lineup change or not, Howard and Utley woke up, and the Phillies pounded out 27 runs in a four-game sweep of the Dodgers.

Did they finally get their mojo back?

There certainly wasn't time for a letdown; the red-hot Mets, which had won 11 of their last 14 games, were in town for a quick two-game set.
What transpired might have been the game of the year.

When fans think of Phillies-Mets during this time, a lot of them will, rightfully so, point to the Utley walk-off hit in August 2007 as the best moment during the rivalry. However, a *strong* contender for number two would be what happened on August 26, 2008.

2008—"WORLD CHAMPIONS, WORLD F%$&IN' CHAMPIONS"

This was a big two-game series. The two teams were neck and neck for the division lead—the Phillies were down a half-game. The two games would be the second-to-last time the two would play each other.

Things were not going well early in the first game; the Phillies found themselves down 7–0 in the fourth inning. The Mets ambushed Jamie Moyer, who up until that point had not allowed more than three runs in a start in his last 14 times taking the hill, to a tune of six runs in three innings. The Mets tacked on another off of steady Clay Condrey in the fourth. However, that's where the comeback started. The Phillies got one back in the bottom half of the fourth on a Pedro Feliz sacrifice fly. Then in the fifth, Rollins, after a leadoff double by Condrey (!), hit a two-run home run off Mets starter Pedro Martínez to make it 7–3. Utley immediately followed up with a walk, and, after a Burrell strikeout, it was Ryan Howard's turn to exit the building, as he hit a two-run home run off Martínez.

Ballgame on.

That score would hold until the eighth before Carlos Ruiz singled to left with one out, which was followed up by a single from Chris Coste (we're burning both catchers here, Skip?) and then another single by Rollins to make the score 7–6. Unfortunately, the rally ended there, and the Phillies would have to wait until the bottom of the ninth to see if they would complete the comeback.

In the ninth, Werth laced a two-out single, which led to pinch-hitter Eric Bruntlett being summoned to hit for Brad Lidge. (Aah, remember when the National League didn't have a DH?) Bruntlett smoked a ball into the right-center field gap, which allowed Werth to come all the way around from first to score. The ballpark was electrified, and it was a brand new ballgame—7–7—heading into extras.

Extras started with no ghost runner then, which meant the fans could be there a while. Neither team scored in the first three innings of extras, and the Phillies bullpen was going on nine innings of shutout baseball. However, that changed in the bottom of the 13th. Victorino led off the inning with a triple. The Mets decided to intentionally walk both Werth and Bruntlett because the Mets knew the pitcher's spot was due up after Bruntlett. Brett Myers came out to pinch hit for Rudy Seánez in what had to be his biggest at-bat of the season, right? *No way* Myers will have a bigger at-bat than this one for the rest of the year. Well, he struck out with the bases loaded, which set the stage for Chris Coste, who was already 3-for-3 on the night. At 12:24 a.m., after a laborious

5 hour and 17 minute affair, Coste made it 4-for-4 as he drove a single into center field and sent the ballpark into a frenzy.

The Phillies were back in the lead in the NL East.

The Phillies closed out August by going 7–3 in their last 10 games but still ended the month a game back of first place. They would have to chase down the Mets again in September if they wanted to capture their second straight division crown.

Now, the page couldn't be flipped to September yet as the Phillies made one more significant move to close out August. The waiver deadline used to be teams' last chance to make an upgrade to the roster before September. Any player acquired before September 1 was eligible for the postseason roster.

In one last shrewd move, Pat Gillick added the final piece to the 2008 Phillies.

Gillick needed a lefty bench bat with some thump. Greg Dobbs was having a phenomenal season, but he was the team's only lefty on the bench heading into the stretch run. Geoff Jenkins was just placed on the IL with a strained right-hip flexor. Gillick found his match in 16-year veteran Matt Stairs. He was in his age-forty season when the Phillies traded for him, but don't let the age fool you. The proud Canadian still brought his lumber to the ballpark.

Make no mistake about it, Stairs was brought here to do one thing, and it wasn't to play the outfield. If it's late in the ballgame and Manuel needed someone off the bench to get in there a pop one out of the ballpark, Stairs was there.

In other words, in case of an emergency use Stairs.

Talk about a trade that aged well.

On to September!

CLOSING IT OUT

It had been a whirlwind regular season for the '08 Phillies. They got off to a hot start for the first time in franchise history (just kidding). They had dealt with some adversity, like their offense going cold, one of their key starters having to be sent to the minors (by the way, Myers was pitching awesome by this point), and their franchise shortstop feuding with fans, but all of that just set the stage for September.

And boy, was September a month to remember for a certain Phillie—more on that later. To kick off September, the Phillies had to finish their season series with the Mets with their final series at the legendary Shea Stadium. The team trailed the Mets by three games heading into the series, and one legendary Phillie knew what was at stake this weekend. Mike Schmidt decided to send the boys a message before the big series up in New York; he penned an email to Manuel to post for the team. He wrote, "One pitch. One at-bat. One play. One situation. Think small and big things result. Tough at-bats. Lots of walks. Stay up the middle with men on base. What it takes to keep the line moving on offense. The Mets know you're better than they are. They remember last year. You guys are never out of a game. Welcome the challenge that confronts you this weekend. You are the best. Good luck. Signed: #20.7"

They got the message. The Phillies took two of three that weekend in New York. Brett Myers went eight shutout innings to bring his post–All-Star break ERA down to 1.55 and give the Phillies a win to open the series. After a rainout on Saturday, Jamie Moyer delivered with seven shutout innings of his own to outduel Pedro Martínez. They would lose the nightcap of the doubleheader, but they won the series and exited New York still two games back for the division.

Obviously, the Phillies' goal was to win the division, but they just had to get in the postseason at this point. Though still hunting down the Mets, they had another foe to chase down, the National League wild-card—leading Milwaukee Brewers. The Brew Crew was coming to town holding a four-game lead for the wild card, and time was quickly running out for the Phillies to make their move.

> The Phillies at this point were maddening to the city. It was like picking the petals of a sunflower with this team. "They love me; they love me not; they love me; they love me not." They have the great four-game sweep against the Dodgers at the end of August and immediately follow that up with the comeback of the year against the Mets. "They love me!" Then they open up September with a series loss to a 59-win Nationals team. "They love me not!" Next, they go up to Shea Stadium and take two of three from the Mets. "They love me!" And finally, they return home and lose two of three to the Marlins, who actually were decent that year (but who cares?). "They love me not!" Even the most perfect season was maddening. If that's not the most baseball thing of all time, then what is?

Now thankfully for the Phillies, they did not have to face CC Sabathia, who was on a tear since becoming a Brewer, pitching to a 1.59 ERA at this point. Still, the Phillies had to make up ground quickly, as there were only 16 games left in the season.

Make up ground they did.

The series started with Moyer pitching on short rest and giving them 5⅔ of three-run baseball. Ryan Howard homered and doubled to drive in three, and Charlie Manuel did something he rarely did. With the Phillies nursing a 5–3 lead in the eighth and Shane Victorino on third with one out, Manuel decided to put the squeeze play on with Carlos Ruiz at the dish. To the shock of many, it worked, and the Phillies got an extra insurance run before closing them out in the ninth. Manuel joked after the game, "I figured I might as well try to start being a National League manager. I think somebody forgot that I knew how to put the squeeze sign on."

For those who don't know the backstory, here's the explanation. One of the main criticisms around Manuel at this time was that he was an American League manager, meaning that he didn't know how to play small ball or know how to double switch. At least for one night, the naysayers had to be quiet.

After a rainout on Friday, the Phillies cooked the Brewers on Saturday with 6 1/3 innings of two-run baseball from Cole Hamels and an offense that jumped on starter Manny Parra for five runs in an inning and a third. The big guns were starting to show up at the right time for the Phillies, as Rollins went 3-for-5 with a homer and Howard drove in another run to take game two, 7–3. Two down, two to go.

On Sunday, the Phillies were tasked with winning both games of a doubleheader if they wanted to complete the sweep against the Brew Crew. The Phillies were starting to roll. Howard and Victorino homered in game one of the doubleheader, while steady Joe Blanton gave them seven innings of three-run baseball to help preserve the bullpen. Finally, in the nightcap behind another strong offensive performance, this time against Brewers starter Jeff Suppan, and a complete game from Brett Myers, the Phillies swept Milwaukee. The September Phillies had arrived and had pulled themselves to within a game of the Mets for the division and to a tie in the wild-card race with the Brewers.

The big boys had finally started to show up for the Phillies. Howard was in the midst of carrying this team, while Rollins had finally broken out of what seemed like a season-long slump. Howard was hitting .354 so far in September with seven home runs in 14 games. Could he come from not making the All-Star Game to win the MVP? We shall see.

The Phillies, for the last month of the season, were playing the game of beating a good team and showing signs of resurgence and then giving it right back the next series against, usually, an inferior opponent. Would now be different?

Thankfully it was. The Phillies had hit their stride. The early-season offense was back, the bullpen continued its lights-out performance, and the rotation was more than holding its own. They went down to Atlanta and swept the Braves, finishing a perfect 9–0 at Turner Field on the season, and took two of three from the Fish in Miami. They had won 10 of their last 11 games to give themselves a 2 1/2-game lead in the National League East. Yes, while the Phillies were surging the Mets were Metsing (it's a word, trust me) and went 7–10 in their last 17 games to lose both the division and a wild-card spot. Aah, that stinks!

Things got a *little* dicey for the Phils when they dropped two of three to lowly Braves in the second-to-last series of the season. As we all know by now as Phillies fans, they never make it easy. The math, however, was heavily on their side. The magic number was three, and they had an 85 percent chance to win the division heading into the weekend set against the Nationals. Manuel said it best when he said before the series started, "If we can't get it done, it's our fault."

For the second straight home series, the white rally towels were broken out to energize the crowd even more. The crowd at Citizens Bank Park could feel it. A rain-soaked stadium cheered as Mr. September, Ryan Howard, went yard in the first to give the Phillies a 3–0 lead. With that, the rout was on. By the top of the third, it was already a 7–1 ballgame. The Phillies would go on to win the game, 8–4, and in maybe more important matters, the Mets lost, which brought the magic number down to one heading into Saturday. Win and you're in.

The Phillies did just that. For the second straight year, the Phillies asked Jamie Moyer to take the hill and send them back to the postseason. The now forty-five-year-old responded by giving the Phillies six innings of one-run baseball. Still, the Phillies weren't in the clear just yet. Leading by a score of 3–2 in the bottom of the eighth, they were looking for some insurance runs. Pedro Feliz delivered with a two-out double to score Shane Victorino from first base; the score was 4–2 heading into the ninth. Manuel did what he had done all year: hand the ball to Lidge. For 40 games meant that the ballgame was over. Would he be able to make it a perfect 41-for-41? It certainly wasn't smooth sailing.

Lidge started off the ninth by striking out Emilio Bonifácio—this was going to be easy, wasn't it? It wasn't. Roger Bernadina singled to right field. Lidge then walked Ryan Langerhans and next allowed a single to Anderson Hernández (who?) to bring Bernadina home from second. It was now a 4–3 ballgame. The next batter, Cristian Guzmán, singled to center field, but thankfully, Langerhans wasn't the most fleet of foot, so he was not able to score from second base. The bases were now loaded with one out in a one-run game with the Nationals' best hitter coming up to the plate in Ryan Zimmerman. To make the ballpark even *tighter*, as Zimmerman came up, the scoreboard flashed that the Mets had won, which meant that if the Phillies lost it all came down to Sunday for them to win the division. The Phillies needed their special players to make a special play. They got their wish. Zimmerman smoked a grounder to Rollins's left; the always smooth Rollins let the ball travel, got in perfect position for a flip to Utley, who made maybe his quickest turn in his history, on to Howard and into October. The Phillies had won their second straight division title ,and Lidge was able to close out his perfect regular season.

The Phillies were hell-bent on not repeating the same mistake they had made last year.

"Believe me," Manuel said on the field to thousands that stayed after to celebrate. "We're going further in the playoffs than we did last year. We want to win a World Series alright!? Thank you alot!"

With that, regular season was over. The first part of their mission was complete; they had won the division. Now, it was time to bring home the first title to Philadelphia since 1983.

No pressure.

SOMETHING WAS BREWING

The Brewers were back in Philadelphia for the second time in less than a month. The last time they were in Philadelphia, the Phillies swept them to tie up the National League wild-card race. In an unprecedented move, the Brewers fired manager Ned Yost after they got swept to try to wake up a talented but floundering ballclub. It worked, as they won 7 of their last 12, including six of their last seven, to chase down the Mets to claim the NL wild card.

2008—"WORLD CHAMPIONS, WORLD F%$&IN' CHAMPIONS"

The Brewers were talented. They finished near the Phillies offense in a lot of categories and had young stars like Prince Fielder, Rickie Weeks, Ryan Braun, and J. J. Hardy. On the mound, they were the CC Sabathia show. Sabathia did everything in his power to get this Brewers team into the postseason, including by throwing on three days' rest a few times. With the Brewers, he pitched to a 1.65 ERA and should have been in MVP discussions. He was a true Goliath; the Phillies just needed to be David one time.

A sun-soaked Citizens Bank Park was the scene for Game One of the NLDS. The Phillies were looking for their first playoff win since October 21, 1993. The young phenom, Cole Hamels, was on the mound for the Phillies, opposed by Yovani Gallardo. Hamels was really starting to come into his own. Even though he didn't make the Opening Day start, it was clear by the time the postseason had rolled around who the ace of this staff was. From July on, Hamels pitched to a 2.77 ERA and held hitters to a .243 average. He was ready; now he just had to go out there and take it.

In what would end up being a nice preview to the magical run that the twenty-four-year-old left-hander was about to go on, Hamels dominated. He retired the first 14 Brewers he faced, before a two-out hit by Corey Hart in the fifth, and ended the day giving the Phillies eight innings of shutout baseball—a masterpiece.

On offense, the Phillies scored all their runs in the bottom of the third in the most nontraditional fashion. Carlos Ruiz led off the inning with a single. This brought up the nine-hole hitter, Hamels. He laid down a bunt toward third base; the Brewers' third baseman, Bill Hall, bobbled the ball and fired across the diamond, but their second baseman, Rickie Weeks, couldn't hold on to the ball. The runners were safe, and all of a sudden the Phillies were in business with guys on first and second with no outs and the top of their order coming up. Gallardo almost got out of it unscathed. He retired Jimmy Rollins on a popup and then struck out Jayson Werth before facing Chase Utley with two outs. Utley scalded a 2-2 fastball from Gallardo into center field. The Brewers' center fielder, Mike Cameron, made the mistake of breaking in on the ball and had to try to scamper back to nab Utley's line drive. He was unable to, the ball bounced off his glove, and both Ruiz and Hamels scored, giving the Phillies a 2–0 lead. Gallardo then intentionally walked Ryan Howard to get to the slumping, and somewhat injured, Pat Burrell. But he walked him as well to load the bases for Shane Victorino. Unbelievably, Gallardo also walked him to score the Phillies third and final run of the inning. All runs were unearned, and the Phillies would need no more.

It was a stress-free afternoon at Citizens Bank Park. Things were easy—maybe too easy. Manuel summoned his perfect closer for the ninth inning in a move that you only second-guess if it goes wrong. Hamels was at 101 pitches and had tallied the second-most innings in the National League that season. The Phillies had to keep him as fresh as they could for what they hoped was a long postseason run. Lidge, while perfect thus far, got by with the skin of his teeth to close out the regular season, needing 33, 26, 29, and 24 pitches to record the save in his last four outings. Game One against the Brewers wouldn't ease any concerns about the Phils' closer. Lidge started the inning by striking out Mike Cameron. He then allowed a single to pinch-hitter Ray Durham. Ryan Braun then doubled home Durham, and it was all of a sudden a 3–1 ballgame with the tying run coming to the plate. Lidge struck out Prince Fielder before walking J. J. Hardy. A wild pitch allowed both Braun and Hardy to advance. The tying run was now on second base with Corey Hart up at the dish. Lidge got him, striking out Hart swinging, and that sound you heard all around the ballpark was a giant exhale. The Phillies took Game One and secured their first playoff win in a generation.

The Phillies needed Game One because that Goliath we talked about a bit earlier was on deck. CC Sabathia would toe the rubber in Game Two with a chance to even up the series before heading back to Milwaukee.

> We can all be honest here, okay? We all chalked Game Two up as a loss, right? I feel like everyone had the same collective thought. Treat Game One like a must-win because the bad man was lurking for Game Two. We know what happened, but I'm trying to bring you into what the feeling was like.

The Phillies had done their job and took Game One; now a win in Game Two would be like playing with house money. Win? Great, the series is over, essentially. Lose? It's CC, so what did you want them to do? One guy who felt good against Sabathia was none other than the wise old sage Charlie Manuel. After Game One, Charlie offhandedly said to reporters, "We might get after Big CC." Then Manuel followed up on it before Game Two by saying, "CC, he's good. He's going to get the ball and mostly come right after us. He's definitely not afraid and he'll control his emotions. But we're going to get balls to hit."[8] Did impromptu "Charlie!, Charlie!, Charlie!" chants just start in your house, or was that just here?

Game Two started shakily. Brett Myers, toeing the rubber for the Phils, allowed a one-out walk to Ray Durham. Ryan Braun followed that up with a double to move Durham to third. Myers intentionally walked Prince Fielder to set up the double play and a force out at every bag. Myers walked the next batter, J. J. Hardy, to force in the first run of the game. Gulp. They certainly didn't need to be giving away runs with Sabathia on the other side. Thankfully for the Phillies, Corey Hart swung at a first pitch breaking ball and hit a dribbler back to Myers, who fired to second base to set up the inning-ending double play.

The bottom of the second is where this one got fun. Jayson Werth ripped a one-out double for his first postseason hit. Pedro Feliz followed that up with a double of his own to plate Werth and tie the game up at one. Sabathia, who was making his fourth start on short rest, was on the ropes early. Carlos Ruiz then grounded out, advancing Feliz to third, to bring up Myers to the plate with two outs. This inning was over. Even among pitchers, Myers was a bad hitter. His 4-for-58 on the season ranked him 58th out of 64 pitchers with at least 30 at-bats. Go get in the beer line, because this inning was donezo. Before you could blink, Myers was down 0-2 in the count. Citizens Bank Park was chuckling. But then, Sabathia missed out of the zone for ball one, and Myers fouled the next pitch up the first-base line. Signs of life? Sabathia's next pitch was into the ground, and all of a sudden it was a 2-2 count. Myers fouled off the 2-2 pitch, which drew a huge cheer from the crowd; took a ball in the dirt (a 3-2 count now); fouled off another pitch after that (the crowd was getting louder and louder); and then somehow, someway, Myers held off on another 3-2 pitch from Sabathia and drew the walk. The crowd was at a fever pitch. A nine-pitch at-bat by Myers completely unraveled Goliath. He walked Jimmy Rollins on four pitches, which brought up Shane Victorino.

Victorino was not usually this team's two-hole hitter. That's spot was usually reserved for Werth. However, Werth was struggling. Manuel said before the game that he was trying to do too much, so he dropped him to sixth in the lineup. That meant it was up to Victorino to man a key spot in the lineup. Would what transpired next have happened if Manuel didn't make that switch? I guess we'll never know.

With two outs, the bases loaded, and the largest crowd in Citizens Bank Park history ready to come apart at the seams, Victorino stepped to the plate ready to deliver a death blow to Sabathia. Victorino crushed a two-strike hanging slider over the fence, into a sea of red, to finish off the Goliath. Citizens Bank Park was sent into a state of euphoria—5–1, Phils.

> The Victorino grand slam, I believe, was the first time it set in for people that this team might be different. Taking down Sabathia was a *big* deal, and the manner in which they did it, in the grandest of fashions (please clap), made it that much sweeter. Now, all we had to hope for was that the Victorino grand slam wasn't like the Iverson stepover of Tyron Lue or the Brian Mitchell kick-off return against the Bucs in the 2002 NFC Championship Game—moments when our team seemed poised to win a title before falling short. Overall, that was a *moment* and the first one that really felt different.

The Phillies chased Sabathia by the fourth after 98 pitches. In a forgotten piece of Game Two lore, Myers worked a 10-pitch at-bat after his now famous nine-pitch walk. While what he did at the plate will be remembered forever, his pitching was much more important, and Myers delivered on that end as well, firing seven innings of two-run baseball and outdueling the great Sabathia.

The bridge to Lidge got the job done, and the Phillies perfect closer made it two-for-two in the postseason. The Phillies took a commanding 2–0 lead and were on to Milwaukee to try to make it back to their first NLCS since 1993.

Game Three—they lost. Who cares? We don't write about losses during the magical 2008 postseason! Onto Game Four.

Putting extra emphasis on a playoff game feels a little odd, but here's what was at stake in Game Four in the NLDS. If they lost, they would return home after losing two straight to the Brewers, having lost momentum in the series and making Citizens Bank Park tight. On top of that, Sabathia would be back on the mound (albeit on short rest); could they beat him again? Maybe, but the stakes were certainly much higher. They *had* to beat Jeff Suppan.

> For as much as Moyer was a marvel to a lot of baseball fans, with his 82-mile-per-hour fastball, that's what Jeff Suppan was for me. I have no idea how this guy got people out. I promise this is not totally a shot at Jeff Suppan, who, if you're reading this book thank you for reading, but if they lost to this guy to blow a two-games-to-nothing lead, I would have been seeing red. Suppan somehow pitched 16 years in the big leagues with *nothing*. Jeff Suppan was at his peak—which feels like an insane phrase to write—from '97 to '09. He had an *average* ERA of 4.64. People complain about the pitching in every era, but, holy cow, although there were some aces, of course, the middle-to-late 2000s saw a bunch of innings eaters. Rant over.

In a close-out game after having lost the day before and being on the brink of blowing a 2–0 series lead, the Phillies needed to have their stars show up to take some of the pressure off. In what would end up being a theme in the postseason, Jimmy Rollins led off the clinching Game Four with a home run. The sound you heard in the Phillies dugout was one collective exhale. Although the 1–0 lead was nice, having runners on second and third with one out in the top of the second and not scoring was not nice. Not taking advantage of key situations in the postseason is how you let teams stay around. Thankfully, for the Phillies they weren't messing around later on.

Pat Burrell had no idea if he would be in the starting lineup in this pivotal game. He was nursing a tight back and had really struggled in the series thus far. The Brewers were pitching around Utley and Howard to get to Burrell, who was not making them pay. Manuel stuck with him, probably because in his career Burrell was 9-for-21 with three homers and two doubles off Suppan. In the third, the bet paid off. With Victorino on second with two outs and Ryan Howard stepping to the dish, Brewers manager Dale Sveum intentionally walked the slugger to bring up Burrell, who was hitting .170 against righties in the last month. On a 2-2 pitch, Burrell didn't miss a meaty 88 mile-per-hour fastball from Suppan and deposited it into the left-field seats for a three-run home run. You could hear a pin drop inside Miller Park. To make matters worse for the Brewers, Jayson Werth followed up with a home run of his own. With the score 5–0, Phillies, it was on Average Joe Blanton to carry them home.

Blanton did just that, firing seven innings of one-run ball and holding a powerful Brewers offense to one solo home run by Prince Fielder. Burrell added his second home run of the day in the eighth, and Lidge closed them out. Good morning, good afternoon, good night.

The Phillies were in the NLCS for the first time since 1993.

A date with the Dodgers was next.

PHILLIES-DODGERS NLCS

The Phillies being in the NLCS wasn't really a surprise. Even though their regular season was up and down, with that offense and bullpen anything was possible. The Dodgers being in the NLCS? That was a bit of a surprise. No, this was not those Dodgers teams of the late 2010s and early 2020s. This was an 84-win ballclub that got hot in September (going 17–8); after trading for Manny Ramírez, they won a truly terrible NL West. Who would ever lose to an 84-win team in the NLCS? (I'm getting mad all over again at the 2023 Phillies.)

> I can't help but find it funny that in this series Larry Bowa was in a Dodgers jersey and Davey Lopes was in a Phillies jersey. For those of you who don't know, Lopes was a great Dodger, and he and Bowa are forever linked in their own franchise's respective history because of Black Friday. Of course, that involved the play in which Bowa threw out Lopes but the ump called him safe, and the Phillies would end up losing the 1977 NLCS to the Dodgers. Lopes was this team's first-base coach, and many of the guys credited him with their success on the bases. Rarely are first-base coaches game changers, but Lopes was one of them.

To the Dodgers' credit, they were hot. They swept out the Cubs in the NLDS and had arguably the best hitter in the series in Ramírez. Thankfully, as the old adage says, momentum in baseball is only as good as the next day's starter, and in this case, the Phils had their best on the mound in Game One.

Hamels was great against the Brewers, but was the twenty-four-year-old really ready for the bright lights of the NLCS? Early on it looked like the moment might be getting the best of Hamels. The second batter of the game, Andre Ethier, drove a double to left field, which created early tension as Ramírez stepped to the plate. Should the Phillies walk him with the base open? They decided not to, and Ramírez hit maybe the furthest ball you could

2008—"WORLD CHAMPIONS, WORLD F%$&IN' CHAMPIONS"

at Citizens Bank Park without it going out, as he laced one off the 19-foot wall in deep left-center field. It was 1–0, Dodgers, just like that. The Dodgers would add to that lead with some small ball in the fourth, as Matt Kemp led off the inning with a double, Casey Blake moved him along to third with a groundout, and Blake DeWitt hit a sacrifice fly. Get him on, get him over, and get him in—2–0, Dodgers.

The ballpark was tight and so were the Phillies. They were facing a hot starter, the thirty-five-year old veteran Derek Lowe. In his last nine starts of the regular season, Lowe pitched to a 0.94 ERA and went 5–1; additionally, he pitched six innings of two-run ball against the Cubs in the divisional round. Lowe and his patented sinker were keeping Phillies hitters at bay through the first four innings, and Citizens Bank Park sounded like a funeral. That started to change in the fifth as Carlos Ruiz and Cole Hamels each hit two-out singles to bring Jimmy Rollins to the plate, and the crowd was right back in it. Unfortunately, Rollins would eventually pop out, but some cracks were showing.

The cracks finally led to a problem for Lowe in the sixth. To open the inning, Rafael Furcal made an error to allow Shane Victorino to reach first base. Chase Utley, mired in a 2-for-15 slump to start the postseason *finally* got going, as he lifted a first-pitch hanging sinker into the right-field stands. The ballgame was tied, with the ballpark in a frenzy. After Howard grounded out, Burrell, who was starting to break out of his slump in a big way, laced a home run to left field that barely reached the flower bed. Ramírez's ball in the first that was struck better than both of those homers by the Phils was not a home run, but both Utley's and Burrell's balls were gone. That's baseball.

Just like that, after their offense sleepwalked through the first five innings of the game, the Phils were alive. It was ultimately all they would need. Hamels had settled into a groove, allowing only one hit after the fourth inning, and finished the day with seven innings of two-run baseball. It was onto the bridge to Lidge, as Madson took down the eighth before giving way to the still-perfect closer. Lidge responded with a one-two-three ninth, and Game One was in the books.

A lot was going on during this time for both the Phillies and the rest of the world. First, the country was in the middle of the stock market completely crashing. Yes, while the Phillies were attempting to go to the World Series, everyone was else was worried about losing a lot of money. It was a tense time. Now for the Phillies it was a bit more somber. Between Games One and Two, both Manuel and Shane Victorino experienced losses in their families. Charlie's mom, June, a lifelong baseball fan, passed away, and Victorino's grandmother passed away back in Hawaii. The Phillies took the field with some heavy hearts in Game Two.

The Phillies secret weapon at the dish, Brett Myers, was set to toe the rubber against future Phillies "great" Chad Billingsley. This version of Billingsley was definitely a different one than the Billingsley who eventually ended up on the Philllies. This was a younger Billingsley who still had his big fastball and had won 16 games for the Dodgers in the regular season. This day, however, would not belong to him.

Myers set the tone early with a fastball over the head of Manny Ramírez (I wonder if this will come back up later in the series) before striking him out to end a scoreless first. The Dodgers would actually take the lead in the top of the second on a fielder's choice before the Phillies came alive. With two outs in the bottom of the second, Dobbs hit a single. Carlos Ruiz followed that up with a double to bring Dobbs all the way around from first. The game was tied at one. With two outs and a runner on second, surely Myers would not carry over his magic against Sabathia from the NLDS, right? Wrong. Myers singled to center field to bring home Ruiz. With the score now 2–1, that brought up Rollins, who extended the rally with a single to bring Myers around to third base. The heavy-hearted Victorino brought them both home with the fourth single of the inning—4–1, Phils, after an inning that included four singles and a double, all with two outs.

Myers would not be done yet at the plate. In the fourth, with the score now 4–2, a single by Burrell to open the inning, a double by Werth, and an intentional walk to Greg Dobbs led to Ruiz grounding into a force play at the plate. It was Myers's turn at the dish again. Bases were loaded with one out, with a chance for the Phillies to blow the game wide open or let the Dodgers off the hook. Myers didn't let them off the hook. He laced a single to right field, which sent Citizens Bank Park into a frenzy and allowed Werth and Dobbs to score. Again, just to hammer this point home, Myers couldn't hit. Even for pitchers, he was among the worst in baseball in 2008. This version of Myers was loose and aggressive and seemed like Charlie Sheen in *Major League*. It was a scene. With the score now 6–2 and Billingsley chased from the game, it was Victorino's turn to be the other star of the game, as he smoked a triple, which allowed both Ruiz and Myers to score. It was 8–2 after three.

2008—"WORLD CHAMPIONS, WORLD F%$&IN' CHAMPIONS"

Game over, right? Not so fast. In the fourth, Ramírez got his revenge on Myers for the fastball in the first that sailed past his head. He deposited a pitch into the flower bed in left field to all of a sudden make this an 8–5 game. Maybe Myers was tired from running around the bases and having to pitch on top of that. He exited after five while allowing five runs. But Myers did mix in one more hit before exiting. He was 3-for-3 at the dish, drove in three, and scored three runs. Maybe this was the year?

Myers gave way to the bullpen to close this one out. Given how well the Phillies starters had pitched to start the postseason, the now famous bridge to Lidge hadn't really been put to work, outside of Ryan Madson. That would not be the case in Game Two, as the Phillies used Chad Durbin, J. C. Romero, and eventually Madson before handing the ball to Lidge. They did their job and thwarted any Dodgers momentum, firing three innings of scoreless baseball. The one stressor, however, came in the seventh. With the Phillies still nursing their 8–5 lead, Madson was brought in relief of Romero with two outs, a runner on first, and the righty Nomar Garciaparra coming up. Nomar singled to move Kemp to third base, which brought Casey Blake to the dish. Once again, Victorino played hero. Blake lifted a ball to deep left-center field, a spot in the ballpark that has led to many, many triples. Victorino sprinted back, felt for the wall, leaped, and then crashed into the wall to secure the catch—a tough play for most center fielders that was routine for the Gold Glover. Madson would fire a one-two-three eighth, and the bridge to Lidge was complete.

Although his inning produced some anxiety, with two runners on and one out before back-to-back strikeouts against Kemp and Garciaparra, Lidge got the job done. The Phillies had won the first two games of the NLCS. With June Manuel and Victorino's maternal grandmother looking over them, they were off to Hollywood to write their final script.

Game Three—much like we said in the Brewers series, they lost! Who cares? On to Game Four.

> Can I start Game Four with a Jack note please? I guess that really is nobody else's choice but mine. Game Four of the NLCS, as we'll describe, might have been the best singular game of the '08 postseason run. From the twists and turns, all the anxiety, some late-game heroics—it truly had it all. Though all these games weren't like the NLCS in 1980, this series was probably the closest. Let's get into it—a game we'll all remember.

The Phillies didn't waste any time jumping out in front in this one. After back-to-back singles by Rollins and Werth to start the game against Derek Lowe, who was pitching on short rest, Utley snuck one past the diving first baseman James Loney for a double—1–0, Phils. Howard, up next, grounded out but was able to bring home Werth from third base—a productive out. However, Howard was mired in a tough slump to start the postseason. He was 4-for-23 heading into Game Four, with no home runs. The Phillies were winning and things were going well, but they needed their big piece to get going if they truly wanted that parade down Broad Street that they all dreamed about. The Phillies had Lowe on the ropes but could only escape with two in the first.

The Dodgers got one back against Joe Blanton in the bottom half of the inning after Furcal led off with a single, Ethier grounded out to move Furcal to second, Manny Ramírez was intentionally walked, and James Loney hit an almost home run to deep center field to bring in Furcal. Blanton escaped a potential disaster and only gave up one in the first. The score would remain the same until the fifth. These next four innings is when this game went from your regular run-of-the-mill postseason game to all-timer in Philadelphia sports history.

It started with Blanton getting himself into trouble. In the bottom of the fifth, Furcal led off with a walk (never a good idea) and Ethier singled, which brought up Manny Ramírez in a key spot. The Phillies could not walk Ramírez this time. There was nowhere to put him, as the Phils would not want to load the bases with one out. Blanton was forced to pitch to Ramírez, who was 14-for-25 lifetime off of Blanton—gulp. In what wouldn't be the worst outcome in the world, Ramírez laced a single into left field that brought home Furcal—2–2 game. The next batter was Russell Martin, who grounded out to bring Ethier home from third base. With the score now 3–2 and first base open with one out, Manuel decided to walk James Loney to keep the double play in order. He got his wish as Blanton got Blake DeWitt to ground into a double play. The Phillies were down, but in the bottom of the fifth they again avoided disaster.

The Phillies tied the game back up in the top of the sixth, but much like the Dodgers, they missed their chance to really blow this game wide open, as they had runners on second and third with one out and were only able to score one on a wild pitch.

2008—"WORLD CHAMPIONS, WORLD F%$&IN' CHAMPIONS"

> I apologize for these Jack notes during this game, and more are to come. This is one for the true baseball sickos. What happened at the end of the top of the sixth was National League baseball at its finest. I know you kids these days grow up with your little designated hitter in the National League, but how *I* grew up (finally getting to use my old man voice even though the DH wasn't in the National League until the 2021 season), we had pitchers hitting and a manager actually had to make decisions.
>
> In the top of the sixth, Chan Ho Park, future Phillie, was on in relief of Clayton Kershaw (wow), who was in relief of Derek Lowe. Manuel decided to pinch-hit for Blanton with an opportunity to blow the game wide open by bringing in Geoff Jenkins to face Park. In a true game of chess, this prompted Dodgers manager Joe Torre to bring in the lefty Joe Beimel, which prompted Manuel to not even use Jenkins and go with So Taguchi instead. Taguchi popped out to end the inning, but still! People told me National League baseball wasn't fun! That's fun! Thank god Manuel didn't use Stairs there and burn him, or else maybe we would have had a different outcome.

The game was now 3–3 heading into the bottom of the sixth. Durbin was brought in to keep it a tie ballgame. That didn't last long. Casey Blake led off the inning with a home run to give the Dodgers the lead. Juan Pierre, future Phillie, followed up with a double, and then Durbin walked James Loney—not a hot outing for Durbin. Manuel had to yank him without recording an out.

In walked Scott Eyre, a waiver claim the Phillies made after the July 31 trade deadline that had done a great, great job for this bullpen. He doesn't get the accolades the other guys in the bullpen that year do, but Eyre was an important piece of this team. With first and second, no out, Torre had Furcal lay down a bunt to the first-base side of the rubber. Ryan Howard came sprinting in, fielded the ball, and threw back to first base, only his throw was errant and bounded off Utley's glove into right field. Pierre scored, Kemp went to third, and Furcal was on second base. The game was now 5–3 with runners on second and third with no outs. After a long at-bat with Ethier, Eyre was able to jam him, and he lined out weakly to Howard. No runners advanced, one out and first base now open. Manuel instructed Eyre to intentionally walk Ramírez and load the bases for Russell Martin.

RING THE BELL

Instead of having Eyre face him, Manuel went to one of his big guns, Ryan Madson, to try to keep the Phillies within striking distance. What happened was game saving. On a 1-2 pitch, Martin laced a ball toward the middle of the field. Utley, shaded that way, dove and caught it, scampered to his feet just enough to dive and tag second base before Furcal could get back. The wherewithal and IQ of Utley was on full display, and the Phillies were able to dodge disaster yet again.

Time was running out on the Phillies. It was now the top of the eighth, and they were still trailing 5–3. Howard led off the inning with a single up the middle. Burrell popped out, which brought up Victorino to face Dodgers righty Cory Wade. It had been a whirlwind series for Victorino. He lost his grandmother before having an unbelievable Game Two, and then in Game Three, Hiroki Kuroda threw at his head, which prompted him to yell back at Kuroda, and the benches cleared. On this night he fulfilled his villain role, as he went down for a Wade slider and parked it into right field to tie the game up.

> Yes, another Jack note—I still think this was the most underrated huge moment of this entire postseason run. If Victorino hadn't hit that homer, then we wouldn't have what happened next, the game *probably* would have ended in a loss, and all of a sudden the series would have been back to 2–2. People don't talk enough about the Victorino home run off Wade, and it definitely gets overshadowed, but that's why the Jack notes are here. We don't forget anything. Victorino was a postseason star.

With two outs and the game tied, Carlos Ruiz hit a measly single. Torre lifts Wade from the game in favor of his closer Jonathan Broxton to face the pinch-hitting Matt Stairs. We all know what happens next. On a 3-1 pitch, with the whole ballpark knowing a fastball was coming, Stairs didn't miss it. He ripped one into the night, 450-plus feet and maybe, besides Schwarber off Darvish in '22, and some old titanic Ryan Howard home runs, the most squared up baseball in my time of watching the Phillies. "In case of an emergency please use Stairs" T-shirts were printed, and he went from afterthought to folk hero. The Phillies dugout erupted, and Dodger Stadium fell silent. What a moment.

2008—"WORLD CHAMPIONS, WORLD F%$&IN' CHAMPIONS"

However, the Phillies weren't out of the woods yet. Brad Lidge was summoned from the bullpen with two outs in the bottom of the eighth to face Ramírez while nursing a 7–5 lead. Ramírez greeted him by ripping a double into right-center field. The next batter was Russell Martin. Lidge got him to strike out, but the ball got past Ruiz, and both runners were safe. Just like that, runners were on the corners with James Loney coming to the dish. After a long battle with Loney, Lidge got him to pop out to the left fielder Bruntlett. In total, Lidge had to throw 16 pitches to get one out in the eighth. That wasn't great, but Manuel had to stick with him for the ninth.

Thankfully, Lidge made quick work of the Dodgers in the ninth, retiring them one-two-three, and just like that the Phillies were one win away from the World Series.

Hollywood in Hollywood. It truly doesn't get any better than that. The hometown kid was on the mound, looking to put the team that gave him a shot into the World Series. To say the twenty-four-year-old was locked in would be an understatement. In speaking with Mike Arbuckle, who was now the assistant GM but drafted Hamels, remembers what he was like on the team bus a couple days before Game Five out in Los Angeles.

"We're on the team bus, and I asked Cole, 'Are your parents coming up for the playoff games?'

He said, 'Oh, yeah.'

And I said, 'Well, how are they doing? Have you talked to them?'

And he said, 'No, they're in a different hotel. I don't want any distractions.'

So I'm thinking, *Here's a kid that went from getting in bar fights to [being] a mature major leaguer.*

Whether it was not talking to his parents or whatever Hamels was doing, it was working, and it worked yet again in Game Five.

However, this one started off the same way the clincher in Milwaukee started—with a leadoff home run by Jimmy Rollins on the eighth pitch of the at-bat. The Phillies just had the look of a team that wanted to end it that night, celebrate in LA, and not have to get on a plane back to Philadelphia to play another game in the series. The tone was set, once again, by their leader, Jimmy Rollins. I don't believe he was set to appear on *The Best Damn Sports Show Period* after this one.

In the third, the Phillies got their 25th two-out run of the postseason. Twenty-five! Rollins drew a one-out walk against Dodgers starter Chad Billingsley and stole second. After Werth struck out, Utley drew a walk of his own to set up first and second with two outs. The struggling Ryan Howard came to the plate. Howard came into the game hitting .185 in the postseason with still no home runs. He did not exit the ballpark here, but he singled into right field to score Rollins—2–0, Phillies. Burrell then followed that up with a single into left field to score Utley. Just like that, the score was 3–0 Phillies, and Billingsley was already chased from the game.

It was probably safe to say that with the way Hamels was pitching that three runs were all he would have needed, but it never hurts to add on to take a *little bit* of the stress away. In the fifth, Rafael Furcal might as well have gift wrapped the Phillies the pennant. On to pitch for the Dodgers was none other than Greg Maddux, who was a waiver claim for Los Angeles, just like Matt Stairs.

> Baseball really is a beautiful game. Multiple times while writing this book, I've cocked my head back and smiled because of how it all seems to just come together in a perfect way. Maddux entering into this game is no different because Maddux was the losing pitcher all the way back in 1993 for the Braves when they lost the NL pennant to the Phillies. Only in baseball would a city go 15 years without making the postseason, make the NLCS, and end up facing the guy who was on the losing end the *last* time the team was in the same spot. Baseball.

With runners on first and second and one out, Pat Burrell drove a groundball to Furcal's right. He dove, but it bounded off his glove into short left field. It was just enough for the always instinctual Utley to never break his stride running around third to score. Furcal then threw the ball away trying to throw home, which allowed Burrell to get to second base—two errors on one play. With the bases loaded and two outs, Maddux got what should have been an inning ending groundout, but again, the ball was hit right at Furcal. On what would be his third error of the inning, Furcal made a brutal throw to first base, which allowed Howard to score and give the Phillies a 5–0 lead after the top of the fifth.

In the bottom of the fifth, things got a *little* dicey for Hamels. Back-to-back singles opened up the frame, and Dodgers fans came to their feet. This was their time to break through. Any feeling of this being a big inning was immediately thwarted after Hamels got Blake DeWitt to ground into a double play and then struck out Jeff Kent looking.

> What a Dodgers team here. The Jeff Kent strikeout, and then strikeouts, really got me going on this. Kent, a former MVP; Maddux, a 300-game winner; Garciaparra, a former batting champion; Juan Pierre, a former Marlins great and world champion; Joe Torre, who obviously was more known as a Yankee but was still a multiple World Series champion; Andruw Jones, who was on this roster at one point; and then Manny, who was still insane at this time, but you get the point. They were a collection of great players who were all past their prime, besides Manny, who was terrifying.

Ramírez scored the only run against Hamels on this night, as he lifted a two-out home run in the bottom of the sixth to cut into the Phillies' lead and make it 5–1. Ramírez, by the way, ended the series hitting .533 with a 1.749 OPS—video game numbers.

The last real chance for the Dodgers came in the bottom of the seventh. After two straight fly outs, it seemed as if Hamels was going to end his night without breaking a sweat. However, he walked both Matt Kemp and then the pinch-hitter Garciaparra. There were two outs, with the still dangerous Kent at the plate. With Madson warm and ready to come in, Manuel walked out to the mound. He wanted to talk to his young ace and look the horse in his eyes to see if he still had it. Manuel stuck with him. In the modern era, Hamels would have been yanked no doubt. "Look at his numbers against righties compared to lefties!" they'd shout from the stands and on social media. But he did not come out in this game. On his 26th pitch of the inning and the 104th of his night, Hamels reared back and fired a 94-mile-per-hour fastball down and away that froze Kent. Kent wiped away tears (kidding) as he argued with the umpire that the pitch was low, but nevertheless, the call was made, and Hamels's night was over.

After Madson worked a scoreless eighth, it was onto the ninth, where Mr. Perfect entered in a non-save situation. After Loney singled, the only stress of the inning was a one-out deep fly ball to center field that Victorino corralled while crashing into the wall. The stage was set. Dodger Stadium for all intents and purposes was dead, and the Phillies were waiting to come bounding out of the dugout to celebrate winning the pennant. On a 3-2 slider, Garciaparra finally gave in, popping up a slider into foul territory. Ruiz threw off his mask, sprinted to the spot, and with two hands (rejoice, Little League coaches) secured the final out. "The Phillies win the pennant!"

> I think this was the first time it hit me that the Phillies were really doing this. It was like an out-of-body experience when they won the pennant. Sure, they had won a division and beaten the Brewers, but trying to wrap my head around my baseball team actually winning the pennant was tough. By the way, I can't tell if I'm the weird one here, but this is our book, so I will continue. I remember by this point that I had found my spot. I'm 100 percent superstitious. I had a spot in '08, a routine in '09, and a spot for the Eagles run in '17. I had found this spot during the Victorino game against the Brewers, and I wasn't moving. Now, I was fourteen, and I just watched playoff games with my parents, so it sure wasn't the sickest set up in the world (love you, mom and dad), but you get the point. If you're superstitious and you find the spot, you're not leaving there until the job is finished.

The champagne was flowing. They had done it. They knew that the ultimate party would commence with four more wins, but also, as the old football coach in town would say, "enjoy the win, man." While his team was celebrating in the clubhouse, Manuel went back to his office to collect his thoughts for a bit. While in there, a couple of reporters stopped in. The manager couldn't stop smiling, and he told reporters, "I've been to the World Series, but I've never won one. This is going to be the year. I can feel it."

On to Tampa Bay.

BRING IT ON HOME

The Phillies clinched the National League pennant on October 15; obviously, the World Series couldn't start until both series were finished. the Tampa Bay Rays and Boston Red Sox didn't want their series to end, so they decided to take their series a full seven games. This meant the Phillies had to wait, and waiting in baseball is not great. It's not like football, where players look forward to having a week off to rest their bodies; in baseball players have routines, they are used to seeing live pitching, and so forth. It can take a little bit to get readjusted to the intensity of the game, *especially* in the World Series. The Rays and Red Sox didn't wrap up their series until October 19, and Game One of the World Series didn't start until October 22. The Phillies had to wait. Was the key to the Phillies staying loose during this time a rubber duck?

2008—"WORLD CHAMPIONS, WORLD F%$&IN' CHAMPIONS"

Apparently so, and who had the idea? No way was it was the most serious man on the face of the planet in Chase Utley, was it? Apparently that was true. See, the thing with time off ahead of the most pressure-filled series of these guys' lives is that it gives them a lot of time to think and get tight. Utley, of all people, had to tell his team to "get the rubber duck out of your butt," a.k.a. relax. Manuel took a liking to the saying and had the Phillies order specialized ducks so that when players showed up in Tampa each one had a rubber duck for at his locker.[9] It's tough to say how much the rubber ducks contributed to the Phillies playing loose to start the series, but it sure seemed like they at least got the message in Game One.

What's the best way for your message to get across to the entire team? Go out there and do it. With the stupid cowbells ringing in the background, Mr. Rubber Duck did just that. With Jayson Werth on first after he worked a one-out walk and Utley tried to lay down a bunt up the first-base line that actually would have been a heads up play, Utley smoked a 92 mph fastball over the right-field wall to give the Phils an immediate 2–0 lead. "And it's a good start for the Phillies," as Joe Buck so aptly put it.

> Let me start this off by saying that I am pro–Joe Buck. I think he's the best. But it really bums me out that we got the version of Joe Buck that was worried about what every fan base thought of him, so he called everything dry and down the middle. Conversely, Joe Buck from around 2016 on didn't care what people thought. It also annoyed me that the year he gave up doing the playoffs to go over to ESPN for *Monday Night Football* was of course the year the Phillies finally returned to the postseason in 2022. Joe Davis was great, but imagine Buck on Bedlam at the Bank? Oh, well.

The home run by Utley was so massive. It was like all the concerns about a slow start or being rusty were wiped away on one swing of the bat. Game on!

While all is well that ends well, Game One of the World Series was an excruciating battle of two fan bases both believing their team was trying to hand the other team a win. After Hamels induced an inning-ending double play in the bottom of the first, the Phillies were back at it on offense, looking to blow the game wide open. Victorino singled to start the inning, Feliz followed that up by drawing a walk, Coste (whom Manuel was giving the first crack at being the DH for the series) flew out to right field, and then Ruiz drew a one-out walk. The golden opportunity was right there for the Phillies with the top of the lineup due up.

Unfortunately, Rollins was late on a 1-0 fastball and popped up a ball to short center field. Given his speed, Victorino decided to test the arm of B. J. Upton in center. It was a bad bet. Even with Victorino's great speed, Upton was able to gun him down and keep it a 2–0 game. If you were a Phillies fan, you had to hope that wouldn't come back to haunt you.

Werth, who killed left-handed pitching, was due up next. He doubled off Scott Kazmir to start the next inning. In what was beginning to become a theme, after the Werth double and Utley moving him to third base, Kazmir struck out both Howard and Burrell to escape yet another jam.

Luckily for the Phillies, the Rays were matching their futility with runners in scoring position blow by blow. In the third, Ben Zobrist singled with one out, Hamels walked the nine-hole hitter, Jason Bartlett, and then Akinori Iwamura singled to right field to load the bases for Upton. There were two things to be worried about with Upton. One, he was scorching hot in the postseason, as he already had seven home runs, and two, with his speed, he was going to be hard to double up. Somehow the Phillies did so, as Upton hit one sharply to the left of Pedro Feliz. Feliz, who was really there for his glove, calmly fielded it and threw to Utley, who whipped it over to Howard for the inning-ending double play—the Rays' second of the night.

The Phillies got their third and final run of the night in the top of the fourth, when Victorino started the inning with a single. That was followed by a single by Feliz. They were both moved over by Chris Coste, and Ruiz was able to put the ball in play to bring Victorino home from third. In the bottom of that inning, the Rays finally got to Hamels, as Carl Crawford, the longest-tenured Ray (and father of Justin Crawford, who at the time of this writing is one of the Phillies' best prospects), hit his first home run of the postseason. Thankfully, it was only a solo shot.

Hamels found himself in another jam in the fifth, as he couldn't get out the nine-hole hitter Bartlett again, this time walking him with two outs. Bartlett stole second to get into scoring position for Iwamura, who laced a ball to the left-center-field wall to bring him around to score. All of a sudden, it was a 3–2 game.

> This game felt like a loss; the Rays might have stolen it, and we would look back and agonize over what the Phillies did after the first-inning home run by Utley. It would have been classic. I know every fan base probably says this about their team, but no team was better at scoring early and then not getting a run for the rest of the game than the Phillies. By this point in the game, they were already 0-for-8 with runners in scoring position. Hamels was dodging in and out of jams; how long could he keep that high-wire act going?

In the bottom of the sixth, it seemed like the missed opportunities were going to bite the Phils. Carlos Peña reached on an error by Howard. Here we go! The door was cracked; it was time for the Rays to break through. Once again, the Phillies were let off the hook, as Hamels picked off Peña on what was probably a balk to first base. Howard redeemed himself by firing a strike to Rollins at second base to apply the tag. Threat neutralized. Hamels then locked in and struck out Evan Longoria and got Crawford to ground out to end the frame.

Don't worry, the Phillies weren't done playing baseball that made you want to rip your hair out just yet. In the top of the seventh, facing tough Rays lefty J. P. Howell with one out, Utley singled into center field. He then stole second and got to third on a wild pitch. The Phillies desperately needed an insurance run for not only themselves but also the millions of us around the country. Howell struck out Howard on a tough down and away slider to keep it a one-run game. With two outs and Grant Balfour now on in relief, Victorino went down swinging with Utley stranded on third base.

By now, Hamels had settled all the way in, as he finished off his night with a one-two-three bottom of the seventh to not let the Rays get any momentum after another escape job by their pitching staff. After Madson retired the side in order in the bottom of the eighth, the Phils gave the fans back home one more shot of pain in the top of the ninth. Werth hit a one-out double, and then the Rays then intentionally walked Utley to get to Howard. Rays manager Joe Maddon countered with lefty specialist Trever Miller to get Howard. After only one hitter, Miller was out of the game, and in came Dan Wheeler. Werth and Utley executed a double steal to set up runners on second and third with two outs for Burrell, who promptly fouled out meagerly to the second baseman. It was on to Lidge to protect a one-run lead like he had done all year.

Thankfully for everyone sitting on their couches watching the game, Lidge made quick work of the Rays, retiring them one-two-three. The Phillies escaped. In total, they went 0-for-13 with runners in scoring position. But, yet again, their young ace was phenomenal, and the duo of Madson and Lidge were dominant. On to Game Two.

And . . . on to Game Three. They lost; it sucked! Who cares?

Some explanations are in order to set the scene before Game Three. The first set has to do with on-field issues. One, the Phillies were 1-for-28 with runners in scoring thus far in the Series, which they simply had to turn around if they were going to bring home the title. Two, a Ryan Howard power surge had to come at some point, right? He *still* hadn't hit a home run in the playoffs. Three, in one of the coolest stories of the '08 Phils, Jamie Moyer was getting set to make his first World Series start at the ripe age of forty-five. He remembered the 1980 parade well as a high school senior, and now 28 years later he had a shot to give the team he grew up rooting for a leg up in the World Series. Now come off-the-field issues. First, rain was becoming a problem. Game Three was delayed an hour and 31 minutes, which meant that first pitch wasn't until 10:08—the latest-starting game in World Series history. Citizens Bank Park had to be in a state of delirium. Second, and this was really cool, throwing out the ceremonial first pitch that night was none other than Tim McGraw—the legendary country music star and obviously the son of Tug McGraw. The star didn't just throw out the first pitch—he also placed some of his father's ashes on the mound to give the Phillies some extra luck. Tugger was on the Phils' side. Lastly, speaking of stars in the building that night, guess who sang the national anthem that night before Game Three? That would be none other than the one and only Taylor Swift, who was just starting to gain some popularity around this time. Wonder whatever happened to her?

If you thought that the hour and half rain delay was going to tamp down fans' excitement, you were sadly mistaken. It started in the first as fans got on the always emotional Rays starter Matt Garza. Garza ran hot and cold—either he was locked in and hard to hit with his mid-90s fastball and heavy curveball, or he was emotional and almost taking himself out of the game. It looked like the Phillies got the emotional Garza early in this one, as Rollins, who was in a slump, led off the bottom of the first with a single, followed by a walk to Jayson Werth. Garza then buried a curveball in the dirt, which got past Navarro and allowed both runners to advance 90 feet. Utley brought in one on a groundball to first baseman Peña, giving the Phillies a 1–0 lead. Unfortunately, the struggles with runners in scoring position continued, as Howard struck out and Burrell flew out to center field. They had a chance to bury Garza early, but let him off the hook. The Rays got one back in the second as Carl Crawford doubled, stole third with one out, and then Gabe Gross drove him in with a sac fly.

In the third, catcher Carlos Ruiz started to become a legend.

> Hindsight is obviously 20/20, but during the '08 regular season and even the postseason, fans were not thrilled with Ruiz. Chooch is obviously a legend now and became a fan favorite, but there were a lot of calls for Manuel to play Chris Coste more. Manuel always trusted Ruiz, and the pitchers even more so, but he never made the move. Had the Phillies panicked about Ruiz's hitting and looked for another catcher, who knows how the next couple of years of Phillies baseball would have played out?

The light-hitting Ruiz, who only hit four home runs during the regular season, took Garza deep and gave the Phils a 2–1 lead. After that, Garza locked in for a few innings. Fortunately for the Phillies, so did Jamie Moyer, who was matching Garza blow for blow. Moyer had not had a good postseason so far. He had a 13.50 ERA through his first two starts, but on this night, when the game probably started after his bedtime (sorry, Jamie), he did a job. The score remained 2–1 into the top of the sixth. B. J. Upton hit a one-out single up the middle, and, as he often did in this series, he stole second to put himself in scoring position with two outs for the dangerous, but struggling, Evan Longoria. With chants of "Eva! Eva! Eva!" filling the stadium—referring to the *Desperate Housewives* star, Eva Longoria—the Rays' third baseman lifted a ball to left field that would have *probably* been a home run on a hot summer night. It was not meant to be this night. Even though the camera operator gave everyone back home a heart attack, the wind did its part in really knocking the ball down, and Burrell was able to haul it in on the warning track. This all led to the famous shot of Jamie Moyer sticking out his tongue while walking off the field—an iconic shot.

Garza was in cruise control—that is, until the sixth, when the Phillies *finally* showed some of their thump they were known for. Utley started it off with one of his patented rockets into the right-field seats to give the Phillies a 3–1 lead. Ryan Howard then joined the party with his first home run in the postseason to give them a 4–1 lead. Citizens Bank Park was on fire, the big boys finally woke up, and it was time to cruise to a 2–1 series lead in the World Series. Welp, the Rays had other plans.

Instead of handing the game over to his bullpen, Manuel let Moyer start the top of the seventh inning. This is where the ole Negadelphia started to creep back in—it was beginning to feel like a loss. The inning started with Carl Crawford attempting a bunt up the first-base line. Moyer shot off the mound, looking spry for a forty-five-year-old. In one fell swoop, he corralled the baseball and flipped it from his glove to Howard at first base. He was out, and the replay showed he was out, but Tom Hallion called him safe. Challenges during this time were not allowed, so the Phillies just had to live with it. It was a miracle play by Moyer and one that we would be talking about for a long time around here had this one gone a different way. Navarro followed up with a double to set up second and third with no outs for Gabe Gross. Manuel left in Moyer to face the lefty and Gross promptly grounded out to bring the run home but give the Phillies an out. That was it for Moyer, who delivered his best start of the postseason, one that every kid around this area dreams of. In to replace Moyer was Chad Durbin, who induced a groundball by Jason Bartlett that made the game 4–3, and then Scott Eyre was brought in to eventually get Iwamura to strike out swinging. All things considered, a potential disaster was avoided. The Phillies still had the lead with their two horses set to take down the eighth and ninth.

B. J. Upton was becoming a thorn in the Phillies' side. With Madson, who had allowed one earned run up until this point, on to lock down the eighth, Upton singled up the middle. Madson got Peña to strike out, which brought up Longoria. On the first pitch, Upton stole second base. With the righty up, stealing third becomes that much more advantageous. Upton did just that, stealing third on the next pitch, and the errant throw by Ruiz got past Feliz and allowed the Rays center fielder to score. Talk about creating a run all by yourself. All of a sudden, Game Three was tied.

It looked like the Phillies were going to take the lead right back in the bottom half of the eighth. Werth drew a leadoff walk. With the lefty Howell now in to face both Utley and Howard back to back, Werth stole second. On a 3-2 pitch, with Utley just looking to put together a productive at-bat, he couldn't lay off a slider from Howell and struck out. Werth was still stuck

2008—"WORLD CHAMPIONS, WORLD F%$&IN' CHAMPIONS"

at second base. He wouldn't be stuck at second base for long. With Howard now up, Howell pulled off an inside move to pick off Werth at second base—a crucial base-running mistake. Then Howell struck out Howard to finish off the frame. Feels like a loss! Remember when it was 4–1 and Utley and Howard went back to back?

After Romero worked a clean ninth, it was on to the bottom half of the inning. The defensive replacement for Burrell, Eric Bruntlett, led off the inning. He got drilled in the leg by Howell, which gave the Phils a baserunner. Rays manager Joe Maddon replaced Howell with Grant Balfour, who probably should have just started the inning. Balfour was sort of like Garza, highly emotional on the mound. If he was on, he was lights out. If he was off, things could get interesting. Balfour yanked a fastball to Victorino who was trying to get a bunt down to get Bruntlett in scoring position. Thankfully, Balfour took care of that himself as the ball cascaded to the backstop. Navarro fielded it and fired down to second base. The throw ate up Jason Bartlett, which allowed Bruntlett to get to third base with no outs. Okay, now we're back in business. Maddon decides to walk the bases loaded to create a force play at all bags. He even decided to get Ben Zobrist an infielder's glove so that he would have five infielders and only two guys in the outfield. He was pulling out all the stops to prevent that run from coming home. Up walked the guy who turning into a legend in Philadelphia, Carlos Ruiz. Talk about a scenario we all created in our minds as kids: "Bases loaded, bottom of the ninth, in the World Series—what is X going to do?" On a 2-2 pitch, Ruiz placed the perfect swinging bunt up the third base line; Longoria did about all he could do, but the flip home sailed over Navarro's head. The Phillies, at 1:47 a.m. and after flirting with disaster, took Game Three.

There was no time to rest after Game Three, as the Phillies and Rays were back at it later that same day, this time without an hour-and-a-half rain delay. On the mound for the Phils was their innings eater, Joe Blanton. Average Joe had one job—give the team six strong innings and a chance to close it out tomorrow night with their young ace, Cole Hamels, on the mound. It turns out, Blanton would do more than that.

To say the 2008 World Series was not an umpiring clinic would be an understatement, and that was evident again in the first inning. With runners at first and third after a leadoff double by Jimmy Rollins (who was starting to heat up just in time), a fly ball to right by Werth to move Rollins into scoring position, and a walk to Utley, Howard stepped to the dish. He hit a little dribbler back to Rays starter Andy Sonnanstine, who at first correctly looked back Rollins, who was a little too far off the third-base bag. The problem was, Sonnanstine, who clearly hadn't worked on his fielding in a while (or his PFPs for those counting at home), took too long to throw the ball to Longoria covering the bag, so Rollins was able to dive underneath the third baseman's tag. Did Rollins avoid the tag though? Both replay and Longoria's explosion on the field would say no, but third-base umpire Tim Welke (our guy), said yes, and the Phillies caught an early break. The bases were now loaded with only one out for Pat Burrell. Could this finally be the moment where they break through with runners in scoring position? The Phillies up until this point in the series were 2-for-33 with runners in scoring position. Talk about excruciating. The Burrell at-bat was a step in the right direction; he worked a walk to give the Phils an early 1–0 lead, but then Victorino grounded out in a comebacker to Sonnanstine, and Pedro Feliz flew out to center field. The Phillies offense, once again, couldn't break through.

However, they would have another opportunity in the third inning, as Utley reached base on an error by Iwamura. Howard followed that up with a single, putting a runner in scoring position. It wasn't looking good for the average with runners in scoring position that was starting to dominate this series when both Burrell and Victorino popped out to the shortstop. Thankfully, to help calm peoples' nerves, Feliz drove a ball through the 5-6 hole into left field to score Utley from second base. The ballgame was now 2–0, with an opportunity for the Phillies to blow this one wide open. Ruiz followed up the Feliz single with one of his own to load the bases for Joe Blanton. Understandably so, Blanton fouled out, and the Phils left 'em loaded again.

Blanton was cruising through three and even racking up some strikeouts that were uncommon for him—he ended with seven on the night. His only blemishes? Two solo shots. One of them was delivered by Carl Crawford in the top of the fourth to make it a 2–1 game.

You know the old saying "better late than never?" That was starting to become the case with the Phils' big thumper in the middle, Ryan Howard. Howard was continuing to have a power outage in the postseason and hadn't hit a big fly until Game Three of the World Series. The tide was certainly turning just in time for the Phils. In the bottom of fourth, Rollins reached on what would have been a tough play by the second baseman, Iwamura, but the ball ate him up, and Rollins was aboard safely at first base. Werth drew a

2008—"WORLD CHAMPIONS, WORLD F%$&IN' CHAMPIONS"

walk next to set up the Phillies, once again, with a pesky runners-in-scoring-position situation. Not a hot start yet again for that stat, as Utley immediately struck out. But the just-in-time power surge by Howard was officially here as he stayed back on a Sonnanstine offering and drove a home run into a sea of red in the left-field seats. The score was now 5–1.

The second solo shot of the night happened in the next half inning, as Eric Hinske—not sure if he'll factor in to end of this series at all—launched a home run off Blanton to deep center field. Still, it was with two outs, and Blanton was able to retire the side with the next batter.

Game Four of the World Series went from just your regular old World Series beatdown to the stuff of legends in the bottom of the fifth. With two outs, and Edwin Jackson—an Immaculate Grid legend—now on the mound for the Rays, Blanton stepped to the dish. Average Joe didn't just bring his glove and spikes to ole ballyard today; it turns out, he brought some lumber too. Blanton got a 2-1 fastball from Jackson and somehow didn't miss it, as he hit a home run. Blanton said after the game that he hadn't hit a home run since high school, and—a fun fact for your local Quizzo games—it is still the last home run hit in the World Series by a pitcher and could very well be the very last. Joe Blanton, forever in the record books. Who woulda thunk?

Blanton had to remember that he's a pitcher, not a hitter, and with a 6–2 lead now, a shutdown inning to keep a stranglehold on the Rays in the top of the sixth was imperative. Blanton loaded the bases, but against what would be his last batter of the evening, he recorded his seventh strikeout by getting Dioner Navarro swinging. The Joe Blanton game—he pitched so well that Rays manager Joe Maddon was bitching to the umpires that he had some sticky substance on his hat. Grow up, Joe!

The game truly turned into a rout in the bottom of the eighth. After a combination of Durbin, Eyre, and Madson pitched the seventh and eighth innings, Jayson Werth popped a two-run home run that followed a double by Rollins. Just for good measure and to really ram home how done this game was, Ryan Howard launched his second home run of the night—a two-run shot off of Trever Miller.

That sound you heard was dads all over the Delaware Valley telling anyone within range that they should save some runs for tomorrow. It was now 10–2, Phillies. Blanton did his job in more ways than one, the Phillies capitalized one some mistakes by the Rays (and some fortunate umpiring), and their back-to-back MVPs had finally arrived. They were one win away from winning the World Series.

What happened next is so Philadelphia it almost hurts.

The city was ready; the players were ready. In a way, Game Five felt like a fait accompli. Everyone could feel in their bones that with Hamels on the mound in front of a crowd that hadn't witnessed a loss yet in this postseason October 27 was going to be the night that Philadelphia was finally a world champion. On a chilly evening with rain in the forecast, the young lefty who was already 4–0 with a 1.55 ERA in the postseason took the hill. He made quick work of the Rays, setting them down one-two-three. Much like Game One, the Phillies were able to get to Rays starter Scott Kazmir early. He served up a one-out walk, his first of six on the night, to Jayson Werth, then he hit Chase Utley and struck out Ryan Howard. Burrell worked a two-out walk to bring up Victorino with the bases loaded. The Phillies entered Game Five 6-for-47 with runners in scoring position, which was good for 12th lowest in World Series history Could they finally make the Rays pay? They could. Victorino smoked a single down the left-field line to plate Werth and Utley, and the Phils had the early 2–0 lead. Citizens Bank Park was rabid in anticipation.

Both pitchers settled into a rhythm after this, until the top of the fourth. If you thought the Phillies' numbers with runners in scoring position were bad, the production the Rays were getting from their two sluggers, Carlos Peña and Evan Longoria, was worse. The duo entered the game 0-for-29 in the Series! They finally got off the schneid in the fourth inning of Game Five, with Peña doubling off the wall in right and Longoria following it up with a base hit just past the outstretched arms of Rollins into center field to cut the Phillies' lead to 2–1.

The first portion of Game Five was a whirlwind of emotions for the Philadelphia sports fan. Not only were they dealing with the elements but also, with two outs and Hamels up to bunt to get Carlos Ruiz into scoring position, our ace got hit in the hand on an attempt. He ended up being fine, but what more were we supposed to deal with on this night?

This is where the game started to get out of control. The rain started to come down in the fourth and had reached monsoon levels by the sixth. However, Major League Baseball had ruled not suspend the game—yet.

2008—"WORLD CHAMPIONS, WORLD F%$&IN' CHAMPIONS"

> Let's be honest here—we all felt like Major League Baseball was just waiting and begging the Rays to tie this game up so they didn't have to deal with any controversy. This isn't confirmed, but I believe we could all see Bud Selig smiling when the Rays eventually did tie it up. Again, the whole thing was so Philadelphia it hurts. For you younger kids who have grown up in the new era of Philadelphia sports where you have a World Series and two Super Bowls, it's hard to wrap your head around how agonizing this was. It had been 25 years! 25! And it was going down like this. This portion of the rant is over.

With two outs, B. J. Upton hit a groundball up the middle that Rollins had gotten to no less than ten thousand times during his career. We've seen him make this play in his sleep. The problem? He was essentially playing on the baseball version of an ice hockey rink. Given the conditions, Rollins was unable to get to the baseball, and the speedy Upton was on first base on a field that no one could get a grip on. Given this, Upton stole second and the now-alive Peña singled into left field to score him. After all that and with some help from Major League Baseball, the Rays tied up Game 5. For the first time in the history of the World Series, and another sick joke for Philadelphia sports fans, the game was suspended. We couldn't even win it normally!

The Phillies were furious. Manuel declined to comment after the game due to his rage, and the team was spewing in the clubhouse. Hamels was most certainly done after only throwing 75 pitches. It had the feeling like Major League Baseball let the Rays back into this series.

So all of Philadelphia sat and waited and waited. The two teams were unable to play the next night as the rain was unrelenting, which meant that they would have to resume Game Five two nights later on October 29.

What transpired was maybe the oddest way to consume a game of this magnitude. The old adage in baseball is that it is a marathon, not a sprint. That goes for the regular season and sometimes, the game itself. Well, this was the opposite. This was a sprint to the finish line—four innings to determine if Philadelphia was to be world champions or if it was back to Tampa for Game Six. Oh, the drama! I'm sure FOX Television was thrilled. In what turned out to be the debate of the city, Manuel decided to have Geoff Jenkins lead off the bottom of the sixth inning, pinch-hitting for Hamels. It sure seemed like every Phillie truly had a moment in this postseason, and for Jenkins, who was brought here as a platoon option only to have Werth take the job and run with it, this moment was his. He scorched a ball off Grant Balfour into the right-center-field gap for a leadoff double. With Jenkins pumping his fists and screaming toward the dugout, Citizens Bank Park was alive again. Rollins was up next; he bunted Jenkins over to third base, which brought up Jayson Werth. Werth got jammed but still got enough of the ball to push it into center field toward no man's land. Rays second baseman Iwamura sprinted out and Upton came in, but the second baseman was going to have to make the play. The ball was hit just weakly enough that Iwamura couldn't turn around to grab it, so he opted to try to haul it in Willie Mays–style. He couldn't, the ball slipped by Iwamura, Jenkins sprinted home from third, and the Phillies took a 3–2 lead.

That would be it for the Phils that inning, but you could *feel* it. They weren't going to be denied this night, and with the bridge to Lidge now in, this one was over. That is, until the player who the Phillies were thinking about taking over Chase Utley, Rocco Baldelli, hit a shocking one-out home run against bullpen ace Ryan Madson. A once fervent Citizens Bank Park had suddenly fallen quiet. The Rays would not go away.

Things went from bad to worse when Jason Bartlett followed up the home run with a single. J. P. Howell bunted Bartlett over, and in an instant the Rays had a runner in scoring position for the top of their order against J. C. Romero. In four innings that might as well have been decided by the defense of the second basemen, Iwamura shot a ball up the middle that looked like it had a shot to tie the game. Utley sprinted over and was able to get it, but he knew he would unlikely get the ball to first base in time to get to the speedy Iwamura. So what did the instinctual Utley do? He knew that with two outs Bartlett was going on anything, so he probably wasn't prepared for what Utley was going to do. Utley faked the throw to first, selling it just enough so that Bartlett put his head down to go home. In one of the most heads-up plays in World Series history, Utley recoiled and, all in one motion, threw a strike home on a bounce to Ruiz to nab Bartlett. Once again, coaches all over the Delaware Valley were fawning. The score remained tied.

In the bottom of the seventh, in what would be his only World Series hit and his last at-bat as a Phillie, Pat Burrell led off the inning with a 400-foot double off the left-center-field wall. Victorino followed that up by getting pinch-runner Eric Bruntlett over to third base. That left Game Five in the hands of Pedro Feliz. Remember when we said that every member of the roster seemingly had his moment in this postseason? It was Feliz's turn now. He smoked a single up the middle off of the submarine pitching Chad Bradford to give the Phillies their fourth and final run.

Romero held the lead with a scoreless eighth, the Phillies couldn't add any insurance runs in the bottom of the inning, and in the blink of an eye it was on to the top of the ninth. Mr. Perfect was looking to write his final chapter.

> I know this whole game has been written in a bit of a woe-is-me tone, but this is how it was at the time. It really would have been so Philadelphia to have Lidge blow his perfect season with a chance to win the World Series. Fans thought, *This is going well . . . too well*, and they were waiting for the other shoe to drop. Nevertheless, this ended up not being the case.

After waiting for 25 years and extra two days, Philadelphia was ready to be world champions. All Lidge had to do was do what he had done the entire season—close it out. The inning started well, as he struck out Evan Longoria. Dioner Navarro, however, followed with a single to right field. Fernando Perez pinch-ran for the catcher and promptly stole second base. All at once, a runner was in scoring position for Ben Zobrist. On a 2-1 pitch, Lidge hung a slider, and Zobrist didn't miss it. The problem for him and the Rays was that the ball was hit right at Jayson Werth in right field. So the stage was set: two outs, top of the ninth, Lidge on the mound, and Eric Hinske up.

After a meeting from Rich Dubee and the catcher, where they all agreed to *not* throw Hinske a fastball, Lidge toed the rubber to work against his final hitter of the 2008 season. What a whirlwind it had been for Lidge—from a hot-shot reliever, to allowing one of the most memorable home runs in postseason history, to being given up on by the team that drafted him, to a trade to Philadelphia and one batter away from a perfect 48-for-48 season and an ever-elusive world championship.

Hinse fouled the first pitch slider up the first-base line. For a crowd waiting with bated breath, it looked like a possible slow roller to Howard for an easy putout, but it was not meant to be. Hinske then went around on a checked swing on the next nasty slider from Lidge to quickly make the count 0-2. The crowd was at a fever pitch. Lidge was, as he later described "gripping the baseball to throw the nastiest slider I could," he released the ball. At 9:58 p.m. EST, Hinske went down on the third of three straight sliders from Lidge, making Philadelphia world champions for the first time since 1983 (and 1980 for the franchise).

It was over.

Lidge dropped to his knees and screamed, "Oh my God!" Howard came in and tackled him to the ground and the dogpile ensued. This team that overcame so much over the last couple of years had finally done it. The homegrown stars, the out-of-nowhere signings, and the perfect acquisitions had all come together in perfect harmony. The journey was complete.

The great Phil Sheridan wrote the following in the *Philadelphia Inquirer* the next day:

> Remember 1964 and Black Friday and Joe Carter, because they're all just a little further away and a little less menacing than they were a week ago. Remember the 10,000 losses, because they will make this one win all the better. Remember the other uncountable losses: the loved ones buried in their red caps and Eagles sweatshirts, the fathers and mothers, spouses and friends who didn't make it to this day. Even the die-hards die in time. Remember the older loved one you weren't sure would live to see it. Make a call. Give out hugs. Bask in this with the people who matter the most. Remember Tug and Whitey. Remember Vuke and the Pope. Remember it all, savor every moment.
>
> After all, you waited forever and a day.

Perfection.

Two days later, on Halloween no less, the city of Philadelphia got to show their appreciation to the team that they fell in love with over the last month. Gone were the days of questioning Charlie Manuel, gone were the days of ripping Rollins for not running or calling us front-runners, gone were the days of people saying the Phillies were too inconsistent offensively to win a World Series—everyone was together and celebrating as one. On a sun-soaked day, somewhere between one million and two million people took over the streets of Philadelphia to get a glimpse of their champions.

Pat Burrell and his dog, Elvis, led the parade on a chair fit for a king. It had to be sentimental for Burrell. He had been through it all in Philadelphia, from being the number one pick with the hopes and expectations of the franchise on his shoulders, to really struggling and falling out of the limelight and giving way to Utley, Rollins, and Howard to carry the mantle as saviors of the franchise. It all culminated in his last year as a Phillie, being able to call himself a world champion. Leading the parade just felt right.

The parade started at 20th and Market Streets, then went through City Hall and eventually turned down Broad Street toward its final stop at the sports complex and Citizens Bank Park. As players have described it, there was a sea of red, with the crowds just expanding and expanding. The whole city, seemingly, was waiting for them at the sports complex, including a young Jack Fritz.

The team then went inside a sold-out Citizens Bank Park and spoke to the crowd. One thought echoed throughout the team that day: *This won't be the last time we're taking a parade down Broad Street in front of you millions of fans.* Of course, the most memorable speech from that day was by Chase Utley, as the soft-spoken second baseman, who *might* have had some liquid courage, started off his speech by saying what everyone was saying and thinking for the past two days: "World champions . . . World f***ing champions!" Citizens Bank Park melted, and so did the producers of local TV and radio as they had to scramble to dump it.

Some would say that was a perfect day to cap off what was a perfect season.

Now, the big question was, could they do it again?

#11

POST-2008 YEARS— NO CIGARS

2009: OH, SO CLOSE

After the dust had settled and all the confetti had fallen, believe it or not, life went on, and there was another season to get ready for.

The first thing the Phillies had to do was name a new general manager. It was always the plan that Pat Gillick would go out on top. After the Phillies won the World Series, Gillick officially retired, and the search was on for his replacement. Easily enough, the Phillies decided to not even leave their own building to hire the man who would replace Gillick. They tapped Phillie legacy Ruben Amaro Jr. to take over the position. It was a culminating move for Amaro, who was the bat boy for the 1980 team, played on the '93 team, and won the World Series as an assistant general manager for this Phillies squad.

His first order of business was what to do with left field. The longest-tenured Phillie, Pat Burrell, was set to hit free agency. Given they hadn't extended him earlier in his career, this felt like the end for the Phillies and Burrell. Still, the team had to replace 30ish home runs, a good on-base guy, and the protection for Ryan Howard in the lineup. Plan A was to trade for the versatile former University of Pennsylvania Quaker Mark DeRosa. The great Jim Salisbury broke that news back at the Winter Meetings in December 2008 that the Phillies were close to acquiring DeRosa in a three-team deal that would have sent Jake Peavy to the Cubs and DeRosa to the Phillies. With the deal falling through, the Phillies had to turn their attention elsewhere. Plan B was to sign thirty-seven-year-old Raúl Ibañez, which the Phillies did, at three years and $30 million. Although the fit wasn't perfect, given his age and adding another lefty bat in the lineup, the Phillies just needed production from that spot, and Ibañez ultimately provided that.

With that, the Phillies entered into the 2009 season with essentially the same roster that had just won them the World Series the year before. That offseason, Amaro Jr. handed out extensions to Jayson Werth, Ryan Howard, Cole Hamels, Ryan Madson, and Greg Dobbs and re-signed Scott Eyre and Jamie Moyer. They were running it back, with the addition of Ibañez, and banking on their experience being enough to put them back on top again as world champs. They were *that* close.

The biggest story in spring training that year was the health of their ace. Cole Hamels pitched more innings in 2008 than he did in his entire minor-league career, and when he showed up to spring training, he felt it. In what would end up being an ominous sign for his 2009 season, Hamels had a sore elbow; after attempting to pitch through it, he was sent back to Philadelphia to get it checked out. Ultimately, the now twenty-five-year-old didn't need Tommy John surgery, but he would miss the start of the 2009 season, which meant that Brett Myers was going to make his third straight Opening Day start. Still, the Phillies headed north in pretty good condition as they looked to be the first repeat World Series champions since the Yankees in the late 1990s and early 2000s.

The Phillies had to mix in some baseball with all the pomp and circumstance to start the season. It was a pretty wild thing to watch unfold. On one hand, you're watching the team get paraded around like kings (they were), and the next minute, players had to try to win baseball games that mattered. On Opening Night, the Phillies raised the championship banner and had a ceremony on the field, two nights later they had commemorative T-shirts to give out, and finally, they had the ring ceremony before the third game of the series. Now, it's normal to have a lot going on after winning a title, and it is hard to flip the switch and get locked in, *especially* given that there were 162 games that had to be played. The Phillies subsequently dropped the first two games of the season and salvaged game three with a monster comeback. Trailing 10–3 in the bottom of the seventh, the Phillies scored eight runs to steal one from the Braves and show Phillies fans that some of the magic was still there.

What happened next, however, would change the Phillies forever.

The upcoming road trip looked to be nondescript for the Phillies, and I'm sure players looked forward to it after all the commotion that had come with the opening series with the Braves. They split the first two games of the series out in Colorado and were tied up 5–5 in the top of the ninth against Rockies closer Huston Street (a name to remember for later in the year). Pedro Feliz led off the inning with a double; he was then moved to third base on a bunt by Chris Coste. Manuel summoned pinch-hitter extraordinaire and recent postseason hero Matt Stairs off the bench. Instead of a boring ole sacrifice fly, Stairs went big fly to give the Phillies a 7–5 lead. Harry Kalas of course was on the call and gave Stairs his patented "outta here!" as the ball flew out of Coors Field.

Little did we know that would be Kalas's last home-run call. With the team in Washington preparing for a day game against the Nationals, Kalas collapsed in his broadcast booth while preparing for the game. After being rushed to a nearby hospital, he was pronounced dead at seventy-three years old. It was a gut punch, and everyone remembers where they were when it happened. The late great David Montgomery said it best: "There are no words to express the sadness that the entire Phillies organization is feeling with the news of Harry's passing. Harry was the voice of the Phillies, but he was also our heart and soul."

The Phillies players lost the man who had called all of their big moments, the broadcasters lost their teammate, and we all lost a friend. It was a tough day. The broadcasters were choked up throughout. The players, led by Shane Victorino, found someone to go buy them cigarettes to light up before the game in honor of Harry, and the team won one for the Philadelphia sports giant.

Phillies baseball was never going to be the same. When they returned home, a funeral service was held at the ballpark, with thousands of fans showing up and a bunch of members from the Phillies organization giving their eulogies to Harry. With heavy hearts and the HK patch now on their jersey and in the outfield, the Phillies had to do what Harry would have wanted: get back to baseball.

> Obviously, if you read the Harry chapter earlier in this book you can tell how much he meant to all of us. He was the best. I remember I was in an assembly in high school when he passed, and when I eventually heard the news, it truly was like I had lost a friend. I think a lot of people felt that way. I'm so glad he was able to get to call a World Series win before leaving us. Had they not been able to do it and then he passed, it would have been so much worse. While everyone was upset, I think many felt some happiness that he was able to call one before he left. Now, the team just had to win number two for H.K.

Jim Bunning is fifth in team history with 23 shutouts, despite playing just six seasons in Philadelphia. Just ahead of him is teammate and fellow Hall of Famer Chris Short (24), who pitched 14 seasons with the Fightins. *(Getty Images)*

The Phillies were 16–8 in Steve Carlton's 24 starts in 1981. Carlton posted a 2.61 ERA in the 16 wins and a 1.98 ERA in the eight losses. *(Getty Images)*

Mike Schmidt, the franchise leader in offensive and defensive WAR, runs scored, home runs, RBIs, MVPs, and Gold Gloves, had a hidden talent: Wheels. He's quietly 15th in franchise history in stolen bases (174). *(Getty Images)*

Manny Trillo's six RBIs earned the second baseman series MVP honors, but Gary Maddox got carried off the field, after his extra-inning heroics in game five of the 1980 NLCS. *(Getty Images)*

Tug McGraw's iconic celebration after securing the final out (with the bases loaded) of the 1980 World Series. *(Getty Images)*

First baseman Pete Rose and manager Dallas Green, both new to their posts in 1979, celebrating the first championship in franchise history. *(Getty Images)*

"In our clubhouse, if you called somebody a psychopathic idiot, it was a pretty good compliment." —John Kruk, from his book *I Ain't an Athlete, Lady* (Getty Images)

Lenny Dykstra batted .313/.450/.729 during the 1993 postseason. His 1.179 postseason OPS is the highest in franchise history (minimum 50 plate appearances). *(Getty Images)*

Darren "Dutch" Daulton. Women loved him, men wanted to be him. *(Getty Images)*

Mitch Williams's wild delivery was more effective than you might remember: his 102 saves are the fourth-most in team history. *(Getty Images)*

Curt Schilling is arguably the greatest postseason pitcher of all-time. Only three pitchers have tossed complete game shutouts in the World Series since Schill's Game Five blanking of the Blue Jays in 1993. *(Getty Images)*

Phils fans letting Barry Bonds know what they thought of his pursuit of Babe Ruth's home run title in 2006. *(Getty Images)*

Ryan Howard's iconic bat point, modeled after Jim Thome, who learned it from Charlie Manuel. *(Flickr: Matthew Staubmuller)*

Howard soared past Mike Schmidt's single season franchise home run mark in 2006, clubbing ten more than Schmidt's 48 in 1980. *(Getty Images)*

Cole Hamels, the other lefty, is second to just Steve Carlton amongst southpaws in Phillies career pWAR (64.6, 42.0). *(Kevin Durso)*

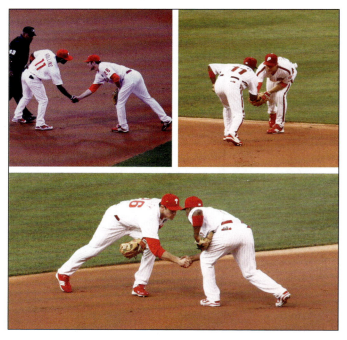

Part of the best double-play combination in team history, Chase Utley and Jimmy Rollins, together from 2003–14, sealed the bond with a handshake before each game. *(Kevin Durso)*

Phinally! The city of Philadelphia was in a major sports championship drought that dated back to 1983 . . . until Brad Lidge closed out Game Five of the 2008 World Series. *(Getty Images)*

World f*cking champions! The city's first championship parade in 25 years. In the background, lunch specials were enjoyed by many. *(Getty Images)*

Through the 2024 season, Cliff Lee and current ace Zack Wheeler had the lowest career WHIP of any Phillies starters since 1930 (1.089, 1.031; min. 100 starts). *(Flickr: Keith Allison)*

Roy Halladay's short-but-sweet stretch of brilliance in 2011 and 2012 (40–16, 2.40 ERA) was enough to cement the right hander as one of the most beloved players in franchise history. *(Flickr: SD Dirk)*

The Phillie Phanatic phlashes the CBP crowd atop the visitors' dugout. This is the only angle we are legally able to display. *(David Christ)*

Philadelphia Phil and Phillis live on in Storybook Land amusement park in Egg Harbor Township, New Jersey. Between them, two sets of Vet Stadium chairs. Photo Credit: Storybook Land. *(Storybook Land)*

Mired in a 1-for-19 slump to start the 2022 postseason, fan favorite Rhys Hoskins opted for the celebratory bat slam after going deep in a Game Three victory over the Braves in the NLDS. *(Getty Images)*

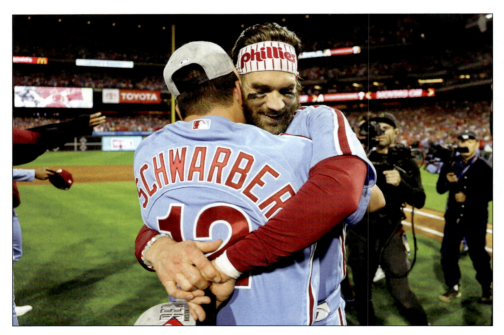

Bryce Harber and Kyle Schwarber embrace after defeating the Atlanta Braves in Game Four of the 2023 Divisional Series. *(Getty Images)*

The Trea Turner standing ovation in 2023, subject of the Netflix film, *The Turnaround*, is just another example of Phillies fans being the best in baseball. *(Getty Images)*

Prelude to a Schwarbomb. Kyle Schwarber holds the record for most lead-off home runs in a single season (15; 2024). *(Getty Images)*

Above: After a 4-1 win on May 11, 2025, Zack Wheeler held the lowest WHIP (1.023) of any Phillie during the Live Ball Era. The only player with a better mark was George McQuillan (1.020), who pitched his final game for the Phillies in 1910. *(Getty Images)*

Left: Aaron Nola led all pitchers in WAR in 2018 (9.7; 17–6, 2.37 ERA) and still finished just third in NL Cy Young voting. *(Getty Images)*

In July of 2024, John Kincade ranked thirty-one-year-old Bryce Harper as the sixth greatest Philadelphia athlete of the twenty-first century. Plenty of time to move up the list. *(Getty Images)*

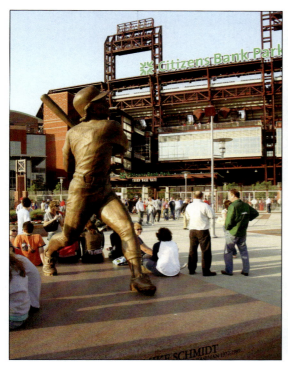 

(Michael Kirk) *(Flickr: Wallyg)*

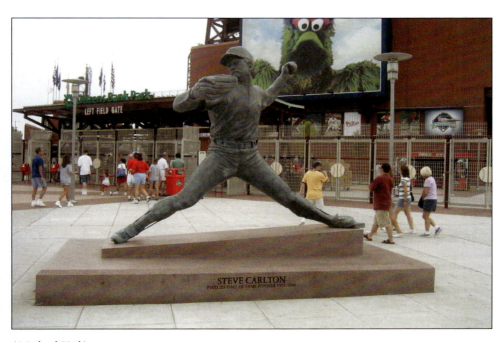

(Michael Kirk)

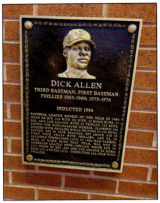 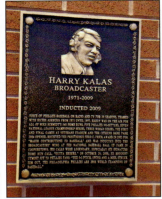 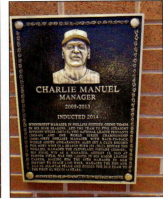

(Photographs courtesy of Matt Albertson)

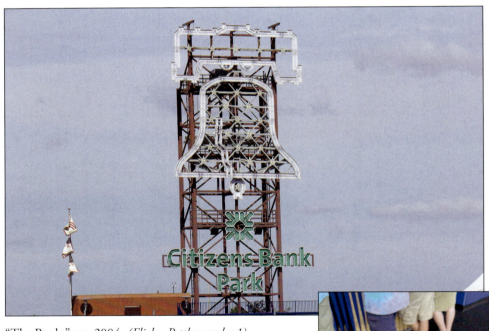

"The Bank," est. 2004. *(Flickr: Pettlesnumber1)*

Photographed and consumed by Kevin Reavy at CBP.

The Phillies finished April with a winning record for the second straight year, and while that shouldn't be a big deal, for this team it was. They were doing what you expected this team to do: mash. However, problems were starting to show with two of their stalwarts. Obviously, when a team plays deep into October, it's harder to bounce back the next year, *especially* for pitchers. That was starting to show with both Cole Hamels and Brad Lidge. Neither looked like last year's version of himself. In fact, both left April with the same ERA—7.27. Was it going to be a *thing* for the rest of the year? We shall see.

In May, the Phils made their trip to the White House, and President Obama quipped, "What an unbelievable run it was, full of come-from-behind wins by an underdog team that loved to prove the prognosticators wrong. And so we share something in common there, because nobody thought I was going to win either." Rollins asked him where the basketball court was, to which the former president replied, "I got a foot on you." It was a kickoff to the Phillies' upcoming 10-game road trip and the end of the early-season distractions that seemed to plague this team. This was a .500 ballclub before the road trip, and it had some work to do to get back to the prior level of play.

Thankfully, players were starting to come alive.

The Phillies started that road trip 6–1 before a three-game set in New York against the Yankees. The Yankees loaded up in the 2009 offseason. With a disappointing 2008 season that saw them miss the playoffs for the first time since 1993 and say goodbye to the old Yankee Stadium, the organization wasn't about to let similar disappointment happen at new Yankee Stadium. So it spent, and spent, and spent to try to give an aging core a shot at a title. In that offseason, the Yankees signed CC Sabathia, Mark Teixeira, and A. J. Burnett and traded for Nick Swisher—in total they shelled out almost $430 million in contracts that offseason. It was truly World Series or bust in New York. That's why the series against the Yankees at the end of May had a decent amount of intrigue. Added to the intrigue was the Phillies' shortstop once again throwing out one of his now famous predictions—although this time, it wasn't in a traditional sit-down interview. No, Rollins's latest prediction was courtesy of *Playboy*, where Rollins had a feature in the June issue. Rollins said, "The Fall Classic? I see our boys vs. the Yankees. They spent all that money. They've got to be there. We've got a title to defend, so we're going to be there." Before the series, one of the beat writers informed Yankees captain Derek Jeter of those comments, to which he replied, "Really? Hopefully he's right. That would mean we're there. I'd take any World Series." After all, Jeet, it's been what? Five full seasons since the Yankees have been in the World Series? What a disaster! Regardless, the stage was set for a possible World Series preview.

The Phillies met the match in more ways than one. They launched three home runs to win game one of the series and then closed it out with a thrilling 4–3 win in extra innings. All in all, it was an 8–2 road trip for the Phillies that saw them reclaim first place for good. The team that we had seen turn into October heroes seemed to have arrived.

The team stayed in first place ahead of another 10-game road trip, except this time it started out on the West Coast. This team was in the midst of tying the club record for road wins on the year and helped add to that with a series sweep of the Padres and a split in the NLCS rematch against the Dodgers. The Phillies closed out the road trip with taking two of three from the Mets up in New York.

A couple of things were starting to become evident with this Phillies club over a third of the way through the season. One, Raúl Ibañez was looking like a free-agent steal. Up until this point of the season, about 60 games, Ibañez was hitting .322 with a 1.051 OPS and 21 home runs. He would be placed on the injured list a few games later with a strained left groin that might have affected him for the rest of the season. After he returned, he only hit .232 with a .771 OPS. The starting staff was going to plague them all season long. Hamels seemed off; his ERA was north of 4.00 at this point of the year, and he didn't change much. Blanton was carrying an ERA in the mid-5.00s, and Moyer's ERA was over 6.00! Brett Myers was hurt and wasn't all that effective; when in there, his ERA was north of 4.50. It was bleak. On top of that, their ace closer was turning into a question mark as well, as Lidge's ERA was in the 7.00. Was it time to hand the reins over to Ryan Madson? The Phillies were evidently going to have to mash their way to victory, and for the most part they did. But with the trade deadline looming, first-year general manager Ruben Amaro Jr. was going to have to get creative in adding some starting pitching to this ballclub that clearly had a championship offense. Oh, and for some reason, this team, world-beaters on the road, couldn't win at home.

That continued after the Phils returned from another productive West Coast swing, as they lost eight games during a nine-game homestand against the Red Sox, Blue Jays, and Orioles—unbelievable. This isn't fact-checked and it could definitely be wrong, but the Phillies might have been the first team in the history of baseball to win the pennant with a better record on the road than at home. (Note that, during the editing process, our wonderful editors informed me that the 1948 Indians also did this. Still, the point remains.) The most notable thing that happened toward the end of June was that Jimmy Rollins and Charlie Manuel were in the news. Rollins was struggling big time at the plate, and it was starting to carry over into the field a little bit, as he made a mental gaffe in the series against the Rays. Rollins was hitting just .211 with a .254 OBP and a .582 OPS at this time in the season, which is obviously a far cry from his usual offensive numbers. Manuel decided it was time to give him a break. Charlie told reporters, "I want him to sit down. I want him to get away. I told him if he didn't want to, he doesn't have to take BP. I want him to just get away for a couple of days and sit and watch and hopefully just relax and try to get his thinking back and the way he feels and everything."[1] This was the value of Manuel; this wasn't a benching for a lack of hustle.

> A lot of the game has been lost due to analytics, and benching players is certainly one of them. In today's era, you don't bench one of your best players because it affects your win probability for that day; it's why Gabe Kapler never benched players. Sometimes you have to bench guys to get them right, and if it costs a few games, so be it. But analytics proponents never factor in getting the player back on track. Though one could not definitively prove the benching was the reason, Rollins turned back into the player he had been for a majority of his career. After this, he finished the year hitting .282 with an .828 OPS—he was Rollins again.

The Phillies ended the month of June 11–15, although almost miraculously still in first place.

Aah, July of 2009—also known as the month the Phillies remembered they were the still the defending World Series champs. With Rollins back to looking like himself, Ibañez and Lidge both off the IL, and a much easier schedule, it was get-right time, and get right they did. In total, they went 20–7 in the month, including a 19–3 stretch in the middle of July that included a 10-game winning streak. The beast had finally awaken and had also given this front office reason to add pieces to this core. The starting staff was still this team's biggest issue even during this stretch. They had called on the rookie Antonio Bastardo (what a throwback) to make some starts and even Rodrigo López, who really had nothing left by this point in his career. The Phillies had exhausted all the internal options; no one in the minor leagues was ready to come up and compete in a meaningful way. They were scrambling, and Amaro was attempting to make deals, but a starting pitcher hadn't pried loose just yet. The deadline was looming and he had to get creative. Given the current state of the rotation, Amaro probably needed two arms for the second half of the season and the postseason. Did the club have the farm system needed to offer pieces to trade partners for two moves? Probably not. So, Amaro threw a Hail Mary and called on a guy who was already getting his bust created in Cooperstown. Who was this mystery man? None other than the one and only Pedro Martínez.

On July 15, in the middle of their run and while half the team was at the All-Star game, the Phillies officially signed Martínez. He finished his last season with the Mets with an ERA over 5.50 and looked done, but Martínez still wanted to pitch, so he did what a couple others had done in previous years and sat out half the season waiting for the perfect opportunity. The Phillies, desperate for starting help, offered that opportunity. In his introductory press conference, Martínez said, "I might surprise you, I might not. But it's going to be really fun to find out." Inspiring!

With that, they were off. The Pedro Martínez show had come to Philadelphia—well sorta. Martíinez still had to ramp up. He likely wasn't going to be ready until mid-August, so Amaro still needed to get another arm to help his rotation at the July 31 trade deadline. The name everyone in Philadelphia, really on the Phillies, was clamoring for was Roy Halladay. Amaro in subsequent years has referred to Halladay as his white whale, and for good reason. Halladay was arguably the best pitcher in baseball during this time, and his Blue Jays team was going nowhere. A Halladay trade felt like the right thing for both parties. Halladay had been a great Blue Jay, and given that he was now thirty-two years old and had never pitched in a postseason game, Toronto owed it to him to trade him to a winner. The most likely fit was the Phillies, who had a World Series core and a gaping hole in the rotation. It truly felt like a match made in heaven.

> The town was on fire at the thought of adding Roy Halladay. Reporters like Jim Salisbury were heading to Toronto to follow the story from up there, the lede in almost every newspaper article during that time had something Halladay related, and heck, even the package it would take to get Halladay was out there. Kyle Drabek, Domonic Brown, and J. A.

> Happ—that was the deal; all Amaro had to do was pull the trigger. Aah, I can just hear the callers into WIP: "They're just prospects!" Regardless, the guy was a horse's horse. Without the trade happening yet, he already *felt* like a Phillie. Modell's (RIP) could already start printing the jersey. No way were the Phillies going to let the best pitcher in the game go elsewhere with the way this team was currently playing. The only thing at this time I could compare the Halladay craze to was the Terrell Owens craze in '04. The town was buzzing, and Amaro *had* to deliver us Halladay.

Even the most perfect matches don't work out; just look at every season of *The Bachelor* and *The Bachelorette*—"Darn, I really thought they were perfect for each other!" Ultimately, the Phillies decided not to pay the huge price that it would have cost to bring Halladay to Philadelphia, and they pivoted. The funny part is that they didn't pivot to some scrub—they pivoted to the guy who beat out Halladay for the American League Cy Young the year before. The town was just so fixated on Halladay that anyone but him wasn't good enough, however. As one rival executive described to Jim Salisbury of the *Inquirer* on the day of the trade, if Halladay was a Mercedes, Lee was a BMW.[2] Ultimately, instead of dealing Drabek, Dom Brown, and J. A. Happ for Halladay, they sent out Carlos Carrasco, Jason Knapp, Lou Marson, and Jason Donald to the Indians (at the time) for Cliff Lee and Ben Francisco. The best part? Even though a majority of the town might not have known who Cliff Lee was before the Fightins traded for him, they were about to get taken on one of the most fun rides of their life. It's funny how things work out.

> You wanna talk about stress? I was on a boat off the coast of Key West on a Boy Scout trip for about 10 days while this whole thing was going on. I got on that boat, with no cellphone at the time, *expecting* Roy Halladay to be a Phillie by the time I disembarked. Every morning, I'd wake up and beg one of my friends' dad to check his phone and let me know if they had traded for Halladay yet. Well, one morning, I woke up, got the dad to check his phone, and *bang!* the Phillies had made a trade—for Cliff Lee. I remember exactly where I was, checking his phone to make sure it was real. "They didn't get Roy Halladay?" The ocean was looking more and more enticing (I'm kidding)—how could they do this to me?

RING THE BELL

> In the end, it all worked out. I still remember being furious that they didn't get him and then waking up the day after Lee pitched a complete game against the Giants in his first start and thinking, *Maybe that Amaro guy knows what he's doing after all.* In my defense, I was just a fan back then, not an objective big-J writer guy like I am now just rooting for the storyline. You believe me, right? Right?

While the town was definitely deflated that the Phillies didn't trade for Halladay, they did get *somebody* who wasn't the Joe Blanton type. Amaro was all in, and he gave the Phillies another legit piece to head into October with to try to win back-to-back titles. The good news for the fans deflated about not getting Halladay is that Cliff Lee quickly won them over. In his first start out in San Francisco, Lee pitched a complete-game four-hitter, but that wasn't enough. He also singled, doubled, scored a run, and pitched 5 2/3 innings of no-hit baseball. "Who is this dude?" and "Halladay who?" Could be heard all throughout the Delaware Valley, and with that, the Cliff Lee experience was here for the remainder of the 2009 season.

August for the Phillies was the story of the two new starters, their older starters, and their closer. How real was Pedro Martínez? Was he a viable option for this team heading down the stretch run and even the playoffs? As for Cliff Lee, how good was he? In Cliff's case, he answered that in a big way. In his first five starts with the team, Lee went 5–0, threw two complete games, and allowed a *total* of three earned runs. Cliffmas came early for the Phillies (please clap). The Martínez situation was murky. With Martínez in the fold, Jamie Moyer was sent to the bullpen, in what Manuel described as the toughest decision of his managerial tenure. Moyer did not agree with the team on this and said that he felt misled when he signed his contract—he was promised he would start. Brett Myers was rehabbing from a torn labrum in his hip in his hometown of Jacksonville when the right-hander was out to dinner with friends and tripped out of his Cadillac Escalade and hurt his eye. Only this is not what Myers told the team; he said he was having a catch with his son and that caused the eye injury. Myers later fessed up and was on the comeback trail to Philadelphia. After famously not blowing a save in 2008, Brad Lidge had the most blown saves in baseball in 2009 with nine at this point in the season, and he was on his way to setting the all-time record for that category. Manuel was stuck; Lidge always pitched better with confidence, but how long can the manager stick with him?

He tried Madson earlier in the season, but that didn't work. Myers was falling out of cars. Although some suggested Pedro, he was just signed to help boost the rotation. Manuel really didn't have a choice but to ride his closer, regardless of how rocky it would get, but don't worry—Charlie had gotten a lot of suggestions from fans and media, so he was taking it all into consideration.

Two events near the end of August were noteworthy. One, with runners on first and second and no outs, it was looking like Brad Lidge was going to blow another save for the Phillies—until Jeff Francouer laced a ball toward the middle of the field. Phillies reserve infielder Eric Bruntlett was already moving in that direction because both runners were attempting to steal on the play. Bruntlett hauled in the lined shot, tagged second base, and then tagged the runner, Daniel Murphy, who was coming from first base, to create the first unassisted triple play to end a ballgame in baseball history. Second, and maybe most important, is that Ryan Howard's now legendary nickname was revealed for the first time at the end of this month. In speaking to reporters after a game in which Howard hit two home runs, Manuel said, "Yeah, that's why I call him The Big Piece," and the rest was history.[3]

The Phillies entered September with an eight-game lead in the division. They just had to play out the string and not lose the intensity as they looked to make it back to the World Series. In the first half of the month, the coolest two moments might have been both by Pedro Martínez. On September 3, he faced the guy who would end up winning his second straight Cy Young Award that year in Tim Lincecum. The two went pitch for pitch, as both went seven innings, but Pedro got the edge, as he only allowed one run and struck out nine. The Pedro Hail Mary was paying early dividends. Pedromania (no one called it that, but you get the point) reached its peak on *Sunday Night Baseball*, against the team that gave up on him; the thirty-seven-year-old fired eight shutout innings to top the flailing New York Mets. Through seven starts, Pedro's ERA was 2.87—it was going just about as well as the Phillies could have hoped. The other moment in September of '09 was Manuel testing out Madson in the closer's role again. Up until this point of the season, Madson had not fared much better than Lidge, given that he too had his own share of blown saves with six. However, Manuel gave him some leeway, and the early returns were solid, but not great. Piecing together the bullpen was Manuel's final task during the stretch run and before the postseason started.

On September 30, the '09 Phils completed the first mission on their journey back to the World Series, demolishing the Houston Astros to take home their third consecutive National League East title. With two outs in the ninth, Manuel summoned his imperfect closer Lidge to remind him who he was and who he could be. He didn't even break a sweat as a slow roller up the first-base line was all that was needed to end the ballgame. They celebrated, and probably exhaled, when it was all over. The coolest thing was an impromptu jog out to left field where the Harry Kalas memorial had been all season. The entire team shared a toast with H.K. that night.

It was a much different NL East run for the Phillies in this season. Instead of a frantic run at the end of the season to chase down the Mets, they were the ones that had to stay sharp and avoid the collapse. When you win the World Series the year before, there's always heightened expectations, and people expect you to play perfect like you did just a few months prior. It's borderline impossible in baseball, but *for the most part* the Phillies did it.

> I have a theory that everyone thinks their baseball team isn't good enough to get the job done until they're hoisting the trophy at the end of October. Seriously, talk to any baseball fan in the middle of the summer about whether their team is good or bad, and I guarantee you'll hear one of these age-old tripes: "They can't hit with runners in scoring position" or "The bullpen stinks; no way they'll hold up in October" or "They can't manufacture runs; all they do is hit solo home runs" or "They don't have enough starting pitching," like starting pitching is just abundant. However, in the case of the '09 Phillies, I got it. Heading into the postseason—and it was evident throughout the season—the Phillies had real flaws. No, it wasn't the nonsense about not being able to hit with runners in scoring position—no fan thinks their team can hit with runners in scoring position—but the bullpen was a legit concern. They still didn't have a set closer—the options were shaky at best, as this was not last year's bullpen. On the starting side, Lee had been about as good as advertised, but Hamels never fully found his footing during the regular season, J. A. Happ was a godsend for this team but was a rookie, Blanton was average, and then there was Pedro, who was a total wild card. Finally, the team in general fluctuated between brilliant and maddening all year long. I don't think anyone had any idea which team would show up in the postseason, but nevertheless it was go-time, and here they were.

COLORADO HIGH

Oh, great, the team that had swept the Phillies just two years prior on their own trip to the World Series—surely they wouldn't let that happen again, right? Even though the Phillies won this series 3–1, it was pretty neck and neck and did require some heroics from a couple of the Phillies superstars.

Cliff Lee was the first such superstar. Even though he was semishaky coming down the stretch run (a 5.59 ERA in September), ole Clifton Phifer Lee gave the fans a nice preview of what their next month was going to be like, as he tossed a complete game six-hitter in his first-ever postseason start. It was an interesting call by Manuel. Hamels was a World Series hero less than a year before, and it's not like Lee was lighting the world on fire heading into the postseason. Was this just a little bit of fire underneath Hamels to get him going? One could only hope. Either way, behind a masterpiece by Lee, the Phillies took Game One, 5–1.

For as easy breezy as Game One was, Game Two was not. The story of the game was decision-making by Charlie Manuel. Hamels could only go five innings and then immediately left the stadium because his wife, Heidi, was giving birth to their first son. Was Hamels distracted? Who knows? This was, however, when Manuel started going a bit nuts. He pitched both J. A. Happ and Blanton, two guys who might have been in line to start Game Three of the series, during the middle portion of the game, and in total the Phils used 20 players to get through the game. For the first time since 2007, the Phillies lost a home playoff game, and one had to hope this wasn't déjà vu all over again against the Rockies. On top of heading to Colorado after losing home-field advantage and throwing everything but the kitchen sink in Game Two was that snow was forecast for Game Three. No big deal!

The weather dominated conversation around the game. Simply put, 35 degrees at first pitch is just not baseball weather. After all the controversy that surrounded Game Two of the series for Manuel, he decided to go with the young left-hander over the experienced Blanton. Unfortunately for Manuel, Happ didn't give him the length he thought he was going to get from him, as he could only go three innings, which forced the skipper to go to Blanton anyway.

With Lee and Hamels slated for Games Four and Five in the series, Manuel could be aggressive. Trailing 3–1 in the top of the fourth, the Phils showed patience and were able to tie the game with the aid of three walks, including back-to-back walks following Ryan Howard's RBI single to Werth and Ibañez. The score was now 3–3 with a chance to tack on more. Unfortunately, Feliz hit into a double play, but Carlos Ruiz was able to sneak a single through the 5-6 hole to give the Phillies the lead. It was 4–3 for a millisecond when, with Blanton in the game now, Carlos González—who was unreal this series—tied the game right back up with a long home run to right field.

In the top of the sixth, once again, the walks were king, and Ruiz was continuing to become a postseason hero. After Ibañez and Feliz walked, Ruiz smoked a single up the middle to give the Phillies a 5–4 lead. However, once again, González was a *problem* for the Phillies, as he led off the top of the seventh with a double off Scott Eyre. The very next batter, Dexter Fowler, laid down a sacrifice bunt right at Eyre. Maybe it was because of the cold weather, but Eyre went down in a heap of pain and could not field the ball. Manuel would have to replace him with Madson in a crucial spot, protecting a one-run lead in the seventh with runners on first and third and one out—gulp. Madson limited the damage by getting Helton to strike out, but then Troy Tulowitzki tied the game with a sacrifice fly. Finally, Madson was able to get Yorvit Torrealba swinging.

We talked a lot about feels-like-a-loss moments in the '08 postseason, and in the eighth after Ruiz and Stairs struck out with runners on second and third and one out, this one truly felt like one too. However, this game was about sacrifice flies, walks, the cold, and some bad umpiring. The Phillies were beneficiaries of that umpiring in the top of the ninth when, with Rollins at second base and one out, Utley hit a checked-swing nubber up the first-base line. The Rockies' closer, Huston Street, made a miraculous play to even get to it and attempt a throw to first base. The umpire ruled Todd Helton off the bag and Utley safe at first. Thankfully, there was no replay yet in Major League Baseball, so there was nothing the Rockies could do. But it would have showed that Utley not only hit himself with the ball running up the first-base line but also was out—a break for the Phils. Howard drove Rollins in with a sacrifice fly—the most exciting play in baseball!

And we were off to the ninth with none other than Brad Lidge in to close it out. Gone were the days of Lights Out Lidge; this postseason's version was "Hold onto Your Butts." Carlos González, because of course he did, worked a one-out walk. He then stole second to put a runner in scoring position for the ancient Jason Giambi. Thankfully, Lidge got him to pop out, which set up Lidge versus a career .337 hitter (at this point of his career) against right-handed pitchers in Todd Helton. Lidge walked Helton, because of course he did, which set up two outs and the winning run on first base for Tulowitski. Feels like a loss? Nope! "Lights Out, Never a Doubt" Lidge got him to pop up, and the Phillies escaped victorious in Game Three and were one win away from a return trip to the NLCS.

Whereas Game Three was more of a professional win by the Phils, Game Four was about superstars being superstars when the team needed them the most. This game's superstar? That would be none other than their prodigious power-hitting first baseman. After what Cliff Lee did on the mound in Game One, you certainly had to feel good about the Phillies chances to close this one out without needing a return trip to Philadelphia for Game Five.

Let's fast forward to the eighth in this one, shall we? This is a quick synopsis: Lee was brilliant—he pitched out of some jams but gave them 7 1/3 innings of one-run baseball. Oh, and Victorino and Werth hit two solo home runs, so the Phils had a 2–1 lead in the eighth. Okay, here we go. Here's another feels-like-a-loss moment. In the top of the eighth, the Phils loaded the bases looking for some insurance runs. Pedro Feliz weakly popped out to left field, and then Ruiz, shockingly, also was not able to come through—the score remained 2–1 heading into the bottom of the eighth. With Lee still on the mound and Dexter Fowler on first base after a one-out walk, Todd Helton hit a soft dribbler toward Utley at second base. Somehow, Fowler jumped over Utley, who was bending down to pick the baseball up; the second baseman, who had to be in a state of shock, made a bad flip to Rollins at second base, and everyone was safe. After a miraculous catch by Ben Francisco, who replaced Ibañez in left, Madson, now in the game for Lee, went to work on Jason Giambi with two outs, protecting a one-run lead. He couldn't do it. Giambi hit a jam shot into short left field and tied the game up at two apiece. Things would go from bad to worse for Madson when the catcher, Yorvit Torrealba, smoked a double into the right-center-field gap to score both Helton and Giambi. Just like that it was 4–2 Rockies—gulp. Madson was able to limit the damage, and it was on to the ninth with the Phillies needing a rally to not return home for a win-or-go-home Game Five.

Now, the mood in the dugout and the mood in the front-office suite were two totally different feelings. Jayson Werth said after the game, "Running off the field, I thought we were going to win this game. Everyone was calm. . . . We knew what we had to do and we did it."[4] Ruben Amaro Jr. did not feel the same. "I was thinking about the flight home. Thinking about whether Cole [Hamels] would be ready for a Game Five start, and how tough it would be to stop their momentum." Thankfully, the mood in the dugout prevailed, and the superstars stepped up. Later it came out that Ryan Howard was telling his teammates ahead of him in the dugout, "Just get me to the plate, boys. Just get me to the plate."

The Phillies would have some work to do as Howard was due up fifth. The inning started with a strikeout by Greg Dobbs. Rollins followed that up with a single up the middle, but Victorino grounded into a fielder's choice, so with two outs, Utley was due up with the lurking Howard on deck. Utley worked a walk, and the Phillies did get Howard to the plate. This is where a great quote and a great story become immortalized. With Victorino on second and Utley on first, Howard smoked a 2-1 fastball off the right-field wall. Utley, going on contact, was able to score all the way from first base to tie the ballgame up. "Just get me to the plate, boys. Just get me to the plate."

The Phillies still had work to do, as the game was only tied up. The comeback would be complete, as Werth, who had the good feeling coming off the field, hit a single over the second baseman's head to score Howard from second base—5–4, Phillies. Now, had this been 2008, Lidge would have been given the ninth without a second thought. This wasn't '08, however. With two switch-hitters due up that were worse from the right-side than the left-side—Gonzalez due up second and Helton lurking in the four spot—Manuel opted to give Scott Eyre the first crack at the ninth. Eyre got Eric Young Jr., but González, of course, fisted a single over Jimmy Rollins's head. With two outs, Helton ripped a base hit up the middle to set up runners on first and second with Troy Tulowitzki coming up. Manuel brought in Lidge to send the Phillies back to the NLCS. Lidge did the job; he threw Tulowitzki five straight sliders, getting the Rockies' shortstop swinging on an 86 mph one in the dirt to end it. Lidge and Ruiz embraced, and the champagne started flowing in the clubhouse.

If this series was any indication, it was going to be a tight rest of October. "They just know how to win," said Tim Kurkjian on ESPN's *SportsCenter* after the Phillies' thrilling comeback victory, and it was hard to argue. Most teams have trouble following up a World Series title with the same intensity the following season, a team with higher goals than just one world title finds it a bit easier. In fact, by winning this series, the Phillies became only the fifth NL team to win a playoff series the year after winning the World Series and the first since the Braves in 1996.

"We have belief, and belief goes further than momentum," Rollins said after the game with his goggles on to protect himself from the douses of champagne.[5]

Oh, how right he was.

ANOTHER DATE WITH THE DODGERS

This Dodgers team was much different than the one the Phillies saw last year in the NLCS. That team that snuck into the playoffs with 84 wins and wasn't supposed to be in the League Championship series. This Dodgers team, however, won 95 games, which meant the Phillies would have to start the NLCS on the road, unlike the year before. It was the same cast of characters for the Dodgers on offense like in '08; however, their big bopper, Manny Ramírez, was busted 50 games for using performance-enhancing drugs. Maybe that's why he hit .800 against the Phillies the year before. Still, Ramírez was dangerous and had a knack for coming up big in key moments. The biggest change on the pitching side from the year before was the emergence of Clayton Kershaw. He was just twenty years old in the '08 NLCS and getting his feet wet in Major League Baseball. In 2009 he broke through, pitching to a 2.79 ERA as a twenty-one year-old and jumping to the front of the line as one of the best young pitchers in baseball. The most jarring thing about the '09 Dodgers was the number of former Phils they sported. Randy Wolf, Vicente Padilla, Jim Thome, and Eric Milton all suited up for the Dodgers, and in the cases of Wolf and Padilla they would have to make postseason starts at Citizens Bank Park, which was obviously a much different animal than when they were in Philadelphia.

Game One was going as advertised. Two of the best young left-handers in the game, Hamels and Kershaw, were cruising through the first four innings on a beautiful night out in LA. It looked like we were getting a classic pitchers' duel—until the fifth, when for the first time we saw Kershaw's struggle in the postseason. After Ibañez singled to left and Pedro Feliz worked a walk, postseason hero Carlos Ruiz stepped to the plate. He smoked an offering by Kershaw into the left-field seats for his second career postseason home run, giving the Phillies a 3–1 lead. This is where Kershaw unraveled. He walked Hamels on four pitches. He threw two wild pitches to allow Rollins to get to third base (after Hamels was forced out at second base), and then he walked Utley to bring up Ryan Howard. The red-hot Howard laced a ball that was eerily similar to his double off of Huston Street in Colorado to give the Phillies a 5–1 lead. Ballgame? Not so fast. You see, the thing that plagued 2009 Cole Hamels was one big inning that got him in seemingly every outing. In an effort to truly go blow for blow with Kershaw, Hamels allowed a three spot of his own in the bottom of the fifth that was capped off by a long home run by none other than Manny Ramírez. The ballgame was suddenly 5–4.

The score would remain the same until the eighth when, after George Sherrill walked both Howard and Werth, Raúl Ibañez went big fly to give the Phillies an 8–4 lead. "All they do is win." Well, sort of. Madson gave two back in the eighth, which meant it was Lidge time to protect an 8–6 lead. The first batter in the bottom of the ninth, Matt Kemp, singled just over the outstretched arms of Rollins. Uh-oh, was it time for heart attack Lidge? It looked like it for a second. the next batter, Casey Blake, smoked a ball right at Chase Utley at second base, who calmly flipped it to Rollins, who then completed the double play. Lidge then got Ronnie Belliard to pop out, and the ballgame was over. Never a doubt, Brad!

> I know, I know. In the chapter on 2008, there were no summaries of games the Phillies lost. They lost; it sucked! However, here is a brief summary of Game Two in a Jack note. One, they couldn't hit Vicente Padilla, seriously? Again, had this happened with the 2022–24 version of Padilla, I would have had to be taken out of Citizens Bank Park in handcuffs. If that seems too extreme, just imagine if Vince Velasquez pitched seven innings of one-run baseball against the best Phillies offense of our lifetime, and tell me how you would feel. Maybe Vinny Velo is too harsh for Padilla, who did make an All-Star team as a Phillie, but you get the point. Their only run of the game was a home run by Ryan Howard, who was having an unbelievable start to the '09 postseason. However, on the other side, Pedro Martínez was brilliant, firing seven shutout innings and handing over a 1–0 lead to the Phillies bullpen. This is where the game turned nutty. With runners on first and second and no outs, Chase Utley threw a potential double-play ball into the first base dugout for the second time in two games. Yips? This tied the game up. Manuel went to J. A. Happ, his fourth pitcher of the inning, with two outs and the bases loaded only to have him walk Andre Ethier to give the Dodgers a 2–1 lead. Manuel went to his fifth pitcher of the inning, Chad Durbin, to

> retire Manny Ramírez and at least give the Phils a shot heading into the ninth. They went down one-two-three with the heart of the order. They lost! It sucked! They always lose Game Two!

Any concern about whether the bad offense was going to carry over from a poor Game Two performance was pretty much erased right away when Howard, who again was having an unbelievable start to the '09 postseason, hit a triple (!) to score both Victorino and Utley—2–0, Phillies. The next batter, Jayson Werth, took a pitch from Dodgers starter Hiroki Kuroda to the ivy in center field to give the Phillies a 4–0 lead after one. With Cliff Lee on the mound in Game Three, that probably would have been enough. All in all, Lee gave the Phillies bullpen a much-needed rest, as he fired eight shutout innings, lowering his postseason ERA to 0.74. Still, even with Lee on the mound, four runs weren't enough. The score was 6–0 in the bottom of the fifth when Pedro Feliz tripled (!) to bring home Ibañez, and then Carlos Ruiz drove home Feliz to make it 8–0 and *effectively* end the ballgame. It was at this point that local dads around the Delaware Valley were begging the Phillies to save some runs for tomorrow.

> Some fun and interesting things that happened in Game Three. One of my favorite things about Philadelphia is how blunt we can be. Gone were the days of the creative chants at the ballpark; sometimes you just have to be honest. So every time that Manny Ramírez came to the plate, the crowd began chanting in unison, "You took steroids! You took steroids!" Again, it's not always about being the most creative, it's about being the most effective. The chants only sort of worked, as Manny still had two hits off of Lee.
>
> The second thing that happened was the crowd gave an extra little bit of cheer when Utley stepped to the plate for his first at-bat. With the throwing errors in each of the first two games, the crowd wanted to let Utley know they had his back. Utley still made two shaky throws on the night, which was all of a sudden a concern here, but still once again—we have a heart.
>
> Finally, you want to talk about a tight ballpark? Before the Phils were set to play a crucial Game Three that could swing the series, the entire city had to watch the Eagles go out to Oakland and score three field goals

> in a losing effort against JaMarcus Russell—yes, *that* JaMarcus Russell, arguably the biggest bust in NFL history. A team with Andy Reid as the head coach, Donovan McNabb at quarterback, LeSean McCoy at running back, and DeSean Jackson on the outside couldn't beat Tom Cable and Jamarcus Russell. Thank God the Phillies got out to an early lead.

The story of the game was, of course, Cliff Lee—who was starting to turn into a folk hero—24 1/3 innings, two earned runs, 20 strikeouts, and three walks. *Who was this guy?* The '08 team had guys that the city had gotten to know pretty well, but with Lee? All of this was new and somehow, someway, he was outdoing what Hamels had just done the previous year, all while pitching like he was on a deadline. It was remarkable.

On to Game Four and Average Joe Blanton starting a postseason game for the first time since he went big fly in the World Series in what would end up being a game and a moment that we'd be talking about for the rest of our lives.

Should we just fast-forward to the bottom of the ninth? That's why you're all here right? No way! What fun would that be? On the mound for the Dodgers was another phrustrating former Phillie in Randy Wolf. Interestingly enough, Pat Gillick tried to sign Wolf back here in both the 2007 and 2008 offseasons—thankfully, Wolf said no, and the rest is history.

> In hindsight, simply no way would the Phillies lose a playoff series to the Dodgers with Padilla and Wolf making starts. Now, had they not won the World Series the year before and the championship drought was still there, then *maybe* you could convince me that the most Philadelphia thing of all time would be losing a playoff series to those two, but not this team and not with this newfound confidence in our sports teams. If Padilla's showing against the Phils would have been like if Vince Velasquez had done it, then I guess Randy Wolf doing it would have been like if Adam Morgan started and dominated against them in a playoff start. I know, Wolf was better than Adam Morgan, and Wolf never pitched out of the bullpen, but during the lean years they didn't have a lefty starter for multiple seasons, so what do you want me to do? Do you want me to compare him to Ranger Suárez? Over my dead body.

The last couple postseasons have had a running trend of games that felt like a loss. Game Four of the 2009 NLCS was no different. Through five innings, local dads were furious that the Phillies didn't save any runs from the night before. The only runs the Phils had through five was a no-doubt home run off the bat of Ryan Howard, who was doing all he could to carry this team back to the World Series.

With the score 3–2 in the top of sixth, after Matt Kemp hit a long home run in the top of fifth, the feels-like-a-loss vibe radiated through Citizens Bank Park. First, the slow-footed Ramírez reached first base on a throwing error by Pedro Feliz; given his defensive prowess, this was a shock to all involved. With one out, Ronnie Belliard fisted a single into no man's land between Rollins, Victorino, and Ibañez, which allowed Ramírez to get to second base. After Blanton got Russell Martin looking, all he had to do was get out Casey Blake to avoid any more damage. He could do no such thing, as Blake hit a bleeder into right field to score Ramírez from second.

With no hard-hit balls and an error, the score was now 4–2 heading into the seventh. The crowd was brought back to life when Victorino laced a triple down the left-field line with one out. Here we go, the Phillies were on the comeback trail. Utley followed up the triple with a single into right field to make it a 4–3 ballgame. They were in business. Howard then walked, setting up first and second with one out for Werth. He hit into what could have been a double-play ball, but Belliard dropped it on the transfer, so the Dodgers only got one out. Maybe this wasn't a loss after all? With runners on first and third, Ibañez laced a sinking line drive into short left field. With the defensive stiff Ramírez in left field, the game was going to be tied, right? Wrong. Somehow, Ramírez made a shoestring catch to rob Ibañez and prevent the game from being tied. This was definitely a loss.

Fast-forward to the bottom of the eighth. The top of the Phillies lineup was up against George Sherrill, or, as he was known around these parts, the Utley, Howard, and Ibañez stopper. The Dodgers traded for Sherrill at the trade deadline specifically for this time of the year, and in the bottom of the eighth it worked. With one out, Victorino got hit by a Sherrill slider, and then Utley grinded out a walk to set up first and second with Howard coming to the dish. Howard was probably the last person the Dodgers wanted to face right now, but again, Sherrill was here to do this job, and he did, striking out the Phils' first baseman. Jonathan Broxton came on to get out Werth, and the opportunity was wasted once again. After Lidge worked a scoreless top of the ninth, it was on to the bottom of half of the inning to see what the thrill ride Phillies had up their sleeve this time around.

In speaking to reporters after the game, Lidge said the Phillies offense was "borderline extremely cocky that they're going to come back every single time," and how right that description proved to be.

The inning started pretty nondescriptly. Ibañez grounded out weakly to the second baseman. With one out, Manuel started to pull some levers and rely on past trauma to maybe get into the head of the Dodgers' closer. He summoned Matt Stairs to pinch hit for Pedro Feliz. While he didn't produce a moon shot, Stairs was able to draw a walk on four pitches and maybe, just maybe, rattle Broxton enough for a breakthrough. That became more evident when Broxton plunked the next batter, Ruiz, on the first pitch to set up first and second with one out. The Phils were in business. However, in true feels-like-a-loss fashion, pinch-hitter Greg Dobbs lined out meagerly to the third baseman Casey Blake. Still, the stage was set for Rollins, maybe the cockiest of the comeback-believing Phils. With a possible tied series and a guaranteed trip back to LA hanging in the balance, Rollins smoked a 1-1 99 mile-per-hour pitch into the gap in right-center field. By now, we all know what happened next. The forty-five-thousand-plus fans all turned into horse racing jockeys, begging Ruiz to get around those bases as fast as he could to deliver the Phillies a 3–1 series lead and one of the most dramatic wins in franchise history. Ruiz sprinted home, and the Phillies took a stranglehold on their second straight National League pennant.

This team was special.

When asked about it after the game, the always wise Charlie Manuel said, "He likes the moment. He wants to be there, and he can control his adrenaline and handle the moment. Jimmy Rollins thrives in that situation. The bigger the stage, the better he likes to play. The more people watching, he likes the mic, he likes to talk, that's the way he is. I like everything about his personality."[6]

And with that, the Phillies were one win away from a return trip to the World Series, with the hero from last year on the mound to try to seal it.

Cole Hamels versus Vicente Padilla in a close out game to send the Phillies to the World Series? Did fans even have to show up to the ballpark to know this one was over? Well, it wasn't 2008 anymore.

Hamels set the wrong tone in the first when he allowed a two-out home run to Andre Ethier, who was hitting in the .190s against lefties on the season.

Manuel said before the game to reporters that his command early will tell you a lot about the performance you're getting from Hamels that night, and early indications were not great. Thankfully for Hamels, the Phillies bats showed up ready to pop some champagne. In the bottom of the first, also with two outs, Padilla walked Utley and Howard to bring up Werth. On a 3–2 count, Werth didn't miss a backdoor sinker from Padilla and deposited it into the right-field seats, making the score 3–1, Phillies. Don't you worry, this one wasn't a laugher just yet, as Hamels made sure to keep the Dodgers around. He allowed a leadoff home run to James Loney the next inning to make it 3–2—so much for a shutdown inning.

Fortunately, Vicente Padilla was the pitcher we had come to know; the talented but frustrating right-hander wasn't ready for that ballpark and that moment and was out of the game in the bottom of the fourth after allowing his fifth run of the game—a double by Ibañez to bring Werth around from first base. Things were looking so bleak for the Dodgers that Joe Torre went to his bullpen ace, George Sherrill, in the fifth to work out of a bases-loaded jam just to try to keep the game close. He eventually got Utley swinging, but that was after he hit Victorino on a backdoor slider to make it 6–2. This one was over, right? Well, it wasn't 2008 anymore. Hamels returned to the mound for the top of the fifth and again, almost immediately, gave a run back on a solo home run by Orlando Hudson. Furcal followed that up with a double, finishing Hamels's night. He had another frustrating start, with a postseason ERA at 6.75. We'll get back to the game in one second, because it's much more fun, but to get an idea where Hamels head was at, read what he said after the game: "I'm glad Charlie took me out, because I wasn't going to help the team win."[7]

Yikes.

Okay, back to the fun stuff. Durbin and Happ combined for a scoreless inning and a third before Victorino put this game on ice with a two-run home run off Clayton Kershaw in the bottom of the sixth. They could feel it. Rollins, who scored on the Victorino blast, seemed to be soaking it all in, as the Flyin' Hawaiian almost caught up to him rounding third base. Werth tacked on his second home run of the game in the seventh inning to make it 9–3. Manuel gave Lidge the ninth, even though it was a 10–4 ballgame, and the suddenly resurgent right-hander made quick work of the Dodgers. One-two-three—the Phillies were National Champions again. What a world.

Rollins said it best, as he usually does, after the game when asked about how this team didn't let complacency kick in. "Strong-willed. We don't have quitters. When Charlie had his meetings, he used some other words, but he didn't want quitters on his team."

They weren't quitters, and they weren't done yet.

On to New York.

NEW YORK, NEW YORK

Talk about a dream for Major League Baseball. Believe it or not, the baseball's dying, argument was going on then too, just like it was in the '90s and the '80s and the '70s. Shocker! The sport's still standing! But for this matchup, the defending World Series champs versus the Yankees—who just added Sabathia, Teixeira, and Burnett in the offseason to the aging "Core Four"—was a big draw. Add in seeing if Álex Rodríguez could bring home his first title? It was a television network's dream. Now, it just had to live up to the hype.

> The '09 Yankees were daunting. It wasn't like the '01 Sixers versus that Lakers team, but in my lifetime, I'd say the '09 Yankees were right behind the Lakers as the second-best team that a Philadelphia team has had to play against for a title. For my money, they were better than the '04 Patriots, although very similar. They were better than '17 Patriots for sure, the '22 Astros, and the '22 Chiefs. The Lakers in '01 were the toughest task; they didn't lose a game until Game One of the Finals.

One guy who knows how to live up to the hype and give predictions of his own was, of course, Jimmy Rollins. Rollins was on a bit of a heater in the predictions category. Everyone remembers '07, but who could forget that back in a June edition of *Playboy* he predicted that this would be the World Series. Well, Mr. Prediction was back again when he appeared on *The Jay Leno Show* and said, "Of course we're going to win. If we're nice, we'll let it go six, but I'm thinking five, close it out at home." Surely that sat well with Jeter and the Yankees.

With that, we were off.

Aah, Game One of the 2009 World Series—one of the most joyous and memorable nights we as Philly sports fans have ever had. On the mound for the Phils was the new folk hero, Cliff Lee, who was making the most of his first-ever trip to the postseason, as he entered Game One with a 0.74 ERA.

Opposing him was none other than CC Sabathia. Whoever wrote the chapter on the '08 Phillies really laid it on thick about how impossible hitting Sabathia was and how daunting a task it was going to be, but interestingly, it didn't seem that scary this time around. I wonder what happened. Much like the year before, the Phillies would have to win a game in the rain. Heck, when the game started you couldn't tell if it was rain or the fog from the Jay-Z and Alicia Keys concert that had just ended. ("Empire State of Mind" immediately pops into all of our heads.)

Both aces did their thing until the top of the third, as Utley, once again, set the tone with a big World Series Game One home run. It was only a solo shot, but it staked the Phillies an early 1–0 lead. Utley wasn't done with Sabathia just yet. In the top of the sixth, he launched a 95 mile-per-hour 0-2 fastball by Sabathia deep into the right-field bleachers. He was owning New York yet again.

By this point, Lee was locked in. He knew it, the Yankees knew it, and their fans knew it. It was borderline psychotic looking how calm, cool, and collected he was on the mound in his first World Series start. They always say when you're growing up pitching, "Just play catch with the catcher!" Well it truly looked like it was Little League for Lee out there. In the sixth, with the game still in the balance, Johnny Damon fisted a weak popup back to Lee. Without a care in the world, Lee, almost nonchalantly, stuck his glove out to nab the baseball. Was he using this as a tactic to let the Yankees know he wasn't scared, or was he really just that cool on the mound? We may never know.

The score remained 2–0 into the eighth; although Utley did get him twice, Sabathia was more like himself in this game than in Game Two of the NLDS the year prior, firing seven innings of two-run baseball. Phil Hughes started the eighth and walked both Rollins and Victorino to start it. Yankees manager Joe Girardi brought on his lefty ace out of the bullpen, Dámaso Marte, to get out Utley and Howard. Like he would annoyingly do for a majority of the Series, he did, and then runners were on first and third with two outs for Jayson Werth. With David Robertson now in the game replacing Marté, Werth drew a walk, which set up bases loaded and two outs for Ibañez, who was dealing with an injury that would require offseason surgery. Thankfully, Ibañez came through, singling through the right side to give the Phils a 4–0 lead. Floodgates open!

To start the bottom of the eighth, Lee showed once again that he was too cool for New York. Robinson Canó hit a groundball back toward Lee.

This time, not so nonchalantly but still cool under the pressure, Lee snared it behind his back and flipped it over to Howard for the out. Even Lee, cool and all, smiled at that one.

The Phillies added two more in the top of the ninth to make it 6–0, but that would be more than enough for Lee. Even with a semishaky ninth (for his standards), he was still able to get the complete game after striking out Rodríguez and Jorge Posada to end it. A complete-game effort by Lee, home-field advantage gone for the Yankees, and they took down Sabathia for the second-straight postseason? It was hard not to feel like they were about to do it again.

> I know they eventually lost this Series—sorry for the spoiler—but Game One of the 2009 World Series was the stuff of legends. We didn't know how the rest of the Series would go, but all we heard about was how good the Yankees are, 26 rings, and on and on, and our guys went up there and stuck it to them. The Cliff Lee stuff was crazy. His postseason ERA after Game One was 0.54, and if you were too young to remember this game, please fire up on YouTube and watch the two plays I described.

In Game Two, Daddy's home. Who could forget that when Pedro Martínez was a dominant starter for the Boston Red Sox in the early 2000s he had his own duels with the big, bad New York Yankees. After a regular-season game in which Pedro allowed five runs in September 2004 as the Yankees and Red Sox were duking it out, he uttered the now famous, "I mean, what can I say—just tip my hat and call the Yankees my daddy." Match lit. Every time Pedro took the hill at Yankee Stadium, "Who's your daddy?" chants would rain down. Martínez and the Red Sox got the last laugh that year, but it was a special time in Major League Baseball. Fast-forward to 2009, and the Yankees fans didn't forget about Pedro and his comments. Once again, "Who's your daddy?" chants filled up the new Yankee Stadium, as the Phillies looked to take a commanding 2–0 series lead.

Overall, Game Two of the World Series was just a loss. (How's that for some high-level writing? Please keep reading.) The Yankees were desperate, and the Phillies always lose Game Two. By the way, that's up to six straight postseason series that have started with them taking Game One, and they lost. The story of the game was A. J. Burnett. Burnett was your classic when-he's-on-he's-on type of starter, and in Game Two he was on, firing seven innings of one-run baseball while striking out nine. Surprisingly enough for the Phillies, Martínez was almost equally as good. Through six innings, he had only allowed two runs, solo shots by Teixeira and future World Series MVP Hideki Matsui. In the seventh, Manuel let Martínez go back out there, but it almost immediately backfired, as the first two hitters singled, causing Manuel to yank him from the game. Before he had completely exited the field, Martínez took one last look around Yankee Stadium and let out a big smile before heading into the dugout. It felt like Martínez's official goodbye to baseball as he left it all on the mound one last time (spoiler alert—it wasn't). The Yankees added on the extra run to make it 3–1, Utley grounded into a double play with runners on first and second with one out in the top of the eighth, and Game Two of the World Series was over. No big deal, the Phillies had done their job up in New York, and it was back to Philadelphia, where they still had only lost once in each of the last two postseasons.

There was something eerie about Game Three falling on Halloween and this version of Cole Hamels being on the mound for the Phillies exactly a year to the day that the Phillies were making their way down Broad Street at the parade. A guy that looked superhuman just a year before now looked human, pitching to a 6.75 ERA and having allowed six home runs in the postseason. Could he just put on the '08 Hamels costume for one night and give the Phillies the Series lead? Fans are pleading, Cole! Ultimately, no—no he couldn't. There would be no Halloween magic for the Phillies on this night.

This game was the worst; let's get into it.

Opposing Hamels was one of the better big-game pitchers of his generation in Andy Pettitte, who has the most postseason wins in baseball history, and things were looking good early. Hamels wasn't Hamelsing yet, and the Phillies offense looked ready. In the bottom of the second, Werth went big fly to give the Phils the early 1–0 lead. Two batters later, Pedro Feliz pounded one off the wall in right field for a double. Pettitte then walked Carlos Ruiz to bring up the pitcher, Hamels, who laid down a perfect bunt into no man's land and was aboard safely. It was early, but did this feel like a win? Big game Pettitte walked the next batter, Rollins, to make it 2–0. The Bank was on fire, Pettitte was on the ropes, and Mr. Grand Slam, Shane Victorino, was coming to the plate. He just missed it. Victorino *just* barely got jammed on a fastball by Pettitte and lifted it to left field for the sacrifice fly. Still, the damage was done, and the Phillies had an early 3–0 lead.

The fourth was when this game went from feels like a win to no, this was definitely a loss. One of the biggest problems for 2009 Hamels was keeping his emotions in check. When he was upset on the mound, you *knew* he was upset. If things weren't going his way, he would become more and more demonstrative, and things would snowball. That's why everyone immediately got nervous when he just missed on a 3–2 borderline pitch to Teixeira to walk him with one out in the fourth.

Fortunately for the Yankees and unfortunately for the Phillies, what happened next was World Series history. On an 0-1 fastball, Álex Rodríguez smoked a ball to right field. It was carrying and hit off the top of the wall for a double—only it didn't hit off the railing in right field, it hit off the camera. For the first time in World Series history, replay was used by Joe Girardi, the call was overturned, and instead of runners on second and third with one out, the game was now 3–2 on an opposite-field home run by Rodríguez. There might be some bias here, but had that camera not been hanging over the wall and into the field of play, that wouldn't have been a home run. It would have hit off the top of the wall and maybe, just maybe, the Phillies still would have won this ballgame. But it wasn't meant to be, and just when you thought that he had his '08 Hamels mask on, it was ripped off to reveal that it was still the '09 version.

Things went from bad to worse for Hamels in the fifth when Nick Swisher led off the inning with a double down the line. Hamels was able to rebound and get Melky Cabrera swinging on a changeup, but he was unable to get out the pitcher, Andy Pettitte, as he looped a single into center field to score Swisher. Nightmare. Derek Jeter then singled up the middle off Hamels to extend the inning and put Pettitte in scoring position. The death blow was delivered to Hamels when Johnny Damon smoked a double into the right-center-field gap to score both Pettitte and Jeter. The score was 5–3, Yankees, and a Halloween nightmare was unfolding right in front of the Philly faithful. Hamels's night was done after he walked the next better, Teixeira. All in all it was 4 1/3 innings and five earned runs—Hamels's postseason ERA stood at 7.58.

> I remember watching this unfold and thinking that this was the first time the Phillies looked like they thought they might have run into the better team. The cockiness that they had shown in their ability to come back just wasn't there, and the ballpark was lifeless. I know when players are not scoring runs and they're pressing, it can look a certain way, but I just distinctly remember watching and thinking that the invincible Phillies felt like they had met their match.

The rest of Game Three felt like a slow death. In the top of the sixth, Swisher hit a long home run off J. A. Happ to make it 6–3. The Phils recaptured *some* momentum when Werth hit his second home run of the game to make it 6–4. He was the only Phillie to really show up in this game. In the seventh, Durbin allowed a bleeder to Jorge Posada that scored Johnny Damon from second, and the final knockout punch was delivered in the eighth, when Matsui took Brett Myers deep out to left field. It was a deflating night at Citizens Bank Park. Hamels didn't have it, and the Yankees offense, one that the Phillies had kept down for a majority of the Series so far, finally looked like the Bronx Bombers—it was a tough road ahead with Blanton on the mound versus CC Sabathia the next night. To make matters worse, Hamels after the game told reporters that, "I can't wait for it to end. It's been mentally draining. At year's end, you just can't wait for a fresh start."

Fun times!

If Game Three wasn't enough of a nut punch, then Game Four didn't help the matter much more. The Phillies had their back against the wall; though the series wouldn't be over if they lost, you would be hard-pressed to believe they would come back from being down 3–1. Would facing Sabathia give this team a little burst by thinking they could slay the beast one more time, or did he create too much doubt with his Game One performance for them to doubt they could get him again?

Things didn't start too hot for the Phils, as Blanton immediately gave up two in the first. Luckily, Sabathia, who doubles as Utley's personal batting-practice pitcher (in the playoffs), gave one back in the bottom of the first, as the second baseman just missed a home run to right field as he doubled to bring Victorino home from second after he hit a one-out double of his own. The score remained the same until the fourth, when Ryan Howard led off the inning with a single up the middle and then stole second in a move that had to leave the Yankees stunned, since it didn't even draw a throw. With two outs, the ever-so-clutch Pedro Feliz drove a ball to left field that ate up Johnny Damon just enough to allow Howard to come around from second to score. The play at the plate was fascinating. Howard lined up like a linebacker going to level a running back in the open field but completely whiffed touching home plate; the naked eye suggested he had to have touched home plate, but the replay showed he didn't. A break for the Phillies? Feels like a win? Not so fast!

In the fifth, Blanton walked Nick Swisher to lead off the inning, and then Melky Cabrera hit a ball up the middle that was just tough enough for Utley to try to flip the ball to Rollins to at least get the force out at second. He couldn't, and the ball bounded away, creating first and second with no outs for Jeter. In what would be his second bleeder of the night, he sneaked one past Rollins at shortstop to bring Swisher home from second. The chants of "Derek Jeter!" rained down as the Giants and Yankees fans that had watched their football team get destroyed earlier in the day by the Eagles had come all the way back to life. The next batter, Damon, one-upped Jeter by fisting one right over the outstretched arms of Utley at second to bring Cabrera home. The feels-like-a-loss vibe had officially taken over Citizens Bank Park, as it was now 4–2 Yankees.

But hold on—maybe this one wasn't over yet. That was because, once again, Utley got Sabathia for the third time in the series with a home run on Sabathia's 107th pitch of the night, to make it a 4–3 game. Then, more improbably, Pedro Feliz took Joba Chamberlain deep in the bottom of the eighth. They weren't dead yet. Citizens Bank Park was fully alive; our guys were back—tie ballgame.

> I just remember the Feliz home run being the first time I had felt life in days. It really all felt like it was going one direction but that home run really seemed to propel us back into the Series. They just tied the game up off Joba Chamberlain, who struggled in the final months of the season. *No way were they losing this ballgame* was pretty much how I thought then, and I believe a lot of other fans felt the same. Suckers.

With two outs in the top of the ninth, it really felt like a fait accompli that this game was going into the bottom of the ninth for the Phils to win. Lidge had popped up Matsui to start the inning and then struck out the slap-hitting Jeter for the second out. There wasn't even a thought that a rally was about to begin. But then Damon singled to left and then stole second during the next at-bat. But with the shift on for Teixeira, no one was covering third base, which let the speedy left fielder get all the way to third base with two outs. Cover the bag! Communicate! Poor local kids had to work on that for months after the Phils screwed it up in the World Series. Okay, but still there were two outs—all Lidge had to do was get Teixeira. He plunked him, which brought up Rodríguez. In his marquee World Series moment, no not his home run, Rodríguez slapped the ball down the left-field line to score Damon from third—5–4, Yankees. The next batter, Posada, ripped a single to score both Rodríguez and Teixeira—just like that it was 7–4, Yankees. The Phillies went down with a whimper in the ninth, and the Series was now effectively over with the Yankees taking a commanding 3–1 lead.

> Just writing and rewatching some of the clips really goes to show how painful these two losses were back to back. Thank God they won the World Series in '08 because had they somehow lost that and then had two-straight games like these two at home against a New York team, I'm not sure the city would be standing the next day. It was brutal. I think part of why it never gets talked about on the Philly sports pain rankings is because they had just won the year before, kind of like the Eagles Super Bowl in '22. Everyone assumed they'd just be back there next year. It's a good lesson to remind yourself that teams need to take advantage of championship runs when they can because, especially in this city, we absolutely cannot take them for granted.

To the Phillies' credit, they didn't just roll over and die in Game Five. Utley homered twice to tie Reggie Jackson for most home runs in a World Series, but Cliff Lee was human, as he went seven innings and allowed five earned runs. Still, the Phillies kept the Yankees just far enough away to where they couldn't come back and steal one to close out the series. They won the game, 8–6, and gave Phillies fans one last glimmer of hope that they could chase down the big, bad New York Yankees.

Unfortunately for the Phils, they might have used up all they had left of Pedro Martínez in Game Two and throughout the playoffs. In what would be his last start of his Hall of Fame career, Martínez only lasted four innings at Yankee Stadium, as Hideki Matsui drove in all of the runs against him on this night. Matsui homered off him in the second and then hit a backbreaking two-out two-run single in the bottom of the third just after the Phillies had made it a 2–1 ballgame. Matsui wouldn't be done yet. In the fifth, with the score now 5–1 and Happ in the game, he doubled to bring home Teixeira and Rodríguez. Matsui drove in six and sealed his World Series MVP. Ryan Howard hit a two-run home run to make the score 7–3 in the top of the sixth, but this one was all but over. Mariano Rivera jammed Shane Victorino one last time to end it, and for the 27th time in their history the Yankees were world champions.

With that, the dream of being champions for the second straight year died. The year before? The Phillies got all the back-breaking hits in the World Series. This year? Virtually none. Last year the bullpen was "Lights Out"—this year, even outside the closer role, not so much. The ace of the staff last year? This year he couldn't wait for the season to be over. It was a fun ride, they were a damn good team, but they just missed out on invincibility. Could we really expect this team to keep getting back to this same spot, or was it time for a changeup?

Guess we'll have to wait and see.

THE STORY OF THE 2010 PHILLIES

Change was on the horizon for the 2010 Phillies. Sure, the core was going to remain the same—Howard, Utley, Rollins, Werth, Victorino, Ibañez, Carlos Ruiz, Cole Hamels (they really needed Hamels to be his ace self); and, of course, our new hero, Cliff Lee. However, general manager Ruben Amaro Jr. needed to tweak. It wasn't the same as 2006 when Pat Gillick essentially said that they've gone as far as they could with this group and now was the time to mix it up. But Amaro was ready for some new blood in the Phillies clubhouse. Gone from the '08 and '09 teams were Brett Myers, Pedro Feliz, Matt Stairs, Eric Bruntlett, Scott Eyre, and Clay Condrey. Amaro made one thing clear in the 2010 offseason—he wanted upgrades. Whether it was the bench, the back-up catcher, the third baseman, or the rotation, if there was an upgrade to be made, the second-year GM was going to make it. It's why the Phillies declined the option on Feliz; they could have picked it up and paid him $5 million to play great defense and not hit very much. It's why they decided to move on from Myers, a good pitcher but just too inconsistent. And it's why Amaro eventually made his boldest move as a GM yet—they wanted an upgrade.

Amaro's first order of business was finding his replacement for Feliz, with whom they'd won two straight pennants. Funny enough, they went back to an old friend to man the hot corner and *maybe* righted a wrong from earlier in the decade. Amaro's replacement for Feliz was none other than former Phillie Placido Polanco, who was coming off of four straight seasons in Detroit in which he hit over .300 and added 30 doubles. Given Polanco's age, now thirty-four, playing in the middle of the infield was no longer as desirable, so Polly switched over to being a full-time third baseman and fit in nicely as the team's two-hole hitter. Local high school coaches loved the way Polanco hit behind runners—the *perfect* two-hole hitter hits the ball the other way!

However, for Amaro, there was still one big fish that he just had to reel in. It was no secret that Roy "Doc" Halladay was Amaro's white whale, and for good reason. He was the best overall pitcher of this decade, a horse, and maybe the hardest-working guy in baseball. Unlike at the previous season's trade deadline, Halladay was going to get traded this offseason—it was just a matter of where to. By the looks of it from the outside, the Phillies were set. Cliff Lee was the toast of the town, and it was reasonable to expect Hamels to bounce back with a much quieter offseason in store. They didn't *need* Halladay per se, but they wanted him. So Amaro kept cool and quiet—laying in the weeds waiting to pounce. Finally, on December 14, the first reports surfaced that the Phillies and Blue Jays had an agreement on a deal that would send Halladay to Philadelphia for a similar package to the one they discussed in the summer. *You mean to tell me they got Halladay to go with Cliff and Cole?!* was the common thought among the locals that day. That was until you saw the other layer to the Halladay trade and subsequent extension for three years and $60 million, which was that Cliff Lee was sent packing to Seattle for a package of prospects to try to replenish the farm after both trades the Phillies had made. It was mass confusion, but one that ultimately ended with Halladay in pinstripes and World Series hero Lee packing.

> I think this was the day I decided I wanted to get into sports radio. I just remember sitting in my car not wanting to miss anything that had happened. I was so confused, yet so excited, which I think summed up a lot of how everyone felt that day. *Why couldn't they just keep both? Imagine that rotation!* However, Amaro was under strict orders to keep the payroll under a certain number, and there were reports that Lee was going to test the market no matter what the following offseason, which might have forced the Phillies hand to get the deal done with Halladay and not leave themselves bare if Lee walked. It was a whirlwind but, holy crap, man, Roy freakin' Halladay was finally a Phillie. *Get us to Opening Day!* God, the offseasons used to be so exciting around that time.

With Halladay finally in the fold, Polanco at third base, and some new pieces in the bullpen and bench, the Phillies were retooled and ready to embark on getting back to the World Series for the third straight year. These windows don't happen very often, they knew that, which is why they were unloading the clip to try to get a parade down Broad Street one more time. Much like Terrell Owens in '04, the fans of the city of Philadelphia were enamored with their new star they had heard so much about.

The team, and city, couldn't wait for the team to head north. The 2010 Phillies started the season in the same place they'd clinch the division title in the upcoming months—the nation's capital. The first game went to plan. Halladay pitched and dominated, going seven innings and only allowing a run, meanwhile the offense put up an 11 spot. The Phillies certainly looked the part in the first week of the year, as they won five out of their first six games. Was another hot start in order for this ballclub?

Come on, don't count your chickens before the eggs hatch. The story of the first month of the year was injuries and a big extension for the Big Piece. At the end of April, in what would go down as an infamous contract, the Phillies inked Howard to a five-year, $125 million extension that made him the second-highest paid player in the sport, with the contract being the biggest in franchise history. Although the city has seen its stars exit, it certainly didn't seem like Howard would wear another uniform. At the time, it seemed like a no-brainer; he was going to be a free agent after the 2011 season, he had put up prodigious power numbers for multiple seasons, and he was a homegrown Phillie. Reward those who have rewarded you, and take out any doubt about their future. Notwithstanding a bogus offseason ESPN report that the Phils were considering trading Howard for Albert Pujols, the Phils rewarded Howard.

The other storyline of the first month of the season was not as good, as the injuries were already a key storyline for the 2010 Phillies. First, Brad Lidge, J. C. Romero, and Joe Blanton all started the season on the IL. Lidge had to get offseason surgeries on both his knee and his elbow—great! Blanton was dealing with an abdominal strain, and Romero had elbow surgery. The first in-season injury of note was Rollins, who, sometime in warm-ups, hurt his calf, which put him on the shelf for the first month of the season. The next was Polanco, who got hit by a pitch on his elbow down in Atlanta, which would affect him for the entire season and require offseason surgery. The starting staff was the next to get it, as J. A. Happ was shut down for three months with an elbow strain. Finally, to close out the month and add insult to injury (get it?), Ryan "Mad Dog" Madson kicked a chair after a bad outing and broke his toe. Madson had been closing for Lidge, and things had not been going well. For as good as Madson was as a set-up man, when the ninth inning started—he just didn't seem to have *it*. On April 28, after failing to hold another lead, Madson said, "I went downstairs to cool off and I slipped on the way down and that just set me off. There was a chair at the end of the stairs and I tried to kick it over and I caught my toe underneath the chair instead of on top. I'm frustrated and I'm embarrassed."[8] Hey, who knows? Maybe the chair was asking for it. Seriously, how excited do you think the headline makers at the newspapers were after the Madson injury? The puns were simply out of control.

> I don't know if this part of 2010 has to be added, but it's a funny story nonetheless that lived on in Philadelphia for years to come. On May 4, not even "The Force" could protect seventeen-year-old Steve Consalvi from being tased after he ran onto the field at Citizens Bank Park. In a moment that will go down in history as one of the top Philly fan moments of all time, much like snowballs at Santa and whatever nonsense people throw at us, a kid was tasered after being on the field for too long and evading cops. It was the first time in sports history that it had been used to subdue someone on the field, and I think it had to be the last because it's not like a wave of people have been getting tasered for running onto the field, and people certainly haven't stopped doing that. More history for the Phils was made: the first taser in sports history. With history like that on their side, it's hard not to imagine a parade down Broad Street.

Much like 2009, 2010 would have another massive loss in the Phillies family. This time it was former pitcher and Hall of Famer Robin Roberts, who died of natural causes at his home in Florida at eighty-three. The Phillies would wear the No. 36 patches on their jersey for the rest of the season, and the 1950 pennant flag that hung in center field would be at half-mast for a bit. He was a titanic force in the Phillies organization, and he used to be around the team and loved talking to the players. He wasn't just a legend who went away from the city when his time was done. In maybe the only way a Phillie could honor Roberts, two nights after his passing, Jamie Moyer fired a complete-game shutout, becoming the oldest pitcher in baseball history to accomplish such a feat. His hardest pitch of the night? An 83-mile-per-hour fastball. The author of 305 complete games (yes, Robin Roberts threw 305 complete games) had to be smiling down at that one.

> Much like the taser story, I'm not sure if this *has* to be included in the story of the 2010 Phillies, but for those that weren't around during this time it has to be discussed—especially with what happened in 2017 with the Astros. In a series in mid-May against the Rockies, Phillies bullpen coach Mick Billmeyer was seen on TV with binoculars staring in at Phillies hitters when they were at the plate. The Rockies were fearful that he was relaying signs from the bullpen to tip off Phillies hitters about what was coming. They filed a formal complaint to Major League Baseball about it, much like the Mets had just done at the start of the month. It seemed like this was a *thing*. I'm sure if the Phillies were stealing signs, they'd be much more discreet than the hefty bullpen coach (sorry, Mick) looking in with binoculars in broad daylight. It was so obvious, it was caught on TV. Furthermore, the quotes from Charlie about this were amazing. The first concerned the Mets complaint: "Somebody maybe ought to check on the Mets. Their [expletive] home record is out of this world. They're losing on the road. That's a good indication sometimes if they're stealing signs." The second was about the Rockies and why he thought they were accusing them of stealing signs: "Because we beat them. That's why. What the hell? Keep crying." Put that on a T-shirt. I think it's safe to say Charlie didn't believe that his team was cheating and stealing signs.

There wouldn't be a Phillies season without the most powerful offense of our lifetimes hitting a rough stretch during the season. It's hard to compute, but, yes, even the best struggle in baseball. Heading into a series in late May in Florida, the Phillies had been shut out in three straight games and in four out of their last five—shut out! During such times, teams have to lean on their starting pitching, and fortunately for the Phillies they had the best in baseball on their side. It was an exciting time in Philadelphia when Roy Halladay took the mound in what was supposed to be a pretty nondescript night in South Florida. For a majority of Philadelphia sports fans, when Doc pitched it was must-see TV However, on this night he would be on TV number two in the house or not on at all because the Flyers were playing for their first Stanley Cup since the mid-'70s.

Two points should be made before getting to the game. First, he was roughed up in his last outing. The Red Sox somehow, someway tagged him for six runs. I guess he was human after all, but it was hard to envision him putting together two stinkers in a row. Second, Rich Dubee might have helped take Halladay to even another level before the 2010 season. Halladay was a famed workaholic, and he always looked for ways to get better, whether it be his conditioning or learning new pitches. Heck, Mariano Rivera taught Halladay his Hall of Fame cutter at the All-Star Game in 2008, much to the chagrin of his Yankees teammates because it made him even tougher to hit. Halladay always seemed to have one pitch he could never master—a changeup. The changeup had evaded Halladay for years, and he often spent spring training tinkering with it. Dubee had another idea for him: the split changeup. It was a game changer for Halladay, as he finally felt like he had completed his repertoire. That would be an important pitch on this night and one a little later down the line.

At 7:17 p.m. on a muggy night in South Florida, Roy Halladay fired his first pitch of the ballgame, and by 9:23 p.m., he had accomplished perfection. It started pretty harmlessly, a 19-pitch first inning, his most strenuous of the night, which featured two three-ball counts—he had only five more the rest of the game. After that, Doc was in session. With Halladay you almost went into every start wondering if tonight was going to be the night he threw a no-hitter. There was no pressure; he was just that good. So when he had gone through the fourth inning after not allowing a walk or a hit, you just *knew* something might be brewing down at Sun Life Stadium. As the night continued, the buzz kept growing. Local bar owners were in a panic, as people were getting wind that Halladay was flirting with perfection. The Flyers were locked in a tight battle in the first game of the Stanley Cup, but there was Doc. The buzz continued to grow as Halladay went through eight innings perfectly. When Doc took the field to start the ninth, a funny thing happened—an ovation. Now maybe it was because of the amount of Phillies fans in the building that night, but an ovation for an opposing player throwing a perfect game sure was odd. The hardest hit ball of the night was off of the bat of pinch-hitter Mike Lamb to start the ninth. He hit a ball to deep center field off Halladay that *might* have been a home run at Citizens Bank Park, but nevertheless, Victorino calmly sprinted back to the warning track to reel it in. Halladay then struck out former Phillies great Wes Helms for the second out of the inning. All Halladay had to do now was get out the light-hitting Ronny Paulino and his night would be complete.

Scott Franzke told it like this: "Halladay steps back up onto the mound, tucks the baseball in his right hand. Now into the glove. Holds it in front of the letters. Nods yes. The wind, the one-two pitch. Swing and a ground ball left side. Castro's got it. Spins, throws. He got him! A perfect game for Roy Halladay! Twenty-seven up and twenty-seven down! Halladay is mobbed at the mound as the Phillies celebrate perfection tonight in Miami!"

After the game, Halladay was greeted by his teammates in the clubhouse with a huge ovation and some celebratory pops as well. Halladay gave a short speech, he talked to the vice president of the United States at the time, Joe Biden, and even cracked a smile. Through the first two months of the season, Halladay was certainly living up to the hype.

In June 2010 the annual question as to whether this core had it anymore popped up. However, this time may have felt more real. Honestly, the best thing the Phillies had going for them in the beginning to the middle of June was the cover they were getting from the miracle Flyers Stanley Cup run that unfortunately ended in six games. One of the main themes of the season was all the injuries the team was dealing with, whether nagging ones the guys were playing through or more serious ones with key guys missing time, like Rollins, who was still out. Still, there should have been enough talent there to produce—but the production wasn't there. In June, Manuel had to give Werth a day off because, in his words, "he's worrying too much about his contract," which didn't sit well with the Phillies right fielder who said, "The contract is the last thing on my mind right now."[9]

Still, Werth was struggling, Utley's numbers had fallen off a bit, and Davey Lopes said he was dealing with a knee injury (oh, no!). Howard was hitting for average, but his power numbers were down, and it looked like Father Time was *maybe* starting to catch up to Ibañez. Things were looking so bleak for the Phillies famed offense that a couple of scouts who talked to reporters from the *Philadelphia Inquirer* were raising serious questions about whether the Phillies were actually cheating with the binoculars, given how many top players had fallen off since it was exposed.[10]

What was going well, however, was the top of the Phillies rotation. Halladay was great, but maybe the most important Phil for this team to get back to glory was Hamels, who famously had the brutal 2009 season. In the middle of June, Hamels had three straight starts of seven-plus innings and was starting to look like the pre-2009 version of himself. Still, the Phillies *felt* an arm short in the rotation as the deadline was looming. They got good production out of Kyle Kendrick and Jamie Moyer, but there were legitimate questions about how long those two could keep it up, and Blanton's ERA was still over 6.00 after offseason surgery.

Finally, it felt like the Phillies had settled into the season when Jimmy Rollins came off the IL. They needed their swagger back, and no one was better at delivering that than Rollins. In his second game back, he hit the first walk-off home run of his career to give the Phillies two straight wins with him back in the lineup. They won five of six against the Indians (at the time) and then the Blue Jays, even though the Phillies were visitors in their own ballpark because of the G20 Summit happening in Toronto, and they were *starting* to look like the true Phillies. However, just when it looked like they were about to take off and join the baseball season—after all, they were in third place in the National League East at this point—the nagging injuries came up again. On the same day at the end of June, the Phillies had to place Placido Polanco and Chase Utley on the injured list. Utley sprained his thumb sliding into second base and would end up missing eight weeks, and finally, the elbow was too much for Polanco, who needed time off after it wasn't responding to cortisone shots. Asked by reporters in Cincinnati if he was keeping up, Charlie Manuel responded with, "I don't know if I'm keeping up or not. I'm getting ready to throw up."[11]

It was fair to wonder at the end of June if this team just didn't have it anymore. Without two more starters in the infield, the 2010 Phillies truly felt snakebitten.

Things weren't getting any better to open the month of July, as they started 2–5 and fell to six games back in the NL East. This was their lineup on most nights at the time: Rollins, Ibañez, Werth, Howard, Ben Francisco, Greg Dobbs, Wilson Valdez, and Dane Sardinha. Dane Sardinha! Still, to this point in the season, they had the exact same record as they had had the last two years; the difference was the rest of the division came to play in 2010.

> Similar to how I now feel that no one thinks his or her baseball team has enough to win a title until the parade happens, I believe a specific game or series during the regular season triggers fans to think the team is done, even though 100 or so games are left to play. In 2010 I think that would have been when the Braves came in here and took two of three to put this team six games back in the NL East. Players were all hurt, they were struggling to hit, they had gone so hard the last two postseasons that maybe they were finally hitting a wall. Six games back with 79 games to go is when I declared the 2010 Phillies dead, for those of you keeping track at home.

The Phillies were now six games back, and they had to get hot quickly, *especially* with the July 31 trade deadline now 20 some games away. The Phillies started to pick themselves off the mat against the Reds the next series, winning three straight games in walk-off fashion. During the second game of the series, a younger Jack and Jill Fritz (yes we're Jack and Jill—no, you're not the first person to figure it out) were in the building to see the Phillies storm back from being down 7–1 in the ninth with a six-run bottom half to tie it up. Ryan Howard got a walk-off hit in the bottom of the 10th against former Phillie great Arthur Rhodes. Finally, the Phillies had some wind at their sails. On this same night, the first trade deadline domino fell, as the Mariners traded Cliff Lee to the Texas Rangers. There was some talk about the Phillies possibly reacquiring Lee to add to this rotation, but come on, adding the lefty back into this rotation was a pipe dream. Stop living in fantasyland. Still, Amaro was on the prowl for a starter before the deadline, and one of the biggest ones had just landed elsewhere.

> Before we get to the trade the Phillies made, we *have* to discuss the other move that almost happened around this time; had it not been for a little luck it might have gone down. Yes, another injury came the Phillies' way heading into the trade deadline—this time it would be Victorino missing three weeks with an abdominal strain. However, this injury might have kept Jayson Werth in a Phillies uniform for the remainder of the season. You see, during the weeks leading up to the trade deadline, the

> Phillies were shopping Werth, who was a free agent at the end of the year and was already hinting at wanting to hit the market. The Phillies also were obsessed with making sure their prospect cupboard was not bare. They could have used existing prospects to get a frontline starter and then replenished the farm with a trade of Werth. It was basically what they did in the offseason with the Lee-Halladay swap.
>
> You might be thinking, *Isn't this just cutting off your nose to spite your face?* You would be mostly correct; *however,* you are misremembering the legend of Dom Brown. Yes, Dom Brown was ready and could play right field for the remainder of the season and the postseason if Werth were gone. It would have been ballsy, but Victorino got hurt, so we got Brown up here anyway without having to move on from Werth. Thank God. Brown's first at-bat was legendary. He was the third-best prospect in baseball behind Mike Trout and Bryce Harper—he was a *dude*. After a huge ovation from the Philly faithful, Brown smoked one off the fence in right field for a ringing double. The 2010 Jack and the rest of us fainted; we had another superstar who was going to carry us in the post–Howard, Utley, and Rollins days. What a blessing. That is, until, well, you know. Regardless, that moment was awesome, and so was May and June of 2013.

The final game of the Reds series was wild and memorable. Roy Halladay pitched nine innings of shutout baseball; however, the Phillies headed to the bottom of the ninth to try to win this one because Reds starter Travis Wood had a *perfect game* going. Thankfully, the Phillies scraped out a hit in the inning and then won it in the 11th off the bat of Rollins, his second walk-off hit of the month. But still, what a memorable game. If he had gone through the bottom of the ninth without allowing a hit and the game went into extras with him out of the game,. would that have counted as a perfect game?

Three straight walk-offs might have been the momentum this team needed heading into the All-Star break. That is, until the Phillies came out of the All-Star break flat, much like the inconsistent and maddening team of the first half. Remember just earlier here when someone declared the 2010 Phils dead after dropping two of three versus Atlanta to begin the month? Whoever wrote that really means it now that they lost five of six coming out of the break and were now seven games back of the division crown. A fourth straight division crown seemed a ways away. On July 22 the Phillies pulled the first lever a struggling team does to try to find a spark—fire the hitting coach. Yes, on July 22, the Phillies fired Milt Thompson in a message that they were serious about turning this thing around. Most people around the team knew it wasn't Thompson's fault; even Manuel, the guy who had to fire Thompson, said, "He's not the one doing the hitting."[12] To their credit, it worked. Maybe it was getting healthier—Polanco and Ruiz were now back—or the firing of Thompson; whatever the explanation, they reeled off eight straight wins after the move. It was just what the doctor ordered for Amaro and Company to get a starting pitcher.

The next day, after Brown's arrival, Amaro landed his latest big fish—Astros ace Roy Oswalt. Oswalt was the talk of the town for weeks, much like Halladay the year before, and once again, Amaro put this team in position to go after a world title. Of course, the convo that dominated was, "He should have just kept Lee if he was going to trade for another ace anyway," and one could see the point, but the nice part of the Oswalt deal was he was guaranteed to be here through the 2011 season. The two Roys and Hamels—it was time for the Phillies to chase down the Braves.

That campaign didn't get off to the hottest start, as the 2010 Phillies were bit again by the injury bug—this time Howard went down with an ankle sprain that would sideline him for three weeks. Now the Phillies lineup was without Howard, Victorino, and Utley for the time being. Amaro didn't sit on his hands; he swiftly acquired the veteran Mike Sweeney from the Mariners. It would be the first time in his 16-year career that Sweeney was on a team contending for a playoff spot.

> Two memorable moments for the 2010 Phils happened in mid-August. First, there was nothing like the Phillies owning Jonathan Broxton during this time. No, it wasn't a big playoff game like the Stairs home run and the Rollins walk-off hit. The Phillies came back from three runs down in the ninth on August 12 against him, a nice cherry on top of a tough three-year stretch for the closer.
>
> Second, and not so fun but equally as memorable, was when the Astros came to town later in the month. This series sucked. The Phillies just started to have some mojo, and then a bad Astros team swept the

Phillies in four games. Two of those four games were pitched by former Phils, Brett Myers and J. A. Happ. In the bottom of the 14th inning in game two of the series, Ryan Howard went around on a checked swing that he vehemently disagreed with. Howard threw his bat and yelled at the third-base umpire, Scott Barry, who subsequently threw the Phillies' first baseman out of the game. The mild-mannered Howard sprinted toward Barry and had to be restrained while yelling and waving his finger at him. Tensions were high on the field and in the radio booth as Phillies radio announcer Larry Andersen went on a legendary rant about umpires, saying, "What did he just throw him out for? Why did he throw him out? He has no business being thrown out of this game. They need to watch a replay of this and send this guy out. I'm telling you right now, this is a travesty, and it's what's wrong with these umpires today is that they can't control themselves and they have no composure. That is wrong on Scott Barry's part, plain and simple. That's terrible." Legend.

With that, Howard was out of the game, and the Phillies didn't have a first baseman, which meant Ibañez had to shift from left to first and the newly acquired Oswalt was summoned to play the outfield. That's not the position they had traded top prospects for him to play, I assume. What a night. They lost, but I'll never forget Roy Oswalt's bleep-eating grin as he was standing in left field. Damn you, ghost runner, for robbing us of moments like that.

The good news for the 2010 Phillies was that the Houston series was the last time this team would really face any adversity for the 2010 regular season. Sure, they were two games down in the division at this point, but September was this team's month—a different kind of confidence takes over the ballclub when the calendar flips. After the Houston series, the Phillies went 27–8 to close out the regular season, including a nice 15–1 stretch in the middle of it. Their toughest test in the stretch was a showdown against the Braves to really put a final nail in the coffin of that Atlanta team, which had fallen three games behind the Phillies for the division heading into the matchup. The Phillies really flexed their pitching muscle and gave the fans even more hope heading into the postseason that the three-headed monster at the top of the rotation wasn't to be messed with. First, the resurgent Cole Hamels, who had an ERA under 2.30 since July 1, fired eight innings of one-run baseball to give the Phils the early edge in the series. Not to be outdone, Roy Halladay then followed that game up with seven strong innings of his own to deliver the Phillies an automatic series win and also nail down his 20th win of the season, which was the first time a pitcher had won 20 games here since 1982. Finally, to round it all out and give the Phillies the three-game sweep, and, more important, a six-game lead in the division, Roy Oswalt fired seven innings of shutout baseball to finish off the Braves. Their three aces, the horses that were hopefully going to carry them to a championship, allowed four runs total in the three-game series in front of the rally towels and an electric Citizens Bank Park. Whoever wrote this team off earlier in the season was a fool and should not be writing a book about the Phillies.

The first step of the 2010 team's hopeful return to the World Series was completed on September 27 when their horse, Roy Halladay, fired a complete-game shutout against the Nationals to deliver the Phils their fourth straight division title and the first champagne celebration for the thirty-three-year-old ace.

With 97 wins and the best record in baseball, the 2010 Phillies were in a dangerously good spot heading into the postseason. Some thought the team was Manuel's best yet and, given the injuries throughout the year, the season was his best managing job yet. Rotationwise, Halladay was getting MVP buzz while locking up his second Cy Young Award; the 2009 stink was almost off Hamels, but he obviously needed the playoffs to completely rid himself of it; and Oswalt had been just what the doctor ordered, as he pitched to a 1.74 ERA in the red pinstripes. H2O, as they were called, were ready for the postseason. The only question about the lineup heading into the postseason was what version of Jimmy Rollins would show up. He battled nagging injuries down the stretch run as well, and Victorino had done an admirable job all season filling in at the leadoff spot when the shortstop was down. If Rollins didn't look right, would Manuel unseat him for Victorino?

On the positive side, Ibañez had his best stretch since the first half of 2009; Utley posted an OPS over .900 in September, as did Howard and Werth. But maybe the most surprising was Carlos Ruiz, who had a .960 OPS in September and finished the year with an average over .300. So, the lineup was clicking, the rotation was firing on all cylinders—what about that pesky bullpen? After returning from his heavyweight bout with the chair in San Francisco and no longer in the closer's role, Madson pitched to a 1.64 ERA and Lidge allowed two earned runs total in the final two months of the season.

Outside of those two, the bullpen was a *little* shakier, but this team was more than poised and ready for a deep run into October.

Why not start it off with a little magic?

DOCTOBER

This might sound cocky: given how the Phillies were playing, and the expectations placed upon this baseball team, you could have put the '27 Yankees in front of Phillies fans in the first round of the NLDS and the message would have been the same—Phils in three. By this point, the sentiment in the city was that it was a forgone conclusion that this baseball team would be back in the World Series trying to take the title back from the New York Yankees. Attempting to stand in the way of the buzzsaw was the Cincinnatti Reds, not a bad baseball team! They scored the most runs in the National League! Joey Votto was an MVP candidate, Jay Bruce was a good player, and they had Snot—sorry!—Scott Rolen at third base! Scared? Nope.

"There's no way this is happening, right?" is what every Philadelphian was saying when Roy Halladay singled off Edinson Volquez to give the Phillies a 2–0 lead in the bottom of the second. The Phillies did score three in that inning to give themselves a 4–0 lead in the ballgame, which was more than enough for Halladay on this day. Why? Because what we saw on October 6, 2010, was a man etching himself into baseball immortality.

> I don't think there was ever a doubt in the mind of any Philadelphian that night that Halladay was going to put on a show. It didn't matter that it was his first start in the postseason; the moment was not going to be too bright for him. The confidence that this city had in that man was borderline arrogant. With Cliff Lee the year before, you could make the case about being worried about him heading into the postseason; after all, he was left off the '07 Indians playoff roster and really only had one special year in the big leagues before coming over here. Not Doc! He was built for this and we all couldn't wait to see what he had in store. But I'm not sure any of us thought that he had this in store.

It started pretty nonchalantly—a ho-hum, one-two-three start in the top of the first, but you could tell early in the ballgame that Halladay's stuff had "the look." Votto said so in an MLB Network feature about the no-hitter when Halladay was about to go into the Hall of Fame. Halladay jammed Votto, one of the game's best hitters, on a cutter that Votto weakly grounded to Utley at second base. Votto then said to himself, *Whoa, whoa, whoa, you gotta get going now. This guy is really sharp today.* Votto nailed the scouting report, but it ultimately didn't end up mattering. Jimmy Rollins, in the same feature said, "I'll tell you, after the first inning, I said, 'These boys are in trouble—they don't stand a chance today.'"[13]

Rollins was right. Early on, Halladay was mowing down the Reds, which, besides leading the league in runs, were atop the National League in home runs. The only thing that kept this game from being even more unbelievable was a one-out walk to future Phil Jay Bruce in the fifth. If you look at that at-bat, you'll see that Halladay got squeezed twice by home-plate umpire John Hirschbeck. That was the only blemish on an absolute masterpiece. In the top of the seventh, the Reds had their best "shot" against Halladay with Orlando Cabrera, Joey Votto, and Scott Rolen due up. With one out, Votto was up again against Halladay and tried to throw the pitcher's rhythm off by calling timeout on him twice. This didn't rattle Halladay, as he got Votto to ground out to third base for the second out. Just because it didn't rattle him didn't mean he forgot what Votto was trying to do. At the All-Star Game the next year, Votto said that Halladay said to him that he wanted to walk to home plate and strangle him. Doc was locked in. After retiring the heart of the Reds' lineup in the seventh, the pathway to a no-hitter was set. All he had to do was navigate the bottom of the Reds order and it was over. Around this time, everyone around the city was starting to think to themselves, *Is he really about to do this?* He was. Halladay struck out two more in the eighth to bring his total in the game to eight.

On to the ninth! No one had moved from whatever spot he or she was in—history was about to be made in South Philly. Reds catcher Ramón Hernández started the ninth with a weak pop fly to Utley at second base. One out. Then Miguel Cairo popped out into foul territory on the third-base side to Wilson Valdez. Finally, it was up to Brandon Phillips. Scott Franzke, take it away:

"Just about a quarter to eight, October the sixth, 2010. The first postseason start for Roy Halladay. He winds, the oh-two. A dribbler, out in front of the plate. Ruiz out to get it. The throw from his knees is in time, and it's a no-hitter! Unbelievable! Ruiz and Halladay embrace and the Phillies, once again, celebrate around Roy Halladay!"

He had done it. The first postseason no-hitter since Don Larsen's perfect game in Game Five of the 1956 World Series. After 320 regular-season starts and 11 seasons, Doc wasted no time making his presence felt in the postseason in the most dramatic fashion.

> When it was all said and done, you couldn't help but laugh when Halladay got the job done. Of course he threw a no-hitter in his first postseason start. I know this sounds crazy, but it wasn't surprising. He was a different animal. A couple things have to be pointed out. One, the play that Chooch somehow made routine was insane. That ball was moving every which way, and seemingly hit Phillips's bat lying on the ground one or two times. Rollins out at shortstop said that he didn't think Chooch was going to make the play. "My first thought was that there was no way we were getting him out," Rollins said in the MLB Network feature on the game. "The ball's going to hit the bat, and something is going to happen screwy." But it didn't, and Chooch calmly got on knees and fired a strike to Howard at first base. Second—I got chills writing this—if you read the great book by my friend Todd Zolecki, *Doc*, Victorino tells an unbelievable story about seeing Halladay before the game in the training room. Victorino walked in, and Halladay was on the stationary bike, glued to the TV, and had a fiery look in his eyes. What was he watching? It was the city's former hero, Cliff Lee, carving up the Tampa Bay Rays with seven innings of one-run baseball while striking out 10. According to Victorino, he believed that Halladay knew how much the city loved Lee and he wanted to prove he was the man for the job. Halladay proved that once again

With a playoff no-hitter added to the lore that was this magical couple of years of Phillies baseball, the 2010 postseason was underway. What did they have in store for us next?

Things weren't looking too good for the Fightins in Game Two early. Roy Oswalt started the game and struggled, and the Reds, reeking of embarrassment after Game One, looked ready to go. Game Two provided the first feels-like-a-loss moment of the 2010 postseason. Brandon Phillips led off the game with a home run, Jay Bruce followed it up two innings later with a long ball of his own, and Joey Votto hit a sacrifice fly to make it 4–0, Reds heading into the fifth.

However, the Phillies started to show their might in the fifth. With two outs and Dom Brown on first base, Victorino lined one hard in the hole between first and second, and the ball ate up Brandon Phillips, which allowed both runners to be safe. The next batter, Placido Polanco, smoked a ball at the usually surehanded Rolen, who bobbled it and threw wide of Votto at first base. Just like that, the bases were loaded with two outs for Utley against Reds starter Bronson Arroyo. Utley ripped one into right field to bring home both Brown and Victorino, making the score 4–2, Reds. The ballpark was revived, the Phils were back in the ballgame, but unfortunately the next hitter Howard struck out with the bases loaded. In the sixth, with Arthur Rhodes on the mound and Werth on second base, the forty-year-old left-hander hit Carlos Ruiz to put runners on first and second with one out. Logan Ondrusek was then brought in to face Ben Francisco, whom *he* hit. Bases were loaded, two out, for Shane Victorino, who followed that up with a walk of his own, making the score 4–3, Reds; however, Polanco grounded out to end the frame. That was two bases-loaded opportunities they couldn't capitalize on—still sort of feels like a loss?

That feeling flipped in the bottom of the seventh. You know how Aroldis Chapman always has that look of disbelief when something bad happens in a playoff game? We were to witness to the first Chapman face in this inning. At the time, Chapman was a sensation—a 105-miles-per-hour-throwing southpaw who could shut down any game he entered. It seemed like a tall task for the Phillies in the seventh, but Utley led off the inning by getting hit by a pitch. Two batters later, Werth hit a soft grounder toward Rolen at third base, but he couldn't get the ball to Phillips at second quickly enough. Runners were at first and second with one out for Rollins, who was batting sixth in this one. Rollins lifted an easy fly ball to right fielder Jay Bruce for what should have been the second out of the inning. But Bruce either lost it in the lights or in the rally towels, which allowed both Werth and Utley to come around to score. Were the lights too bright for the little old Reds? Get it? It was now 5–4, Phils, and the Bank was shaking—a bad time to be the Reds. Two batters later, with runners on first and third with one out, the Reds couldn't turn two on a soft grounder to shortstop by Ruiz, which allowed another runner to come home.

The Phillies then tacked on one in the eighth, and Lidge closed the door with a stress-free ninth inning. The Phillies were on to Cincinnati after taking the Reds' best punch and were looking to return to their third straight NLCS.

Game Three was a big test for just how good and how far this Phillies team was going to go in the 2010 postseason. Halladay passed his test, Oswalt was shaky, but the real key was what would Hamels look like. Obviously, if you're this far into the book you don't need the backstory. Hamels looked "back" for a majority of the regular season, but we all know the ultimate test is the postseason. As things turned out, he would reintroduce himself in pretty grand fashion.

How about a complete-game shutout to send the Phillies back to the NLCS to remind everyone that Cole Hamels was still himself? That's just what Hamels did. The Phillies only mustered up two runs, on an error in the first and an Utley home run in fifth, but it was all that was needed. In the ballpark where he made his major league debut and where he was 6–0 lifetime, Hamels pitched a gem. Had it not been for a no-hitter in the first game, it would have been the pitching performance of the series. In total, Hamels struck out nine in the game. The final out was a strikeout of Rolen, his third of the night, which led to an emphatic fist-pump from the usually calm Hamels.

> I remember being so happy for Hamels after this game. The '09 season really sucked, but Cole was still *ours*. Even though new aces were in town, something is different about a homegrown guy. You *felt* his fist pump to end the game—it was like an unleashing of all the frustration he had felt in the last year was let out on one 95 mph fastball to get Scott Rolen. Welcome back, King Cole.

Winning series was becoming the norm for this baseball team. After the Phillies beat Milwaukee in '08, a massive celebration ensued. After they beat the victory over the Reds was a lot of this-is-the-first-step talk. Oh, how far we had come.

H2O had been a success. Worryingly, though, the Reds made seven errors, and the Phillies had only four extra-base hits in the entire series. The offense was going to have to show up in a much bigger way in the NLCS. Unfortunately for them, a freak and a journeyman were in their way.

RING THE BELL
A GIANT PROBLEM

> The confidence the fan base exuded heading into the playoffs had turned into complete cockiness after the takedown of the Reds in the NLDS. The stories published heading into the next series sent a cold shiver down my spine. At this point the Phillies were even money to *win* the World Series. Even money! In Philadelphia? Are you kidding me? The *Inquirer's* preview of the series had matchup advantages, like who had the edge at every position. The Phillies had the edge at every position besides shortstop, which felt like a throwaway—Juan Uribe better than Rollins? Reading all of this and watching the games all over again really made me wish I could go back in time and be the Paul Revere to the Phillies fan base—they needed to be warned. "The Giants are coming! The Giants are coming! The Giants are coming!" as I run outside Citizens Bank Park. Sigh. All right, here we go.

The series set up perfectly for the Giants. No one in the sports world gave them any chance, and the pressure was all on the Phillies The Giants seemingly went into this series with house money. That's crazy, given that they had won 92 games; it wasn't some scrappy 84-win ballclub. (What team would ever lose to an 84-win team in NLCS? I'm getting mad at the 2023 Phillies again.) The Giants had a rotation that stacked up with that of the Phillies. Even though all the hype was around Lincecum, who in his career had eaten the Phillies' lunch, Matt Cain had the better season, Jonathan Sánchez was talented, and, wouldn't you know, they had some young pitcher who would go on to be the big-game pitcher of his generation in Madison Bumgarner. Although the offense wasn't overwhelming, they did have an emerging young superstar catcher in Buster Posey and a collection of guys who were pesky and knew how to play the game. God, this series sucked.

Rarely does baseball do a good job of hyping up its own product, but it did not do a poor job of that in Game One. The short, but long-haired hippie-looking Lincecum took on the poised, hard-working, and stoic Halladay. Oh, the TV drama! The hype was living up to the billing early, as Halladay had retired the first seven batters he faced, continuing his no-hit streak from the Reds start. He looked locked in and dominant against the weak-hitting

Giants. That is, until the unlikeliest of thorns in our sides entered the stage. Cody Ross, who was on the Marlins' team that Halladay threw a perfect game against earlier in the year, was picked up off waivers by the Giants later in the season and was now starting in right field for them. He was eight-hole hitter! You've got to be kidding me! Anyway, he hit his first home run of the night off Halladay in the top of the third to give the Giants an early 1–0 lead. Did it just get tight in here?

It wasn't all bad though; our postseason hero, Carlos Ruiz, led off the next inning with a home run off Lincecum. Both aces have drawn blood early in this heavyweight bout—Game One was back to all tied, until the top of the fifth, when the bad man came back to haunt the city of Philadelphia again. Ross took Halladay deep to left for his second home run of the night, and all of a sudden visions of Joe Jurevicius running down the sideline went through everyone's head. Who was this guy? This was the kryptonite for Halladay? Cody Ross?

The game was now 2–1 in the fifth, and the tightness at Citizens Bank Park was palpable. What transpired in the sixth didn't exactly help matters. With two outs, Posey harmlessly singled into right field—no big deal. However, did we all forget that this was a Pat Burrell–revenge spot for letting him go after 2008? Maybe it was the 10-foot sign in left field, PAT, ELVIS [his dog] ROOTS FOR THE PHILLIES, that gave Burrell the extra motivation. He lifted a ball to deep left field off Halladay. It looked like it had a chance to go, Ibañez was tracking it and was nearing the wall. Instead of just getting back to the wall, he stopped running, misread it, and jumped to try and haul the baseball in—he didn't. This allowed Posey to come around from first base to score and give the Giants a 3–1 lead. Surely, Doc was going to keep it there right? Wrong. Uribe then singled up the middle to bring home the pinch-runner Nate Schierholtz from second: 4–1, Giants in the sixth—gulp.

The Phillies weren't dead yet! With one out and Utley on first, Werth launched a home run to right field off Lincecum to bring the Phils right back in this one at 4–3. Had they caught the ball in the top half of the inning, this would have been even bigger. In classic fashion, all the hype surrounding the pitching matchup and had led to a 4–3 score in the sixth inning. You can't script baseball.

In the bottom of the eighth, the score still 4–3, we were introduced to a guy who presented a problem for the Phillies this entire series. Much like adding Cody Ross was a shrewd midseason move by the Giants, so was trading for lefty specialist Javier López. Much like Pedro Feliciano with the Mets, López was a side-winding, soft-tossing lefty who was seemingly built in a lab to get out Utley and Howard. Well, in his first opportunity in the series he did just that, as he retired them both to start off the top of the eighth. Was Charlie going to have to split his mighty lefties up? We shall see.

You know how a common theme throughout this book has been playoff games feeling like a loss? Of course, this one *reeked* of a loss throughout, but in the top of the ninth it sort of felt like a win. Lidge had just escaped a bases-loaded, one-out jam to keep the Phils a run behind heading into the bottom half of the inning. But they were facing the National League leader in saves in Brian Wilson (remember this guy?), who was developing into another problem for the Phillies. It was not meant to be. Even though Ruiz got hit by a pitch to get on base, they could do nothing, and for the first time in seemingly forever, the Phillies had lost Game One of a playoff series. Cancel the parade route; we might have a problem here.

The Game Two pitching matchup was not hyped as much as that of Game One, but it was still a darn good one. Roy Oswalt was looking to bounce back after a mediocre NLDS appearance, while Jonathan Sánchez was young and talented. The first move in the chess match between these two managers was done by Manuel heading into Game Two, as he split up his lefties, Howard and Utley, against Sánchez, and seemingly, against López for later in the game.

Things were looking good early. With the bases loaded and two outs, Rollins walked to give the Phils the early 1–0 lead. However, in classic feels-like-a-loss fashion, the Phils could only get the one run home, as Ibañez struck out. The score remained the same until the fifth, when the bad man showed up *yet again*; yes, Cody Ross went yard to make it a 1–1 ballgame. Was this all because Halladay threw the perfect game? We take it back! We take it back! (No we don't, but still.) You've got to be kidding. Thankfully, the Phillies answered back in the bottom half of the inning on a sacrifice fly by Polanco to give them a 2–1 lead.

The Phillies put this game on ice in the seventh. Manuel let Oswalt hit to lead off the bottom of the seventh, which felt insane in viewing this game through the modern baseball lens, but he was rewarded as Oswalt singled up the middle. Obviously, if you're going to let him hit, you can't pinch-run for him. With runners on first and second, Polanco drove a single up the middle and rounding third to come home was Oswalt. For some reason, Giants first baseman Aubrey Huff cut the throw off, and Oswalt was able to get in safely to give the Phillies a 3–1 lead. The game became a rout when Rollins, batting with the bases loaded, doubled off the top of the wall to bring everyone around to score. Just like that, it was 6–1, Phillies. Crisis averted. Oswalt handled the eighth, and Madson locked down the ninth to tie this series up. Even though Cody Ross was doing his best to make everyone in Philadelphia nervous, the series was headed back to San Francisco tied one apiece.

Game Three felt like a must-win for the Phillies. The big three for the Phillies was obviously very good, but the fourth? He was a little shaky. Joe Blanton was set to toe the rubber in Game Four, and Manuel had said previously that he didn't want to start guys on short rest just yet, so it was likely just going to be the Phils' fourth starter. The other problem for the Phillies as they headed out west was that they did not play well at AT&T Park (the name at the time), as they were 14–24 there since it opened in 2000, which was the worst record they've had in any of the National League parks, and they hadn't won a series there since 2006. Not great! Matt Cain, the Giants' starter, had never beaten the Phillies, however, and his ERA was over 6.00. Something had to give. Let's get into Game Three.

Through four-and-a-half innings, this pitching matchup was developing better than that of Game One. Hamels was perfect heading into the bottom of the fourth and Cain was pitching a shutout as well. That changed when with two outs, Hamels walked Burrell to bring the boogeyman to the plate again in Ross. Now, he didn't go yard this time, but he did line one into left field to score Edgar Renteria from second base to give the Giants a 1–0 lead. Things went from bad to worse when the next batter, Aubrey Huff, weakly singled into right field off the glove of Utley. From my vantage point, if Utley had reeled that one in, he *probably* would have gotten up and thrown out Huff at first base, but it was not an easy play. The Giants were up, 2–0. With the Phillies offense failing to really put anything together against Cain, it was important for Hamels to keep the score at 2–0 to give this offense a shot.

Plans changed in the fifth, with former Phil Aaron Rowand on second with a leadoff double, Giants second baseman Freddy Sanchez knuckled a ball toward Utley at second base. It completely ate him up, as the ball bounded into center field, allowing Rowand to come around and score. A 3–0 lead, given the current feebleness of the Phillies offense and the pitching of Cain, might as well have been 10–0. The Phillies only threatened in the seventh with runners on first and second and two outs, but Victorino grounded out sharply to Sánchez. They were turned away yet again. Javier López handled the eighth, getting out Utley and Howard yet again, and Wilson got the ninth. The Phillies went down without much of a fight against the Giants pitching staff and had their backs up against the wall against a team they were so heavily favored to beat. The 2010 season was on the brink.

The offense was turning into the Phillies' biggest problem in this series and postseason. There were signs in the Reds series: only four extra-base hits in the entire series. But with the Giants' pitching combined with no errors killing San Francisco in the field, the Phils could muster up little on the offensive side. Now down 2–1 in the series, would Manuel change it up and have Halladay go on short rest in a vital Game Four? In what could have been viewed as controversial when the series was over, Manuel opted not to start Halladay in Game Four, instead leaving it up to Joe Blanton. The Phillies skipper was sticking to his guns.

In the '08 chapter we said, "They lost; it sucked. On to Game X!" Unfortunately, at this point of the book, the losses are the stories, and we're reliving the pain these ones brought. Game Four of the 2010 NLCS was a good example of that because this one actually felt like a win. That's what always makes the losses hurt so much worse. Game Four was pivotal in this series; if they lost, it was *essentially* over. But with a win, they might have a shot in this thing. Trailing 2–1 in the fifth with runners on first and second with two outs, Placido Polanco shot a perfectly placed double to the wall in left-center field against Giants reliever Santiago Casilla to bring in both runners on base. After all the momentum was seemingly on the Giants' side in this one, the Phils all of a sudden had the lead. This was starting to feel even *more* like a win when Casilla loaded the bases up against Jimmy Rollins. He ushered a wild pitch to bring home Polanco—4–2, Phils. But as they always say, it's the hope that kills you.

The bottom of the sixth was where this game flipped from "this kind of feels like a win" to "no, this is definitely a loss." It started with Chad Durbin walking Pat Burrell, then Cody freakin' Ross doubled into short left field. Runners were at second and third with no outs—gulp. Wasting no time, Pablo Sandoval smoked a ball past Victorino in left-center field that got all the way to the wall. Everything felt like it was moving in slow motion, as it felt like the season was slipping away from the Phillies.

God, this game is brutal to relive. So it's hard to admit that the feeling like the Phillies might be able to steal one was coming back. In the seventh, Rollins made a brutal error off the bat of Cody Ross (because of course), which loaded the bases for Sandoval. Sandoval grounded into a double play to keep the deficit at one run. They were getting breaks? Then in the top of the eighth, Ryan Howard led off the inning with a double against Javier López—which seemed like an impossible task. Werth followed that up by doubling down the left-field line off of Sergio Romo. In the blink of an eye, the Phillies tied this one up. They weren't dead yet!

With the game still tied in the bottom of the ninth and Manuel out of his good options in the bullpen—he had been aggressive, knowing that he would still need Lidge to possibly close it out if they got a lead. So he brought in Game Two starter Roy Oswalt. It didn't go well; Huff and Posey both hit one-out singles to set up first and third with one out for Juan Uribe, who promptly lifted a ball to left field to end the game on a sacrifice fly. The Phillies fought, but ultimately it was all for naught. The team that we had grown accustomed to seeing win series and reach the World Series was down, 3–1, to an opponent it was heavily favored against. What an odd feeling.

What happened in Game Five, however, was chill-inducing.

In the second inning, with the Phillies already down 1–0, starter Roy Halladay reached back for a little extra in an at-bat against none other than Cody Ross and felt immediate pain in his groin. After the inning, he got checked out by the trainers, who determined he pulled his groin. Most pitchers in this moment might be done for the night, but not Doc. "He wasn't going to let us take him out," Manuel said after the game. So the Phillies, with their back up against the wall, facing the back-to-back Cy Young champ Tim Lincecum, had to win a game with their ace ailing. Sounds fun! In the third, the Phils took the lead when Victorino smoked one off of Aubrey Huff at first base that allowed both Ibañez and Carlos Ruiz to come around and score. The next batter, Polanco, singled up the middle to bring home Victorino to make it a 3–1 ballgame.

With that, the nursing Halladay went to work. Given his state, Halladay had to change from the pitcher he usually was. His push-off leg was compromised so that bite on his fastball just wasn't there. Halladay had to turn crafty and use his off-speed pitches more to keep the Giants off balance. It worked, as Halladay allowed only one more run and ended up firing six innings of two-run baseball to keep the Phillies' hopes alive. Let's add this performance on one leg in the biggest game of his life to the growing list of legends for Roy Halladay. Had they come back and won this series (sorry for the spoiler), it would have been talked about for years. The Phillies did end up winning this one. Jayson Werth homered in the ninth for an insurance run, and the bullpen trio of José Contreras, Madson, and Lidge fired three shutout innings.

After the game, Manuel went up to Halladay and offered up a joke. "When are you going to be available? Next year?"

Halladay, stone-faced as ever, replied, "Five days."

They were still alive.

> I don't want to write about Game Six. I hate Game Six, but for you, the wonderful readers of this book, I will write about it. Just know that I am reliving the pain so you don't have to. But you are reading this portion, so maybe you're just a glutton for punishment like I am? The pain is what makes the great moments that much sweeter. What if the next great moment didn't happen until like twelve years later—*it was all worth it.* Sigh. Let's get to Game Six.

If the Phillies were to come back in this series, they needed their stars to shine. The first was on the mound; they were in a pretty good spot there. Of course, people were freaking out about Oswalt being on the mound in Game Six after he had just pitched in Game Four, but that was essentially a bullpen—he threw 18 pitches. Also, in a potential Game Seven, the resurgent Cole Hamels was locked in and ready to go. The other stars were in the lineup. Ryan Howard was getting some hits, but up until this point, he didn't have a home run or RBI, and his partner in crime, Chase Utley, was currently enjoying the worst postseason of his career—hitting only .200. They needed their stars to shine.

Early on in this one, things were looking good. The Phillies jumped on Jonathan Sánchez, as he walked Polanco—following that with a wild pitch, sending Polanco to second—to bring up Utley, who greeted Sánchez with a ringing double off the right-field wall to give them a 1–0 lead. Howard then followed that up with a single to move Utley to third with one out for Jayson Werth. On a summer night, the ball that Werth hit would have ended up in the bushes or a few rows back in left—he *just* missed giving the Phillies a 4–0 lead in this one, but it was deep enough to get Utley across the plate. Oh, the pain. Still, the Phillies exited the first inning up 2–0. Things were looking good.

That feeling would die a cold death in the top of the third when Sánchez led off the inning with a single up the middle that Utley should have had. Andrés

Torres followed that up by smoking a ball to deep center field. Victorino didn't look like he got the best read on it, and the ball kept carrying and carrying toward the wall. In a Willie Mays–like way, Victorino caught the ball, but then collided with the wall, which jarred the ball loose. He did not secure the catch and two feet were not in bounds (this is just a joke). Uh-oh, the feeling of doubt was starting to creep in! After a bunt to move runners into second and third with one out, Aubrey Huff smoked a single up the middle to at least plate one. But the problem for the Giants was that Victorino had a cannon for an arm and gunned down Torres at the plate. It was still a 2–1 ballgame at this point with Buster Posey coming up. Oswalt *had* to get him out here, and it looked like he had done just that, as the Giants' catcher hit a slow roller to Polanco. The Phils' third baseman charged it, brought it in, but made an errant throw to Howard at first base to allow Huff to come around and score from second. The game was now tied on a brutal defensive inning from the Phillies.

What transpired after this was nothing other than absolute torture that you wouldn't wish on your worst enemy.

> I watched this game in public because, being sixteen, I thought I had to be the cool guy and be with others. I realized then, though, that I was not built to watch Phillies postseason games around people. Now at the ripe old age of thirty, I know to never do that again. Shoutout to my best friend and fellow absolutely diseased Phillies fan, Tom O'Neill, and, of course, my now wife, and girlfriend at the time, Jill—who had to be questioning her decision to date me at this point.
>
> The last moment of life I felt in this one happened in the bottom of the third inning. After a leadoff walk by Polanco, Utley was hit in the top of the back by Sánchez. As he ran up the first-base line, the ball bounced right to him. Calmly, Utley flipped the ball to Sánchez, who seemed irked by the move. He jawed at Utley, who replied back with an expletive and a nonchalant wave of his hand. This caused Huff to get in Utley's face a bit and the benches to clear. This should have been a galvanizing moment for the Phillies to show they weren't going down without a fight. Sánchez was removed from the game and they had runners on first and second with no outs. *Come on!* Nope, Howard struck out, Werth popped up to short right, and Victorino grounded out weakly to first base. Kill me.
>
> The slow march to death was on.

In the bottom of the fifth, with the speedy Rollins on first base, Howard smoked one off the wall in left-center field. You would think Rollins would score on this; however, it was going to be a bang-bang play at the plate, so third-base coach Sam Perlozzo decided to hold him. With two outs, that was a tough call. Giants manager Bruce Bochy then walked Werth to set Madison Bumgarner on Victorino with the bases loaded. He grounded out back to Bumgarner—opportunity wasted. We marched on.

After a double play ended a Giants threat in the top of the sixth, the Phillies were looking poised to capitalize on the momentum when Ibañez led off the next inning with a double and was bunted over to third by Ruiz. But pinch-hitter Ben Francisco struck out, and Rollins popped out to end another golden opportunity. You could just *feel* this one coming; you just didn't know when or how it was going to happen.

It happened in the eighth. With Madson working his second inning of relief and two men down already in the inning, Juan Uribe, on the first pitch from Madson, lifted one to right field. Eerily similar to Álex Rodríguez's ball the year before, Uribe's fly ball went over the fence to give the Giants a 3–2 lead. Absolute pain.

But again, the Phillies couldn't just die quietly and not give us any hope. In an absolutely absurd move, Bruce Bochy went to Tim Lincecum, who had just thrown 104 pitches two nights before, to try to shut down the Phillies in the eighth. It backfired, as back-to-back Phillies hitters singled off Lincecum to give them first and second with one out. Bochy then brought in Brian Wilson to put out the fire. He would do just that as Ruiz ripped a ball at Huff at first base, and he calmly threw it to second to double off Victorino. They couldn't break through. Maybe in the ninth they would?

With Wilson still in there, Rollins drew a one-out walk. Polanco followed that up with a grounder toward third that the Giants couldn't turn two on. With two outs and the season on the line, Utley drew a walk to bring up Ryan Howard. This was his moment—no RBIs in the postseason just yet. It was going to be the 2010 version of the "Get me to the plate, boys." On a 3–2 pitch, with an entire crowd holding their breath, Wilson fired a backdoor cutter that froze Howard and ended the Phillies season.

It was about as excruciating a game as you could imagine. After two runs in the first, the Phillies offense couldn't score a run for eight innings and wasted multiple opportunities to steal it. The season was over; 97 wins, a perfect game, and a postseason no-hitter all for naught. The fun that it looked like players were having early in their string of runs had turned to the pressure of having to get it done for a second time. You could just see the tension on their faces as another year passed by without the most talented team in club history having a parade down Broad Street.

Overall, for a season that ended the way that it did, the 2010 team had a lot of magical moments—most of them orchestrated by Roy Halladay. However, the squad had a glaring problem. It was starting to get long in the tooth. Heading into 2011, the Phillies didn't have a starter in the lineup under the age of thirty, their ace was thirty-three, their closer was thirty-three—all of a sudden it was getting late fast on this Phillies core, which made 2011 that much more imperative.

On to 2011.

DOMINANCE AND DESPAIR

Aah, the 2011 Phillies—this one is going to hurt to write. It was another off-season of transition for a ballclub that still had the core and dreams of having another title down Broad Street, except this time they'd have to do it without one of their best.

Jayson Werth, after months of speculation, finally did end up leaving the Phillies. Armed with his new agent, Scott Boras, Werth ended up taking a seven-year $126 million deal to go join the Phillies "rival" Washington Nationals. It was a shocking move and one that it sure didn't seem like the Phillies saw coming given that their offer to Werth was reportedly around $65–$70 million. Maybe Werth was right when he said, "I don't know what they were thinking. It's something they're going to have to answer. Unfortunately, it didn't work out. I did have a great time in Philadelphia. Once you get to a point where you feel unwanted or you get a sense you're not a part of the plans, it's time to move on." Werth would say more as the season was getting closer, but it was clear he was hurt by the Phillies seemingly undervaluing what he brought to the table, and make no mistake—they would miss him. In a year where the offense had a step-back season, Werth was their best player, hitting .296 with a .921 OPS. Dom Brown, his perceived replacement, had talent but for a team with World Series aspirations, it would be a stretch to believe he could put up similar production. Still, with a young player like that who was still one of the top prospects in baseball, you have to give him some runway to see if he can take the job and run with it. Hindsight is always 20/20, but in this case, it is hard to fault the Phillies, who had a lot of money tied up in position players already, for not wanting to see if their young, talented outfielder could do the job.

With Werth officially gone, it was on Amaro to get creative, and he did.

When Cliff Lee got traded to the Mariners in the offseason before the 2010 season, the left-hander said that he was "shocked" and that he was planning to sign an extension in Philadelphia. Thankfully for us, the left-hander didn't harbor much ill feelings because on December 14, 2011, Ruben Amaro Jr. made a move that sent shockwaves through Major League Baseball. He brought Cliff Lee home. No one even mentioned the Phillies with Lee; it was perceived that he was going to either return to the Rangers or take the Yankees' money and go to New York. However, that was until the longing of playing at Citizens Bank Park in the postseason again took over Lee and he was able to get a deal done here. Oh, the city of Philadelphia was on cloud nine; a star player wanted to come here *again and* he turned down the YANKEES (!) to do it. Build the Clifton Phifer Lee statue right now.

> The night was wild. This was the first time I had followed a story not in the newspaper or on *SportsRise* the next morning. The story was happening in real time. I didn't know what Twitter was yet, but apparently news was being talked about on there. No, the site I was using for the first time was MLBTradeRumors.com, which I must have refreshed a million times that night. For those of you who don't remember, Jon Heyman tweeted earlier in the night that there a mystery team was vying for Lee's services, but no one knew who it was.[14] As it turned out, that team was the Phillies, and when I woke up the next day, after following this as late as I could (I had school the next day; you know—education?), I vividly remember waking up with a text from my buddy that simply stated, "We got him." What baseball team were we following? They spend big money and have a rotation of Halladay, Lee, Hamels, and Oswalt? Is this heaven? Nope, it was Philadelphia.

Surely, Werth felt burned that they were able to pay Lee essentially the same salary the Nationals paid him, but maybe his departure expedited the pursuit of another top talent like Lee. Regardless, the Phillies had stretched their wallets to bring home a guy who never wanted to leave, to create arguably the best rotation, on paper, in baseball history. Now, they just had to go win the World Series.

No pressure.

The Phillies showing up at spring training 2011 was the baseball version of The Beatles coming to the United States in 1964. There was excitement in each of the last three spring trainings, but when they added Lee to formulate one of the best rotations in the history of the game, there was a different kind of buzz. The story of spring unfortunately was the injuries, and they were big ones. Dom Brown went down with a broken hamate bone on an awkward swing, which sidelined him for three to six weeks. He was supposed to be the Werth replacement in right field. The next was one that had been bubbling under the surface for a couple of years now and would plague him for the rest of his career and was Chase Utley's knees. He would miss the first six weeks of the season with knee tendinitis. Finally, which seemed like a spring tradition by now, Lidge was dealing with a shoulder injury that would sideline him until late July. Oof. Still, this is why you assemble R2C2, which was definitely not on a shirt that one of the writers of this book had.

However, despite the question marks, and there were real ones, the Phillies headed north for what was the most anticipated season in Philadelphia baseball history. Let's get into the 2011 regular season.

It started how you would have liked, with a John Mayberry Jr. walk-off hit after trailing by three in the ninth on Opening Day and then a sweep of the Astros behind the aces doing their thing. Ho hum, stress-free—what a breeze this season was going to be—sorta.

Interestingly, the story of the 2011 Phillies' regular season really was about who was going to step up with everything a lot of the stalwarts of the team were dealing with—besides the aces. Ben Francisco was getting the lion's share of playing time in right field. Antonio Bastardo and Mike Zagurski (look up this hoss if you've never seen the legend) were filling in for J. C. Romero. Wilson Valdez and Pete Orr were taking down second base and, eventually, Vance Worley and Michael Stutes would make their presence felt. For all the star power that the '11 Phillies had, the guys who helped keep them afloat while others were getting healthy were the real story during the regular season.

One fascinating situation that was brewing had to do with Ryan Madson. He was in a contract year and wanted to close, for obvious reasons—closers get paid. The Phillies drew ire from Madson when they opened up the season and named the thirty-nine-year old José Contreras their closer. The quotes from both sides were shocking. After the decision was made, Madson said, "My only comment is I'm here to play for the other twenty-four guys, my family and the fans."[15] Oof. Rich Dubee offered his own opinion on Madson not closing when he said, "Ryan Madson is Ryan Madson. What did he do, take a crash course in how to close or something?" Obviously, the Phillies didn't think Madson had the mental fortitude it took to close out ballgames for them. Regardless, at the end of the April they had no choice. Contreras went down with a flexor strain in his elbow, which opened the door for Madson to take the closer's job and run with it. Ultimately, he would.

In early May, Jayson Werth made his first return trip to the city he helped bring a championship to. Oh yeah, this was going to go well. (Why don't books have a sarcasm font yet?) The war between the fans of Philadelphia and Jayson Werth was still bubbling—it hadn't reached its boiling point just yet. It obviously started when Werth left and took the huge contract with our "rivals" to help teach them how to win down in Washington, but it also was aided by some comments Werth made to the *Washington Post*. In spring training, Werth was at the batting cage when the Nats' GM, Mike Rizzo, quipped that he "[expletive] hates the Phillies," to which Werth replied back, "I hate the Phillies too."[16] That's not the best match for the ole Philadelphia faithful, but he clearly wanted to stay, and the Phillies chose Cliff Lee over him—he was mad. Werth's first at-bat was a bit rocky, but we got there. When he started to the plate, it sounded like a good amount of boos, but as he tipped his cap and the umpire called time, the boos were drowned out with cheers, which was good to see. The Werth-Philly thing would eventually turn ugly, but at least for one night it wasn't too bad. After all, he was a key figure in the best run in franchise history.

With the Werth return over, the wait for Chase Utley to return was officially on in Phillies land. Utley had been rehabbing in Clearwater to get ramped up to make his return north to help a Phillies offense that was in more than just a skid—it was downright brutal. With Utley out of the lineup, Dom Brown rehabbing in Lehigh Valley, and both Ruiz and Victorino missing time during this stretch—the Phillies offense was scuffling. Before Utley's return, the team had scored three runs or fewer in 27 of 42 games, had scored three runs or fewer in nine straight, and had managed six or fewer hits in eight of nine. Hey, no pressure on the four aces or anything, but they better be perfect, or else we might not win. The middle of the last couple of regular seasons saw questions about whether this Phillies offense was going to be good enough in October, but this might have been the most legit of all of those years. Still, with Utley returning maybe it would spark this offense.

In Utley's third game back, on May 25, we would have the regular season game of the year against the Cincinnati Reds. Fast-forward to the 10th inning when Jay Bruce untied the game with a home run to right off Antonio Bastardo. Ryan Howard followed that up with a dramatic home run of his own to retie the game in the bottom of the frame. With that, we went further into extra innings. Remember, this was pre–ghost runner, so these games could take a while. With the Phillies not wanting to use any of their starters to win this one, they turned to their bullpen pieces to navigate however many innings this one was going to go. The first hero was David Herndon, who fired 2 1/3 scoreless. Then Manuel told Danys Báez essentially to pitch until his arm fell off. I'm not sure if the real conversation went that way, but it sure seemed so, as Báez threw *five* innings in relief, which was something he hadn't done in nine years.

The game turned into the stuff of legends when Wilson Valdez took the hill in the top of the 19th inning to face the heart of the Reds order in Votto, Rolen, and Bruce. This game was about to be over, right? Wrong. Valdez got the reigning NL MVP in Votto to pop up on a 90 mph fastball, Jay Bruce flew out to the wall, Wilson hit Rolen, and then he got Carlos Fisher, a pitcher, to fly out to short right field. This wasn't what you see from these position players that pitch now where they lob it up there. Valdez was legit trying to throw hard, and it worked. He ran off the mound to a standing ovation, he fake-threw his glove at teammates who were making fun of him—it was a great moment at the ballpark. Thankfully, Ibañez ended it in the bottom of the 19th because it may have been another Valdez inning, and we all would have been robbed of Wilson Valdez being able to be mentioned in the same sentence as Babe Ruth. With that feat, Valdez became the first player since Ruth in 1921 to start the game in the field and end up with the win on the mound—take that, Sultan of Swat.

As the calendar flipped to June, one member of the four aces wasn't really living up to the hype. Entering into the month, Lee's ERA was—gasp!—3.94, which for most pitchers is fine, but for this team? Come on, Cliff—pull your weight around here. He exited the month of June with an ERA of 2.66. The Phillies left-hander threw 32 scoreless innings to close out the month and pitched three-straight complete game shutouts. It was only, at the time of writing this book, 13 years ago, but that seems insane. Hell, if a pitcher throws a complete game in today's game, there's talk of giving him an extra day to get right. Lee found his groove in a big way and only allowed one run for the entire month. Welcome to the season, Cliff.

As the Phillies exited June, they were the first team in baseball to reach the 50-win mark. It was an interesting dichotomy watching and listening to fans talk about the ballclub. They were in one of two camps with them. The first camp was appreciating what we were watching with this pitching staff and marveling at a rotation that had so much hype and was living up to it. The second camp already had their eyes on October and had a fear that this offense was going to hold back the team from reaching the ultimate goal. Both were legitimate. The starting staff was absurd; unfortunately, in June they lost Roy Oswalt to a nagging back injury that would sideline him for a little bit, but in his place Vance Worley was more than carrying his own. In 2011 Vanimal (his nickname) was a little cocky and had a nasty two-seam fastball that would start at the lefty's hip and end up on the corner, a perfect combination for the Phillies' faithful to get behind. The Phillies had the best record in baseball but had scored three runs or fewer in 44 of the first 81 games; they were 34–3 when they scored four or more runs and were 36–14 in games started by Halladay, Lee, and Hamels. It was just going to come down to October and if Amaro was going to make another splash at the deadline.

While Manuel was publicly pushing for another bat around this time, Amaro stated that they probably weren't going to be in the mix for the big names at the trade deadline, namely Hunter Pence or Carlos Beltrán. Suuuure, Rube. Regardless, the first 81 games were finished, and it was evident that we were watching one of the greatest regular seasons in Phillies franchise history.

Multiple times while writing this book, I sat back, laughed to myself, and said, "Baseball." That was on display yet again when the Phillies went to the Rogers Centre in early July to take on the Blue Jays in Halladay's return to Toronto. It was an emotional day for Doc. While warming up, he got a three-minute ovation from a Toronto faithful that had over forty-four thousand people in the stands that day. A bedsheet in center field read, WELCOME HOME, DOC. PLEASE BE GENTLE. He threw a complete game—because of course he did. Sure, this could have been enough for you to kick back, chuckle to yourself and say, "Baseball," but what really hammered it home was that it was 10 years to the day that he got recalled by the Blue Jays after getting demoted all the way down to Single A to fix himself. Ten years later, he was in the middle of authoring a Hall of Fame career. Now, that's baseball.

The rest of July was more of the same for the Phillies: pitching dominated, but the hitting was starting to really come together. They took two of three from Atlanta, including a 14–1 walloping in the final game of the series to increase their lead in the NL East to 3 1/2 games heading into the All-Star break. In total, the Phillies sent five guys to the All-Star game: Halladay, Lee, Hamels, Victorino, and Polanco. In a pretty cool moment, Doc started the game, threw two innings, and then gave way to Cliff Lee for an inning and two-thirds. Look at how far we've come—our guys opening the All-Star Game. I never thought we'd see the day. The National League won, 5–1.

With the All-Star break in the rear-view mirror, it was officially Amaro season. What move did the general manager have up his sleeve this deadline? Unfortunately and fortunately for Amaro the expectation was now that he was going to land a star—when you trade for Lee and Oswalt in back-to-back deadlines, that expectation is warranted—but could they really purge more from the farm system? This was the cat and mouse game they were playing with the media in the weeks leading up to the deadline. "We're probably just going to add around the edges of the roster" was coming from the front office. However, when a team is on pace to set the franchise wins record, the GM just has to bite the bullet and go all in. Maybe it was a different move that forced the Phillies hand in making another major trade at the deadline. The Giants were in town right as the hot stove was heating up at the end of July. The Giants at this point had four less wins than the Phillies but, obviously, had a ton of real estate in the players' heads. While in Philadelphia, the Giants not only took two of three from the Fightin's but also completed a major trade for Mets outfielder Carlos Beltrán, which was a major power move in the National League at the time. Interestingly, the guy they traded for Beltrán? That would be none other than Zack Wheeler, who was viewed as one of the best prospects in all of baseball at this time and a major coup for the Mets. With Beltrán in the fold, many viewed the Giants, and not the Phillies, as the best team in the National League, which had to irk Amaro. So, on July 29, the date that he also traded for Lee and Oswalt the two previous years, Amaro traded for Hunter Pence from the Astros. This time they sent out Jared Cosart, Jonathan Singleton, and Josh Zeid to get it done. The trade for Pence was significant; unlike Beltrán, he wasn't a free agent at the end of the year—the Phillies had control of Pence for two more seasons after this, which clearly pleased them. The Werth replacement was officially here, and Manuel landed the right-handed hitter in the lineup that he so coveted.

With Pence in the fold, and not that it wasn't already, it was officially World Series or bust time in Philadelphia.

> I don't know if it comes across here that I'm a bit of a goofy, sometimes sappy, dork when it comes to the Phillies. I would say '11 was the peak of this, and I'll let you be the judge of whether this was cool. When they got Pence, it was the summer heading into my senior year of high school. In his second game as a Phillie, he scored the winning run on a walk-off hit by Ibañez and was interviewed by "The Sarge," Gary Matthews, after the game. When asked what he was thinking as he rounded third base and was coming home, Pence uttered the phrase, "Good game; let's go eat!" That phrase might as well have been my calling card the rest of the summer and my senior year, so much to the point that I believe my senior yearbook quote was that phrase. There's no way *that* was cool. I should be embarrassed.

Nothing that gets this city's juices flowing like a good old-fashioned rivalry. Certainly, one was brewing with the Phillies and Giants. The Giants had just upended the Phillies the year before, both teams made big swings before the trade deadline, and neither really had much respect for the other. When the Giants were in Philadelphia about two weeks before their rematch in San Francisco in early August, Charlie Manuel had stated that both Tim Lincecum and Matt Cain were good, not great starters—hell of a take, Chuck! This irked Lincecum, but it did set up a real playoff-like intensity for a regular-season series in August on the West Coast. The series started with Cliff Lee throwing a complete-game shutout as the Phils won 3–0, but this was just the appetizer. The main course was an all-out brawl that happened the next night, August 5, when the Phils already had a six-run lead in the sixth. Everything was fine until Ramón Ramírez drilled Victorino in the back with a 92 mph fastball. Victorino made a move like he was going to charge the mound, which made the Giants' catcher, Eli Whiteside, rush out and start jumping up and down in front of Victorino like an absolute loser (opinion). Before you knew it, benches had cleared, Whiteside and Polanco were going at it, and for a baseball fight the scrum was legit. Just when it seemed like tensions had cooled off, Victorino laid a Brian Dawkins–like hit on Ramírez once he was able to find him among the Giants. A good old-fashioned fisticuffs rivalry—I miss it. The Phils exacted some revenge on the Giants from a couple weeks prior and took three of four in San Fran.

> I'll tell you what, Victorino must have been really annoying to other teams because it sure seemed like guys were always throwing at him. Leave Victy alone!

The Phillies were in the midst of their best 10-game road trip ever. They ended the run 9–1, thanks to a getaway day comeback against the Dodgers that started when they were down 6–0 in the contest. During the span, Lee fired 17 innings of shutout baseball, and Pence was finding his footing, as he launched three home runs. The Phillies were 37 games over .500, had opened an 8 1/2-game lead in the division and were firing on all cylinders as October was right around the corner. The Phillies were officially approaching "too good" territory. What's that? It's that feeling that every Philadelphia sports fan has when things are going too well. Philadelphia sports aren't about greatness; we don't even know what that word means. We like being the underdog and get uncomfortable being the top dog. The best record never wins the big prize, and the locals were begging for a losing streak: "It's not supposed to be this easy. Make it harder!" It's a weird feeling and pretty unique to Philadelphia.

As the Phillies were ready to exit August and head into September and the stretch run of the season, Mother Nature had some other plans. Thanks to multiple rain delays due to Hurricane Irene, the Phillies played just one game between August 24 and August 29, which meant they would have to play 33 games in 31 days to make it to 162. Maybe file that one away for the end of this chapter.

On September 17 the Phillies completed the first step on what was shaping up to be a historic 2011 season. No other team in the 129-year history (at the time) had clinched the division as early as they did, and they were officially four wins short of setting the club's all-time wins record. Interestingly, they got to celebrate after beating the Cardinals, of all teams, to clinch the East. Again, file that one away for later.

> The different camps of Phillies fans during this time had to be so fun. The older camp was maybe around for 1964 but definitely was there during the lean times; fans here had to be having an out-of-body experience as the Phillies wrapped up their division title. Then you had the younger camp, my camp, fans who were 100 percent taking this all for granted. Those idiots—the finger pointing right at me—were naive to believe that this is just how it was with the Phillies. We win all the time. Oh, the blissful ignorance of the youth.
>
> One of my favorite parts of watching the Phillies clinch during those years was getting to see someone who's never won before experience it for the first time. It started with Cliff Lee in '09, then Doc in '10, and, finally, Pence in '11. Professional athletes turned into little kids again, albeit without the beer showers—nothing better. When they clinched in '11, the entire clubhouse was waiting for Pence to walk through the door, and then they celebrated. Little stuff like this brings a team closer together.

What happened after they clinched was not ideal, and the feeling of doubt crept into every single Philadelphian. There's a bit of a blessing and a curse when a baseball team clinches early in September. The blessing is the playoff spot and, after the long, grueling regular season, players can take their foot off the gas. Players can rest and make sure they're fresh heading into the postseason. The curse is that the intensity in place for over five months is gone. In baseball, if teammates just play out the string, given the mundane nature of the sport, it is hard to pull themselves out of it. Also, rest is great, but rust is worse, *especially* in a sport like baseball that is so dependent on rhythm and routine. Unfortunately for this great team, players slipped, and the question was whether they'd be able to flip the switch back on when the postseason started.

After they clinched, the '11 Phillies lost eight games. Eight! There's taking the foot off the gas, and then there's whatever they did. The downturn started with losing three of four at home to the St. Louis Cardinals. Once again I started running through the streets of Philadelphia like Paul Revere: "This was a bad idea!" They then followed that up by getting swept at home in a four-game set against the .500 Nationals. Hunter Pence was pulled from the first game of a doubleheader against the Nats with a knee injury, and Ryan Howard sat for a week with left-ankle inflammation—file that last one away. After the losing streak reached eight, enough was enough for Manuel, who put all of his regulars in the lineup in the last game of the Mets series, and they won the game, 9–4. Was that enough to calm the nerves in Philly? The last series of the year in Atlanta had a good amount of intrigue for a team playing out the string. The first was that the Phillies needed a sweep to set the franchise record for wins, and if they were able to do that, Manuel would become the all-time winningest manager in club history. The Braves had a nine-game lead in the wild-card race heading into September, but their free fall had them only a game up on the Cardinals heading into the series. It was a nice little playoff atmosphere at Turner Field before the real thing started.

The Phillies did their part. They swept the Atlanta Braves (what a choke job, by the way), and it wasn't like the Phillies played all their regulars. Integrity of the sport is great, but ultimately a manager has to do what's best for the ballclub. Behind Lee and Oswalt, the Phillies won the first two games of the series, and in the finale they started Blanton, who was fighting for a postseason roster spot. The game would take over four hours, the Phillies would use nine pitchers (including Hamels), Craig Kimbrel (who had 47 saves on the year) blew a lead in the ninth, and they were finally able to squeak out a run in the top of 13th to give themselves the lead. The Braves' season ended on the bat of Freddie Freeman as David Herndon fired a scoreless bottom of the 13th. The Cards won two of three in Houston to clinch the National League wild card. At the time, the sentiment was definitely, "Ha ha, Braves!" In about a week and a half, letting the Cardinals in would be no laughing matter.

Before we get into the playoffs, Kevin wanted to make sure we *properly* put this 2011 regular season into perspective for the Phillies rotation.

The following excerpt was originally printed in 2016's Incredible Baseball Stats *by Ryan Spaeder and Kevin Reavy:*

Simply put, that regular season, the Phillies had the *greatest starting rotation of all-time.* Well, at least among five-man rotations. Maybe.

The five-man has roots that date back to the early part of last century, but it didn't become a staple of the game until the 1970s. In terms of ERA, the best rotation during the Live Ball era (post-1919) was the 1981 Houston Astros' unit (2.43 ERA), but they're penalized by playing just 110 games during a strike-shortened season. The

Phillies' 2011 quintet, featuring, predominantly, Roy Halladay (19–6, 2.35 ERA), Cliff Lee (17–8, 2.40 ERA), Cole Hamels (14–9, 2.79 ERA), Vance Worley (11–3, 3.01 ERA), and Roy Oswalt (9–10, 3.69 ERA), ranks third during the five-man era (40th during Live Ball) and is the best in baseball since 1985.

That year, the Mets qualify as the best five-man ERA (2.84), but they were top heavy, with Doc Gooden at his peak of complete domination (24–4, 1.53 ERA). The Phillies rank a tad behind at 2.86, but they were deep and dangerous, top to bottom.

During the Live Ball era, regardless of rotation size, the Phillies' Five ranks eighth in WHIP (1.110) and fifth in K/9 (7.9; NL record until 2014), with the very best strikeout-to-walk ratio (4.22). Of course, it's hard to quantify "best," and no one ever seems to agree on a team, or even method.

What's in a win? The 1971 Baltimore Orioles have often gotten the moniker, because they were just the second team since 1920 with four 20-game winners—but the 1972 O's actually had a better ERA (2.58 to 2.91), with the fourth-best WHIP of the Live Ball era (1.094).

For simplicity's sake, let's assume the Phillies fielded the best five-man rotation all-time. And five is better than four. So, the 2011 Phillies had the greatest rotation of all-time. Maybe.

Now that the important stuff is out of the way (I sigh and pour a strong glass), let's get into the Cardinals series.

A REDBIRD DISASTER

Before fully diving into each game here, it's important to put some things into perspective. One, the Phillies just got done playing 33 games in 31 days. There was no wild-card round for the top seeds in baseball anymore, so the regular season ended on Wednesday and the divisional series started on Saturday. Also, the Phillies were a bit banged up. Howard was dealing with an ankle issue, Pence was dealing with a knee injury, Rollins and Utley were just getting off the IL, Oswalt was working through bulging discs in his back, and Carlos Ruiz had an ankle injury he was dealing with as well. These are not excuses; I'm just setting the scene. Also, Dick Stockton was on the call, so maybe that was a reason as well. (He didn't deserve that shot; the emotions of this series are just starting to kick back in.)

Things were not going according to the plan early in Game One. In the first, Halladay allowed a three-run home run off the bat of Lance Berkman. To Halladay's credit, that would be all he would allow, as he went eight innings and struck out eight. It wasn't a no-hitter, but Halladay retired 21 straight Cardinals after a Skip Schumaker single to lead off the top of the second. Trailing 3–1 in the sixth in what was definitely turning into a tight ballpark, the Phillies came to life. Rollins and Pence both singled off Cardinals starter Kyle Lohse to bring up Ryan Howard with one out. Howard wasted no time collecting his first home run and RBI in this postseason as he launched a high, 3-2 changeup into the sea of white rally towels in right field. Just like that, the ballpark was alive, and Lohse was on the ropes. They didn't let him off the ropes either, as the next batter, Victorino, singled up the middle, and then Ibañez followed that up with a home run of his own. *This was more like it.** After this, the Phillies turned this one into a rout. Howard, Victorino, and Ibañez each had an RBI in the bottom of the seventh to make it an 8–3 game, and they added two more for good measure in the bottom of the eighth. Unfortunately, Manuel had to get his closer, Madson, into the game because Stutes couldn't close the door easily, but, regardless, Game One was a convincing 11–6 win for the Phillies.

Game Two, however, was one of those games that will keep you up at night.

Oh, it started off so well, too. It was the perfect elixir for the Eagles blowing a 20-point third-quarter lead against the Niners earlier that afternoon at the Linc. In the top half of the first, Cliff Lee stranded Furcal at third after a leadoff triple, and then in the bottom half of the inning the Phils bats jumped on Chris Carpenter. Rollins led the inning off with a ringing double off the right-field wall, and then Carpenter issued back-to-back walks to Utley and Pence to load the bases up for Howard—who proceeded to single up the middle to give the Phils a 2–0 lead early. They weren't done yet, either, as two batters later, Ibañez hit a single into left field to plate Pence and give the Phillies a three-run lead. Do you remember the last time Lee was in the postseason in a Phillies uniform? This game was *over*—well, until it wasn't. The Phillies tacked

---

*Here's a short note on the cruelty of the sport of baseball. The ball Ibañez hit here was eerily similar to the one he'd eventually hit in Game Five—sorry for the spoiler.

247

on another one in the bottom of the second to make it 4–0; however, it was in the top half of the fourth where this one turned.

Lee had been flirting with allowing runs in each of the first two innings, escaping a leadoff triple and double without allowing any runs, but it was fair to wonder how long that was going to hold up. In the fourth, Berkman led off with a walk and then Molina hit a one-out single up the middle to set up runners on first and second with the light-hitting Ryan Theriot due up. He singled down the right-field line to bring home Berkman, and then Jon Jay had his own single to right field to plate Molina. In a gutsy move, Cardinals manager Tony La Russa pulled his starter Carpenter in favor of the pinch-hitter Nick Punto, who ended up striking out for the second out of the inning. The opportunity was right there for Lee to keep this a 4–2 ballgame with Furcal coming up, but he just couldn't do it. Furcal singled into left field to plate at least one Cardinal, but a strong throw from Ibañez was able to nail down Jay at the plate.

The damage was done, but the Phillies still had a 4–3 lead. The score remained the same until the Cardinals finally came all the way back in the top of the sixth—you could just feel it coming. Theriot started it with a two-out double off the wall in left field, and Jon Jay finished it with a single to left field. This time, Ibañez was a little high with his throw and Theriot was safe at the plate—we had a brand new ballgame.

To win a World Series, Charlie Manuel was going to ride his horses that got him there. Even though Lee clearly didn't have his best stuff, Manuel viewed it as better than the alternative, so he let him start the inning against the right-handed hitting Allen Craig. Craig smoked Lee's 106th pitch of the night to deep center field; it was going to be a tough play for Victorino, who was tracking it. It looked like Victorino got stuck feeling for the wall and trying to make a play on the ball at the same time. It bounded off his glove and allowed Craig to lead off the inning with a triple. With Lee still in the game, the next batter, Pujols, laced a single into left field to fully complete the comeback. You could hear a pin drop in Citizens Bank Park.

The Phillies offense felt this too, as they could barely stage a rally to come back and take this one. Fireworks early, a power outage late, led to this series being tied at one game apiece.

Still, the point of the four aces was that in a playoff series, each one of them was going to get a chance to toe the rubber, and in Game Four they had another pretty one going in Hamels. Before we get into this one fully, Hamels was a bit of an afterthought after Halladay and Lee, but the guy pitched to a 2.79 ERA in '11 and had fully blossomed into all the promise he had shown coming through the minor leagues. He had one hiccup in '09, but the guy was a stud. He proved that once again in Game Three.

Game Three was truly playoff baseball at its best: a tight ballpark, pitchers shoving, both teams wondering who's going to blink first. Playoff games with a ton of runs are fine, but low-scoring, tight playoff games—that's when the men separate themselves from the boys. On this night, we saw the old Phillies, the ones who were going to show off their championship mettle at some point. It started with six brilliant innings of shutout baseball from Cole Hamels. Cardinals starter Jaime García was matching him pitch for pitch.

> There has never been a bigger kryptonite for every single Phillies team in my lifetime than a crafty lefty starter who won't overpower hitters with stuff but gets them out by moving the ball around and keeping them off balance. It's foolproof. I do not mean to give away any secrets to teams wondering how to stop the Phillies, but if they just find a lefty starter that knows how to pitch, there's the answer. It's awful!

In the top of the seventh, Manuel got aggressive. With the score still 0–0, Victorino led off the inning with a single up the middle. With two outs and Victorino now at second base, La Russa opted to force Manuel's hand and walk Ruiz to bring up the pitcher's spot in the order. What was Manuel going to do? He's ridden his aces all the way here, and there were two outs. Was this the time to go for it? It was, and he opted for Ben Francisco, who ended up making Manuel look like a genius when he took García deep to left field to give the Phillies a 3–0 lead. The problem now? This game was left to the Phillies bullpen to hold the lead—they were going to have to walk the tightrope to close this one out.

Manuel opted to give Worley the first crack at it in the bottom half of the inning, and he held, only allowing a run, in a situation that could have gone much worse. Things got even tighter in the eighth, when Manuel opted to stick with Worley instead of having Lidge start the inning. Worley allowed a leadoff single and was yanked from the ballgame in favor of Bastardo, who got pinch-hitter Nick Punto out. With the dangerous Matt Holliday now hitting in the pitcher's spot, Lidge was brought in to get him out. That didn't work out, either, as he ripped one through the 5-6 hole and into left field. *This was starting to feel like a loss.* It got even worse for Lidge and the Phils as Furcal singled into left field, but it was shallow and the Cards decided not to run on Mayberry Jr. in left field. Manuel lifted Lidge from the game and brought in his fourth pitcher of the inning—this time it was his closer, Madson. No pressure, but it was bases loaded, one out, and the heart of the Cardinals order up. They escaped. Allen Craig smoked a ball right at Utley, who took matters into his own hand, as he tagged second and fired to first to complete the double play.

However, the Cardinals wouldn't go away, as Pujols led off the next inning with a double, he scored on a two-out single with Yadier Molina, but that was it. Mad Dog did a job and held the lead, getting Theroit to ground out to end the game—pretty good for a guy who they didn't think had the mental fortitude to close out ballgames!

> It's a shame that Ben Francisco's home run won't go down as an all-time Phillies home run given how this series turned out. He was a light-hitting outfielder who provided all the offense they would need to win a playoff game on the road. I just want to make sure that we give a shoutout to Benny Fresh before we move on.

The Phillies took command of the series by winning a game that took some serious stones in St. Louis. All they had to do was win one more game to advance to their fourth straight NLCS. The beauty of the four aces in a five-game set is that there's an ace for each game. It was hard not to feel good with Oswalt and Halladay each lined up in the next two games.

These next two games are going to suck to have to relive. *How do you lose a playoff game to Edwin Jackson?* By the way, if you play the Immaculate Grid, which had a good run in the summer of 2023 and is *maybe* still a thing when you're reading this book, Jackson should not be allowed as an answer. It's too easy; he pitched for 16 teams! Find a different answer! This is all just deflecting from Game Four.

It started off so well too. Rollins led off the game with a ground-rule double, Utley tripled down the line, and Pence singled up the middle to make it 2–0 after the first three batters of the game. *Yup, this is what this team just does* was going through the minds of fans all through the Delaware Valley. However, Pence got thrown out on a strike-'em-out-throw-'em-out double play with Howard at the dish, and the threat was over.

If a soft-tossing left-hander was one kryptonite of the Phillies, the other was scoring early. Although this might not make sense, nothing sums up Phils baseball quite like scoring early and then not scoring again. Well, this squad was in the midst of doing that on this night—they were going to need their ace to be one. Oswalt gave up the lead in the third when, after walking and hitting a batter in the inning already, St. Louis's future hero, David Freese, lined a double down the left-field line to plate them both—3–2, Cardinals. By now, we all know that Chase Utley is a heads-up baseball player. Who could forget the '08 World Series and countless examples all throughout the years? In the top of the sixth, the aggression and instincts came back to bite him. Utley went on a 3-2 pitch that Pence grounded toward the shortstop. Given that the runner had started, the Cardinals couldn't have turned two, but the Phils' second baseman never broke stride and Pujols—the heads-up player he is—stepped off the bag, got the throw early, and threw out Utley at third base. One of the cardinal sins of baseball is making the first out at third base. The heady Utley did just that to stymie a potential Phillies rally. In the bottom half of the inning, Freese would continue his magical postseason, as he launched a two-run home run into the same grass in center field where he would hit the biggest home run in his life two weeks later.

The Phillies lost Game Four, 5–3. They had a mini-rally going in the eighth, but Howard struck out with two outs and a runner on second base. They managed only four hits after scoring twice in the first inning. The offense was choosing a really bad time to go cold, but sadly, it was hardly a surprise. Now, the Phils were back to Philly with their horse on the mound against one of his best friends, Chris Carpenter. The two had come up through the Blue Jays organization together and maintained their friendship even though Carpenter was sent to the greener pastures in St. Louis. Here we were, the last breath of the greatest run in Phillies history:

Game Five.

> I'm not kidding—and by now I think it's pretty obvious and not surprising—it took me really until the '22 run to feel all right watching highlights of this game. Every once in a while, I'd look at the two should-have-been home runs, but this game took me personally about a decade to get over. I'm barely over it now, but you couldn't even mention it to me before '22 without me getting all worked up all over again.
>
> Fine, I'll do it. I'll write the thing.

The old adage in baseball is that you have to get to an ace early because if he settles in, it's game over. That was true with Halladay, who usually took an inning or two to settle into the game. His ERA in the first inning was 3.66 during the '11 regular season and that same issue would come back to bite him in this one. Rafael Furcal led off the game with a triple into the right-center-field gap, and he came home on a double by Skip Schumaker. A tight ballpark somehow got even tighter. Halladay had already given up a run in the first in a do-or-die Game Five? Great!

Luckily, Halladay settled down and started to really dominate this game. But Carpenter was matching him pitch for pitch. That was until the fourth, when with a runner at first base already, Victorino shot one past Pujols and into right field to set up runners on the corners with two outs for Raúl Ibañez. In one of the most painful camera shots of all time, Ibañez lifted a 3-2 pitch to deep right field. In July, it was gone—in October, it was dead. Fitting. He just missed a three-run home run, but nevertheless, the score remained 1–0.

In the sixth, Utley's aggression got him again. After he singled with one out, he attempted to steal on a 0-1 pitch that was primed for a Carpenter curveball. He got the curveball; the issue was that arguably the best defensive catcher of his generation, Molina, was behind the plate, and he gunned down Utley at second base. The Phillies were trying to do anything to score a run—they just couldn't. The score remained the same until the ninth. The Phillies had escaped a bases-loaded, one-out situation in the eighth that the locals were *hopeful* could jolt this team, but it was to no avail. To make matters worse, Utley led off the inning, with Carpenter still in the game, and shot a ball that, again, would have been gone in July but died at the wall and fell into Jon Jay's glove. The air left Citizens Bank Park at that moment—you just knew it wasn't their night. On a 2-2 count with two outs and Ryan Howard at the dish, the Phillies' window to win a championship slammed shut. Howard grounded up the first-base line but immediately went down in a heap of pain. The ankle injury that had been bothering him for weeks finally reached a breaking point. The Phillies' titanic slugger had torn his Achilles on the final pitch of the game.

It was over—a 1–0 loss in a deciding Game Five at the home ballpark with arguably the greatest rotation of all time. It was going to take a while to get over this one.

> I cried that night. I'm not going to lie and didn't come this far into this book to not admit that. An angry cry is a pretty sad thing to look at; I don't know what to tell you. I remember watching this whole game at Jill's parents' house, and attempting to remain calm around such nice people was a very big challenge. When they lost, I didn't say goodbye, stormed out of the house, dropped an f-bomb that the entire town could hear, and drove back to my parents' house crying. Jill's parents let their daughter marry this guy, by the way.

A picture is worth a thousand words, and Howard on the ground writhing in pain as the Cardinals celebrated really was the salt in the wound of a brutal postseason series. They couldn't even lose normally; it all had to come crashing down with one swing. You know the rest: the core got older, Howard was never the same, Utley's knees never bounced back, they traded Pence and Victorino the next year, Halladay was starting to decline heavily with all the work he had put on his body for a decade-plus. It was over, just like that. Although the run from '07 to '11 was one that was fruitful and full of good times, it's hard not to look back and think of what could have been. That was a dynasty that wasn't meant to be—we don't get those in Philadelphia. Tough times were ahead for baseball in Philadelphia, but nevertheless, that was the story of the post–2008 Phillies—unmet expectations.

#12

THE HARPER PURSUIT

The 2018–19 offseason was a massive one for the Phillies, and it was one they'd been planning a while for. Why? Two of the best players in all of baseball were going to hit the market at twenty-six years old, which is very rare, especially in today's game where teams usually look to buy out the arbitration years of their young stars. However, for Bryce Harper and Manny Machado, they've almost been destined to be in this situation since they were kids. They could afford to wait and get to free agency as fast as possible.

The Phillies had been a sleeping giant in the spending market for a couple of years. They were keeping their books as clean as possible to make sure they were in position to offer those guys upward of $300 million. Sure, the Jake Arrieta signing was on the books, which didn't need to happen, but we know what that was—a classic case of buttering up to old Scott Boras to ensure he'd give the Phillies a seat at the table this offseason. The Phillies were in desperate need of a facelift and a jolt because, much like we all remember, they were mostly dead to a majority of the city of Philadelphia. I'm sure sickos like those of you reading this book appreciated Jeremy Hellickson making two straight Opening Day starts for your beloved franchise or often wonder what would have happened had Charlie Morton not torn his hamstring off the bone and turned into one of the best big-game pitchers in the sport or remember exactly where you were when Vinny Velasquez struck out 16 Padres. Although all of those were great memories, I'd argue that if John Middleton ever read this book he would disagree on how fun all of that was. The best part about being awful for that long stretch is that even with a ton of high picks, the farm system was barren with no true next star coming through the pipeline. Rhys Hoskins and Aaron Nola were there, but they needed more. They needed a star—Manny Machado or Bryce Harper.

What transpired, however, was four-and-a-half months of pure torture and one that would put the fan base through the ringer. It truly was like the old school line about a girl with her sunflower picking off the petals saying, "He loves me! He loves me not!" seemingly every single day with whatever new "report" was out there. Four-and-a-half months waiting on pins and needles to see if your franchise was going to be able to land the star player they so coveted.

Let's get into it:

The signing of Bryce Harper.

On September 12, 2018, the Phillies lost a game, 5–1, to the Nationals in which their young ace allowed a home run to Harper in the first inning of the game. After the game, the Phillies' manager, Gabe Kapler, made a statement that might as well have been, "Please sign here!" Kapler, often the pontificator, had this to say when asked about Nola: "His stuff looked good. Their lineup is exceptional. We knew that from the very beginning of the season. It got healthier and it is as deep as it possibly can be. Juan Soto is one of the best young players in baseball. Bryce Harper might be the best player in baseball." Wait, what? Harper was good but his OPS was sub-.900 in 2019, so it was certainly an odd time to make that claim. The Phillies weren't shy when showing they wanted Harper. Earlier in the summer of '18, a game got called due the Phillies not laying tarp on the field properly, and the grounds crew had use blowtorches to try to dry the field enough to play. During this time, Hoskins and Harper were seen on TV laughing and talking in the infield. Of course, we were reading into everything around this time, and it sure seemed like Hoskins was trying to sell Harper on Philadelphia. Thanks, Rhys!

Early in the offseason, John Middleton sent a message to his fan base by way of Bob Nightengale at *USA Today*. That was before Middleton had become a public face with the Phillies; the team's owners for years were all behind the scenes, and you never really saw them in public. You knew the names of course, but you couldn't put a face to the name. It was largely David Montgomery (may he rest in peace) who would speak for the owners, but the organization was changing, and Middleton was charging through as the new steward of the ship. Whereas we fans had heard about Middleton wanting to spend money and be "Steinbrenner South," as Jimmy Rollins once said, we also wanted to see him put his money where his mouth was. It's why there was some extra excitement heading into free agency when Middleton told Nightengale that the Phillies were "expecting to spend money and maybe even be a little bit stupid about it." That became the catchphrase that we would say on WIP day in and day out for 118 days, the catchphrase you'd say to your friends when talking about the offseason, and the catchphrase that would eventually get said in a mocking tone because the whole thing dragged out so long: "stupid money." Think of this with a Philly accent: "I tHOuGhT yOu wANted tO spEnD sTuPid MOneY?" Sorry, some PTSD I got from the callers during this time came back.

Middleton's quote was a tone-setter, and even though it was a long process, we can look back now and appreciate the aggressiveness that it was said with. Part of stupid money wasn't just meant to be spent on Harper—the Phillies had to build out the rest of their ballclub, as they had signaled to the fans that 2019 was going to be the year that they were going to get back to playing competitive baseball. First, they signed their new leadoff man and former NL MVP, Andrew McCutchen, for $50 million over three years. Second, GM Matt Klentak righted his wrong from a year prior when he traded first baseman Carlos Santana and shortstop J. P. Crawford to the Mariners for Jean Segura, Juan Nicasio, and James Pazos. The move allowed Rhys Hoskins to go back to first base (thank God), got them out from under the Santana deal, and gave them a quality major-league shortstop in Segura, who could consistently put the bat on the baseball. Crawford has turned into a Gold Glove–caliber player at short for the Mariners, but the Phillies wouldn't have won the pennant in '22 without Segura. The trade was a true win-win.

Fittingly enough, the Winter Meetings in the offseason of 2019 were held in Las Vegas—the home of Harper and also where big gambles don't always pay off. The Phillies met with Boras and Machado's agent, Dan Lozano, out in Las Vegas during that week, and rumors were percolating that the Phillies were more interested in Machado than Harper given the similar production but Machado's more premium position.

> I think if you put truth serum in Klentak and the other front-office members during this time, they'd say they viewed Machado as the better fit for the club. However, although Machado was a great player, Harper was a box-office attraction, and both Middleton and Boras knew this. Boras played this card well out at the Winter Meetings when he said, "I think when you're talking about Bryce Harper it's just a different situation. There are a lot of really good ballplayers out there. They are exceptional. But Bryce's situation has a dynamic about it in terms of what he brings to an ownership and the iconic side of it. It certainly has an appeal because he is really a player that has the ability to economically pay for himself independent of the performance." Box office.

THE HARPER PURSUIT

Nine days later, after meeting with both agents, the Phillies welcomed Manny Machado into town for his visit. You want to talk about not looking ready for the moment and not exactly giving much confidence to your fan base? That was what Phillies president Andy MacPhail and Matt Klentak did on this day. It looked like a clown show. First, Machado showed up outside Citizens Bank Park instead of being brought to the private parking lot or garage, which meant that the superstar was subjected to the public on his way in. As Machado got out of the car and walked toward the doors at the ballpark, an electrician came out of nowhere and first asked Machado for a photo—the Phillies' brass had to be sweating at this point—and then yells at the superstar in a beautiful Philly accent, "Super Bowl champs over there, World Series champs here, do the right thing and sign! Take the money!"[1] Oh lovely. Welcome to the city, Manny! To make matters worse, the doors weren't even open to let Machado in! They made him wait outside and be subjected to more of this! Now, it wasn't like five minutes he was waiting there, but it looked like Machado had to knock on the freakin' door to be let in—are we serious? Oh, watching this video was just brutal. Finally, Klentak opened the [expletive] door and, as if he were greeting his in-laws at the holidays, said in a boyish voice, "Hey, Manny, what's up! Come on in!" It was so bad.

> At this point I was convinced that they weren't going to sign either one of these guys. You had to wow star players, not subject them to the locals. The Phillies are not a clown show, but holy cow, it sure looked like amateur hour with Klentak and MacPhail involved. It was also at this point that I'm sure Middleton said, "You know what? I'm going to probably have to take matters into my own hands from this point forward." Thank God he did. If you haven't seen any of the videos of that day, please look them up.
>
> It was a really tense time around here for people who cared deeply about ever seeing playoff baseball in Philadelphia again.

To the shock of this reporter, Machado left Philadelphia without signing a contract. The day after the Machado disaster, the Dodgers freed up right field by moving Matt Kemp and Yasiel Puig, which also freed up $25 million. Harper, a historian of the sport, obviously would be drawn to Dodger Stadium or the team he grew up rooting for, the Yankees. Thankfully, the

Yankees didn't make a similar move to free up an outfield spot or any money because Harper might very well have been a Yankee. The Dodgers were now a problem for the Phillies.

Christmas passed, and still no Machado or Harper under the tree. A meeting was happening, however, just after the New Year out in Las Vegas between the Phillies brass and the Harper's people, with Scott Boras merely sitting off to the side. As detailed by Matt Gelb of The Athletic, Middleton, Gabe Kapler, and Matt Klentak did most of the talking for the Phillies, but Harper drove the conversation from his side. He wanted to know two things from Middleton and the rest of the Phillies brass: from the ownership side, were the owners committed to winning? From the front-office side, were team officers willing to be aggressive to do what it took to win? Then Harper shocked Phillies officials by admitting to them that he didn't want an opt-out in his contract—he wanted to stay in one place and go to Cooperstown wearing that cap. It might have been in that moment that Middleton decided to end the pursuit of Machado and turn his entire attention toward Harper. The Phillies by all accounts left that meeting blown away by the twenty-six-year-old.[2]

Also around this time, Harper was open to the idea of signing a short-term contract at a record average annual value (AAV) to hit the market again before the age of thirty—Boras was pulling out all the stops to make the Phillies fidget. Apparently, this was a way for the Dodgers to get involved at around $45 million a year for only three years, but the Phillies believed Harper at his word when he said he wanted to stay in one place for the remainder of his career.

While the pursuit of both Harper and Machado was ongoing, an offseason was still taking place, and the Phillies *still* had to get better even with one of the two superstars in the fold. They got better when they acquired J. T. Realmuto from the Marlins on February 7 in a move that surprised a lot of people in Philadelphia. He had hung around in the offseason just long enough for the Phillies to reengage with the Marlins and bring the best catcher in baseball to Philadelphia. It didn't hurt, either, that Harper in years past had said multiple times that Realmuto was his favorite player in baseball, and at the All-Star game, with the Nationals looking for a catcher, he put a Nats cap on Realmuto during introductions. *Surely* this had nothing to do with the Phillies parting ways with pitching prospect Sixto Sánchez, whom they had prized for years. Realmuto, McCutchen, and Segura already made for a massive offseason, but one more prize fish was still to be reeled in.

> This whole offseason was not only painstaking, but also funny for reading into every move. Like the Realmuto news, it wasn't just about getting the best catcher in baseball, it was about getting Harper's favorite player. Earlier in the offseason, the Phillies signed infield coach Bobby Dickerson. That couldn't just be about hiring the best guy for the job; no, it had to be about Dickerson being Machado's mentor. The Phillies had covered their bases by appealing to both players.

By this point, spring training had already started, and everyone was starting to get impatient—even the writers and talk-show hosts. Todd Zolecki was so bored that he put up a Twitter poll simply asking which player fans hoped would sign with the team. A whopping 86 percent of over nine thousand votes wanted Harper over Machado. This poll was mentioned as something that Middleton considered when talking about the fan reaction to signing Harper. It was clear where his people landed on the matter.

Finally, the first domino to drop in this whirlwind offseason was that of Machado, who on February 20 signed with the San Diego Padres. Phillies front-office guys might have preferred Machado due to his defense and also elite offense. but by this point it was clear who their boss wanted. However, with Machado gone now, the pressure only intensified on the Phillies to land Harper. This isn't confirmed, but somewhere, most likely in Vegas, Scott Boras let out an evil laugh when he saw Machado had signed. He had the desperate Phillies right where he wanted them.

The bar was now set. Machado got $300 million, which meant the Phillies were *at least* going to have to top that—it was reported that the Phillies offer to Machado was 10 years for $225 million. By this point, the team knew it was going to take a record contract to land Harper, but there was still convincing the superstar that Philadelphia was the right choice for him. That's why Middleton, along with his wife, Leigh, got back on the plane and flew to Las Vegas for another meeting with Harper. This time, however, business talk was put to the side, and the two families truly got to know each other over a dinner at a Las Vegas restaurant. The next morning, business was back on the table because Middleton and Boras met over breakfast for four hours—surely the conversations were different here than at dinner the night before. But Middleton wanted to meet Harper again even after the dinner and breakfast to nail down some things that he wanted made clearer. What did he really want?

What mattered to him the most? This had to impress Harper, who wanted to see an owner who was aggressive and wanted to compete at the highest level.

The Phillies made their first offer to Harper a few days later on February 24: 15 years, $330 million. Imagine! Tension was building through the offices down in Clearwater, as after receiving the Phillies offer, the Dodgers and Giants both flew to Vegas to meet with Harper. The Phillies were worried about being hoodwinked by superagent Boras, but the most powerful voice, Harper? He marched to the beat of his own drum on these negotiations. It wasn't all about the money for him. The Dodgers and Giants both came in with shorter years and bigger average annual values to try to woo Harper—the Phillies told Boras if this was what he wanted they could do the same thing. Luckily, it wasn't what Harper wanted.

On Wednesday the 27th, Middleton and Boras engaged in two phone calls that were so contentious in nature, it left the Phillies top brass thinking that Harper was never going to wear red pinstripes. Boras wanted a higher number than $330 million. Middleton told him if someone is making you an offer north of that, then take it—the two sides were at a stalemate.

The next morning, Boras called Harper with the Phillies' offer—13 years, $330 million. The Phillies budged on the length of the deal, and Boras budged on the overall dollar number, even though it was still a record. Boras told Harper that he was waiting for a final offer from the Giants, but in the meantime, to talk over the final decision with his wife, Kayla. Harper, during a sit-down interview with Ken Rosenthal after he signed, gave this description of this moment: "So we sat there and talked for a little bit and I remember standing there and giving her a hug and saying, 'We're going to Philly.' This was before a final offer or anything from San Fran. San Fran called and made their offer but by that point I already felt like I was a Philadelphia Phillie. In my heart, I was already a Phillie."[3]

Back in the Phillies offices, Boras had called Middleton a couple times already that morning. After the phone calls the day before, the Phils front-office people had decided to wait until they got in the office to hash out their response. They decided to have Klentak, not Middleton, call back Boras—the Phillies' young GM was working at his condo in downtown Clearwater instead of the stadium on this day. In what had to be the longest hour of Middleton's life, Klentak called back and said, "Well, we have the makings of a deal."[4]

It was a signature moment for Middleton and his tenure as Phillies owner. It wasn't always like Phillies ownership to be so public facing, but times were changing, and the new face of ownership was looking to make his mark. He had done just that, as he landed one of the biggest free agents in sports history and totally changed the fortunes of his franchise. Now, Middleton probably would have liked to have seen a playoff appearance earlier than four seasons after he signed him to the megadeal, but '22 made up for all of that. Bryce Harper was a Phillie, and it's pretty safe to say he will be donning that Phillies *P* when he enters Cooperstown in 2038.

#13

2022

John Lennon famously said, "Life is what happens while you're busy making other plans." Since the Phillies' inception in 1883, the *plan* was to win as many games, and championships, as possible. To that end, the next-most apt quote might be from David Gerrold: "Life is hard, and then you die."

That's, of course, a very negative and thankfully very fading view of the Philadelphia Phillies these days, but it wasn't that long ago that the plan seemed *almost* as lousy as the 76ers' "process."

Injuries and age forced a rebuilding following the post–2008 championship era, ushering in some very lean, seemingly rudderless seasons.

Following a franchise-record 102-win regular season in 2011, the Phils returned a lot of the same players with a lot less productivity. They fielded the oldest hitters in the league (average age 31.1 years) and sputtered to an 81–81 record in 2012. Things just went off the rails from there.

2017

A lineup that used to feature MVPs (Ryan Howard, Jimmy Rollins, Cole Hamels), Cy Young Award winners (Roy Halladay, Cliff Lee), and world f*cking champions (Chase Utley), all in their primes, slowly-but-surely shifted to a who's who of "Who the Hell are These Guys?" All-Stars. Take a look at the Phils' lineup in 2017:

C Cameron Rupp (.217/.299/.417)
1B Tommy Joseph (.240/.289/.432)
2B César Hernández (.294/.373/.421)
SS Freddy Galvis (.255/.309/.382)
3B Maikel Franco (.230/.281/.409)
OF Aaron Altherr (.272/.340/.516)

OF Odúbel Herrera (.281/.325/.452)
OF Nick Williams (.288/.338/.473)

An argument could be made that Altherr was the club's most productive bat that season. And just three years later, he'd be playing for the NC Dinos of the KBO League in Changwon-si, South Korea. Free-agent signee Michael Saunders, an All-Star outfielder for the Blue Jays the season prior, either forgot how to hit or stubbornly refused to, slashing .205/.257/.360 in 214 plate appearances; after batting .158 in 154 PAs in the minors in 2018 for the Orioles and White Sox, he was out of baseball for good. On the pitching side, things weren't much better.

Number-two starter Nick Pivetta finished the season 8–10 with a 6.02 ERA in 133 innings. His .846 OPS-against bested Cleveland shortstop Francisco Lindor (.842), who finished fifth in AL MVP voting that season. Pivetta became just the fourth Phillie in 83 years to post an ERA over 6.00 in 100 or more innings pitched. The third pitcher in Phillies history to accomplish this dubious feat? That would be Adam Morgan—just *one season prior* (6.04 ERA, 113.1 IP). Dang.

Sometimes, the plan fails and life's a bitch. But, the Phillies were far from dead.

The 66–96 club had a couple promising outliers that would form a foundation for future success:

- Aaron Nola, in his first full season in the big leagues, shone with a 3.54 ERA and the fifth-best FIP (fielding independent pitching) in the National League (3.27).
- Outfielder Rhys Hoskins had one of the best debuts in baseball history, clubbing 18 homers in his first 40 games, an MLB record. It was the most in the NL since Wally Berger hit 15 through his first 40 games back in 1930.

Through trades, preseason top prospects J. P. Crawford (ranked first) and Jorge Alfaro (ranked third) brought back players who would cement their legacies in Phillies history forever.

RING THE BELL

THE PLAN

Between 2017 and 2022, the Phils executed a series of strategic moves to transform from a rebuilding team into National League champions. These decisions encompassed key player acquisitions, managerial changes, and front-office restructuring.

2018: LAYING THE FOUNDATION

- **Managerial Change**: On October 30, 2017, the Phillies appointed forty-two-year-old Gabe Kapler as manager, signaling a shift in team leadership.
- **Jean Segura**: Following an improved 80–82 showing, the front office shook up the core on December 3, 2018, dealing Carlos Santana and top prospect Crawford to the Seattle Mariners for second baseman Jean Segura.
- **Andrew McCutchen**: Veteran outfielder Andrew McCutchen signed a three-year deal about a week after the Segura deal, bringing experience and leadership to the club. He was off to Milwaukee by 2022, but Cutch was a massive fan favorite during his time in red pinstripes and helped shift clubhouse culture.

2019: AGGRESSIVE OFFSEASON ACQUISITIONS

- **J. T. Realmuto**: Prospects? They don't need no stinkin' prospects. Two months after dealing Crawford, they unloaded Alfaro and 2018 tippy-top prospect Sixto Sánchez for the best catcher in baseball, J. T. Realmuto.
- **Bryce Harper**: Reminiscent of the statement signing of Jim Thome in 2002, the Phillies made a landmark move by signing the best player in baseball, outfielder Bryce Harper, to a 13-year, $330 million contract. Legitimacy established.

2019 Season Outcome
Despite significant additions, the Phillies finished the season with an 81–81 record, leading to the dismissal of manager Gabe Kapler on October 10, 2019.

Kapler's clichéd coach-speak and relentless reliance on "analytics," at least perceptually, made him a pariah among Phillies fans.

"There was bound to be a reckoning," said Scott Lauber of the *Philadelphia Inquirer*. "Someone had to take the fall. A manager with one year left on his contract and a lower Q-rating than a Dallas Cowboys quarterback was easy to sack."

"Drink a toast, then, all you champions of the #FireKapler movement. The Phillies finally heard you. Gabe is gone."[1]

2020: LEADERSHIP AND PITCHING ENHANCEMENTS

- **Joe Girardi**: On October 24, 2019, the Phillies hired Joe Girardi as manager, bringing championship experience to the clubhouse and signaling a tonal shift in managerial direction. Kapler was new school and stubbornly innovative; Girardi was traditional, a poster boy for NPC (non-player character) managers, for better or worse.
- **Zack Wheeler**: Always great to stick it to the Mets. The team strengthened its starting rotation by signing pitcher Zack Wheeler to a five-year, $118 million contract on December 9. In Wheeler's ten seasons of professional baseball before joining the Phillies, his best WHIP was in 2018 with the stinkin' New York Metros (1.124). Through his first five seasons with Philly, Wheeler *averaged* a WHIP of 1.031. Nothing tops the Harper signing, but this is close.

2020 Season Outcome

The Phillies ended the COVID-shortened 2020 season with a 28–32 record, missing the playoffs. This led to the resignation of general manager Matt Klentak on October 3, 2020.

2020 Offseason: Front-Office Restructuring

- **Dave Dombrowski**: On December 11, 2020, Dave Dombrowski was appointed as president of baseball operations, bringing a track record of building championship teams.
- **Sam Fuld**: Shortly after, Sam Fuld was promoted to general manager, signaling a new direction in player development and analytics.

2021: BUILDING MOMENTUM

The Phillies achieved their first winning season since 2011, finishing with an 82–80 record. Bryce Harper earned the National League MVP Award (.309/.429/.615, 35 HR), and Zack Wheeler led the league in strikeouts. These were small but important victories.

RING THE BELL

2022: FINAL PIECES

- **Kyle Schwarber**: In March 2022, the Phillies signed outfielder Kyle Schwarber to a four-year contract, adding significant power to the lineup. Schwarber said in his introductory press conference, "I'm excited to help bring a World Series back to Philly . . . I'm in the business of winning baseball games . . . and this team is a very good ballclub."
- **Nick Castellanos**: The team further bolstered its offense by signing outfielder Nick Castellanos, an unexpected move that really showed the franchise's commitment to taking things to the next level.

THE SEASON

"We got excited about a lot of different things with the Phillies. . . . They signed [Jake] Arrieta, we got excited. Then they signed Bryce [Harper] a year or two later and we got excited. But this is just different. This has the capabilities of being something the Phillies fans should want to see every single day."
—John Kruk, 2022 spring training, referencing the additions of Schwarber and Castellanos.[2]

Colloquially, it feels like the Bryce Harper signing was the moment things turned around for the franchise. In reality, the Phils were an unremarkable two games under .500 for Harper's first three seasons in red pinstripes (191–193). It was a tidal shift for the woebegone franchise, but significant moves still needed to be made, and even with the key offseason additions, the Phils started the 2022 season dreadfully slow. Again, as it had many times over the previous decade, it seemed as though the postseason was just out of reach.

Castellanos started hot, but cooled off significantly, batting .234/.274/.414 in May. After a 2–1 loss to the Rangers on May 4, the Phillies were 11–14, and the bats were colder than a "wooder ice"—soaked wet blanket—new DH Harper (.232/.292/.453), Schwarber (.193/.309/.482), Hoskins (.195/.297/.356), and Segura (.231/.277/.333) were struggling to hit their stride.

On the mound, 2021 Cy Young runner-up Zack Wheeler started 1–3 with a 5.79 in his first four starts, and the Phils were 1–8 in Aaron Nola's first nine outings. Nothing was going according to plan.

As is so often the case in professional sports, when the team on the field is not reflective of the talent on paper, the skipper gets the blame. The slow start was a severe top-to-bottom failure, so it wasn't a total surprise that manager Joe Girardi got fired on June 3, with the club sitting at a woeful 22–29, having failed to win their previous five series.

"There's not just blame on Joe," Harper said after the firing. "We haven't played to the best of our ability. We haven't done the things to be the team we should be."[3]

Everyone within (and probably outside of) the organization recognized that the team was too good to be this bad, and it was too late to not do something about it.

"I still think it's early enough that we have a chance to make the postseason," said President of Baseball Operations Dave Dombrowski prior to the Phils' June 3 contest. "From my perspective, a different voice was needed in the clubhouse at this time, just somebody that can give a message in a different way, and I think that Rob Thomson was the right guy to give that message."[4] Thomson, promoted from bench coach to skipper, turned out to be very good message deliverer.

He was nicknamed "Topper" by Hall of Fame Yankees manager Joe Torre because he seemed to always be on top of things; it was fitting. He wasted no time getting the Phils to the top of the wild-card standings.

With Topper at the helm, the club won eight straight games, and 14 of 16. On June 1, they were eight games below .500, and by August 9, they were in sole possession of the top NL wild-card slot, and miraculously just five games behind the Mets for the division lead.

"Oops, there goes another rubber tree plant."

KEVIN'S NOTE

In Comes the Skipper, Out Goes the Captain. There are so many instances in Phillies history when fate seemed to be an active opponent, working to balance the scales should good tidings ever happen to slide in Philadelphia's favor. Remember when the Phillies landed All-Star Andy Ashby in 2000, and he immediately forgot how to pitch (4–7, 5.68 ERA)? He was quickly dealt to Atlanta where he miraculously regained form and helped them win the NL East (8–6, 4.13 ERA). Or how about three years later, when the Phillies landed All-Star Kevin Millwood, and he also managed to forget how to effectively throw baseballs? (In two seasons he went 23–18 with a 4.34 ERA, though he did throw a no-hitter against the Giants on April 27, 2003). Millwood won the ERA title a year after leaving town, and Atlanta ended up with a Silver Slugger catcher in Johnny Estrada from Philly in the Millwood trade. F%$& Atlanta, man.

Being a Phillies fan comes with the expectation that bad things are always lurking around the corner, so while it was demoralizing, it wasn't a total shock when Bryce Harper took a high fastball to the hand on June 25, fracturing his left thumb. The next morning, the Fightins were riding the high of a 17–6 June, while simultaneously facing the possibility of being without the reigning NL MVP for the remainder of the season. So it goes.

Funny thing about fate, though—it probably isn't real. Somehow, someway, the Phils followed up their 19–8 June with a 15–10 July, and an 18–11 August, mostly without their (seemingly) essential player. A month after the beanball, the Harperless club went on a 12–1 heater. It doesn't really make sense, except for the fact that Philadelphia had maybe finally built a *team* of talented players who liked playing together, enjoyed playing in Philadelphia, and were capable of brushing off misfortunes that historically proved devastating.

What didn't show on either of Ashby's or Millwood's stat sheets was the complete lack of desire to be a part of something special in Philadelphia. Fate favors front offices that build beyond the numbers. When Harper went down, the Phillies started to show the city, and the rest of baseball, that this team was something special.

Finally, the Phillies were back on track to return to the postseason, after a harrowing 10-year drought. Though Harper was certainly the face of the franchise, the team was deep, and plenty of players stepped up to fill the void.

TRADE DEADLINE MOVES

- **Noah Syndergaard**: The Phillies acquired starting pitcher Noah Syndergaard, aiming to solidify the rotation for the playoff push.
- **David Robertson**: Veteran reliever David Robertson was added to strengthen the bullpen, addressing a critical need.

- **Brandon Marsh**: The team traded for center fielder Brandon Marsh, improving outfield defense and adding a young, controllable player.

On October 3 the Phils defeated both the Astros and the dubious distinction of having the longest playoff drought in the National League (11 years).

> "[The fans] asked for Red October the last several years, and guess what? They have stormed into Red October!"
>
> —Tom McCarthy[5]

NL WILD-CARD SERIES VS. ST. LOUIS CARDINALS

The Phillies entered the playoffs as the sixth seed in the National League, which meant they had to face the third-seeded St. Louis Cardinals in the wild-card series. This was a best-of-three series, in consecutive days, all in one location. Advantage, St. Louis.

Game One: Phillies 6, Cardinals 3
(Phillies lead, 1–0)
The Phillies won Game One behind a dominant performance from Zack Wheeler. He pitched 6 1/3 innings of shutout ball, allowing just two hits before José Alvarado surrendered a two-run home run to Juan Yepez with two outs in the seventh inning. With the Cardinals still leading 2–0 in the ninth, the Fightins mounted a rally. J. T. Realmuto started with a single, followed by walks to Bryce Harper and Nick Castellanos, loading the bases. Ryan Helsley, the Cardinals' closer, hit Alec Bohm with a pitch, scoring the first run. Jean Segura then hit a go-ahead single, leading to a six-run ninth, flipping the game from a 2–0 deficit to a tone-setting 6–3 shocker. This was the first time in 94 postseason games that the Cardinals had blown a lead of at least two runs in the ninth inning.

Game Two: Phillies 2, Cardinals 0
(Phillies win series, 2–0)
Picking up where Wheeler left off, Nola channeled his inner Roy Halladay and dominated in his postseason debut. He scattered four hits over 6 2/3 scoreless innings, while Harper (solo homer) and Kyle Schwarber (sacrifice fly) provided more than enough offense. The bullpen shut it down the rest of the way, handing the Phils a 2–0 game—and series—win.

RING THE BELL

NL DIVISION SERIES (NLDS) VS. ATLANTA BRAVES

The Phillies faced the defending World Series champion Atlanta Braves in the NLDS. Momentum was on their side, after thrilling consecutive wins over St. Louis, juxtaposed with the Braves having to sit and wait out a first-round bye. This was a best-of-five series.

Game One: Phillies 7, Braves 6; Truist Park
(Phillies lead series, 1–0)
Max Fried, a Cy Young runner-up with a 14–7 record and 2.48 ERA for the Braves during the regular season, didn't make it out of the fourth inning in this one. The Phils had a 7–1 lead going into the bottom of the fifth inning, and a 7–3 lead going to the bottom of the ninth. That's where things got interesting.

Zach Efflin surrendered a one-out, three-run home run to Matt Olson, after giving up two singles to start the inning. Efflin, the sixth Philly reliever of the game, retired the next two batters, and the Phils won the squeaker, 7–6.

Game Two: Braves 3, Phillies 0; Truist Park
(Series tied, 1–1)
This game was a pitchers' duel, with Braves starter Kyle Wright outdueling Wheeler. The game remained scoreless until the sixth inning, when the Braves finally broke through, scoring three runs. Matt Olson, Austin Riley, and Travis d'Arnaud each contributed with RBI singles. The hot-and-cold Phils offense never broke through, and the Braves tied up the series with a 3–0 statement win.

Game Three: Phillies 9, Braves 1; Citizens Bank Park
(Phillies lead series, 2–1)
Finally, Phils fans could flex their muscle. The tension had built for a while, as the Phillies faithful had four games to sit and watch at home before exploding with fervor typically reserved for the all-or-nothing dramatic intensity of an Eagles NFC Championship game.

Braves starter Spencer Strider had dazzled during the regular season, compiling a 2.67 ERA through 131 1/3 innings pitched. The Philly crowd broke him.

In the third inning, Strider gave the crowd a reason to explode, moving one-out baserunner Brandon Marsh to third base after an errant pickoff attempt at first. Next was an RBI double by Bryson Stott; Strider was clearly shook, and the crowd had been cranked up to 10. And, just like that, it turns out, this crowd goes to 11.

Strider intentionally walked Schwarber next, and then Rhys Hoskins hit one of the most memorable home runs in Phillies history. The Bank went wild as the struggling fan favorite Hoskins immediately threw his hands up and slammed his bat down in celebration. Scott Franzke had the call: "A three-run home run for Rhys Hoskins! His first postseason home run. . . and he's sprinting around third base! What a moment here at Citizens Bank Park!"

The Phils were not going to be denied in this one. That was the moment the greatest home-field advantage in baseball had been awakened, and Philadelphia arrived as a force in the National League.

The good guys scored six runs in total in the third and added three more in the seventh for a 9–1 spectacle. Nola picked up his second win of the postseason, surrendering just the single, lonely unearned run through six innings.

Game Four: Phillies 8, Braves 3; Citizens Bank Park
(Phillies win series, 3–1)
Brandon Marsh got things started early, mashing a three-run homer in the second inning off Braves starter and former Phillie Charlie Morton. Not to be outdone, J. T. Realmuto pulled one of the most exciting feats in sports, hitting an inside-the-park home run, the first for a catcher in postseason history. After three innings, the Phillies led, 4–1. After three straight RBI singles (Hoskins, Realmuto, Harper) in the sixth made it 7–2 Phillies, the game was essentially put out of reach.

Reliever Seranthony Domínguez struck out Braves catcher Travis d'Arnaud to end the game, 8–3, winning the series for Philadelphia, to the delight of its 45,660 standing (mostly cell phone–videographer) fans. They were headed back to the NLCS for the first time since 2010.

NLCS VS. SAN DIEGO PADRES
In the NLCS the Phillies faced the San Diego Padres in a best-of-seven series. Like the Phils, the Pads were overachievers, knocking off the heavy favorites in the previous two rounds (New York Mets and Los Angeles Dodgers, respectively). Both were underdogs, though entirely different breeds.

RING THE BELL

> Let's be honest—the Padres were cooked the minute a group of clueless San Diego "super fans" performed their super cringy original rally song on *Good Morning San Diego* before the game on October 18: "Harper's gonna lose, and Manny's gonna cruuuise—*that's what's in!*"[6]
>
> When something like that goes viral for all the wrong reasons, you're just not allowed to win an NLCS, especially against Philly, with a rich history of badass, sometimes criminal, internet virality. This one was just too lame. The baseball gods presumably have pride (and Wi-Fi), and they'd never reward that kind of behavior.

Game One: Phillies 2, Padres 0; Petco Park
(Phillies lead series, 1–0)
This was good, old-fashioned baseball. Wheeler, dominant as ever, pitched seven scoreless innings, allowing only one hit and striking out eight. Padres ace Yu Darvish was nearly as effective, surrendering just four hits over seven innings, but the Phillies capitalized on their opportunities. Harper's solo home run in the fourth inning was the first and deciding run in the game.

Game Two: Padres 8, Phillies 5; Petco Park
(Series tied, 1–1)
This game and series looked like it might be a cruuuise for Philadelphia early, after a five-hit, four-run second inning off former (and future; 2023) Cy Young winner Blake Snell, the pitcher who sidelined Harper with an errant fastball in June. The Padres showed some fight, overcoming the 4–0 deficit and taking the lead for good in the fifth inning with a five-run outburst that chased Nola from the game.

Nola was charged with six earned runs in the loss; before surrendering the first two runs to the Pads in the second, he had gone 13 2/3 innings without giving up an earned run to start his postseason career.

Game Three: Phillies 4, Padres 2; Citizens Bank Park
(Phillies lead series, 2–1)
Kyle Schwarber (second in Phillies leadoff home runs all-time, with 33 through 2024) led off with a first-pitch dinger, giving the Phils an early lead.

Jean Segura was pivotal with a two-run single in the fourth, after an error by Segura had given the Padres a run in the top half of the inning.

Suárez pitched well, surrendering just two runs (one earned) in five innings. The Phils bullpen kept the Pads scoreless the rest of the way, with Domínguez securing the save.

Game Four: Phillies 10, Padres 6; Citizens Bank Park
(Phillies lead series, 3–1)
Bailey Falter (fal ter | 'fôlter | verb [no object] | start to lose strength or momentum) was not the ideal choice to start Game Four. He had pitched well during the regular season (6–4, 3.86 ERA), but this was not his night. He surrendered four runs to San Diego before handing the ball over to Connor Brogdon with two outs in the first inning. Thankfully, as had become a trend for the Phillies in the 2022 postseason, the falter was brief.

Rhys Hoskins, on the ninth pitch of the game for the Phillies, quickly cut the Padres' lead in half with a two-run home run off starter Mike Clevinger. As rough an outing as it was for Falter, Clevinger was credited with three earned runs total and zero innings pitched.

> Clevinger has plausible deniability here. He can tell his grandchildren he never even played in this game, because zero innings pitched is the same amount of innings I pitched. And I was at a Buffalo Wild Wings that night.

The Phillies took control with a four-run fifth inning, establishing an 8–6 lead they would not relinquish. The squad's 10-run outburst featured multihit performances from their core offensive four: Schwarber, Hoskins, Harper, and Castellanos.

Game Five: Phillies 4, Padres 3; Citizens Bank Park
(Phillies win NLCS, 4–1)
On paper, it feels silly to consider this result was ever in question. Perhaps it wasn't. Historically, only 14 teams had overcome a 3–1 postseason deficit since the first World Series in 1903. Still, Philadelphia is not typically a town to count its San Diego Chickens before they hatch.

The Phillies scored first in the third inning when Rhys Hoskins hit a two-out, 3-0 pitch into the left-center-field stands to establish a 2–0 lead. He had just four base hits in the series, but all were homers—can't knock a guy for only playing the hits.

The Padres responded in the fourth with a solo home run by Juan Soto, making it 2–1. It was a rare mistake by Wheeler in the start, credited with two earned runs in six innings pitched, taking his ERA in the postseason to a stellar 1.78.

The seventh was wild, literally. Domínguez threw three rain-aided wild pitches in relief, which contributed to two Padres runs and a relinquished lead.

After a Realmuto single to open the bottom of the eighth, down 3–2, Bryce Harper hit a go-ahead two-run homer, giving Philadelphia a 4–3 lead, and the franchise its latest iconic moment. Foreword-writing Scott Franzke had the call:

"It is bedlam at the Bank as Bryce Harper has put the Phillies on top! His tenth career home run of the postseason, and he may never hit a bigger one!"

Cool customer Ranger Suárez came in for the save in the ninth. The Padres managed to get two runners in scoring position with two outs, but Suárez, as usual, looked unfazed.

> The stress of it all—and probably also elevated Cheez Whiz and alcohol intake—sent my blood pressure through the roof in this moment, while looking on from the infield stands. Alternatively, Ranger Suárez doesn't get high blood pressure. High blood pressure gets Ranger Suárez.

Suárez, fighting through one of his classic fits of stoicism, induced the game-ending pop-up and Phillies fans everywhere rejoiced.

What a game. What a journey. No matter the incidental details of what would lie ahead, we'll always have *Bedlam*.

THE WORLD SERIES!
Philadelphia Phillies vs. Houston Astros

It had been 13 years since the Phils previously made the World Series (2009), and there was a 14-year hiatus between the club's 1993 trip and the trophy-winning 2008 squad. And while 29 years seems like a lot of time between three World Series appearances, we are talking about a franchise that took nearly 80 years to go to its first three (1915, 1950, 1980).

The Phils' World Series run was unlikely—but so were all of them. The year 2022 was as good as any other.

Game One: Phillies 6, Astros 5 (10 innings); Minute Maid Park
(Phillies lead, 1–0)
The Phillies staged a dramatic comeback in this game. Houston initially took a 5–0 lead, but Philadelphia fought back with small, consistent hits rather than relying on home runs. The game went into extra innings, where J. T. Realmuto hit a solo home run in the 10th to give the Phillies their first lead of the game, securing the win. This was the largest deficit overcome in World Series Game One history.

Game Two: Astros 5, Phillies 2; Minute Maid Park
(Series tied, 1–1)
The Astros bounced back with a strong performance by their pitching staff, particularly Framber Valdez, who managed to keep the Phillies bats quiet. Houston's offense found its rhythm, with significant contributions from Yordan Alvarez, who hit a home run, helping the Astros even the series.

Game Three: Phillies 7, Astros 0; Citizens Bank Park
(Phillies lead, 2–1)
Philadelphia dominated this game with Ranger Suárez pitching brilliantly for five shutout innings and the bullpen following suit the rest of the way. But the story of the game was Harper blasting a home run on the first World Series pitch he saw on Philly soil. It was the MLB record-tying five home runs in all for the Phillies. It was a blessing on this day and a curse for the days to come. A 7–0 rout looks great on its face, but the Phils collected just seven hits in the contest. While no one could predict what would take place the following day, the signs were there that an offense issue was afoot.

Game Four: Astros 5, Phillies 0; Citizens Bank Park
(Series tied, 2–2)
An absolute gut punch—Houston's pitching took over, with Cristian Javier, Bryan Abreu, Rafael Montero, and Ryan Pressly combining for a no-hitter, the first such occurrence in a World Series game since Don Larsen's perfect game in 1956.

RING THE BELL

The offense had gotten tragically one-dimensional at the worst possible time. After the no-no, the series was tied, but it was also over. There was no other way. Terence Mann or Mr. Mertle might explain the dogma more eloquently than I, but simply, the Fightin' Phils could not outslug the (probably imaginary) cosmic forces of a postseason no-hitter.

Game Five: Astros 3, Phillies 2; Citizens Bank Park
(Astros lead, 3–2)
This game was a nail-biter, with critical defensive plays deciding the outcome. Jeremy Peña hit a home run that proved to be the difference. The game included a highlight moment when Houston's Chas McCormick made an incredible catch to prevent a potential tying run in the ninth inning, securing a narrow victory for the Astros and giving them a 3–2 lead in the series.

The Fightins rebounded valiantly but came up just a little short. Baseball is a game of inches, and McCormick's catch may have been the difference in the Series.

Game Six: Astros 4, Phillies 1; Minute Maid Park
(Houston wins World Series [lame])
Houston closed out the series at home. The Astros' pitching continued to be dominant, with Framber Valdez surrendering just two hits in his six innings of work. Houston, down 1–0 in the sixth, got a three-run homer from Yordan Alvarez that ended up being the game-winner. Dusty Baker managed his team to its second World Series title, showcasing the depth and resilience of his squad. In the end, the 'Stros—one of the most hated teams in baseball—got some shine back from past cheating allegations. Good for them. Bastards.

> ## KEVIN'S NOTE
> Hall of Fame player-manager Frank Robinson is credited with the idiom "Close only counts in horseshoes and hand grenades," but that's just a fancy way of saying, "If you ain't first, you're last." And, of course, Ricky Bobby quotes don't hit with the same resonance, unless you're playing horseshoes hammered on Mickey's malt liquor hand grenades.

Close counts for something. Many generations of Phillies fans were born and died without ever having seen the Fightins take home a championship. Was their fanhood worthless? Hardly. An awful destination doesn't have to spoil an epic journey. Like a North Korean cruise line with a great all-inclusive drinks package, sometimes you just gotta sit back and enjoy the ride.

> "The pieces are all in place—young players who have proven they belong, an incredible core of All-Star veterans, a manager who knows how to get the best from us, a front office and ownership who will do whatever it takes, and the best home-field advantage in baseball."
> —Kyle Schwarber[7]

#14

2023

Thanks to the miracle run that was the '22 Phils World Series run, baseball was back in the city of Philadelphia. and the expectations for a team that had been maddeningly frustrating for a couple of years now had risen to brand-new heights.

> Of all the things I loved about the '22 run, arguably my favorite part was that people were reminded how intense and really fun baseball can be. It really was maybe the biggest switch I've seen from this city ever—from "Meh, who cares?" to "Holy cow, this is amazing." All the fan base really wanted out of the '22 postseason was to get a home playoff game, but once Rhys slammed his bat—the ride was truly on. As always, thank you '22 Phillies.

With the expectations now bestowed upon them, the pressure was on Dave Dombrowski to find the right mix of talent to keep the Phillies near the top of the sport. Ironically, heading into the '23 season, Dombrowski had to make a World Series team better; after all, the '22 team only won 87 games. One could argue they were ahead of schedule in '22. So in '23 the team had to prove the season wasn't a fluke and it wasn't ahead of schedule. Although the Phillies had a high payroll in '22 and already had one $300-plus million contract under their belt, they did have the flexibility to add another high-priced player to their squad. With Jean Segura gone after the '22 season, and Bryson Stott maybe projecting more as a second baseman long-term, the most glaring position of need heading into the '23 season was at shortstop. Luckily for the Phils, this year's free-agent class was a loaded with shortstops.

Xander Bogaerts, Dansby Swanson, Trea Turner, and Carlos Correa were all free agents, and all had World Series rings on their finger. Would

Dombrowski want to get reunited with his guy from Boston in Bogaerts? Would he bank on the upside of Correa and his ability to shine in the postseason? What about the all-around good shortstop in Swanson? Nope, as it had been hinted at since the middle of summer, the Phillies had their eyes on one shortstop—Trea Turner.

The case for Turner was simple—he was a .300 hitter who had pop, was one of the fastest players in baseball, and was a World Series champion. It also helped that he was a former teammate of Harper in Washington and was coached there by Kevin Long. The Phillies wanted Turner, but the problem was so did a lot of other clubs. The San Diego Padres were in the market for a new shortstop as well, and they had their eyes on the twenty-nine-year-old former prospect of theirs—people forget he only became a National because of a three-team trade that involved Steven Souza Jr. and Wil Myers. When it came down to it, the Phillies were short; they had to reach the $300 million threshold or else they were going to lose the shortstop. Middleton and Dombrowski got there, offering Turner a contract that would pay him through his age-forty season. It was a big move, and Turner left money on the table (according to Matt Gelb of *The Athletic*) from the Padres to make the move happen. Two other key factors weighed in for the former Nationals and Dodgers shortstop. One, his wife is from Flemington, New Jersey, so the urge to come back to the East Coast was strong. Two was the fans. Yes, the fans that turned Citizens Bank Park back into the coolest place in sports jumped through the TV screen to Turner. Funny enough, those fans would be a key storyline of the 2023 Phillies. Overall, it was a busy Winter Meetings for Dave Dombrowski, as he also inked lefty Matt Strahm (yay!), and a few days after the meetings signed Taijuan Walker (meh!). He finally closed out the offseason by signing a guy who would play in the All-Star Game in a Phillies uniform before Bryce Harper, in Craig Kimbrel, and trading away two of their depth guys from the '22 squad, Matt Vierling and Nick Maton, for Gregory Soto and Kody Clemens of the Tigers.

On paper, the 2023 team had the look of a World Series team, and to their credit, the Phillies were aggressive in trying to maintain the standard they had just set that past October. They had another star in the lineup, beefed up the bullpen, and added a guy who should have given them quality innings. The Phils had the experience of being on the doorstep of taking home a World Series title. Now, they just had to stay healthy and make it to Opening Day.

That proved to be a challenge. Two key injuries happened in the spring of '23. The Phillies were being very aggressive in their push to have Andrew

Painter join the starting rotation as a nineteen-year-old—maybe too aggressive. After only one spring training start, Painter injured his elbow and would end up needing Tommy John surgery.

> I hope that by the time you read this book Andrew Painter has returned and is turning into a stud for the Phillies. Let me just put this in writing, Andrew Painter is going to go into the Hall of Fame wearing a Phillies *P* on his cap. When this book is still being gifted around the holidays 20 years from now, just make sure to point out this portion. Painter is a star, and he's going to make this city very happy for a long time. If this turns out to not be true, please don't take a photo or screenshot of this, please and thank you.

The other injury was much more significant. Rhys Hoskins had just completed "owning October," in the wise words of sportscaster Joe Davis, and was heading into the final year of his contract with the ballclub. Hoskins was stuck in a situation similar to that of Burrell and Werth a decade prior—Hoskins was a good player, but given the money already allocated for the rest of the roster, it was unlikely that he was going to re-sign with the team. Still, Hoskins had one more year to cement his legacy as a Phillie. In the last week before the '23 season, Hoskins drifted back on a routine groundball that bounced off his glove and into right field. On his turn to get the ball, Hoskins immediately went down in a heap of pain, clutching his right knee. He was helped off the field, and Hoskins was done for the year with a torn ACL—the Phillies would ultimately miss that thump in the middle of the lineup.

> Before we continue with the '23 Phillies, I want to give a special shoutout to Rhys. Nola was our first hope during the rebuild, and Hoskins was the first interesting position player. He truly embraced being the face of the Phillies. His rookie year helped bring life back into Phillies baseball, he crushed it on the biggest stage at the All-Star Game in the Home Run Derby, and he helped carry this team to the World Series in '22. Whenever he was on WIP, he would talk about how he wanted to create new memories and that it was time. Although it totally sucks how it ended for him here, I am glad he was able to get his moment after wanting it for so long.

With those two injuries and the team's star, Bryce Harper, battling back from offseason Tommy John surgery, the team headed west to Texas to start a 2023 campaign that was oh so close to ending in glory.

The 2023 season was a season of change in Major League Baseball and one that the purists of the sport had dreaded for years. The reality was in the ever-changing times of the 2020s when attention spans are shorter and shorter, you either adapt or die. That was what baseball was dealing with when it decided to change some of its oldest rules. The pitch clock was in, the shift was banned, the ghost runner on second base to start extra innings stayed, bigger bases were enacted to try to increase stolen bases, and pitchers could only attempt a pickoff to a base three times. It was a monumental shift but ultimately might have saved the sport.

Things didn't start off too hot for the '23 Phils. They started the season 1–5 after getting swept by the eventual World Series champion, the Texas Rangers, and losing two of three to the New York Yankees. They finally returned home and received the hero's welcome they had clearly been waiting for. That was pretty unfair by Major League Baseball to force the defending National League champs to start the season on the road after everything that just transpired in October and November the year prior. The boys just wanted to get home and get their rings. You would have thought this team won the World Series with the rings they got, but still, it was a huge accomplishment for a team that hadn't been in that spot in over a decade. The biggest ovation was for Hoskins, who headed out to the field in a full leg cast to accept his ring. It wouldn't be the last time Hoskins would take the field to a huge ovation that season. Second year second baseman Bryson Stott, who took down Puddin' Head Jones's hitting streak to start the season with a hit in his first 17 games of the season, was arguably the hottest player. Overall, the Phillies exited the first month a game over .500 and had stabilized after a disastrous start to the season.

The reality was that everyone in Philadelphia was on Bryce Watch as he was on his comeback trail from Tommy John surgery that he got after the season. He was even learning a new position, first base, to play when he eventually got back in the lineup. It was once looking like Harper wasn't going to be able to make his season debut until June, but you don't know Bryce Harper if you thought that was going to be the case. It was looking more and more likely that the face of the Phillies would be able to rejoin the club in early May. Given the tenacity of Harper, no planned rehab stints in Clearwater,

Reading, or Lehigh Valley were planned. He was traveling with the team, taking live batting practice, and doing extra work in the cages. In a rare feat, he was attempting to go straight from being cold to live Major League action with little to no ramp up. If there was one guy who could do it, it was Harper.

> **JACK NOTE:** Harper was taking live batting practice against a lot of Phillies pitchers from the majors and minors to get ready. One of the arms was Ranger Suárez, who was batting back from a preseason elbow injury. However, one arm that stood out above the rest that was thirty-year-old journeyman Jeff Hoffman. Hoffman, the former top-10 pick, had never found his footing at the big-league level, which led to many labeling him a bust. That was before he found his footing in the bullpen with the Phillies. In a now famous story, Hoffman faced the rehabbing Harper six times and struck him out in five of the at-bats. It was reported that Harper went to the front office afterward and reported how nasty Hoffman was and that he needed to be on the big-league roster. The shock was that Hoffman had an ERA of 7.00 at Lehigh Valley somehow, but still, Harper got his wish, and Hoffman was activated a couple days after. He would have a 2.41 ERA the rest of the season and eventually pitch his way into a big payday in free agency of 2024—a truly great story.

Before the first game of a three-game set against the Dodgers, Harper met with the doctor who performed his Tommy John surgery out in LA Harper got the green light and was activated on May 2. While it was aided by the existence of the DH, Harper still completed the quickest return from Tommy John surgery in the history of the sport when he stepped on the field a mere 160 days after getting the procedure done. Unfortunately for the Phillies, he couldn't pitch because the pitching staff against the Dodgers allowed 36 runs in three games. Not great!

Maybe the funniest game of Harper's early return happened against the Rockies on the same day that the Sixers no-showed a Game Seven against the Celtics in Boston in one of the most gutless performances in Philadelphia sports history. Harper, a mere 10 games back from the surgery, started a bench-clearing brawl when Rockies pitcher Jake Bird was jawing at the Phillies dugout after a scoreless inning. Harper didn't appreciate this and charged at

Bird and both benches cleared, including the bullpen, and the Phillies' DH was thrown out of the game. His parting words to the Rockies were, "You're a loser [expletive] organization. All of you."

With Harper fully back and integrated into the lineup, there was an expectation that the Phillies would take off; however, that wasn't really the case. For the second straight year, the Phillies would go either on a winning streak or on a losing streak. It was tough for them to find consistency. For the second straight year, this team seemed to be waiting for June to catch fire. June Schwarber was arguably the greatest hitter to ever live, and when he got hot the rest of the team did too. One cool moment that happened before June was when Phillies All-Star Craig Kimbrel notched his 400th save while closing out a game in Atlanta, of all places. Once again, baseball. Celebrating Kimbrel's 400th save was definitely a weird one for us Phillies fans, since he had been a nemesis for so long. The always classy Phillies had champagne waiting in the locker room for him when he got back to the clubhouse. This will be the last positive thing written about Kimbrel for the rest of this chapter, I promise.

On the one-year anniversary of Rob Thomson taking over as manager of the Phillies, the team was in almost the exact same situation as when he took over—seven games under .500. It was as if that was this team's sweet spot, under .500 heading into June.

> One author of this book declared this team dead after getting swept out in New York. In my defense, they had just scored three runs in three games against a bad Mets team, and they just looked dead. Thankfully, the ever-steady and always clear-headed Ike Reese (shoutout to Ike) talked me off the ledge on the radio that day and assured me that everything was going to be okay. Maybe it was just to reverse jinx this team into playing good baseball; either way, the Phillies got hot almost immediately after I declared the season over at the end of May. You're welcome!

With Schwarber back in the leadoff spot to try to ignite a struggling offense, the Phillies caught fire. The Phillies in June ripped off an 18–8 stretch; the Mr. June himself, Schwarber, paced the team with eight home runs in the month. Within June, the Phillies also took down maybe the most important record in the franchise's history.

> **JACK NOTE:** I am sorry for those of you who were not in on this bit, so I feel like I have to explain a bit more. This is nothing personal against David Bell, but he was my least favorite Phillie growing up. Maybe it was because my granddad and I used to fight about him all the time—I just couldn't stand how miserable he looked playing the game of baseball. Anyway, in 2004 he hit for the cycle against the Montréal Expos (RIP) and the record, against my best wishes, stood for almost 20 years. That was until J. T. Realmuto hit for the cycle against the Diamondbacks in Arizona in a game in which the Phillies blew a 5–1 lead, which isn't all that important. Bell's name was that much closer to being erased from people's memories. Unfortunately, this would be the highlight of the Phillies' season versus the Diamondbacks—not really, but you get the point.]

Out in Oakland, the Phillies made a pretty nondescript roster move when they called up Cris Sánchez to make his second start of the year, and his first since early April. Sánchez had been back and forth between the big leagues and Triple A when he arrived in Philadelphia in 2020 but had never really found much success. Finally, it seemed like the Phillies had found the right formula for the left-hander. He could throw hard, but his command was shoddy, so they told him to dial back some of the velocity to spot the baseball better. He did, and when he got his shot in 2023 due to some other injuries on the staff, he didn't look back. Fast-forward to 2024—Sánchez was an All-Star and armed with a brand new contract extension that pays him through the 2028 season. Sánchez would end the year with a 3.35 ERA as a starter.

The Phillies exited June five games over .500 but still 11, yes 11, games back of the division-leading Braves. The division might as well have been over at that point, but the Phillies were still in a very good spot for the wild card as they entered into trade-deadline month. At the beginning of July, this team faced one of their biggest tests yet—the Tampa Bay Rays. Zach Eflin got to pitch against his old team and was finally able to receive his National League pennant ring. Eflin had an up-and-down career as a Phillie after being traded here in the deal that sent a franchise icon, Jimmy Rollins, to Los Angeles. No pressure or anything. Bad knees have ultimately held back Eflin, but while he was here, he was truly one of the good guys that this team had during the down times. In game one of the series, Eflin got to square off against his best friend on the team, Aaron Nola. Even though Eflin was having a career year and would end up sixth in AL Cy Young voting, Nola outdueled him, and the Phillies took the first game of the series. In what felt like an omen of good things to come, they swept the Rays in Tampa, which was the first time the Florida team had been swept so far this season. The Phillies were riding high heading into Miami, typically a house of horrors for the Phils, for the final road series before the All-Star break. The series started off with a bang as Cristian Pache hit a no-way go-ahead two-run home run in the top of the ninth to turn the game around and give the Phillies the first game of the series in Miami. It was maybe the most shocking home run of the 2023 campaign. After this, the Phillies barely showed up the next two nights in Miami, and they lost another series down there. Overall, though, the Phillies put themselves in a very good position heading into the All-Star break.

The Phillies only sent two All-Stars to the extravaganza in '23, with the Phillies entire coaching staff, of course, managing the game. Nick Castellanos was enjoying a bounce-back season, as his first year in Philadelphia didn't exactly go the way everyone thought it would. The other, as documented, was Craig Kimbrel who, fittingly enough, closed out the game for the National League but not without throwing a lot of pitches for an exhibition and making fans nervous at home. Still Thomson managed the National League to a win for the first time since 2012, and it was onto the second half.

At this point of the '23 season, every fan in Philadelphia was waiting for Harper to test out his new position—first base. He had been working day and night to learn the position in an attempt to add more flexibility to the roster. If he could play first, that would open up the DH spot so that Schwarber could not play left field every day, and Marsh could play left instead, making the defense as a whole that much better. Part of that was the promotion of the light-hitting Johan Rojas, who was called up on July 15. He was a special defensive center fielder and a work in progress at the plate, but the Phillies gave him a shot. After all, the Phillies needed help defensively, considering that they had consistently been one of the bottom-10 defensive units in the sport for some time. Harper finally got his shot to man first base on July 21 in Cleveland, and it didn't take long for Harper to make his presence felt. In the first inning, the Guardians' Steven Kwan lifted a ball into foul territory on the first-base side. Harper, running like he used to in the outfield, flipped over the guardrail by the first-base dugout and fell into the camera well, all to catch the foul ball. He was fine, but everyone's heart back in Philadelphia sank. "Please don't do that again, Bryce."

Toward the end of July and heading into the trade deadline, one storyline raised concern—the play of Trea Turner. He obviously had huge expectations—they always come with the $300 million price tag—and it just looked like he was trying to live up to the contract every single night. On July 24 in Baltimore Turner snapped. He made an error on a routine groundball in the fourth and then got thrown out of the game an inning later after arguing balls and strikes on a borderline, but mostly a strike, pitch. Turner was down to hitting .242 with a .295 on-base percentage and a .674 OPS by the end of July and was making crucial errors in the field as well. This team wasn't going to win a title with one of their stars experiencing the first-year-after-a-big-new-contract blues. The Phillies were trying everything, such as giving him some games off and dropping him in the lineup, but nothing was working—maybe it was time for the fans to try to help?

If the Baltimore game wasn't the low point for Turner, eight games later in Miami would be. With the Phillies leading by one in extra innings, Josh Bell shot a ground ball right at Turner that should have ended the game. However, Turner couldn't get a glove on it, and it shot into center field to tie the game up. The Phillies would go on to lose an inning later. Overall, Turner went 0-for-5, which dropped his average to .237. Turner looked broken, and his postgame interview was a tough watch. Todd Zolecki reported that Turner was hitting in the cage until 12:30 in the morning after the game until Thomson came in, turned the lights off, and forced him to go back to the hotel. Turner was trying; it just wasn't clicking. After seeing his postgame presser and the story of him trying to work through it, an idea was hatched. Give Trea Turner a standing ovation on Friday night against the Royals in an attempt to let him know that we have his back and he can just go play. Crazy idea, right?

> Let's go through the timeline here. There had been an idea of a standing ovation percolating for a little bit; allegedly Joe Decamara threw out the idea on the airwaves at WIP a couple weeks before, but no one remembered that. The first tweet that I saw was from Mitch Rupert, a writer from the Bloomsburg area who had a similar reaction that a lot of us did after the Turner interview in Miami, and called for one. I jumped on it the next morning in a tweet that got the fire burning even more.

> Later in that day, The Philly Captain put out a video to his followers that got traction—maybe there's something brewing here. I put out another video the next morning calling for it, and we on the afternoon show talked about it on WIP after the day game that Thursday. By Friday it was the biggest talking point in the city. The morning show debated it for four hours, the new midday show had maybe its most heated debate in the show's young history on the topic, Eagles offensive line coach Jeff Stoutland brought it up at his press conference, and finally, leading into the game myself, Ike Reese and Jonny Marks hammered it home. Give Trea Turner a standing ovation tonight at the game and keep it going. There was nothing to lose, and it might work. Philadelphia had gotten the message and in his first at-bat, Turner received a huge ovation that still brings chills when you watch it to this day. Turner got cheered all throughout the weekend, but the moment that really showed that it might have worked was the next night when, after the seventh ovation, Turner went yard. He touched home plate and let out a whole bunch of pent up emotion. The crowd didn't stop cheering until Turner came out of the dugout and tipped his cap to the fans. It was truly an unbelievable moment and one that many around the nation didn't think that Philadelphia was capable of. Turns out, they just don't know us. The total group effort obviously helped a struggling player.

Getting Turner to be himself might have been the Phillies' biggest trade deadline acquisition. It was a quiet deadline for the Phils, as the only move of significance Dombrowski made was for Tigers starter Michael Lorenzen, who would help the Phillies in both the rotation and hopefully the bullpen. While it was looking good for a hot minute, Lorenzen really tailed off at the end of the regular season.

That hot minute, though, was special.

On August 9, in his second start as a Phillie, Lorenzen threw the 14th no-hitter in Phillies history and the first one since Cole Hamels threw one in his last start with the team. This was also the first game of Weston Wilson's big-league career that was starting at the age of twenty-nine. He homered in his first at-bat. Talk about an emotion-filled night at the ballpark. With both sets of families, the Lorenzen's and the Wilson's, in tears, on top of the Turner thing that had just happened, if you walked into Citizens Bank Park in August of '23 you might be walking out welling up. It's always a magical ballpark, but the August of this season might have taken the cake, at least for the regular season.

> It was around this time that this season truly felt like "The Year." With all the Turner stuff, the no-hitter, the Wilson home run—an aura seemed to be around the players so that this year felt different. I watch all the video yearbooks (multiple times) and some serious video yearbook moments were piling up. One of the cooler moments of the '23 regular season was when the Phillies players were in the stands for Media Little League's game up in Williamsport during the Little League World Series. As soon as the Phils walked through the door, Media mounted a large comeback to get the crowd into it. Seeing millionaire baseball players turn into fans watching kids play the game the players are paid to play was a really cool scene and unique.

The magical month of August ended with Bryce Harper hitting a two-run home run in the bottom of the eighth against the Angels to give the Phillies an 8–7 lead. Not only was it another clutch home run by Harper, but it was also the 300th of his career—always a flair for the dramatic. However, the Phillies would lose this game in what was slowly becoming a trend. It's hard to quantify and there's no stat for it (I don't think)—at this point in the season it seemed like after every big Phillies home run, the bullpen would immediately blow it. Hopefully it wouldn't happen in the postseason, but it was certainly starting to become a trend.

In mid-September, even though the division was well over, it's always good to see how you stack up against the best of the best. In 2023 the Braves were the best team in the National League during the regular season, winning 104 games. Seven of the Phils' 19 remaining games left before the postseason would be against those Braves. In the first series, the Braves took it to the Phillies, taking three of four and setting the National League single-season home run record in the process—they ended with 307 of them. The most important thing that happened this entire series might have been the Phillies being given the opportunity to watch the Braves celebrate clinching the NL East on their home field. Multiple Phillies players stayed around to see the Braves celebrate, including Nick Castellanos, who was captured by a famous photo while he was looking out with CONGRATULATIONS, ATLANTA BRAVES! 2023 NATIONAL LEAGUE EAST CHAMPIONS on the home video scoreboard.

Castellanos got the first part of his revenge tour against the Braves that season six days later as the Phillies were looking to take two of three from Atlanta and continue to build their lead in the NL wild-card chase. In a tie game in the bottom of the ninth, after former Phil Luke Williams stole second and third with one out, future Phils nemesis Orlando Arcia lifted a ball to foul territory in short right field. It was a tough decision for Castellanos. "Do I catch the ball, spin, and try to recapture my footing and throw out Williams at the plate, or do I let it drop and take my chances the rest of the at-bat?"[1] On the broadcast, it was clear what John Kruk wanted, as he was screaming, "Let it go! Let it go!" when Castellanos eventually corralled the ball in. Luckily enough, Castellanos caught it, made a spin move, and delivered a strike to Garrett Stubbs at the plate to gun down Williams. It was your classic, "No! No! No! . . . Yes!" play by Castellanos. Stott hit a bases-clearing double in the top of the 10th to put the Phils up for good, as they extended their lead in the National League wild card. After the game, as half the team admitted they were screaming at Castellanos to drop the ball, including the manager, Castellanos revealed there was a voice inside his head that said, "Catch it, and throw him out." What an interesting cat that dude is.

> Maybe the most interesting thing to happen as the Phillies were counting down the days until the postseason was the debut of Orion Kerkering. Again, we're writing this in 2024 and 2025, so hopefully when you're reading this book 10 years from now he's the Phillies all-time saves leader, and we can finally erase Jonathan Papelbon from our record book. For me, he is similar to David Bell; first it was the cycle that had to get taken off the books, and next is Papelbon being our all-time saves leader. Anyway, Kerkering had a meteoric rise through the system. Drafted in the fifth round of the '22 draft out of South Florida University, the numbers there didn't really pop off the screen. He had a 5.72 ERA in college, but you know what popped? The stuff. The stuff allowed him to rise through the minor leagues and reach the big leagues in one season. Yes, from Clearwater, to Jersey Shore, to Reading, to Lehigh Valley, and finally to Philadelphia. I hope he was just staying in hotels at those places. Against the Mets, as the Phillies were finishing up

> a sweep, Kerkering made his debut. The Phillies bullpen was good, but adding another weapon couldn't hurt, especially with playoff Kimbrel lurking—so they gave the kid a shot. Kerkering delivered, as he broke off several nasty sliders and flashed his 98–100 miles per hour fastball to sit down the Mets in order and pick up two strikeouts. As he was coming off the field, the camera found his dad, an ex-Marine, overcome with emotion and crying watching what his son had just done.

On September 26 against the Pirates, the Phillies would officially punch their ticket to the postseason, as another kid stepped up in a big spot. This time it was Johan Rojas, who had turned into this team's primary center fielder after being called up from Reading. In the bottom of the 10th inning, he called game as he shot a one-out single up the middle to plate Pache from second base. It wasn't as dramatic as in '22, but they had done it again—from under .500 to number one in the wild card and a ton of moments in between. It was hard to find a true flaw in this group. Turner was looking like himself, Harper and Schwarber were known postseason risers, and the Phillies had a starting rotation that had been there before and a bullpen that had developed into a strong unit. They were a well-rounded team—it was time.

There was no hope to just get a home playoff game heading into October 2023—it was simply time to finish a job. Standing in their way in the first round was the Miami Marlins, who made the playoffs and their fans didn't even realize it.

> I'm not going to lie; I was nervous about the Marlins. They seemed to always trip up the Phillies, especially down in Marlins Park, or whatever it's called, and now they get to play spoiler. *I Hated It!* Thankfully, you could tell within the first like five innings that this series was over, but still, I was nervous. To be fair, I'm always nervous about the Phils, but the Fish Anxiety was real, and thankfully the Phillies just took care of business.

Game One was over before it even started, as Rhys Hoskins got to say goodbye to Phillies fans one last time with an emotional first pitch. After that, it was back to Clearwater for Hoskins. He was attempting to pull off what

Kyle Schwarber had done in 2016 with the Cubs: come back from a torn ACL in time for the World Series, Who knows if he could have done it, but it would have been nice for him to have the opportunity! Sigh.

It was a workmanlike effort by the Phillies in Game One. Wheeler shoved, as he usually does in the postseason, as he fired 6 2/3 innings of one-run baseball. Every member of the Phillies lineup got a hit, Harper ran through a stop sign, the bullpen didn't allow a run, Josh Bell had three hits (he's a Phillie killer), and the ballpark was on fire as they took down the fish in Game One.

> So I have definitely made up for not getting to go to one playoff game during the run from '07 to '11 (does that disqualify me from writing this book?) because I've been at every home playoff game besides Game Three and Four of the NLCS in '22. The coolest part about Game One of the Marlins series was how everyone was just back at the ballpark knowing that something cool was about to happen. Citizens Bank Park was the place you just wanted to be in '22, and people didn't want to miss out on the fun in '23—you could just feel that type of energy in the ballpark. Thankfully, they delivered. It was like seeing an old friend again when I walked through the gates at the ole ballpark.]

If Game One was truly never in doubt, then Game Two might as well have been a lock. Braxton Garrett vs. Aaron Nola at the jungle that was Citizens Bank Park? Please. Nola was in an interesting spot heading into this postseason. He bet on himself heading into his walk year with the hope of pitching well and securing a huge contract in free agency. It didn't go to plan because he struggled a majority of the year and finished the season with an ERA of 4.46. But a mechanical adjustment that had Nola pointing his shoulders more toward the first-base dugout before his final start of the regular season might have been enough to get the good version of Nola in the postseason. Early in this one, it was looking like another workmanlike performance by the Phils. Nola was pitching well—the two horses had already done their job—and the offense was doing just enough. The Phillies had scored three runs heading into the bottom of the sixth, but the first signature moment of the '23 postseason occurred here. With the bases loaded and the entire crowd singing along to Bryson Stott's walkup song, "A-O-K," the Phillies' second baseman did something he normally didn't do—he swung at a first pitch. He didn't miss it; Stott launched one into a sea of red towels in right field to truly put this one away, 7–0 in the bottom of the sixth. The party was on in South Philadelphia—you just had to wait for the game to be over. They finally did get the last out, "Dancing on My Own," blared over the PA system, and the Phillies were celebrating like mad men in their clubhouse. It truly felt like '22 all over again—it was good to be back.

Winning the division is cool, but you know what's cooler? Beating the Braves in the postseason. That was the task as the Phillies and Braves squared off again in the NLDS. This time, the pressure was even more on the Braves side. After all the whining they did in '22 about the long layoff between the end of the season and the playoffs, the main crybaby, manager Brian Snitker, tried something different. He had the Braves play simulated games and pump in crowd noise to try and emulate Citizens Bank Park for when they would eventually have to travel up here.

Game One was a Rob Thomson master class. There's something about Game Ones and Thomson pulling all the right strings to win a ballgame. For the second straight year, Ranger Suárez started Game One down in Atlanta—his opposition this year, however, was much tougher. While we never want to admit that Spencer Strider wasn't healthy in Game Three of the NLDS in '22, the '23 version was a whole different animal. He was fully healthy after coming off a top-five NL Cy Young Award finish. The Phillies drew first blood when Stott doubled home Harper from second base for a 1–0 lead in the top of the fourth. However, the bottom half of the inning was when the chess match started. With two outs and runners on first and second, Thomson pulled Suárez for the resurgent Jeff Hoffman. Initially, the decision didn't look so hot as Hoffman walked the first batter he faced to load the bases. Luckily, Hoffman rebounded and struck out Michael Harris II to end the frame. The Phillies would go on to dodge more trouble in the fifth when, noted playoff riser, Seranthony Domínguez, struck out Ronald Acuña Jr. and Austin Riley back-to-back with runners on first and third with one out. Feels like a win?

The next inning, Strider allowed his only earned run of the night when Harper joined the party with a home run to right—2–0 Phillies, as they were in the heart of their bullpen. With the Phillies now up 3–0, thanks to a catcher's interference call with the bases loaded, Kerkering was out for his second inning of work. After he walked the leadoff hitter, Strahm was brought in, and he let up a single to Austin Riley. Uh-oh, first and second with no outs—here come the Braves. Strahm was able to just miss the barrel against Matt Olson, the next batter, who flew out to deep center field. Then, Ozzie Albies smoked a ball to Turner's left. Turner, not exactly known for his defense, fielded it, flipped to Stott, who turned and fired on to Harper at first base to turn the double play. It was the defensive highlight of the night and one that killed the Braves' spirit. At this moment, everyone in the minor-league stadium that is Truist Park started to think, *Not again*. The Phillies were unafraid of the Braves, and it showed. Kimbrel somehow, some way worked a one-two-three ninth, and just like the year before they had a 1–0 series lead over the Braves.

    The Phillies entered Game Two with house money. They had already done their job; now it was time to get greedy. That plan was looking good early too. This was one of those games that, had they not taken the series, would have been heartbreaking, but they did so it was all good. The Phillies jumped out to a 4–0 lead in this one thanks in large part to a home run by Realmuto. At 4–0 with big-game Wheeler on the mound? This one was over.

    Well, until it wasn't. Wheeler was brilliant through six, striking out a career high in the postseason with 10, and he held the Braves hitless through five. They got a run back in the sixth on an error by Turner, but still it was 4–1 heading into the bottom of the seventh. That is, until Travis d'Arnaud hit a two-run home run off Wheeler—the Braves had life. Their minor-league stadium got as loud as it could. The Braves completed the comeback when in the eighth, Austin Riley one-armed a home run to left field off Jeff Hoffman.

    The real drama in this one happened in the ninth, when Nick Castellanos shot one into right-center field with Harper at first base. It looked like it had a shot, and Harper decided to get aggressive. In his head, he's thinking either it's gone or it's going to bound off the wall, and he had to score to tie the game up—only there was one problem. Michael Harris II leaped and caught the baseball, slammed into the wall, and fired into almost no man's land in the infield. Riley came sprinting over, a la Derek Jeter, and in one motion threw Harper out at first. It was insane and pandemonium at Truist Park. The Braves had recaptured momentum in the series after it looked like the Phillies were going to put a stranglehold on it.

    The Braves had momentum in the series until postgame when they got a little chirpy. Now, he probably didn't say this like an evil villain from a comic-book movie from childhood, but in all of our minds that's what this quote sounded like. With reporters in the clubhouse, Orlando Arcia was walking around saying, "Atta boy, Harper! Atta boy!"[2] Oh what a grave, grave mistake that would be. This also wouldn't be the first time this series the Braves' words would come back to bite them.

Before Game Three, back in Philly, you could just feel the city wanting to bury the Braves. The ballpark has a different level of electricity when one of the rivals comes in during the postseason. You could rename Game Three the Bryce Harper game or déjà vu all over again—whichever you prefer. Why déjà vu? Well it would be that damned bottom of the third inning in Game Three back in Philadelphia all over again. Who could forget that a year earlier the Phillies had their humongous third inning against Spencer Strider that included a big Stott double, the Rhys bat spike, and a Harper home run?

They were back in this one. It started with Castellanos tying the game back up at one with his first home run of the postseason. Then, with two outs, Harper came up looking for some revenge for Arcia's postgame antics—he got it, launching a three-run home run to right. As he was rounding second base, he stared down Arcia to let the Braves' shortstop know that he had heard him. The Phillies were up, 4–1, but they weren't done. Braves starter Bryce Elder stayed in the game after the home run and immediately allowed a single to Alec Bohm and a walk to Bryson Stott and got removed from the game. Realmuto capped off the two-out rally with a double into the gap to plate both Bohm and Stott and give the Phils their fifth and sixth runs of the inning. Déjà vu all over again. With this, the rout was on, and once again, local dads everywhere were begging the Phillies to save some runs for tomorrow. In the fifth, Harper hit his second home run of the game, off '22 Phil Brad Hand, for his second staredown—hence why it was the Bryce Harper game.

Then in the following innings, Turner, Castellanos, and Marsh all chipped in with home runs of their own. The final score ended up 10–2—it was a massacre in South Philly and, man oh man, did Arcia hear it from the Citizens Bank Park crowd. After the game, the Braves whined about the quote getting out and Harper, when asked about the staredown said, "Yeah, I stared right at him. That's what this is all about, right?"[3] This series was over; it was just a matter of how much of a fight the Braves would put up in Game Four.

The second comment the Braves wish they could have back was from Spencer Strider, who during the regular season wished that he could pitch where there with no fans in the stands. "Get rid of the fans, it's too loud. It's too loud, everybody be quiet. We don't need the cheering, we know you're watching. I don't need the fans."[4] Whether he was joking or not, he was walking into a hornets' nest at the ballpark that night. That quote, combined with the baby blues and playoff Ranger Suárez? A recipe for disaster.

The long ball was the main course for the recipe to win Game Four. Believe it or not, the city was aware of what Strider had said about no fans in the stadium, as the ballpark was filled with signs wondering if he thought it was too loud. The first player to take him deep on this night was Castellanos, who for the second straight night had tied the game up early with a home run. Then an inning later, Turner, who entered the game hitless against Strider, picked up his third hit and a home run off him in the sixth. And Castellanos put the cherry on top when he became the first player in postseason history, yes history, to have back-to-back two-home-run games, as he turned around a 100-mile-per-hour offering from Strider. His night was done as he heard it one last time from the Philly faithful. Suárez's night was done after five, but much like Wheeler and Nola before him, he had done a job and kept the best offense in the National League at bay.

It was the bullpen's turn to hold on to this one—and they did, but by the skin of its teeth. In the bottom half of the seventh, Alvarado was got the first two outs of the inning no problem, but then he walked the seventh and eighth hitters to bring up d'Arnaud. Thomson wasted no time in bringing in Craig Kimbrel. In classic Kimbrel fashion, he walked d'Arnaud to load the bases for the league's MVP in Acuña. It was a tight ballpark. It got even tighter when Kimbrel yanked the first pitch past Realmuto, only Pillar froze and didn't try and score from third base—a costly mistake. On a 2-2 pitch, Acuña drove one into left-center field—gulp. If it wasn't gone, it was going to at least hit off the wall. But it died and Johan Rojas was able to scamper back, get under it, and crash into the wall. It wasn't a 10 out of 10 on the toughness scale, but it was just tricky enough to cause most center fielders problems, but not the sure-handed Rojas. The next point of tension was in the bottom of the ninth. The always nerve-racking Gregory Soto started the inning with the score still 3–1. He allowed a walk and single to start the frame, which prompted Thomson to bring on Matt Strahm with runners on first and third with one out. Tight ballpark! Feels like a loss? Strahm got Pillar to pop out with no outs and then got the lefty Eddie Rosario—a postseason menace—to pop out to short left field. Just like that there were two outs. A tight ballpark turned to pure jubilation when Strahm got pinch-hitter Vaughn Grissom on a checked-swing slider to end the game. The Phillies had done it again. They had slain the best team in the National League for the second straight postseason and had the feeling of invincibility when they walked through the gates at Citizens Bank Park. Once again, "Dancing on My Own" was blaring, and all just felt right in the world. Guess this is just what we should expect from this team from now on? Regular season they're regular, and in the postseason they turn into demons? We could get down with that.

> This was an especially cool night. My podcast partner, James Seltzer, and our good friend, the Eagles beat reporter you need, Eliot Shorr-Parks, went into the Phillies clubhouse to see what the scene was like down there. We got some beer doused on our heads, met Trea Turner (thanks to Eliot), and soaked it all up with our guys.

They were back in the NLCS, and that feeling of invincibility was back as well. Bring on the Diamondbacks. Sigh.

> Usually I can feel it coming. It's almost like a coping mechanism for me when I tell people to be nervous about this or nervous about that. It all comes from this same place. I need the Phillies to win, and when I let my guard down that's when trouble happens. As you've read in this book, I wish I could have been the Paul Revere of Phillies baseball to warn people about the danger ahead and prepare—but even I fell into the trap. They had "the look," and no 84-win baseball team was going to beat this Phillies team. Again, 2023 was the year—until it wasn't.

Things started off so well too.

The Game One starter for the Diamondbacks was none other than Zac Gallen, a South Jersey native, whose whole family are diehard Phillies fans—except he was a Cardinals fan growing up. The Phillies simply had no choice but to punish him, and they did. In fact, they ambushed him. There was a lot of talk about this postseason feeling eerily similar to '22; that was true for Schwarber, who was quiet once again until the NLCS. He awoke with a 117-mile-per-hour bullet home run to right on the first pitch of the game from Gallen to give the Phillies a 1–0 lead. Two batters later, also on the first pitch, Harper went yard, on his birthday no less. Phillies were up 2–0, and it was a state of euphoria inside Citizens Bank Park. Things got even better for the Phillies when Castellanos exited the ballpark in the bottom of the second inning. It was a resurgent postseason for Castellanos, who performed better with his glove in the '22 playoffs than with his bat, which was not why the Phillies signed him. Still, he was providing some thump at the bottom of the lineup and joined Reggie Jackson as the only players in postseason history with five home runs over three consecutive playoff games.

The lead ballooned to 5–0 after five when Harper and Realmuto each drove in a run in the fourth and fifth, but this was also when the Diamondbacks started showing signs of life. It started with Wheeler allowing his only runs of the night—a two-run home run to Geraldo Perdomo. Wheeler was brilliant again as he had held the Diamondbacks hitless after the first batter of the game until that inning, while the Phils built up their lead. Then in the seventh, they navigated a first and third with no outs situation by only allowing one run to make it 5–3. Still, the ballpark wasn't tight—yet. That changed once Kimbrel came into the ballgame. To his credit, Kimbrel had done his job until this point of the postseason, but it was just never easy, and it was looking like another escape job was going to have to happen on this night. He walked Gabriel Moreno with one out to bring the tying run up to bat for the third straight inning. The Diamondbacks had no business winning this ballgame, but they were one swing of the bat away again. The Phillies, however, were one swing of the bat away from ending it as well, and they did—Lourdes Gurriel Jr. shot one toward Bohm, who fired it to second, and on to first to end the game. Fireworks early, tension late—that's playoff baseball, and once again, the Phillies took the all-important Game One in a playoff series.

If Game One was the shot, Game Two was the chaser. If you're following the script of these last two postseasons, the Phillies would win Game One in dramatic fashion and then have a letdown in Game Two. The difference now, however, is that they were at home and they were favorites. How would they play as the Big Men on Campus? At least on this night, like big men.

For most of Game Two it was looking like a tight, grind-it-out type of affair. Sure, Turner and Schwarber both went yard in the first three innings of this one, but the score was still 2–0 heading into the bottom of the sixth. The story of the game to this point was Nola, who was pitching big, right when the team and his wallet needed him most. Nola fired six shutout innings and struck out seven. He pitched so well even the naysayers didn't have an opportunity to mumble under their breath, "bleepin' Nola." His postseason ERA was down to 0.96. Yes, this was a ballgame until the bottom of the sixth when Schwarber led off the inning with his second home run of the night. He was going off in the NLCS again. Later in the inning, with runners on second and third with two outs and Joe Mantiply in the game now, Realmuto broke it wide open when he laced a double into the left-center-field gap to make it 5–0. The rally was capped off with a Brandon Marsh double to plate Realmuto—a four-run sixth to break the game wide open and have Citizens Bank Park wondering if this was real life. The Phillies poured it on from here, and for once, local baseball coaches were right when they were asking for them to save some runs for the rest of the series. The final ended up being 10–0. The Diamondbacks looked totally overwhelmed, almost like big bad Citizens Bank Park had claimed another one. For Phillies fans, the guard was down, there wasn't another shoe to drop here. This is what this team did and no way was this little upstart Diamondbacks team going to stack up with our billion-dollar ballclub. Things were easy—too easy.

> Call it overconfidence or whatever you want, but something changed when the Phillies went to Arizona. To this point in the playoffs, they were the most explosive offense in baseball history—that would change. At this point, the Diamondbacks went into the lab and devised a game plan that, even at the current writing of this book, the Phillies haven't been able to recover from. It was simple, too—make them expand the strike zone. The Phillies were an aggressive group of hitters; a large portion of them weren't working the pitcher—they were up there to launch baseballs. So the Diamondbacks figured, why play to their strengths? From Game Three on, you saw a different Diamondbacks ballclub, and it started with the plan on how to pitch to the Phillies. Or Garrett Stubbs tempted fate when he said they would celebrate in the pool at Chase Field, I don't know.

We now go to Game Three, or as it's called in the house of one writer of this book, the march to a slow death.

We pick up Game Three in the top of the seventh. Both starters are out of the game after brilliant efforts. Brandon Pfaadt executed the new Diamondbacks game plan perfectly, as he struck out a career-high nine in 5 2/3 innings, scattering only two hits, and Ranger Suárez for the Phils matched him nearly pitch for pitch with 5 1/3 innings of shutout baseball. In the bottom of the sixth, Jeff Hoffman just escaped a situation with a runner on third with one out without allowing a run. It was time for the Phils to make their move. In the top of the seventh, they did. With two outs, Harper at third base, and Realmuto at the dish, the Diamondbacks' Ryan Thompson unleashed a wild pitch that let the Phils' first baseman sprint home for the game's first run. The Phillies were six outs away from a commanding 3–0 series lead. But the Diamondbacks just wouldn't die. "Snakes alive," was their motto, and they came alive in the eighth. They tied the game on a double down the line by Lourdes Gurriel to plate Alek Thomas all the way from first base. Not good. However, what was good was what happened with Alvarado now in the game for Kerkering with runners on first and third with no outs. He ushered a ground ball to Turner, who calmly looked back the runner at third base, fired to Stott, who then rifled it over to Harper for the massive double play. Alvarado then got the next hitter, Perdomo, to end the threat. To be honest, the feeling in the building after that was that of a win for the Phils. Oh, to be young and naive.

In the bottom of the ninth, after the Phillies couldn't capitalize on the momentum, Kimbrel was brought on after some heroics from Alvarado. He promptly loaded the bases, even after a miracle defensive play from Turner to get the first out of the inning, and the Diamondbacks' hotter hitter, Ketel Marte, hit a humpback liner into center field to walk it off. This wouldn't be the end of the Kimbrel nightmare in Phoenix.

No, that would continue in Game Four. Instead of going with 15-game-winner Taijuan Walker (made myself chuckle with that one), Thomson elected to go with Cris Sánchez for his first-ever playoff start. Sánchez was not expected to have a long leash, and Thomson could be ultra-aggressive with his horse on the mound in Game Five in Zack Wheeler. In a game in which runs were going to be a premium, giving one away on a mental error is just brutal. That's just what Sánchez did when he didn't throw to second base on a comebacker in the bottom of the second inning. Instead of firing to second to at least get the lead runner, he threw it to first and only got one out. Christian Walker, the lead runner, would eventually come around to score. Was the moment too big for Sánchez? Thomson might have felt that way as he lifted him from the ballgame after just 2 1/3 innings.

With the Phils down 2–0 heading into the fourth, they were awakened by none other than Kyle Schwarber, Mr. NLCS, as he launched one to right to cut the lead in half. An inning later, Brandon Marsh tied the game up with an almost home run to left-center field to plate Realmuto from second. Momentum was swinging back in the Phillies direction here, and, heck, they even got a patented Nick Castellanos feet-first diving catch in the top of the fifth. They never lost when Castellanos made one of those types of catches. By the way, if you're reading this 10 years from now or whatever, just go look up some of the Castellanos catches in '22 and you'll understand that reference and why it was important.

Some of their big horses in the bullpen were being used, however, and Alvarado was being protected after his efforts in Game Three. Kimbrel was going to have to take down some big outs in this one. At least when that situation was going to happen, they would be handing the ball to him with the lead thanks to some work by the offense in the top of the sixth. With the bases loaded, up stepped maybe the Phillies' most important hitter in this series, Alec Bohm. Why? He was protecting Harper, and teams were going to start pitching around Harper if Bohm couldn't make them pay. Well, he did here as he hit a slow roller up the third-base line. The DBacks' third baseman, Emmanuel Rivera, fielded it and threw a bouncer to home plate; it couldn't be corralled, and it bounded away from Moreno behind the plate to score two Phils. Unfortunately, that was all the Phillies could score that inning but the score was 4–2 heading into the bottom of the sixth. Again, when I was in the building for this, it felt like a win.

Things got even better for the Phils as Turner hit a sacrifice fly in the top of the seventh to score Johan Rojas, who had tripled earlier in the inning. But this was the last moment that this one felt like a win. One of the problems for Thomson in the '22 and '23 playoffs was trust in his guys. It's great when it works, but when it doesn't and when it looks obvious to those at home, the reaction is much stronger. We'll get to the Kimbrel situation in a bit, but the first thing was his trust in the rookie Orion Kerkering. They were treating him like he was a vet in this series, and they brought him in during the bottom of the seventh with two outs and runners on first and third. Kerkering walked Moreno and Walker back to back to bring the score to 5–3 Phillies—thankfully, that was it, and he was able to retire the side. That was just the first crack in the Phils' armor.

Thomson went back to Kimbrel in the eighth, after he was unable to get the job done the night before, because his starter was only able to give him two-ish innings of work. Lourdes Gurriel greeted him with a double to start the inning, and then Kimbrel got Evan Longoria to pop out to bring Alek Thomas, who was pinch-hitting for Rivera, to the plate. Yes, Alek Thomas, who had nine home runs on the year, was able to catch up to a 3-2, 94-mile-per-hour fastball (WTF, Craig?) and tie the ballgame up. Thomson's faith in Kimbrel came back to bite him again. It's not like there's a long history of him struggling in the playoffs or anything! Speaking of Alvarado, he was brought on after Kimbrel allowed two more baserunners after this, and given that he was gassed, he allowed the game-sealing single for Moreno. In the top of the ninth inning, Schwarber hit a two-out double, but it was to no avail as Turner struck out against Paul Sewald. Just like that, the snakes were indeed alive, and this series was all tied up.

> Unfortunately for everyone involved, we've reached the point in the book where when they've lost these heartbreaking series that the game losses were far more interesting than the wins. That's why Game Five will be wrapped up fairly quickly. What was supposed to be a fun work trip to Arizona to watch the Phils clinch a trip to their second straight World Series was quickly turning into an [expletive] nightmare. They needed Game Five to stabilize themselves in the series, especially with Wheeler on the mound. They had to get back to Citizens Bank Park with two chances to punch their ticket to the World Series in a place where they hadn't lost yet this postseason. They would do just that. Wheeler was brilliant, again, this time firing seven innings of one-run baseball, and the stars came through. Harper hit a home run and stole home; Mr. NLCS, Kyle Schwarber, went yard, as did Realmuto; and the bullpen pitchers did their jobs. While Games Three and Four were absolutely gutting, one could chalk that up to a desperate team that didn't want their season to end just yet, but the boys were back after their Game Five victory in the desert. There was just no way they were going to lose two straight at home given everything that had gone on there during this magical year. Not this year, not this team. Until . . .
>
> Sorry to continue the Jack note here, but it's important. I am being completely open and transparent when I say that I felt like Game Six was a loss just from the vibe I was getting doing the pregame show on the radio. Do you want to know why? Because I felt a sense of cockiness in the air and in this town. Cockiness makes me nervous—it's how you get clipped when you least expect it. I know these younger sports fans who got to see a Super Bowl early in their lives expect good things to happen in Philly sports, but not us hardened veterans. Aah, I was so mad, I wanted angst, I wanted nervousness. Not this! This was a recipe for a disaster, and boy, was it ever.

RING THE BELL

You know how we joked earlier in this chapter about how it had been a while since the naysayers could mutter under their breath, "Bleepin' Nola"? They got their time to shine in Game Six. It's not that Nola was bad; he just wasn't great. A couple interesting things happened in Game Six. The first was that the starting pitching, which up to this point had been unbelievable—faltered. Nola allowed four runs in 4 1/3 innings, including back-to-back home runs to start off the second inning. All of a sudden Tommy Pham and Gurriel were exiting the ballpark, and that cockiness that was sensed pregame was gone. It was a regular-season Nola inning, too, because he couldn't just stop the bleeding there., He had to allow another run to come home on an Evan Longoria double. The other interesting thing that was developing was that Diamondbacks pitching staff. They had the book on Turner and Castellanos by this point, making them expand the strike zone. But they also avoided Schwarber and Harper when they could. They clearly walked into Citizens Bank Park wanting to make Turner, Bohm, and Stott beat them because Schwarber and Harper were just too locked in. If the Phillies were going to win Games Six or Seven, it was likely going to have to be the other guys who would have to do it. They failed their first test. The Phillies offense mustered just three measly singles after the first inning to help deliver them their first home loss of the postseason.

The sense of cockiness was replaced with anxiety and people wondering, *Are they really about to do this? Is this team going to join all the teams that have let us down throughout the years?*

> The feeling in the ballpark on this night just from doing the radio pregame was much more like I wanted it. People were juiced but not overly confident—that's my Philadelphia. With Suárez on the mound, the confidence level was even higher. Unfortunately, we never got the full Jack Fritz flu game for this one. I was battling something, and if you listen to the open of the full-game highlights on YouTube, your boy sounds horrible. They should have a warning saying, VIEWER DISCRETION IS ADVISED before that video is allowed to be shown in Philadelphia.

It was the first Game Seven in the 140-plus years of the Phillies. Philadelphia baseball fans have witnessed elimination games, but when it comes to the best two words in sports, never. To be honest, we don't need to see another one for a while! Suárez vs. a rookie in Pfaadt pitching in this environment should have been advantage, Philadelphia, but again, that damned Diamondbacks' game plan was back, and they had the perfect guy on the mound to execute it.

Trailing 1–0 in the bottom of the second, however, one of the "other guys" was finally able to beat them, as Bohm launched a home run to left field. He pointed toward his ring finger as he ran up the first-base line, and we all hoped that was going to be the moment that woke up this team. It was looking good, too, because a couple of innings another "other guy" stepped up in Stott, who drove a double to the wall in left-center field to bring Bohm all the way around from first base to score. The ballpark was on fire—they had the lead in Game Seven. They also the Diamondbacks, and Pfaadt, on the ropes, as the next batter, Realmuto, followed up Stott's double with a single. Runners were on first and third with one out for the now struggling Castellanos, who was mired in an 0-for-20 slump. That slump would continue as he swung and missed at another Pfaadt sweeper to give the Diamondbacks two outs in the inning. Pfaadt then pitched around Marsh to set up the bases loaded with Johan Rojas coming to the dish, which created a situation for Thomson. Do you pinch-hit for Rojas and try to deliver the death knell to the Diamondbacks? Or, with two outs and already having the lead, do you stick with the premier defender in center field? He opted to stick with Rojas, who promptly struck out.

In the fifth, with the bullpen warming up, another Thomson decision was put under the microscope, as they often are in the biggest games. With two outs and a runner on second base, Thomson elected to let Suárez pitch to Corbin Carroll, instead of lifting him for perhaps a fresher reliever. In Thomson's defense, it's lefty-lefty, he just struck out Ketel Marte, and there were two outs. If you could just sneak Suárez through this inning, it would make the bullpen's job that much easier. Ultimately, the pitcher just has to get the job done, and he couldn't. Carroll singled to tie the ballgame up, and Suárez was out of the game. In came Jeff Hoffman who, after Carroll stole second to get into scoring position, allowed a bleeder to Moreno to bring the speedy Diamondback home and give them the lead in the top of the fifth.

In the bottom of the inning, the Phillies were looking to get right back in this one as Schwarber led off with a double. But Turner, now slumping, grounded out to third base and Bryce Harper just missed "Bedlam at the Bank, Part II" as he flew out to the wall in left field. Bohm couldn't make them pay, either, and the leadoff double was squandered. The Phillies would continue the squandering in the seventh when Andrew Saalfrank walked both

RING THE BELL

Pache and Schwarber back to back to set up first and second with one out for the big boys in the lineup, but once again, Turner was slumping. He popped out weakly to center field to set the stage for Harper. There was nowhere to put the October legend; Kevin Ginkel, now in the game, was going to have to pitch to him, and the Phillies were thrilled. On a 2-1 pitch, Harper got the fastball he was looking for, and he just missed it by a millimeter. Instead of it being barrelled up, it shot high into the air and fell softly into Alek Thomas's glove in center field. There was no bedlam this year at Citizens Bank Park.

The march was on. The Phils brought Wheeler in to relieve to maybe spark the ballclub and keep the score 4–2—he did kept the score as it was, but there was no spark. Ginkel struck out the side in the eighth and Sewald executed a one-two-three ninth to end it. It was over. The year that felt like "it" ended with a whimper. The Phillies had blown it, and the 2023 Diamondbacks joined the pantheon of *We lost to those guys?* alongside the 2002 Tampa Bay Buccaneers, the 2003 Carolina Panthers, and the 2020–21 Atlanta Hawks. Just crushing.

> The 2023 season hurt way more than the '22 season, and I know that sounds crazy given that 2022 ended in the World Series and you had a 2–1 lead and Game Five of that Series will haunt us forever, but that run was magical. There were no expectations, we barely even knew those guys, and the moments were still unbelievable. It was hard to be mad when they lost in '22; fans were more appreciative because the Phillies reintroduced the city to baseball again. After the '23 season, it was fair to be mad; they had no business losing that series, especially when they had leads of 2–0 and 3–2 with two games to close them out at their ballpark. I don't know what would have happened in the World Series. The Rangers that year were a juggernaut, but I sure would have loved the opportunity. As I finish out this chapter, I hope that we don't look back on the 2023 opportunity as the one that got away. As we sit here after a 2024 campaign fell short in the NLDS, it's looking more and more like the one that got away.

The Lists

THE BEST AND WORST OF TIMES

This part is completely arbitrary and self-indulgent, but it's a proper ending. It feels appropriate to rank the players covered in this book, and beyond.

PHILLIES MT. RUSHMORE

Mount Rushmores, when overused and overanalyzed, can be a stale, pedantic ritual, especially when they're the primary focus of a three-hour block of drive-time sports talk radio. But they're fun. It's really just a visual aid, so let's not get angry about it.

[We all know what Mt. Rushmore is, right? This doesn't need further explanation? Good.]

JACK'S RUSHMORE:
I already know Kevin is going to have some really old players on his that is going to drive me nuts. This guy and his history.

Mike Schmidt
The first face on the Phillies Mt. Rushmore, no doubt about it, and if you have another answer you're just wrong. Blah, blah, blah about a portion of the fan base not liking him, the guy is the greatest third baseman to ever play the game, is the only Phillie to hit his 500th in a Phillies uniform and was the World Series MVP in the team's first ever championship. Was he treated the best? Probably not, but it feels like there's been a big turn in the fan base with Schmitty and hopefully that can continue.

Quick side note—I would have loved to hear Schmidt's truth serum reaction to the Turner standing ovations. This was a guy who was undoubtedly one of the best to ever play the game of baseball, who was held to the highest standard and put through the ringer by the fan base regularly . . . and now fans are giving out emotional support standing ovations??? I'd imagine Schmidt felt a certain kind of way about that.

Steve Carlton

Greatest player and greatest pitcher in Phillies history, in my opinion, gets Carlton on my Mt. Rushmore. As I've gotten older (again, I am writing this at the ripe old age of thirty-one), I've gotten much better at appreciating the true greatness that we have had in this city. Because, believe it or not, we haven't had many truly all-time great players. We've had a bunch of really good players, Hall of Famers, MVPs, etc. But rarely true generational game-changers. This city did, however, have it with Schmidt and Carlton. By now, you know "Lefty's" resume and if you go back and look at his Baseball Reference page and compare it to the modern game—it breaks your brain.

Quick side note II—It's a shame that someone's Baseball Reference page is the new "look at his back of the baseball card." My generation might be the last to even understand the greatness of the baseball trading card. Maybe I'll hand it down to my sons and they'll carry the torch, but man, baseball cards were the best. I still remember a misprint I had on Marty Cordova's card that had him hitting 55 home runs in one of his seasons—I thought I struck gold and this card was going to be worth a lot of money. A Marty Cordova mint condition with a misprint? Sheesh, there might as well have been a line outside my parents house of people trying to get that card. Anyway, Steve Carlton. Lefty. Carve it in.

Ryan Howard

This one was tricky for me. It's almost as if you have to just pick one face for that 2008 era, but how can you just pick one? Well, I did, and while I think Utley was the best overall player, and Rollins was the straw that stirred the drink, there was one man that kept opposing pitchers up at night—Ryan Howard. Those guys were great players, Utley should be a Hall of Famer, but Howard was the anchor for all of them. During this stretch specifically, the most feared sluggers in the game were Howard, Pujols, Miguel Cabrera, and the insane, out of nowhere run that Josh Hamilton was on—it matters.

So while his WAR wasn't high enough for most people's modern standards, those that watched back then knew.

It is nice that the tide has turned on Howard and we've gotten back to remembering the good times. People were too hard on him, maybe because he was the first $100 million deal we had seen in this city, and subsequently the first to get hurt and not play up to it. As fans, we were all frustrated, but as time has gone by, I think it's been easier to put a little more respect on the "The Big Piece's" name.

Bryce Harper
That's right, I'm doing it. Harper should be on the Phillies Mt. Rushmore, preferably with the Phanatic headband on. This is a tad bit of a projection but, when it's all said and done, he's going to go into the Hall of Fame as a Phillie, he's going to his 500th home run in a Phillies uniform and he's *going* to have a parade down Broad Street (please let that last one be true). Listen, whether you want to admit it or not, this has been one of the most fruitful eras in Phillies history. 1950, 1964 and 1993 were one-offs; great memories in short spurts. This version of the Phillies has a pennant, a division title and three straight postseason appearances under its belt. That means something.

Harper gets credit for a couple of things. One, he chose us and brought Phillies baseball back from the dead. He chose to be a Phillie when they hadn't had a winning season in seven years. He could have been a Dodger, a Giant or even stayed with a loaded Nats team, but he chose us and that matters. He also hit arguably the biggest home run in Phillies history to send the team to the World Series in 2022, and has been a clutch player all around. In his postseason career as a Phillie (through 2024), he has a 1.153 OPS. To put that in perspective, with a minimum of 100 at-bats in the postseason, which is a pretty large sample, it puts him right behind Babe Ruth and Lou Gehrig in the history of the sport (eerily, both with the exact same 1.214). Pretty good!

KEVIN'S RUSHMORE

Defense doesn't matter. Not *really*. It's not that I don't respect flashy leather—I think Rey Ordonez was poetry in motion. I just don't agree with categorizing a player's overall value by the position they played.

Chase Utley was a great hitter. But, if he'd played the majority of his career at first base instead of second, NO ONE would be pushing for his Hall of Fame enshrinement. Which is weird, because I've never seen a player bring their mitt with them into the batters box . . .

With that being said, with all due respect to Utley and Rollins, my mountain doesn't discriminate by position.

Mike Schmidt

No surprise, and no reason to repeat Jack's accurate reasoning. Schmidt and George Brett are the most obvious Rushmores for their respective teams in all of baseball.

Steve Carlton

There have been a lot of great pitchers in Philly before and after Lefty, but none live up to the master. You know the strikeouts, the Cy Youngs, and the absurdity of his '72 season. He deserves it for all those reasons, but also for being a total freak.

He was eccentric as hell, was a sports-health nut decades before TB12, and simultaneously had insane insights while also refusing to talk to the media. If there were podcasts around back then, Lefty and Bowa would destroy the Kelce Bros.

Cole Hamels

Nick Foles is a godlike figure in Birds history, and that's based on one playoff run, if not just one single game.

When we're talking about a franchise with just two championships in nearly 150 years, I've got to show deference to the 2008 World Series MVP. There were plenty of guys who were more dominant, but he was a reliable rotation staple at a time when the Phillies needed it most.

Chuck Klein*

This will annoy Jack. It was a toss-up between him and Howard.

We forget how great Howard was, mostly because of stat nerds who use and abuse WAR as a substitute for common sense. Howard was the best non-pitcher on the 2008 team. It's all about those baseball card stats Jack was talking about. Klein's were ridiculous.

There are only five .320+ BA/ 30+ HR seasons in Phils history and Klein owns four of them. Sorry. I considered being a total jerk and listing the guy with the fourth season: Lefty O'Doul. Google him. He was a legend.

O'Doul cliffs notes: He holds the Phillies/NL single season hits mark (254; 1930); introduced baseball to Japan; first American inducted into the

Japanese Baseball Hall of Fame; was partly the inspiration for "The Natural" Roy Hobbs; has a bridge and a bar named after him; had absolutely nothing to do with the non-alcoholic beer.

In fact, he's going up there.

Lefty O'Doul

The great O'Doul takes the last spot. Heroes get remembered, but legends never die.

ALL-TIME STARTING NINE

Now, you can't cheat when you do this—you can't take a guy that was an obvious right fielder and make him your left fielder; have a take.

JACK & KEVIN'S STARTING NINE
C: Darren Daulton

This was, admittedly, a tough one. The problem is that all of these guys were similar—great peaks and big wins but not a long enough track record of greatness to make it obvious. While there's truly no wrong answer between Daulton, Ruiz, Realmuto, or Boone, we went with Dutch because he was "The Man" and the real-life version of Crash Davis from *Bull Durham*. It didn't hurt that at his peak, he was the unquestioned leader of the '93 Phils and also hit in the middle of the lineup.

1B: Ryan Howard

While there have been some great first basemen in Phillies history, Howard stands above them all, with a Rookie of the Year Award, an MVP, and a ring. Among just the first baseman, Howard played the most games (1,572), had the most plate appearances (6,531), scored the most runs (848), had the most hits (1,475), the most doubles (277), the most home runs (382), and the most RBIs (1,194). While it's obvious that Howard is the first baseman, let's not forget how good ole John Kruk was as a hitter. I know he makes his jokes in the broadcast booth, but from 1989–93 he made three All-Star teams and had a line of .305 AVG/.399 OBP/.459 SLG/.858 OPS. A player like that in today's game is getting $100 million. Just saying, put some respect on Kruky's name.

2B: Chase Utley
Not to totally bore you with stats that you might already know, but Utley's bWAR from 2005–14 ranked third in all of baseball, behind Albert Pujols and Adrián Beltré. Pretty good!

SS: Jimmy Rollins
It's either him or Bowa and while Bowa was great, Rollins is a fringe Hall of Famer, an MVP, the club's all-time hits king and a world champion.

Could Trea Turner be in the conversation on the rewrite of this book? We can only hope.

3B: Scott Rolen
Kidding, it's **Mike Schmidt**

LF: Greg Luzinski
With all due respect to Sherry Magee and Del Ennis, Greg Luzinski is pretty underrated in all-time Phillies lore. Sure we think of "The Bull" for his wonderful barbeque at Citizens Bank Park and his banter with John Kruk during games, but the guy was a heck of a hitter. From 1975–78 he finished second in the MVP voting twice and his stat line during that time was .295 AVG/.386 OBP/.535 SLG/.922 OPS and he averaged 32 home runs a year. We ranked him just outside the top four pillars of the 1980 squad, but he deserves more credit than he gets.

CF: Richie Ashburn
Time plays tricks with players' legacies, and Ashburn's is constantly evolving.

Entire generations, too young to see him play in person, had "Whitey the Broadcaster" as their only frame of reference.

Now, the majority of the Gen Z and millennial fan base has never heard the man speak.

Of course, that doesn't erase Whitey from Phillies history, but stat lines preserve better than audio clips. Baseball fans will always dig into the sports' rich statistical history, and that's where Whitey comes alive.

While he wasn't the biggest home run hitter, no one had more hits during the 1950s than Ashburn with 1,875. During that time, he also led the National League in hits three times, walks three times, and won batting titles in 1955 and 1958. While he was only able to make one World Series with the

RF: Bryce Harper

Alright, let's address the elephant in the room here: "but guuuys, you said no cheating, so how could you put Harper in right with him being a primary first baseman now?" Fair critique, smart reader, but this is OUR starting nine and in OUR starting nine we're putting Harper back in right field. Also, at the time of writing this book he's played more right field than any position as a Phillie so we're going with Harper in right field. Listen, if you want to argue Bobby Abreu or Chuck Klein above Harper, knock yourself out, but come on—it's Harper.

JACK'S NOTE: Please read the above in a semi-sarcastic and fun way. I know it comes across as aggressive but please note that we are writing this all with a smile on our faces.

THE ALL-TIME STARTING ROTATION
1. Steve Carlton
2. Robin Roberts
3. Cole Hamels
4. Curt Schilling
5. Zack Wheeler/ Jim Bunning

Not to totally diminish the accomplishments of Grover Cleveland Alexander but come on, it was 1911 to 1917—over a century ago, when baseball was played with broom handles and billiard balls. Carlton and Roberts are the two locks on here and then it's personal preference. Hamels and Schill had similar careers in Philadelphia, slated fourth and fifth in franchise pWAR, respectively (42, 36.8). Hamels gets the edge with postseason heroics that sealed the deal in 2008. In the final spot, Wheeler [detailed below] and Bunning [detailed below] are both deserving. Wheeler (Jack's pick for the fifth spot) is still a bit of a projection, but it's fair. The Wheeler signing is one of the best acquisitions in the history of Philadelphia sports, not just the Phillies. He has two Cy Young runner ups, (he should have won it in '21), and he's turned into a legitimate ace and one of the best big game pitchers in the sport. Among players that have thrown 50 or more innings in the postseason, Wheeler has the lowest WHIP of all time. He's tied with Hamels for the most postseason strikeouts in Phillies history. There's been three postseason starts in Phillies history where a starter has gone seven or more innings and allowed only one or fewer hits—Wheeler has two of three. Still, the argument for Bunning is fair.

Bunning (Kevin's pick for the fifth spot), who had five of his nine All-Star seasons before landing with Philadelphia, was his most dominant self with the Fightins. Recency bias is always a factor, as neither one of us was alive for the 1980 championship, let alone the 1964 collapse, but we also wrote this book for the people who were!

Bunning's first four seasons with the team was probably the most dominant stretch for any Phillies pitcher of the Live Ball Era (post-1920). During that period, he was 74–46 with a 2.48 ERA, which is lower than any single season ERA from Robin Roberts. Of course, his perfect game on Father's Day 1964 helps keep his memory alive each June.

JACK'S FINAL THOUGHTS

If you've made it this far in the book, I just want to thank you from the bottom of my heart. Kevin and I are so proud of this book and the work we put into it. It was designed as a "love letter" to an organization that has meant so much to us and I hope we accomplished that. This team means the world to me and I can't wait to pass the traditions and all the stories down to my kids. If Walker or Sutton (and hopefully our third child, eventually) are reading this portion, just know that it took everything in my power to not name you Chase or Bryce; maybe the third I can convince to at least go Harper—just kidding. We weren't sure how to end this thing so a final thank you felt right. So thank you and I hope you enjoyed reading it as much as we enjoyed writing it.

KEVIN'S FINAL THOUGHTS

Funny thing about this book is that Jack and I both started it as brand new fathers. I remember discussing the premise over lunch in West Chester, maybe a month before my daughter was due. I told him this "fatherhood thing" couldn't possibly get in the way. That was pretty dumb. Anyway, like the Phillies have been over the course of my lifetime, the process of bringing this book to life (while caring for a new human life) was both confounding and

THE BEST AND WORST OF TIMES

extremely rewarding. We set out to tell the stories that shaped our collective Phillies fandom, and we hope we succeeded. May the bell never stop ringing. Unless it's just in your head. That could be tinnitus. Get that checked out.

Kevin Reavy

ACKNOWLEDGMENTS

We are eternally grateful to the following for helping make this book a reality: Glen Macnow, Ray Didinger, Chris Wheeler, Scott Franzke, Ryan Spaeder, Jason Katzman, Jim Eisenreich, Bobby Shantz, Larry Bowa, Tom Burgoyne, Larry Andersen, Joe Frantz, CJ Shumard, Logan Weisbach, Brian Startare, Matt Albertson, Jim Salisbury, Michael Kirk, Kevin Durso, Meredith Burton-Sassmannshausen, Tom McCarthy, Dan Zdilla, Andrew DiCecco, the Lititz Public Library, the Phillies, Mike Arbuckle, Mike Schmidt, Amy Mac, Keith Shook, Video Dan Stephenson and the Phillies video yearbook crew, Baseball Reference, and the *Philadelphia Inquirer*. Special thanks to Ike Reese, Spike Eskin and all of WIP for letting us shamelessly plug this 24/7; to James Seltzer and the High Hopes community for getting behind the book.

A note from Jack:
This *might be*, and let's be honest probably will be, the only book I ever write or co-author (unless Kevin has any more ideas), so there are many people to thank. To Jill, thank you for being the rock of our family and putting up with the countless hours of me watching, talking, and thinking about Phils baseball. I can't and couldn't do this without you. To Walker and Sutton, the two greatest things that have ever happened to me. May the Phillies bring you much happiness and success during your lives, but not too much—we don't want to lose our edge. To my parents for maybe not completely understanding why their only son loved the Phillies so much but always supporting along the way. Thank you. Finally, to my Granddad. Thank you for teaching me the game, taking me to my first Phillies game, always having a catch with me in your backyard, and for being right about Charlie Manuel.

A note from Kevin:
This book was kickstarted by a phone call with a kind and generous person. Meet your heroes, it's worth the risk. Big thanks, as always, to my great family and friends. To Carrie, for raising baby June while I made a book. Someday, long after the feeding tube of "Miss Rachel" is removed from her cerebral cortex, Junie will read this book and roll her eyes at all the lame jokes daddy made.

ENDNOTES

Chapter One: 1964
1. Joe Queenan, "Day Five," diary, *Slate* (website), October 18, 1996, https://slate.com/human-interest/1996/10/joe-queenan-2.html.
2. Ray Didinger, in discussion with authors, January 23, 2024.
3. Bobby Shantz, in discussion with the authors, January 15, 2024.

Chapter Two: 1980 Franchise Pillars
1. Chris Wheeler, in discussion with the authors, March 9, 2024.
2. Glen Macnow, in discussion with the authors, September 10, 2024.
3. Wheeler, discussion.
4. Mike Schmidt and Glen Waggoner, *Clearning the Bases: Juiced Players, Monster Salaries, Sham Records, and a Hall of Famer's Search for the Soul of Baseball* (New York: Harper, 2006), 183.
5. Wheeler, discussion.
6. Wheeler, discussion.
7. Wheeler, discussion.
8. Larry Bowa, in discussion with the authors, September 4, 2024.
9. Stan Hochman, "The Time Steve Carlton Talked," *Philadelphia Inquirer*, May 6, 2013.
10. Shantz, discussion.
11. Jerry Crasnick, "Phillies '80 Team Honored," Bloomberg News Service, June 16, 2000.
12. Crasnick, "Phillies '80 Team Honored."
13. Crasnick, "Phillies '80 Team Honored."
14. Larry Bowa, discussion.
15. Bowa, discussion.

Chapter Three: 1980—The First One
1. *Glory Days: The Story of the 1980 World Champion Phillies*, written and edited by Dan Stephenson, produced by Dan Stephenson and Larry Shenk (Philadelphia, PA: Philadelphia Phillies, 2000), https://www.youtube.com/watch?v=BSZi4aZ4hCw.
2. Kevin Freeman, "Black Friday Revisited: Phillies 1977 Loss to Dodgers Still Haunts Garber," *LNP* (Lancaster, PA), October 18, 2007, https://lancasteronline.com/sports/black-Friday-revisited-phillies-1977-loss-to-dodgers-still-haunts-garber/article_95a98267–18e9–571a-abec-fead1938a375.html.
3. Freeman, "Black Friday Revisited."

4   Frank Dolson, "A Horrible Loss . . . but, for Phillies, There Is Tomorrow," *Philadelphia Inquirer*, October 8, 1977.
5   Bowa, discussion.
6   Freeman, "Black Friday Revisited."
7   Bill Conlin, "Urban Renewal in the Outfield," *Phiadelphia Daily News*, April 11, 1980.
8   Bowa, discussion.
9   Bowa, discussion.
10 Bowa, discussion.
11 *Glory Days*, https://www.youtube.com/watch?v=BSZi4aZ4hCw.
12 Bowa, discussion.
13 *Glory Days*, https://www.youtube.com/watch?v=BSZi4aZ4hCw.
14 *Glory Days*, https://www.youtube.com/watch?v=BSZi4aZ4hCw.
15 Bowa, discussion.
16 Tug McGraw, interview with the authors.
17 "City Salutes Champion Phillies," *Philadelphia Inquirer*, October 23, 1980.
18 TV parade coverage. WCAU Philadelphia, October 22, 1980.

Chapter Four: The Phillie Phanatic
1   "Facts & Figures . . . 1978 Phillies Promotions," *Philadelphia Inquirer*, April 5, 1978.
2   Tom Burgoyne, in discussion with the authors.
3   John Corr, "You're Not Gonna Believe This," *Philadelphia Inquirer*, June 12, 1978.
4   Lauren Amour, "How the Phillie Phanatic Came to Be America's Favorite Sports Mascot," Si.com, December 15, 2021, https://www.si.com/mlb/phillies/opinions/how-phillie-phanatic-came-to-be-americas-favorite-sports-mascot-mlb.
5   Burgoyne, discussion.

Chapter Five: 1983
1   Macnow, discussion.

Chapter Six: 1993—Worst to First
1   Bernard Fernandez, "Parrish Becoming Pleasant Sight for Phils," *Philadelphia Daily News*, July 7, 1987.
2   Paul Hagen, "Confirm Rumor: Parrish Dealt to Angels for Pitching Prospect," *Philadelphia Daily News*, October 4, 1988.
3   Hagen, "Confirm Rumor."
4   Bill Plaschke, "For Kruk, 1988 Was Year of Fear," *Los Angeles Times*, January 11, 1989.
5   Peter Pascarelli, "Thomas Takes Steps on Phils' Road to Recovery," *Philadelphia Inquirer*, June 19, 1989.
6   Pascarelli, "Thomas Takes Steps."
7   Scott Miller, "Confessions of a Steroid Pioneer: My Dinner with Lenny Dykstra," *Bleacher Report*, June 27, 2016, https://thelab.bleacherreport.com/confessions-of-a-steroid-pioneer/.
8   Macnow, discussion.
9   Lenny Dykstra, (@LennyDykstra), Twitter/X, March 10, 2022.

ENDNOTES

10   *Whatever It Takes, Dude*, written and edited by Dan Stephenson (Philadelphia, PA: Philadelphia Phillies, 1994), https://www.youtube.com/watch?v=vFSpxgXWwZY.
11   *Whatever It Takes, Dude.*
12   *Whatever It Takes, Dude.*
13   *Whatever It Takes, Dude.*
14   Craig Hardee, "Possum Whitted," Society for American Baseball Research, n.d., https://sabr.org/bioproj/person/possum-whitted/.
15   Jim Eisenreich, in discussion with the authors.
16   Chuck Darrow, "WIP: An Oral History," *Philadelphia Inquirer*, May 14, 2012.
17   Darrow, "WIP: An Oral History."
18   Macnow, discussion.
19   Mike Bertha, "1993 Phillies Had Bellies Full of Beer, But Only Baseball on the Mind," *Philadelphia* magazine, March 30, 2012.
20   Eisenreich, discussion.
21   Scot Johnson, "Jim Eisenreich," Society for American Baseball Research, last modified July 26, 2021, https://sabr.org/bioproj/person/jim-eisenreich/.
22   Eisenreich, discussion.
23   Eisenreich, discussion.
24   Dan Shaughnessy, "A Rookie's Battle," *Boston Globe*, May 5, 1982.
25   Eisenreich, discussion.
26   Eisenreich, discussion.
27   *Philadelphia Daily News*, October 22, 1993.
28   Brian Startare, in discussion with the authors. Brian was formerly with 94.1 WIP, 97.5 FM; he coauthored the cult classic *This Day in Philadelphia Sports*.

Chapter Eight: The Fans

1   Peter Gammons, "Rolen: 'I've Gone to Baseball Heaven,'" ESPN.com, July 30, 2002, https://www.espn.com/gammons/s/2002/0729/1411564.html.
2   "Michael Jack Schmidt." MLB Network Presents documentary. 2024.
3   Doug Glanville, (@DougGlanville), Twitter/X, October 13, 2023, https://x.com/dougglanville/status/1712906953276465429?s=46&t=SpBSOuw—h3pgcYEEP-4STg].
4   Never forget the "Everybody Hits! Woohoo!" Guy.
5   Matt Albertson interview.
6   Ken Rosenthal (@Ken_Rosenthal), Twitter/X, September 21, 2020, https://x.com/ken_rosenthal/status/1308142198073053190?s=48&t=SpBSOuw—h3pgcYEEP4STg
7   Bob Brookover, "Phandemic Krew Loudly Supports Phillies from the Outside Looking In at Citizens Bank Park," *Philadelphia Inquirer*, August 5, 2020.
8   Matt Breen, "Randy Wolf Is Now a Professional Poker Player and the Wolf Pack Is Still Howling after 25 Years," *Philadelphia Inquirer*, June 27, 2024, https://www.inquirer.com/phillies/randy-wolf-poker-phillies-wolfpack-anniversary-fans-20240627.html.
9   Sporting News, *Philadelphia Inquirer*, April 15, 1895.

Chapter Nine: The 2008 Pillars
1. Mike Arbuckle, in discussion with authors, August 15, 2024.
2. *Team Whistle*, October 21, 2022, https://www.youtube.com/watch?v=1ZCFg0tNh_Q&t=68s.
3. *Team Whistle*.
4. Larry Bowa, in discussion with authors, September 4, 2024.
5. Mike Arbuckle, in discussion with authors, August 15, 2024.

Chapter Ten: 2008—"World Champions, World #$%&in' Champions"
1. Todd Zolecki, "Phils sign Werth," *Philadelphia Inquirer*, December 20, 2006.
2. *The Perfect Season: The 2008 Phillies Video Yearbook*. Written, produced, and edited by Dan Stephenson (Philadelphia, PA: Philadelphia Phillies, 2008) https://www.youtube.com/watch?v=cL1qWh4lpjM&t=4380s
3. *The Perfect Season*.
4. *The Perfect Season*.
5. Todd Zolecki, "Rollins Gets the Message," *Philadelphia Inquirer*, June 6, 2008.
6. Todd Zolecki, Jim Salisbury "Drastic Move for Myers" *Philadelphia Inquirer*, July 2, 2008.
7. Todd Zolecki, "Schmidt Sends Team Encouraging Words," *Philadelphia Inquirer*, September 6, 2008.
8. John Gonzalez, "Fightin's not Frightened," *Philadelphia Inquirer*, October 3, 2008.
9. Todd Zolecki, "Loose and Lighthearted," *Philadelphia Inquirer*, October 21, 2008.

Chapter Eleven: Post-2008 Years—No Cigars
1. Andy Martino, "For Phils, Pitching Woes, Free-Fall Continue," *Philadelphia Inquirer*, June 26, 2009.
2. Jim Salisbury, "Phils Deal for Cliff Lee," *Philadelphia Inquirer*, July 30, 2009.
3. Jim Salisbury, "Phillies' Giants of the Game," *Philadelphia Inquirer*, August 25, 2009.
4. Andy Martino, "No Mountain Too High," *Philadelphia Inquirer*, October 13, 2009.
5. Jim Salisbury, "Phils Somehow Pull One Out of Thin Air," *Philadelphia Inquirer*, October 13, 2009.
6. Andy Martino, "Rollins Lifts Phillies to Win," *Philadelphia Inquirer*, October 20, 2009.
7. Andy Martino, "Werth Repeating," *Philadelphia Inquirer*, October 22, 2009.
8. Frank Fitzpatrick, "Madson Loses Cool, Phils Lose Madson," *Philadelphia Inquirer*, May 1, 2010.
9. Marc Narducci, "Manuel Accenuates the Positive on Werth," *Philadelphia Inquirer*, June 10, 2010.
10. Bob Brookover, "Good Health May Be all Team Needs," *Philadelphia Inquirer*, June 13, 2010.
11. Matt Gelb, "Double Whammy for Phils' Infield," *Philadelphia Inquirer*, June 30, 2010.
12. Matt Gelb, "Phils Fire Their Hitting Coach," *Philadelphia Inquirer*, July 23, 2010.

ENDNOTES

13 MLB Network, *Halladay's No Hitter*, https://www.youtube.com/watch?v=0MS7qAKCnus.
14 For those of you that don't remember, this was around the time that there was a "mystery team" vying for Lee's services. Of course, no one in baseball seemed to think it could be the Phillies—until this fateful night.
15 Bob Brookover, "Give Madson a Chance to Close," *Philadelphia Inquirer*, April 3, 2011.
16 Thomas Boswell, "Can Jayson Werth Bring Swagger to the Washington Nationals?" *Washington Post*, February 26, 2011.

Chapter Twelve: The Harper Pursuit

1 "Machado Arrives," NBC Sports Philadelphia, December 20, 2018, https://x.com/NBCSPhilly/status/1075807242572742656.
2 Matt Gelb, "The Craziest Phillies Offseason Ever: Inside the Winding Path that Led to Bryce Harper," *The Athletic*, March 4, 2019.
3 Ken Rostenthal, "Bryce Harper one-on-one interview with Ken Rosenthal," FOX Sports, March 30, 2019, https://www.youtube.com/watch?v=qf7gT-RYJog&t=493s.
4 Jim Salisbury, "The Complete Timeline of Phillies Path to Signing Harper," NBC Sports Philadelphia, March 26, 2019.

Chapter Thirteen: 2022

1 Scott Lauber, Inside the Phillies, *Philadelphia Inquirer*, October 11, 2019.
2 *Bedlam at the Bank: The 2022 Phillies Video Yearbook*. Written and directed by Dan Stephenson, produced by Dan Stephenson and Sean Rainey (Philadelphia, PA: Philadelphia Phillies, 2022), https://www.youtube.com/watch?app=desktop&v=j38ckdv4zPA.
3 ESPN News Services, June 3, 2022. "Philadelphia Phillies fire manager Joe Girardi after 22–29 start." https://www.espn.com/mlb/story/_/id/34031182/philadelphia-phillies-fire-manager-joe-girardi.
4 *Bedlam at the Bank*.
5 Tom McCarthy, Phillies postgame broadcast, October 3, 2022. Via MLB Highlights, "Phillies vs. Astros Game Highlights (10/3/2022)," https://www.youtube.com/watch?v=9_hc537KNi0.
6 Fan lyrics, *Good Morning San Diego*, October 18, 2022. Via KUSI News, "CRINGY San Diego Padres Rap," https://www.youtube.com/watch?v=xw2M6Guxe7E.
7 "Bedlam at the Bank."

Chapter Fourteen: 2023

1 John Kruk and Tom McCarthy, "Phillies vs. Braves" NBC Sports Philadelphia, September 20, 2023.
2 Jake Mintz, "Inside the Braves Unbelievable Comeback Against the Phillies," FOX Sports MLB, October 10, 2023.

RING THE BELL

3   Bryce Harper, "Bryce Harper Gives Iconic Press Conference Following Heroic Effort in Game 3," NBC Sports Philadelphia, October 10, 2023, https://www.youtube.com/watch?v=Xy_6ArXfDhg&t=151s.
4   Alex Tantum, "Spencer Strider's Hottest Sports Take," *MLB Fits on Instagram*, September 27, 2023.